S0-BYZ-932

INSTRUCTOR'S RESOURCE MANUAL

DISCOVERING LITERATURE
Stories, Poems, Plays

SECOND EDITION

Hans P. Guth • Gabriele L. Rico

Contributors:
Karen Harrington
Brian McLaughlin

A BLAIR PRESS BOOK
PRENTICE HALL
Upper Saddle River, New Jersey 07458

A BLAIR PRESS BOOK

© 1997 by PRENTICE-HALL, INC.
Simon & Schuster / A Viacom Company
Upper Saddle River, New Jersey 07458

All rights reserved

10 9 8 7 6 5 4 3 2 1

ISBN 0-13-573171-2
Printed in the United States of America

A LETTER FROM THE AUTHORS OF *DISCOVERING LITERATURE,* Second Edition

Dear Colleague:

We have put this book together for teachers who love literature and who love to teach literature. Our common challenge as teachers of literature is to pass our enthusiasm for poetry, fiction, and drama on to a new generation—to hand over the torch, to initiate a new group of readers and viewers. As every teacher knows there is nothing automatic about such an enterprise—no patented risk-free method, no "success-or-your-money-back" guarantee.

A book like this is a labor of love, and our enthusiasm as teachers and textbook authors for favorite writers and selections is likely to show through—Mary Robison's "Yours" and fiction by Yukio Mishima or Gabriel García Márquez; poems by John Donne, the Countess of Dia, Li-Young Lee, Gwendolyn Brooks, or Sharon Olds; *Hamlet* and David Mamet's *Cryptogram* or Marsha Norman's *Getting Out*. However, a book like this also has an underlying philosophy, overt or implied. Assumptions like the following are among the articles of faith that have guided us in our teaching and writing:

- The students in our literature classes today are as intelligent, imaginative, and idealistic (under whatever "cool" surface) as any previous group ever was. There may or may not be more of a distance between today's world of video games and net surfing on the one hand and imaginative literature on the other than there was between the fraternity parties or Ugliest-Man-on-Campus contests of an earlier generation of Shakespeare. It may be true that few of today's students already swear by favorite poets or writers of fiction or love the theater of the absurd. Some of them may come from earlier classroom experiences with a teacher who had been brainwashed to believe that students hate poetry.

As our own offspring might say: "So?" Our assignment is to help our students discover imaginative literature—to discover how a storyteller opens a window on the world; to discover how a poem can find words for powerful feelings; to discover the contagious excitement of live drama in a student production or video performance.

- The literary canon is not a static inheritance to be protected by George Will and other guardians of culture but a living evolving legacy. The canon has not been set in concrete since Matthew Arnold ruled on the best that has been thought and said. Our thinking about drama was forever changed by Henrik Ibsen (not to mention Eugène Ionesco), just as our definition of poetry was forever changed by Emily Dickinson's cryptic, sparse, teasing, and provocative poems. Part of an anthologist's privilege is to help canonize today's classic—from Toni Morrison and Alice Walker to Louise Erdrich, Tim O'Brien, or Wole Soyinka.

• The definition of a classic is that it speaks across gulfs in time and space to each new generation. As teachers and critics, we help today's readers and spectators hear the voices. We serve a new generation of readers and spectators as translators and interpreters, somewhat the way the blind prophet in a Greek tragedy helps point the way for other mortals. As we see it, the function of criticism is to serve literature, not the other way around. Our aim in drawing on the rich resources of current criticism is not to make literature serve theory but to draw on critics who can help illuminate the human meaning and contemporary relevance of writers for our students.

Teaching imaginative literature gives us the chance to keep alive the joy of reading. It gives us a chance to help students discover the rich diversity of their cultural heritage. We treasure the privilege.

Hans P. Guth
Santa Clara University

Gabriele L. Rico
San Jose State University

CONTENTS

Note: Page numbers in parentheses refer to the student text and are followed by page numbers for this manual.

Overview: Drama 356

Teaching Suggestions and Answers to Questions: Drama 358

TO THE INSTRUCTOR

As a poet I hold the most archaic values on earth. They go back to the late Paleolithic: the fertility of the soil, the magic of animals, the power-vision in solitude, the terrifying initiation and rebirth, the love and ecstasy of the dance, the common work of the tribe.

GARY SNYDER

The purpose of *Discovering Literature* is to help you share your love of literature with today's students. This manual suggests ways of drawing students into the literature. It sketches ways of implementing a program of close reading, personal response, and creative participation. It provides an ample sampling of student responses for class discussion, work in groups, and written work. New "Perspectives" mini-essays for many selections provide critical, scholarly, or biographical backup material.

OVERVIEWS In the overviews for each genre, we explain the rationale for placement or sequence of selections. Providing a "way in" to the literature, *Discovering Literature* takes students from the more accessible to the more challenging, from the traditional to the more experimental, or from the contemporary to an established classic. "First Readings" at the beginning of most chapters bring a major critical or thematic concern into focus. "Juxtapositions" of classic and modern, male and female, or mainstream and minority authors help students see continuity in diversity, helping them bridge the gap between different periods, styles, and cultures. Departures from familiar course patterns are not arbitrary but reflect our sense of what it takes to capture and hold the attention of students. For instance, while including Sophocles' *Oedipus the King,* the book introduces students to Greek drama through Sophocles' earlier *Antigone,* the story of a young woman whose private conscience puts her on a collision course with a self-righteous, patriotically correct establishment.

PERSPECTIVES ESSAYS New "Perspectives" essays for many selections provide you with material for mini-lectures or context for class discussion. Perspectives essays may focus, for instance, on the range of critical responses to a much analyzed story or poem, on a rereading of a work from a current critical perspective, on reassessments of the critical reputation of a major author, on critical reevaluations or rediscoveries of major female writers, or on introductions to major authors from minority or culturally diverse backgrounds. Sample topics for the "Perspectives" mini-essays:

QUEST IMAGERY IN JOYCE'S "ARABY"
MULTIPLE IRONY IN "EVERYTHING THAT RISES"
RITA DOVE ON POETRY AND ELITISM
A CLASSIC CRITICAL READING OF "THAT TIME OF YEAR"
PLATH'S "MIRROR" AND THE UNRELIABLE NARRATOR
KEATS' "URN" AND NEO-PLATONISM

DISCUSSION STARTERS Discussion starters suggest ways you may want to approach a selection in class. What is a good way to arouse interest or prepare the way for a story, poem, or play? Suggested questions may ask students to take stock of what they bring to a literary work. What expectations do they bring to the selection? What attitudes, preconceptions, or relevant experiences will influence the reader's response? Other questions may help steer the reader's attention, bringing into focus a central theme, key issue, organizing metaphor, or central symbol.

OPEN-ENDED ANSWERS TO QUESTIONS Suggested answers to questions are not meant to be exhaustive or to give the "right answer." They are meant to put at your fingertips key quotations, revealing details, or explications of central metaphors and symbols. Sample answers are not meant to be the last word. They may be followed by a question mark rather than by a period to suggest that the answer is subject to discussion. Students should feel welcome to explore, to think, and to venture tentative and incomplete responses. Often a fuller understanding of a work will evolve from the give-and-take of a range of personal reactions or individual interpretations.

THE CREATIVE DIMENSION The manual provides illustrations of student responses that bring the student's own imagination and creativity into play. Examples of re-creations and other imaginative responses are meant to help you nudge passive readers of literature into becoming involved, participating, interacting readers. Sample responses show why students enjoy writing sequels, prequels, updates, and rewrites (such as "The Second to the Last Time We Heard about Dummy"). The basic assumption of *Discovering Literature* is that imagination and creativity are not the exclusive domain of a few gifted individuals but are part of the birthright of every human being.

ACKNOWLEDGMENTS Among the many students who have given us permission to use or adapt journal entries or creative work in this manual, we want to thank particularly Amy Angaiak, Vanessa Camones, Kelly Hannibal, Gena Harris, Kathryn Harrison, Timothy Lin, Katie Mercer, Hugo Rodriguez, and Amy Timpe.

PARTIAL LISTING OF "PERSPECTIVES" ESSAYS:

FICTION

INTRODUCTION
Teaching *Discovering Literature*

How do we share our love of literature with a new generation of students? The questions we take to class with us are similar, regardless of the varying geography and demographics of our institutions. We ask ourselves:

- How do we help our students overcome negative attitudes or preconceptions about literature that they might bring to our classrooms?
- How can we help students discover the power of literature to illuminate and enhance their lives?
- How do we get students to sense the excitement of good fiction? How do we help them overcome the assumption that poetry is not for them? How do we help them discover the human drama of the great plays?
- How do we help them discover the classics that speak to us across distances in time and place?
- How can we help them experience the richness of our diverse cultural heritage? How can we counteract the influence of those who use terms like *multiculturalism* or *diversity* as divisive slogans?
- How do we involve students in the way today's writers shape our sense of self and our changing awareness of our world?

Whatever our individual strategies, we need to believe in the potential of our students. We need to believe in the untapped potential—potential untapped by routine methods. We need to believe that the students in our classrooms are as intelligent, as capable of experiencing true emotion, and as capable of curiosity and empathy as any previous generation. Our reward as teachers comes when students written off by testing experts and pundits discover unsuspected resources of intelligence and imaginative sympathy. Imaginative literature has the power to kindle interest where there was apathy, to expand horizons, and to awaken and refresh the human spirit.

To believe in our students' potential does not mean ignoring familiar day-to-day classroom realities. Students today often have had little experience with close, responsive reading. Most are the products of a television culture, attuned to its glitz and surface appeal, its sound bites. Many come from homes with few books or none. Many are reading and writing English as a second or third language—dealing with challenges that their monolingual classmates cannot imagine. Many of our students have had negative experiences with literature—especially poetry and Shakespeare—taught in too dutiful a manner as a tour through the literary monuments. For many of them, the riches of the literary tradition are an uncharted continent.

Issues in Teaching Literature

Our purpose in writing this book has been to give teachers the resources they need to help students realize their potential. Reviewers of the first edition praised its "invitation to students" and its ability to encourage reading. We try to do more than the authors of comparable books to appeal to the students' native intelligence; to help them deal with challenging, difficult materials; and to help them bring their own imagination and creativity into play. We have worked to address issues like the following in working on the current second edition:

THE RELEVANCE OF LITERATURE At a time when pundits announce the death of literature and the closing of the American mind, textbooks need to reaffirm our faith in the power of literature to illuminate lives and in the native intelligence, imagination, and idealism of our students. As teachers of literature we share a basic commitment to the students in our classes. Regardless of our theoretical disagreements, we believe in the power of imaginative literature to open windows on the world. We have faith that literature will enrich the imagination, educate the emotions, and nourish the spiritual growth of our students.

THE PARTICIPATING READER Over the years, our profession has seen a successive paradigm shift from emphasis on the author (the life, the times, the milieu), first to emphasis on the text (the form, the theme, the built-in tensions), and then increasingly to emphasis on the critic (the theoretical perspective, the critique of language, the critique of society). We encourage a further shift to emphasis on the student as the participating reader. Imaginative literature is an interaction between writer and reader. It comes to fruition when the responsive reader brings the poem or story to life in the theater of the mind.

THE SHARED COMMITMENT A key issue in the teaching of literature today is the tendency toward polarizing the faculty: the "circle-the-wagons" mentality of traditionalists versus the "political correctness" of advocates of socially committed, gender-conscious literature. Our aim is to help teachers live with this dichotomy: Regardless of theoretical and political differences, our common aim as teachers of literature is to help students discover the true richness and diversity of their literary heritage. We resist the use of labels like *multiculturalism* or *Eurocentric* as divisive slogans.

RETHINKING THE CANON Each generation rediscovers the classics, discovers tomorrow's classics, and rethinks its list of canonical works. This book does more than other anthologies to give students a "way in" to the reading of Sophocles' *Antigone*, Shakespeare's *Hamlet*, Emily Dickinson, John Steinbeck, John Donne, Gwendolyn Brooks, or Flannery O'Connor. At the same time, we stress the continuity between the present and the past. We integrate treatment of the classics with the best current writing. Among today's classics new to this edition are stories by Louise Erdrich, Toni Morrison, Tim O'Brien, and Sandra Cisneros; poems by Maurya Simon, Rita Dove, Edward Hirsch, and Alison Hawthorne Deming; and plays by David Henry Hwang and David Mamet. A basic strategy of *Discovering Literature* is to juxtapose selections from the traditional canon with thematically related work by women or work from culturally diverse sources. Andrew Marvell's "To His Coy Mistress" is linked with the Countess of Dia's "I Speak of That Which I Would Rather Hide." A modern adaptation of the medieval play *Everyman* is juxtaposed with Luis Valdez' contemporary *Everyman* play about a Chicano GI going to Vietnam.

GENDER AND ETHNIC BALANCE Imaginative literature transcends boundaries of gender, ethnicity, race, or sexual orientation. Among the poets in this volume, women from earlier periods include Juana Inés de la Cruz, the Countess of Dia, Christine de Pisan, and Aphra Behn. New selections include fiction by Paul Laurence Dunbar, Guadalupe Valdés, and Lesléa Newman. New poetry includes poems by Quincy Troupe, Janice Mirikitani, Chitra Divakaruni, Maya Angelou, and Martín Espada. The drama section includes plays by Susan Glaspell, Lorraine Hansberry, Wendy Wasserstein, and Marsha Norman.

THE RELEVANCE OF CRITICISM In the "age of theory," we examine the currents and countercurrents of contemporary literary theory for their relevance to the student reader's response to literature. New or strengthened "Perspectives" sections in the student text introduce students to the range of critical approaches to fiction, poetry, and drama. Critical perspectives covered include reader response, author biography, literary history, the New Criticism (or formalism), myth criticism, psychoanalytic criticism, political (often neo-Marxist) criticism, structuralism and poststructuralism, deconstructionism, and feminist criticism. Critical revaluations focus on writers seen in a new light as current critics bring new criteria and expectations to bear.

THE CREATIVE DIMENSION An exclusively analytical approach to imaginative literature is a contradiction in terms. If students are to enter fully into the spirit of poem or play, we cannot neglect honoring the students' own imagination. *Discovering Literature* encourages students to cease being passive readers and instead bring their own imaginations into play. A unique "Creative Dimension" strand encourages students to discover their own creativity.

VALIDATING STUDENT WRITING Writing about literature makes students more intelligent and more responsive readers. *Discovering Literature* provides guidelines for writing and model papers with each chapter. Writing workshops repeatedly take students through major stages in the writing process, from preliminary exploration and note taking through shaping and drafting to revision and rethinking in response to feedback from instructor and peers. A wealth of motivated, well-developed student writing provides model papers for class discussion of writing strategies and for peer review.

ACCESSIBLE TEXTS We have cautiously modernized punctuation (and sometimes spelling) where needed to make poems of earlier periods intelligible, enjoyable, and inspiring for a new generation. Where obsolete printers' conventions or dysfunctional marks impede the modern reader, we update punctuation somewhat to help today's student follow the syntax of a poem by John Donne or the rhythms of a poem by John Keats. Two glossed (rather than footnoted) student editions—*Hamlet* and *A Midsummer Night's Dream*—offer students a more inviting, intelligible, and motivating introduction to Shakespeare than competing books. Close at hand and available at a glance, the glosses illuminate difficult passages and provide the closest modern meaning in the context of a line.

A TEXT FOR TODAY'S CLASSROOMS Traditional literature textbooks have often appealed to teachers by talking to them about the literature they love, using the insider's language or the style of the literary sophisticate. Today, a major concern of teachers is to make sure that the great majority of students does not tune out early in the course, convinced that poetry and sophisticated modern fiction are not for them. What does it take to convince them that literature is not just for an in-group audience? A textbook today cannot assume that the job of initiating future readers of literature and of converting them to the cause has already been done. By the same token, a textbook today cannot put women and new poets or "multicultural" writers in optional separate sections serving as literary ghettos. If we believe in inclusiveness and balance, we need to give teachers books that offer an organic, inclusive vision of the literary heritage.

Teaching Strategies and Teaching Helps

Discovering Literature helps teachers bring literature to life with specific teaching strategies and teaching helps. It sets directions and sets up perspectives for fruitful work with today's students.

NON-ROUTINE APPARATUS What kind of apparatus helps teachers make imaginative literature accessible to today's students? We aim at providing introductions and supporting materials that bring works and authors to life for the student reader. The book offers a rich array of contemporary testimony, provocative critical reactions, and candid student responses that provide "a way into" the literature. Going beyond routine author biographies, we try to help the student reader conjure up the contemporary context of creative work or to reenact vital confrontations. We try to dramatize the personal vision, the personal way of looking at the world, of writers from Emily Dickinson and William Stafford to Lorraine Hansberry and Alice Walker. We give students a sense of how the great writers from William Blake to Gwendolyn Brooks were vitally embroiled in the contemporary issues and challenges of their time.

FUNCTIONAL TERMINOLOGY How do we keep technical terminology from becoming an end in itself? We should not ask students to read a poem for the sake of taking inventory of its images, symbols, metaphors, rhymes, or meter. We study crucial formal features of literature because they serve its human meaning. In this book, "starter quotes" show that major critical concepts are not entries in a reference file but are vital concerns of creative men and women. Introductory discussions of key terms treat them as focal points for our exploration of literature. Setting, for instance, in many a compelling story, is not just a location, a convenient backdrop. It's where people lead their lives; it in many ways shapes and limits who they are.

VALIDATING THE PERSONAL RESPONSE Imaginative literature educates the emotions as well as the intellect. An exclusively intellectual analysis of a work of the imagination is a contradiction in terms. Throughout the book, we try to suggest the right balance of intellectual analysis, emotional involvement, and imaginative participation. We aim at a fruitful balance of close reading and the personal response.

Our student readers cannot read a poem like William Stafford's "Traveling through the Dark" as if it were a dispassionate report on a roadkill. It is true the poem starts on a matter-of-fact note: A deer is dead on the road (the speaker in the poem calls it a "heap"); the "road is narrow." In such cases, it is "usually best to roll them into the canyon." But the poem soon makes it hard for us to remain aloof: The side of the dead doe is still warm; she is large with a fawn, "alive, still, never to be born." For all the speaker's understated, muted account of his momentary hesitation, we cannot help feeling a twinge of futile regret; of rebellion against things as they are; of unavailing, unspoken guilt. In the words of one student reader, "for a brief moment" the speaker in the poem "makes us think of the impossible task of saving the fawn."

THE RANGE OF INTERPRETATION Once we honor the emotional and imaginative dimension of literature, we validate the range of interpretation. We validate the range of reader response. Critics and teachers today are more open than they have been in the past to what readers *bring* to literature. The readers' responses are fashioned in part by their own emotional needs, their preconceptions and previous conditioning, their subjective point of view. A story has a special fascination when a central conflict becomes a mirror for something in the reader's own experience, perhaps bringing to the surface and illuminating an almost forgotten incident. Images in a poem acquire a special meaning when readers discover a personal connection. In Peter Meinke's poem "Sunday at the Apple Market," there is "apple smell everywhere!" People crowd around the testing table, laughing, "rolling / the cool applechunks in their mouths." Here is one student's personal response:

Reading the poem, I was struck by the image of the dogs barking at the children in the apple trees. It brought to mind a time when my grandparents' orchard was for me a "free and happy" world of its own. I remember a Sunday when I was hiding from my cousins in my grandmother's apple tree, stifling giggles on a high branch, my Sunday dress torn on the rough bark. I wrote a brief poem recalling the experience; it ends as follows:

> In Sunday black and white like spotted puppies
> my brothers sniff and search under apple carts

and behind the stacked up empty wooden crates.
Behind heavy leaves red apples hide.
I hide, too.

In reading a story or poem, readers who have learned to love literature respond to the writer's intentions while yet reading the story or poem in their own way. Once we conclude that seemingly absolute standards are personal standards writ large, we can learn from the drama of literary influence and reputation. We can understand why a writer like Edna St. Vincent Millay can for a time enjoy a vogue, then be devalued by changing critical trends, and finally be rediscovered by a new generation of readers. We can help students see how Dickinson was in her time considered willfully obscure—to be recognized today by many as America's greatest poet. Much of the vigor of current criticism stems from feminist rereadings and reevaluations of work by both men and women, with critics listening to the "unheard voices" of characters like Shakespeare's Ophelia or Arthur Miller's Linda Loman.

CLASSROOM INTERACTION Ideally, our students will be active learners rather than passive absorbers of inert knowledge. Our aim in this book is to help teachers provide students with a rich classroom experience that will change passive, isolated readers into active readers—readers who interact with the literature and with other readers. Students have to learn or relearn to translate the letters on the page into sound and image. They should hear the rhythms of poetry and react to the thrust-and-parry of dramatic dialogue. They should be reading aloud and hearing passages and poems read aloud. Formats might vary from Quaker readings (where one reader leaves off and another picks up as the spirit moves them) to readers' theater readings and choral readings of poetry. Students should experience the contagion of involvement as they witness other students getting excited about a poem or story—or rebelling against its implications. They should learn from the range of interpretation, joining in the playing off and synthesizing of individual perceptions.

A SAMPLING OF SPECIFIC TEACHING STATEGIES

• You may want to read with your students the *opening lines* or paragraphs of a story. What world is taking shape, with what implied assumptions, customs, or code? What mood is being set? What expectations are being created? The opening page of a story like Eudora Welty's "A Visit of Charity," Charlotte Perkins Gilman's "The Yellow Wallpaper," Stephen Crane's "The Open Boat, " or Franz Kafka's "The Country Doctor" can provide a striking example of how a story creates its own characteristic world.

• Have your students *complete* an "unfinished" story—a story of which they have heard only a part or from which the original ending has been omitted. Or have them do sequels or updates that show how well they have entered into the spirit of a story. The following is a sequel to Shirley Jackson's "The Lottery" that dramatizes the timelessness and contemporary relevance of Jackson's story:

Winning the Lottery

Over the years, many of the old buildings have been torn down to make room for Seven Elevens and a large SUPER-mart with a cafeteria. Young women come in for the latest cosmetic or fashion magazine. There's even an aisle for the devout; it has Bibles and plastic Virgins that customers can attach to the dashboards of their cars. People are remodeling, improving, and accessorizing their homes, their bodies, and their televisions. The annual lottery has been moved to the large SUPER-mart parking lot. This year, the person drawing the marked slip of paper—is Mr. Stanfield! He was a pretty good man, and he watched television regularly too. The crowd moves to his home and dismantles it piece by piece. Pictures of his family are distributed, clothing passed around, and patterned dishes lovingly packed in bubble wrap. He wanders slowly down the road, past the store where he used to rent movies and the station where he used to put gas in his car. He ambles slowly in the single pair of sneakers he was allowed to keep; of course it's taboo for anyone to give him a ride. He dejectedly holds on to a hand-lettered sign that says he'll work for food, but he knows it's against the rules for anyone to help him. Every morning he leaves the old cardboard that's his cover during the nights under the overpass and stands in line at the Bureau with the other lottery winners of years past. The lone window opens for a short span at ten. The person working the window tells the waiting line of winners that the forms they need to get sustenance stamps were delayed at the printers but that they can expect them any day.

• You will often want to explore with your students key metaphors or central symbols. Have them *cluster* a key image or central term, with different lines of association branching out from the term that provides the central core. Here is a cluster that explores the range of associations for a term fraught with rich symbolic overtones and implications:

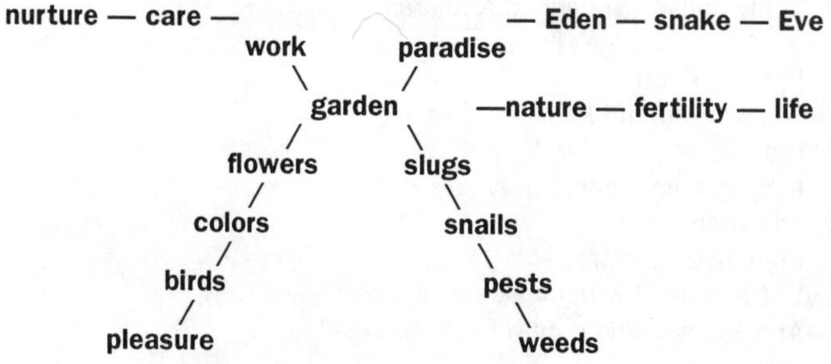

nurture — care — **— Eden — snake — Eve**

work **paradise**

\ /

garden **—nature — fertility — life**

/ \

flowers **slugs**

/ \

colors **snails**

/ \

birds **pests**

/ \

pleasure **weeds**

• Have your students do *re-creations* of a provocative image, a central symbol, or a dominant mood. Often a key metaphor—like John Donne's "twin compasses" in his "A Valediction: Forbidding Mourning"—lingers in our minds and seems to sum what the poem says. A weighty phrase echoes in our minds—as when Stephen Crane says about the survivors of his story about the sea, "They could then be interpreters."

Re-creations invite the student to get into the spirit of a story or a poem, to verbalize its impact on the reader. Some re-creations will take off from a striking detail that lingers in the reader's mind. Others will respond to the whole—to the movement of a story, to the shape of a poem. The following re-creation focuses on the pumpkins that become a central symbol in Mary Robison's story "Yours"—her beautiful parable on youth and age, sickness and health, love and death:

Pumpkins in orange October,
        their sweet soggy smell
        rises from carved insides
        on wet news
Their fierce pumpkin faces, lit by candles,
        glow till morning,
        the live flame softening their shells
Pumpkin, a child's toy,
        not for May or December,
        but for late October, ushering in
        November and a Thanksgiving of sorts
Pumpkins from the brittle vine
        the last sweet
        harvest

Here is another student's re-creation of the elegiac mood in N. Scott Momaday's "Earth and I Gave You Turquoise." It shows a student in her own way capturing the essence of the poem—going to the heart of the poet's message. In this re-creation, a woman rather than a man is the grieving survivor:

We walked the earth together.
In my house we danced and drank
        coffee till morning.
I planted corn.
You wanted children.
But you became ill.
I thought love could heal you.
The years drag,
I'll dance no more.
But one day I will speak your name,
And you will come on a swift horse.

- Have students work in groups to prepare a class presentation of a group of *thematically related* poems. For instance, a group might collaborate to present poems about nature, by and about women, or about a part of the country. It can be an eye-opener for students to listen as their peers recite with passion and commitment poems by lesbian poets, poems against war, poems about the environment, or poems on religious themes.

- Experiment with changes in *point of view*. Essential to the life of the imagination is the willingness to look at something familiar from a fresh perspective. Ask students to retell a story from the point of view of someone other than the narrator or the protagonist. Have a minor or unheroic character in a play—Polonius, Ismene, Linda Loman—present his or her version of events, as seen from the point of view of an ordinary, unheroic person. Give the antagonist—Sophocles' Creon, Ibsen's Torvald, or Molière's Célimène—a chance to tell his or her side of the story. Have Ophelia or Gertrude tell Hamlet what they might have said if less conditioned to let their men do the talking.

- Experiment with *mini-productions*. The difference between reading *Everyman* and playing the part of Everyman, Kinship, Good Deeds, or Death is the difference between listening to a CD and playing the second violin in a Vivaldi concerto. It is a revelation for students to see their peers act out characters in a play and bring them to life. Have students act out selected scenes from a play. Have a group prepare a contemporary adaptation of a classic play or story. One class did an adaptation of the medieval Everyman play called *Everywoman*. In another class, Everyman was a rock musician, who electrocuted himself when plugging his electric guitar into a defective reading lamp. (In one class, students who had trouble memorizing their lines for an *Antigone* production pasted their lines to the inside of their masks.)

The Writing Strand

One of the central aims of this book is to do more than other textbooks to integrate literature and writing—to integrate reading literature, talking about literature, and writing about literature. Students do not learn to write by dutifully practicing papers written to the same one-size-fits-all format. They learn to write by writing papers that respond to a range of assignments and rise to a variety of challenges. *Discovering Literature* presents a structured writing program that builds students' competence and confidence by moving from relatively simple to gradually more sophisticated writing tasks.

JOURNAL WRITING *Discovering Literature* provides a writing workshop devoted to *journal writing* for each of the three genres: short story, poem, and play. After the "Preview" chapter for each genre, students have a chance to look at suggestions for journal writing and be inspired by sample entries written by fellow students.

Journal writing helps students develop the writing habit. It gives them informal practice in the most basic of writing skills: to put what they think and feel into words. At the same time, it provides an essential *prewriting* stage for their writing about literature. The journal allows students to record first impressions and spontaneous responses—in a less structured form than in a formal paper. It gives them a chance to do a running commentary as they see a story or a poem take shape. It offers them an opportunity to register their queries and think about tentative answers. It gives them a place to record their confusions and epiphanies.

The rich backlog of significant details, personal reactions, questions, and tentative answers in a well-kept journal provides a rich resource for more formal, more structured papers. It provides the antidote to anemic, dutiful student papers that have not gone through the essential preliminary stage of taking in possibly significant detail, wrestling with initial confusion, and seeing tentative patterns take shape.

THE WRITING PROCESS Writing a paper is a process, like baking one's own bread. Focus on process moves student writing away from uncommitted papers written at the last minute from vague memory of skimmed reading. Students need a sense of the process that produces real writing. The writing strand focuses on how a well-motivated, substantial, and effective paper takes shape. Students can see again and again how a successful paper moves from the original question in the writer's mind through the process of gestation to near final form. Prewriting, laying out a rough draft, and revision in turn receive major emphasis in successive writing workshops.

What sets a paper in motion—what is the writer's need, purpose, or motive for writing? What has the writer done to work up the material—to build up a rich backlog of telling details, apt examples, quotable quotes, insider's insights, or expert opinion? How is the writer going to bring the subject into focus and work out a workable overall plan? What feedback from peers or instructor will guide the revision of a first or second draft? What rethinking and re-vision will make sure a paper undergoes more than cosmetic revision?

These dimensions of the writing process are not clearly distinct or separate stages. They overlap, and they are "recursive." One writer may start revising after completing the first two paragraphs; another may still be hunting for supporting material or a missing piece of evidence when proofreading the final draft. A realistic definition of the writing process makes full allowance for false starts, changes in direction, and painful reappraisals. A paper honestly worked out is the richer for the thinking and rethinking that the writer has invested in it.

USING STUDENT MODELS Each chapter of *Discovering Literature* is followed by a writing workshop that includes a model student paper. (In one of the workshops, paired student papers juxtapose two different readings of a story.) Often the workshop material demonstrates how a paper moves through different stages—from prewriting to writing, from a first to a second draft.

For instance, following the chapter on metaphor, Writing Workshop 14 shows a student's reading notes on John Donne's "A Valediction: Forbidding Mourning" and then shows the successful finished paper. Like other model papers, this paper has an authentic voice (it was not written by the authors of the textbook). It has a clear focus and a well-thought-out overall plan. It cites and interprets relevant evidence from the poem exceptionally well.

A sampling of the student's reading notes:

Telling others of the speaker's intimate, private love (through loud display of grief) would be like priests revealing the mysteries of their faith to "the laity," that is, to lay people—to unappreciative, unprepared outsiders. The lovers would then "profane" the mysteries of their love—desecrating something sacred by taking it down to the level of ordinary reality.

The upheavals in the lives or ordinary lovers are earthquakes ("moving of the earth"). But any disturbance in the more refined loves of the two people in this poem is "a trepidation of the spheres"—it is like the far-off trembling in the crystal spheres of the heavens, which is "innocent" or harmless as far as actual damage in the world around us is concerned.

The "souls" of ordinary clods are not really soul but sense—they stay on the level of sense perception and sensual feeling; they don't really have a "soul."

True love is like gold—it can be stretched incredibly thin like gold leaf without breaking.

The student author of the paper used the idea of the journey—which is the subject of Donne's poem—as the organizing principle for the paper:

Excerpts from model paper:

(intriguing, evocative title:)

Thou Shalt Not Cry When I Am Gone

(introduction establishing a link between Donne and today's world:)

In a favorite scene in yesterday's romantic movies, someone is boarding a train, going off to war or to some far-off assignment or tour of duty. The person left behind is fighting back tears as the train slowly pulls out of the station. The traveler is trying to stay calm, forestalling the "tear-floods" and "sigh-tempests" that John Donne dreads in his farewell poem, "A Valediction: Forbidding Mourning." Scheduled to leave on a journey to France, Donne pleads with his wife Anne More to accept his departure in a spirit of calm acceptance, confident that the strength of their love will triumph over their physical separation.

(focus on the journey as organizing principle of the paper:)

In arguing against mourning and emotional upheaval, Donne takes us on a journey through a sequence of bold unexpected images, each one a metaphor or a simile for the love between him and his wife. Finally we reach the circle drawn by the twin compasses in the final stanzas as the metaphor for a perfect love that will bring him back to the starting point of his journey, making "me end where I begun." The structure of the poem, a progression from one striking metaphor or simile to another, is the more appropriate when we consider that the poem was presented to his wife before he departed on a journey.

(major stages in the overall plan of the paper, leading up to the culminating metaphor:)

The journey begins with an unexpected analogy between the impending separation of the lovers and death. The poet says "So let us melt"—go quietly, like snow that melts in the March sun, making "no noise" (5). . . .

Their love is in fact almost sacred. It would be profaned if it should be made known to others, who could not comprehend love on such a high spiritual plane. Since it is almost holy, the lovers should not cheapen or defile it through such ordinary demonstration of grief as weeping or lamenting. . . .

We next move to a larger circle than the temple where love is protected from the uninitiated. Even the earth is not adequate to contain true love. For more common lovers, the earthquake of separation would bring "harms and fears" (9). But the love between the poet and his wife is above the reach of such earthly upheavals. It is as if their love resided in the heavens, among the crystal spheres of the Ptolemaic universe. Even when there is "trepidation" or trembling of the spheres, it is "innocent"—it will cause no harm here below. . . .

However, the culminating metaphor is that of the twin compasses, which "are two" only in the sense that there are two legs joined permanently at the top. The "fixed foot" of the stay-at-home "leans and harkens" after the other that "far doth roam" (25–30). As the foot that actually draws the circle travels around the stationary part, that part must incline at the right angle. (It cannot just forget about the "roaming" part.)

(conclusion circling back to the original journey motif:)

Together, the twin compasses create a circle, to Donne's contemporaries the most perfect shape in the universe. The firmness of the "other foot" enables the poet to come full circle; it makes his journey "end where I begun" (36).

The questions following a model paper give the writer's peers a chance to compare their own reading of a story, poem, or play with that of the student author. They remind students that writing is not complete until it has found a reader—who responds, interacts, agrees, and disagrees. Here is one of the questions following the paper on the Donne poem:

> 3. One reader thought the poem "terribly romantic," since the poet wants the love between him and his wife to be perfect, better than anyone else's. At the opposite end of the spectrum, another reader found the poet to be romantic on the surface but really insensitive, lecturing a silent, passive partner about what she should feel and think. Where do you stand? How do you respond to the poem?

DEMYSTIFYING RESEARCH AND DOCUMENTATION *Discovering Literature* includes instruction in research techniques, guidelines for documentation, and a sample research paper for each genre. Workshop 10 deals with a documented paper for fiction. Workshop 23 discusses research techniques for writing about poetry. Workshop 29 does the same for drama. Depending on the scope of the course (one quarter, one semester, or a two-term sequence), teachers may choose to make one of the three genres the focus for a term paper—or to give students a choice among the three.

Every teacher knows the danger in teaching the research paper: The finer points or micro-concerns of documentation tend to crowd out concern with the larger purposes of research and research-based writing. We need to keep research from becoming a mere ritual and to keep attention focused on the *why* (as well as the *so what*). Students need to develop their competence in marshaling evidence and integrating materials from a range of sources. They need to learn to make good use of both primary and secondary sources, learning how to draw on authoritative support from biographers or critics.

Guidelines, sample entries, and model papers in this book follow the current MLA guidelines for research papers. Instructions are designed to help students who are easily overwhelmed by the ramifications of documentation style. The instructions focus on the reasons for and major principles of documentation before they explain and illustrate specifics and finer points. Sample papers were selected to serve as examples of effective writing, not merely to serve as a vehicle for illustrating technical points.

Part One FICTION

THOUGHT STARTERS

This introduction to short fiction focuses on "storying," on the making of stories, as one of the oldest ways human beings give shape and meaning to experience. What do your students bring to the reading of stories? You may want to ask your students starter questions like the following:

- What do we mean when we ask people to "tell their story"?
- Was the age-old tradition of storytelling alive in your own family or cultural background? Are there any storytellers among your friends?
- What writers you know do you think of as storytellers—and what kind of stories do they tell?
- Which practitioners of the modern short story have you encountered—John Steinbeck? Ernest Hemingway? Shirley Jackson? Flannery O'Connor? What short stories do you remember, and how did you react to them?
- Have you read any short stories by writers from minority or non-Western backgrounds? For instance, have you read stories by Alice Walker, Toni Cade Bambara, or Sandra Cisneros? What for you was new or different about them?

Overview

THE ELEMENTS OF FICTION How do the formal elements of the short story serve its human meaning? This introduction to short fiction focuses on how features of form—setting, character, plot, symbol, point of view—shape and carry an author's vision of the world. How do these elements of literature give shape to a story as a finished whole? The treatment throughout here does not treat the elements of fiction as ends in themselves. Throughout, the treatment of the short story validates the student's personal response, recognizes the range of interpretation, and fosters creative participation.

REDEFINING THE CANON The selections help the teacher redefine and revitalize the canon. They include classic stories as well as tomorrow's classics. They are drawn from both the traditional canon and the larger multicultural range. They encourage students to honor diversity while seeing how literature from diverse cultural traditions deals with constants in human experience. More than half of the stories are written by women, from Eudora Welty and Charlotte Perkins Gilman to Alice Walker, Bharati Mukherjee, and Alice Munro. "Juxtapositions"—Anderson and Kincaid, Parker and Bambara—enable students to see the continuity of the literary enterprise and the presence of the past. Many of the stories have attracted serious critical attention while at the same time they are accessible to what Virginia Woolf calls "the common reader."

INTERACTIVE APPARATUS The apparatus encourages close reading and the personal response, encouraging students to find the personal connection in what they read. It encourages creative participation, allowing students to bring their own imagination and creativity into play.

Guide to Contents

1 PREVIEW: THE WORLD OF FICTION The opening chapter focuses on the making of stories, on "storying," as an age-old way of giving shape to experience. This chapter introduces a special feature of this book: the use of "short shorts" that can be read aloud in class and give students a chance to focus on a major dimension of fiction. Short shorts by writers from Sandra Cisneros, Grace Paley, and Chinua Achebe to Ernest Hemingway, Mary Robison, and Tobias Wolff give students a preview of major elements of the storyteller's art: setting, character, plot, point of view, symbol, theme, style.

2 SETTING: LANDSCAPES OF THE MIND Writers of fiction put characters in a setting and set them in motion. Setting is typically more than a physical location. It creates a world with its own assumptions, its own ways of living, its own universe of thinking and feeling. James Joyce's classic "Araby" demonstrates how a great story creates its own world. Bobbie Ann Mason and Yukio Mishima similarly take us to a setting that becomes authentic and compelling. However distant from our own, the world they create becomes believable, enabling us to accept the premises set up by the context of the story.

3 CHARACTER: THE BURIED SELF The writers in Chapter 3 respond to the reader's innate curiosity about what it means to be human. They create characters who become more than cardboard figures and evolve into live human beings. Raymond Carver, Louise Erdrich, Sherwood Anderson, and Jamaica Kincaid give readers a strong sense of the mystery of personality, helping readers piece together their understanding of characters that may be puzzling and elusive (like real-life characters). Alice Munro probes the way gender roles help shape our identity, our sense of self. These stories take us beyond social masks, surface impressions, and stereotypes to probe for the past histories and current motives that define complex fellow humans.

4 PLOT: THE CHAIN OF EVENTS Plot rivets the attention of the reader. In this chapter, stories by Doris Lessing, Bernard Malamud, Shirley Jackson, and William Faulkner invite the reader to look for the mainspring of the action in character, in chance, or in fate. Malamud's "The Magic Barrel," told in the manner of the traditional storyteller, makes the readers follow the action in linear chronological order, creating suspense and leading up to a surprise ending that at the same time resolves the basic agenda of the story. Shirley Jackson's literary horror story takes us to a deceptively normal setting only to make us witness evil surfacing in the context of ordinary lives. William Faulkner's "A Rose for Emily" abandons the traditional linear plot line, asking readers to reconstruct a pattern of events from the clues furnished by the author.

5 POINT OF VIEW: WINDOWS ON THE WORLD Chapter 5 focuses on point of view as a dominant preoccupation of modern writers and critics of fiction. What window does a story open on the world? Who is the "reflector" whose necessarily limited or subjective perceptions define the reality created by the story? Stories by Anton Chekhov, Joyce Carol Oates, Tillie Olsen, and Katherine Anne Porter show the constraints and opportunities that come with the point of view from which the author chooses to see the events of a story. Each of these stories leaves behind the convention of the omniscient author to take us into the world of the narrator or of a central character in the story. Successive stories employ narrative techniques that more and more get us inside the minds of their characters: third-person narrative from the point of view of the naive observer (Chekhov); third-person narrative limited to the central character's world (Oates); first-person confessional (Olsen); partial stream of consciousness (Porter).

6 SYMBOL: THE ELOQUENT IMAGE Readers read the images as well as the words of a story. In Chapter 6, stories by John Steinbeck, Charlotte Perkins Gilman, and Gabriel García Márquez show how the language of symbols enhances or supersedes the language of words and the language of actions. Steinbeck's short story classic uses an overt symbolism that nevertheless has allowed readers and critics to read their own meanings into the story. Gilman and García Márquez, in the modern vein, use ambivalent, disturbing symbols whose meaning shifts and develops as the story takes shape.

7 THEME: THE SEARCH FOR MEANING At the end of Stephen Crane's "The Open Boat," the survivors, hearing the sound of the sea from the shore, "felt that they could then be interpreters." In the chapter focused on theme, stories by Luisa Valenzuela, Alice Walker, Stephen Crane, and Nathaniel Hawthorne make us ponder the meanings we read into or out of a story. The stories range in explicitness from Crane's use of thematic passages and overt symbols to Hawthorne's intentionally perplexing ambiguities. Each of these stories has a powerful message—that, however is not spelled out in the manner of editorial writers, preachers, and moralists. It is *acted* out, for us to ponder and read according to our own lights.

8 STYLE: THE WRITER'S VOICE In imaginative literature, style is more than a matter of style. Chapter 8 focuses on how style helps shape the impact of a story as a whole. Styles range from the ironic John Cheever's mingling of realism and fantasy to Franz Kafka's anxiety-ridden exploration of a surreal nightmare world. Style is the outward manifestation of how an author defines reality and his or her own identity.

9 A WRITER IN DEPTH: FLANNERY O'CONNOR Chapter 9 looks at one of the great moderns in depth. Critical theory has moved between the poles of emphasis on the story as a self-contained artifact and focus on the shaping, informing creative intelligence behind the story. Flannery O'Connor's probing, disturbing stories make her a towering figure in the Southern tradition in American literature. How was her art shaped by her Southern roots, her Catholic faith, her debilitating illness? A range of her stories, the author's personal testimony, and critical commentary give students a chance to examine major recurrent themes in O'Connor's art.

10 PERSPECTIVES: THE READER'S RESPONSE Chapter 10 explores the range of critical interpretation and introduces the student to a range of scholarly and critical approaches to fiction. Capsule definitions of critical points of view and sample essays cover approaches from author biography and the formalist tradition of the New Criticism to deconstructionism and a multicultural perspective. Kafka's prophetic and enigmatic fiction, touching on archetypal anxieties of modern humanity, provides a test case for Freudian, Marxist, and feminist critics. Assignments for documented research papers in the Writing Workshop focus on the range of interpretation for major authors included in this book.

11 OTHER VOICES/OTHER VISIONS: A WORLD OF STORIES This mini-anthology of short stories ranges from classics like Edgar Allan Poe's "The Black Cat" and Eudora Welty's "A Visit of Charity" to rediscovered classics like Kate Chopin's "The Story of an Hour" and to new voices like Bharati Mukherjee, Lesléa Newman, and Amy Tan.

FICTION
Teaching Suggestions and Answers to Questions

Chapter 1 PREVIEW The World of Fiction 3

In introducing students to imaginative literature, how do we do justice to the organic relationship between the language of literature and its human meaning? This book follows the prevailing pattern of organizing introductory courses according to major dimensions, such as setting, character, plot, point of view, and symbol. However, we make a special effort to keep such "elements of literature" from becoming ends in themselves. We try to keep in view throughout how setting or character or symbol helps give shape to a work of literature *as a whole*—what it contributes to an author's vision of the world. We focus on how formal elements serve the human relevance of literature. How, for instance, does the setting of a story shape people's outlook or their lives?

DISCUSSION STARTERS

How much exposure have your students had to the traditional "elements of literature"? You may want to put the key terms from this preview on the board and ask students for their own tentative definition of each. Why is each important? What does it contribute to a story as a whole?

SETTING—CHARACTER—PLOT—POINT OF VIEW—SYMBOL—THEME—STYLE

Sandra Cisneros, "Mericans" 6

PERSPECTIVES—CISNEROS AND CULTURAL DIVERSITY

Traditionally, Americans have prided themselves on the country's capacity for absorbing or integrating people from many diverse backgrounds. In recent years, the traditional melting pot theory of assimilation has come in for much reexamination, with the mosaic metaphor or the tossed-salad metaphor, for instance, being suggested as alternatives. At the same time, there has been a strong conservative backlash against the "cult of diversity" and "multiculturalism." Where are we headed as individuals and as a nation? Cisneros' characters live in a setting where ethnic and cultural diversity is a basic fact of life. Her people, like many Americans, are in transition from a traditional past to a not-yet-defined future. In an age of identity politics, she often writes about young Mexican Americans finding their own way in the world, shaping their own identity. They are steeped in American popular culture (like young people around the world). They are neither entirely beholden to the closed world of the traditional Mexican religion and culture nor to the obtuse, condescending, parochial world of stereotypical "Anglos" (where they are still taken for foreigners). Bebe Moore Campbell says in "Crossing Borders" in *The New York Times Book Review* (May 26, 1991) that Cisneros' characters "aren't European immigrants who can learn English, change their names and float casually in the mainstream. These are brown people with glossy black hair and dark eyes who know they look different, who know the score."

DISCUSSION STARTERS

What does the term *minority* bring to mind? Do any of your students want to be identified as members of a minority? Why, or why not? Have any of them found themselves in a setting where they were openly or tacitly considered "the other"? Are America's minorities on the way to fuller integration into American culture and society or on the way to increasing isolation?

THE RECEPTIVE READER

1. The Mexican-American narrator of the story, who along with her two brothers is apparently on a family visit to Mexico, is outside a Catholic church and waiting for their Mexican grandmother to finish her prayers. (The church is dedicated to "La Virgen de Guadalupe": In December of 1531 a Christianized Indian claimed to have been visited by the Virgin Mary, and a shrine dedicated to Our Lady of Guadalupe was subsequently built on a hill known as Tepeyac.) When the narrator lists what she is not allowed to do while waiting, the items themselves help the reader visualize the location: she cannot "wander over to the balloon and punch-ball vendors," she is not to spend her allowance on "fried cookies or Familia Burrón comic books," and she most certainly should not "climb the steps up the hill behind the church" to play in the cemetery. When the narrator emerges from the church she reenters the plaza outside where the sunlight is so dazzling she has to squint her eyes as if she has just come "out of the movies." These and other details help to bring the setting to life.

2. The children in this story are culturally somewhere between traditional Mexico and heartland America. The "awful grandmother," with her "crystal rosary" and "mustache hairs," is the representative of traditional Mexican culture. Unlike the other family members, she remains extremely pious, she talks Spanish, and she views her United States–born grandchildren as natives of a "barbaric country" with "barbarian ways." At the opposite end of the cultural spectrum are the two tourists. To them, the church is a tourist attraction, and to confirm that they have indeed been there, they arrange to take photographs. Trying to buy favors for a pittance, the woman arranges to photograph the narrator's brother in exchange for a handful of Chiclets. The tourists are dressed in a tourist style totally inappropriate for church: "They're not from here. Ladies don't come to church dressed in pants. And everybody

knows men aren't supposed to wear shorts." The tourists are amazed that children who don't look Anglo speak English.

3. While the children have an easy and extensive familiarity with both cultures, they appear to identify more fully with the apparent freedom of American popular culture. The Mexican culture is represented by the "awful grandmother," and for the children it tends to be boring ("When I get tired of winking saints, I count the awful grandmother's mustache hairs while she prays"), confining ("we may stay near the church entrance"; "we cannot run off and have our pictures taken on the wooden ponies"), and only partially comprehensible ("The awful grandmother says it all in Spanish, which I understand when I'm paying attention"). Among themselves, the children play games more American than Mexican: "I'm a B-Fifty-two bomber, you're a German" or "I'm Flash Gordon. You're Ming the Merciless and the Mud People." On the other hand, the tourists represent the more obtuse, blinkered, and condescending streak in American culture.

THE PERSONAL RESPONSE

Readers with a Catholic background are likely to relate to many of the particulars of the grandmother's actions and the symbols of the church. Any church is more of a place for solemnity than it is for lighthearted frolic; Cisneros effectively contrasts the darkness and mustiness inside the church with the bright light of freedom outside. The grandmother is an immediately believable symbol of the somewhat repressive piety of the matriarchal family member who is a fixture throughout the world. With impressive economy of words, Cisneros presents the history of the family: the grandmother who is the last believer, the grandfather who is permanently soured by politics, and their children who are scattered and untethered by tradition.

Grace Paley, "Wants" 9

DISCUSSION STARTERS

Read to your students (or with them) the first four lines of the story. How much do these few *opening lines* tell them about each character and about the relationship between them? What kind of mood is being set? Where does the story seem to be headed?

THE RECEPTIVE READER

1. The narrator is a woman with an informal style, avoiding confrontation ("I don't argue when there's real disagreement"). She is middle-aged and has been married twice but acts younger than her age—sitting on the library steps, letting a library fine go unpaid for years. She does appreciate the small things in life that were made possible by her husband's taking "adequate financial care"—like a house that's warm in winter, "nice red pillows," and

being able to send the children to camp. She seems to like living in today, not fretting about the future (thus accumulating a $32 library fine) or regretting the past ("Don't be bitter . . . It's never too late," she tells her ex-husband). She has a self-deprecating sense of humor. For instance, she wants to be a "different person"—effective, returning library books on time, lecturing on the "troubles of this dear urban center."

2. The husband serves as a *foil* because he seems humorless, hostile, and pompous. He sounds self-righteous and critical—he pontificates ("I attribute the dissolution of our marriage to the fact . . .") When he's not grudgingly remembering the one good thing about their marriage ("A nice thing I do remember is breakfast"—actually, the narrator claims, just coffee), he speaks about it with "a great deal of bitterness." He criticizes his ex-wife, saying "as for you, it's too late. You'll always want nothing." He wanted something grander, something bigger (freedom, represented by a sailboat). He assumes she wants "nothing," which highlights what she *does* want: "to have been married forever to one person."

3. Will your students identify with the narrator and her wry sense of humor? Will anyone (perhaps some of the male students) defend the ex-husband? (QUESTION: Do men tend to be more pompous and self-righteous than women?)

Chinua Achebe, "Why the Tortoise's Skin Is Not Smooth" 12

DISCUSSION STARTERS

What *beast fables* do your students know? What fables about animals who talk and act out little scenarios with a moral do your students remember? What is their perennial appeal? (Does the tortoise in this story have any parallels in the cartoon characters of American popular fiction?)

THE RECEPTIVE READER

1. Tortoise is believable because the details about him offer a composite personality: he is cunning, tricky, yet eloquent, and he uses these skills to get what he wants. The birds are believable because as a group they get fooled by this slick, well-traveled "man"; however, they finally catch on and are angered at Tortoise's greed. And as many people might, Parrot devises a revenge that helps the victims of the trickster get even.

2. Audiences have always had a sneaking liking or admiration for the successful trickster. Some of the earliest folk tales and the most recent Hollywood movies seem to glorify (rather than condemn) the person who perpetrates an ingenious scam—and gets away with it. Ask your students to cite some examples. You may want to ask your students to do a modern rewrite in this (more cynical?) vein.

3. For many readers, the *turning point* of the story occurs when the cheated birds take back the feathers that enabled Tortoise to fly. How is he going to get home?

4. Tortoise leaves home to journey to the feast in the sky, encounters a challenge there that puts his ingenuity (and his morals) to the test, and returns home again, a changed person.

THE CREATIVE DIMENSION

If possible, have a sampling of the students' creative responses read or distributed to the class.

Tobias Wolff, "Say Yes" 14

PERSPECTIVES—TOBIAS WOLFF: A SIXTIES-GENERATION WRITER

Tobias Wolff tells his life story in his memoir *In Pharaoh's Army* (Knopf, 1994). Wolff, who had determined at age sixteen to be a writer, flunked out of prep school and served a one-year tour of duty in Vietnam. Unlike many of his generation, he went into the military looking for adventure and "honor," discovering instead the senselessness and brutalizing effect of war. He served as a Green Beret adviser to a South Vietnamese battalion, and he credits the failure of nearby Viet Cong guerrillas to kill him to their understanding of how unimportant he was to the war effort. On the brutalities charged against American GIs in Vietnam, he says, "When you're afraid, you will kill anything that might kill you." Wolff remembers the prosaic, shabby, everyday stretches between the bloody, desperate encounters of war, as in his story about his trying to save an abandoned puppy from being cooked and eaten by his comrades in arms. As a writer, he recognizes the difficulty of finding anything like the right tone or point of view in writing about the war experience: "But as soon as you open your mouth you have problems, problems of recollection, problems of tone, ethical problems. How can you judge the man you were now that you've escaped his circumstances, his fears and desires, now that you hardly remember who he was?"

DISCUSSION STARTERS

Tobias Wolff said about the authors in a collection of short stories he edited that they write "about what happens between men and women, parents and children." They write about "the feelings that bring people together, and force them apart" (from his introduction to *Matters of Life and Death*). You may want to start discussion of the story by reading to your students one student's journal entry that focuses on "the mystery of union." Do your students agree that this theme is central to the story? Do they read the story the same way?

Wolff's story involves a series of issues including race, creed, man/woman relationships and the mystery of union. A couple participating in domestic activity (dishwashing) get into an argument about interracial relationships, something they have never before discussed. The man seems biased against such relationships. Is he racist? Both are faced with a side of the other person that they have never experienced before, and at the end of the story they both seem strange to each other. The question the story asks is about the mystery of union: How and why can two people be a part of each other and yet be so different?

THE RECEPTIVE READER

1. At the beginning of the story, the world seen from the point of view of the man in the story is simple and uncomplicated. He considers himself a good man, a good husband, because he helps out with the dishes or puts a Band-Aid on his wife's bleeding thumb. He thinks he knows his companion well; after all, they've spent years together and have at least thirty to go. He does not want life to be complicated—thus his belief that people from different races or cultures should not marry.

2. We have to remember that we see everything in the story from the male narrator's point of view. He seems to feel that the question about interracial relationships is unfair, and he gives a spontaneous sincere answer (that makes him sound racist) when a glib insincere one would have gotten him off the hook.

3. Readers will vary on whether the story does or should lead to a "happy end." Should the woman accept the offer of marriage? Why is the last word of the story stranger?

THE CREATIVE DIMENSION

What is going on in the mind of the woman in the story?

Why did she ask the key question in the first place? (Is it really about race?) At the end, is she going to be hostile, accepting, confused?

Mary Robison, "Yours" 18

DISCUSSION STARTERS

You may want to ask your students what struck them as different about this story. For instance, what is meant by a "May-December" relationship? What are the usual associations or stereotypes that cluster around it? How does this story turn the tables on these stereotypical associations? How does it invite us to take a fresh look at youth and age, sickness and health?

THE RECEPTIVE READER

1. We learn about Allison's illness when we're told that, in bed that night, "a few weeks earlier in her life than had been predicted, Allison began to die." However, important clues are revealed in the story's beginning, with Allison struggling and "limping." Other clues: Allison wore a wig and Clark had been a doctor. Also, although she is thirty-five and he's seventy-eight, they look "something alike in their facial features," which may suggest the illness has aged her.

2. We learn by the letter from "Clark's relations up North" that Allison and Clark are recently married and that they think he's "an old fool . . . being cruelly deceived." They assume that she married him for his money, while others may assume that he—an old man—married her for sex or status. But when we discover the truth of their lives, we know they married for love.

3. Pumpkins are rich, plump, sweet-smelling fruit, associated with the rich flavor of homemade pumpkin pie. In one way, they are a *symbol* of the rich bounty of autumn, the season of harvest. But they are also associated with late October, the crossing over of fall into winter, just as Allison is passing from life to death. Also, Clark, who is in the "autumn of life," is moving from a life with Allison to one without her. At the same time, the different personalities represented by the carved pumpkins might suggest that we shape our own lives and personalities the way we carve different faces on the pumpkins.

THE PERSONAL RESPONSE

Do younger students in your classes find this bittersweet story less meaningful than older ones—or vice versa?

Aesop, "The Wolf and the Lamb" 21

DISCUSSION STARTERS

What, in fable and folklore, are the traditional associations of the wolf, the fox, the bear, the lamb, the tiger, the goat, the owl, the coyote? (Have we come to question some of these traditional associations?) You may want to have several students tell their favorite among Aesop's fables and ask the class to formulate the moral.

THE RECEPTIVE READER

1. You may want to put on the board and discuss with your students their possible suggested morals for this fable. Example:

> The best cannot live in peace if their neighbor plots treason.
> (German proverb)

2. Discuss with your students what is behind their varying answers to this question. (People who find this story too pessimistic have led a sheltered life?)

Ernest Hemingway, "Hills like White Elephants" 22

PERSPECTIVES—HEMINGWAY AND THE DISTRUST OF LANGUAGE

Arthur Waldhorn in *A Reader's Guide to Ernest Hemingway* (Octagon, 1983) focuses on the "silences and near silences" of Hemingway's characters. "In Hemingways's dialogue as in his narrative prose, the testimony of feeling is conspicuously minimal." (In *The Sun Also Rises*, Brett Ashley says to Jake Barnes, who wants to talk about his love for her, "Let's not talk. Talking is all bilge.") Waldhorn draws a parallel between Hemingway and writers like Samuel Beckett, where "silence is a wordless metaphor expressing outrage against the chaos of the universe and the isolation of the individual." Reticence or silence "is the only response several of Hemingway's characters can make when they have been shocked into psychic disorientation, whether by love or violence . . . or by the demands of a society whose values they reject." For Hemingway, "the brusque understatement of everyday speech . . . is the most efficient way to communicate emotional truth." In "Hills like White Elephants," Waldhorn points to the contrast between the talk-talk of the male lover—who talks like others in Hemingway's fiction who lie "to themselves or to others"—with "the simple, though bitter, honesty of the young woman" being pressured into having an abortion.

DISCUSSION STARTERS

Hemingway is one of the most widely known and translated writers of fiction around the world. What have your students read by him? Are they aware of the macho stereotype of the strong silent Hemingway hero? Do they associate Hemingway with stories about bullfighting, deep-sea fishing, great white hunters in the African bush? How is this story different?

THE RECEPTIVE READER

1. Their opening dialogue consists mainly of deciding what to drink. They speak in short, repetitive sentences, suggesting boredom or frivolity.

2. Elephants are large and fecund and swollen as the young woman might become if they don't decide to abort the fetus. Looking at the hills, the woman imagines white elephants resembling full-term pregnant women stretched along the hills. (The man is likely to think of a white elephant as a

present that nobody wants.) On the far side of the river, the trees are green and the fields are ripe with grain. The river, trees, and fields may symbolize life and growth, but the couple are on the barren, sterile, and unproductive side of the river. As one student said, "Jig finds herself in barren surroundings at this moment in her life, and she will have to cross the Ebro some other day."

3. We may first realize they are talking about a decision when he says, "It's really an awfully simple operation, Jig. . . . It's not really an operation at all. . . . I know you wouldn't mind it, Jig. It's really not anything." He repeats "really" and her name to persuade and convince. At first she looks down and does not respond, and then she asks him a series of questions, such as "Then what will we do afterward?" and "What makes you think so?" She feels he is simplifying the issue; she is concerned about what effect terminating their child will have on their lives. He continues to try to convince her, and she responds with sarcasm ("And afterward they were all so happy") and anger ("But I don't care about me. And I'll do it and then everything will be fine").

4. Throughout the piece tensions exist between the two characters. A possible high point is the exchange in which she counters every one of his statements with a negation of what he's said:

> "We can have everything."
> "No, we can't."
> "We can have the whole world."
> "No, we can't."
> "We can go everywhere."
> "No, we can't. It isn't ours any more."
> "It's ours."
> "No, it isn't. And once they take it away, you never get it back."
> "But they haven't taken it away."
> "We'll wait and see."

5. By the end of the piece, the young woman is no longer fingering the bead curtain or looking down. She puts up a brave front: When her companion asks if she feels better she responds, "I feel fine. . . . There's nothing wrong with me. I feel fine." Does her smile at the waitress and the man suggest an inner peace—has she come to a decision? Her emphasis on "I" and "me" perhaps implies there is something wrong with *him*. She is no longer trying to convince him of anything. Has she decided to go it alone? Or will they drift on as before in their aimless relationship?

THE PERSONAL RESPONSE

The following two responses, the first by a young woman and the second by a young man, suggest the possible range of reactions:

(a) In this story, we see the inexplicable barrier of communication between men and women—the inability for people to get into another's mind and understand the chemistry. A woman's frame of mind is much different than a man's frame of mind. In this story, both the man and the woman are thinking about the abortion, but he simply does not understand the pain that she faces. He thinks it's all over after the air is let in, but she knows things will never be the same for her. Every time I have a hard time communicating with my boyfriend I think of this story. I usually turn silent and remain quiet for a time. With such an emotional issue as abortion, it may very well be impossible for a man to understand the inner chemistry of what a woman is experiencing.

(b) For me the man in the story is not as despicable as he seemed to be to the rest of the class. I thought of him as a tired, uncaring fellow but not a deceiver or a deliberately evil person. I found him unsure of himself, unsure of his relationship with the girl. Why did she just not want to talk about the procedure for the abortion?

FOLLOW-UP—THE CREATIVE DIMENSION

How well did the student who wrote the following re-creation get into the spirit of the Hemingway story? How well did the student recreate the Hemingway style?

Espresso like Chocolate

The coffee beans in the glass containers lining the wall were small and dark. The shop was in a busy airport and there were no windows to let in the warm sunshine.

"What should we drink?" the man asked. He had put on his jacket that he had been carrying when they were outside.

"It's pretty chilly," the woman said.

"Let's drink some hot coffee to warm us up."

"Two coffees, please," the woman said to the waiter.

"Sugar?"

"Sure, two spoonfuls," the man responded.

The waiter returned from the counter with two cups and two saucers and set them on the table, turned, and returned to his place.

"What's that on the poster behind the counter?" the man asked.

"It says 'espresso.' "

"It looks like chocolate."

"I have tried it before," the woman said mixing the sugar into her coffee.

"What does it taste like?"

"I don't remember."

"I want to try it, it looks like chocolate."

"I don't think you should. Some people say it isn't worth the money."

"One espresso, waiter," the man said in a loud voice.

"Sugar?"

"I don't know, is it good with sugar?" the man asked the woman.

"You should have it with sugar."

"Well, I will try it without sugar to see what it is like," he said to the woman. He told the waiter, "No sugar, thank you." "That sure wasn't as good as I thought it would be," the man said putting down the cup. "I thought I heard people talk about it. They all said it gave them energy."

"I told you you shouldn't have ordered it," the woman said wiping a kleenex under her nose. "At least not without sugar."

"Why do you say that?"

"Because sugar always covers up any unanticipated bad tastes."

"Well, it did look like a big solid piece of rich chocolate in that mug. Wasn't that creative?" the man asked ponderously.

"That was creative," the woman said.

A cool draft rushed across their feet from the opening door.

"This coffee is good," the man said.

"It sure is," the woman responded through a cough.

"I really hate to see you go," the man said. "You have been taking more and more of these business trips lately."

The woman took some aspirin.

"It is hard for me to see you board that plane by yourself," the man continued.

"I dread them, but it is all part of the job that I committed myself to."

"I wish I could come with you."

"No, you don't. Where I am going, no one would deliberately go."

The woman stood up and walked across the coffee shop and set the empty coffee cup on the counter. The waiter stared at her as she weakly walked back to her chair.

"You can't come on the plane. I don't want you to," the woman said. "Besides, if both of us go, Laura would be all alone. It is better that I go alone."

A nasal voice came over the intercom and announced, "All passengers bound for Bermuda must board through gate C-6 at this time. Thank you."

The couple stood up and walked through the terminal to the gate.

Chapter 2 SETTING
Landscapes of the Mind 35

In much fiction that draws us into its world, setting is more than a mere location, more than the physical backdrop for a story. The term *setting* is used here in the larger sense of the context a story creates, the world to which it takes the reader. You may ask students to draw on their previous reading or viewing to offer tentative examples of major categories sketched out here: "The Setting as Mirror," " The Setting as Mold," "The Setting as Challenge," "The Setting as Escape," and "The Alien Setting."

FIRST READING: Larry Fondation, "Deportation at Breakfast" 37

PERSPECTIVES—LARRY FONDATION AND THE BANALITY OF EVIL

The German-Jewish sociologist and historian Hannah Arendt made herself unpopular by claiming that ghastly crimes are not necessarily committed by monsters but by ordinary people. In her *Eichmann in Jerusalem*, she used as her key example Adolf Eichmann, the colorless Nazi bureaucrat responsible for the rounding up and extermination of tens of thousands of Hungarian Jews. Writers such as Franz Kafka and Larry Fondation suggest that ghastly things are not only done by ordinary people but happen in ordinary surroundings—while ordinary people continue to go about their business, eating their eggs and toast. W. H. Auden said in Musée des Beaux Arts, (1938),

> About suffering they were never wrong,
> The Old Masters: how well they understood
> Its human position; how it takes place
> While someone else is eating or opening a window or
> just walking dully along; . . .

DISCUSSION STARTERS

Do your students stay away from places where they expect bad things to happen? Do they know places that they have a "bad feeling" about? Conversely, have they seen something bad happen unexpectedly, "out of a blue sky," in ordinary, nonthreatening surroundings?

THE RECEPTIVE READER

The story's setting is a small restaurant. At seven-thirty in the morning, the narrator notices that the restaurant is neat, "family-run and clean."

Descriptive touches that help to convey the utter normalcy and familiarity of the place include the chalkboard printed menu, the green-and-white awning over the door, and the red swivel stools at the counter. The story takes a Kafkaesque turn with the arrest of the short-order cook. Does the cook's fate indicate that the restaurant is located in an area where the arrival of the immigration authorities would cause neither surprise in the cook nor alarm in the customers? Because his name is Javier, is the cook about to be deported to someplace in Central or South America? His lack of resistance and absolute silence as he is being handcuffed shows that if this has not happened to him before, he is at least quite familiar with the process. There is a definite Orwellian aura to the cook's disappearance—are we supposed to feel that "it can't happen here"—but it does?

Fondation uses an excellent ironic touch when he has the two elderly women pay their breakfast bill. When they ask the narrator how much they owe, "they seemed surprised" that he does not know. Does the fact that he looks the part to the ladies point to the interchangeable nature of cogs in the machine that is the running of restaurants? Another nice touch is that just as the narrator is getting ready to resume his place in the world ("I put the plate at my spot at the counter, right next to my newspaper"), the process is interrupted by the arrival of more customers ("As I began to come back from behind the counter to my stool, six new customers came through the door"). When he presents such twists of fate as the arrival of the immigration authorities or six new customers walking in through the door, does Fondation make a point about the unpredictable, absurd course of human experience?

Settings: The Sense of Place

James Joyce, "Araby" 39

PERSPECTIVES—QUEST IMAGERY IN JOYCE'S "ARABY"

Readings of "Araby" have ranged from the majority view seeing the story as the first bitter clash between adolescent idealism and drab reality to a dissenting view seeing the story as an acerbic portrait of the adult narrator, whose capacity for joy and idealism has been sapped by a dour Irish asceticism. John Wyse Jackson and Bernard McGinley, in an afterword to "Araby" in *James Joyce's Dubliners* (St. Martin's, 1993), trace the different strands they see woven together to create a story of adolescent aspiration ending in painful disillusionment. The nineteenth century, with the British empire at its peak, had brought to the British Isles "a rapid growth of interest in things oriental." The name of the Araby Bazaar (a real bazaar that the young Joyce had visited in 1894) evokes the then fashionable "allure of the East," with its mingling of the exotic and the erotic.

The boy, in the manner of a medieval knight setting out on a quest, "promises to seek a prize for his fair lady." The "quest will test his abilities to overcome the obstacles" ahead—"notably the lateness, drunkenness, and possible stinginess of his uncle." Like a knight "riding through solitary lands and crossing distant and nameless rivers, the boy journeys alone amid ruinous houses until he reaches the place with the 'magical name.' "

The boy is not simply a knight on a quest; "he is on a holy quest." The boy's passion for Mangan's sister is "expressed in the powerful language of the church. His love is a chalice, borne through a throng of foes, and her name is invoked 'in strange prayers and praises.' " The boy's search "is as serious as that of the Knights of Arthur's Round Table for the Holy Grail—not just a cup but also the plate that was used by Jesus at the Last Supper, which later received his blood at the cross." When the boy reaches the bazaar, "it reminds him of an empty church." In the darkness, "but significantly lit by a pool of colored light, the first people he sees are two men counting money on a salver." However, "if this is the Holy Grail, it has been debased by the commerce of Dublin."

Also debased "is the ideal of adoring love that sent him on his mission. Romance is an illusion, and the reality of love is overheard in the flirtatious conversation between the young lady and the two young men."

DISCUSSION STARTERS

For your students, what associations cluster around the words *infatuation, love, romance, passion, desire*? What images, memories, regrets, or apprehensions does each bring to mind? How is each different from the others? You may want to ask your students to cluster one of these and write a short passage based on the cluster, to be shared with their classmates.

THE RECEPTIVE READER

1. The house is on a "blind" street, and the "former tenant" of the house, who died there, was a priest. The houses "gazed at one another with brown imperturbable faces." The boys played in the cold stinging air till their bodies "glowed." There is much play between light, dark, and shadow: The boys play in "the dark muddy lanes," the "dark dripping gardens," and the "dark odorous stables." In the story the boy moves from the darkness into the light, from innocence to experience. Or he may be moving from light into darkness—the light of youthful hopes into the dark of adult disillusionment?

2. Joyce's description of Mangan includes a nimbus of back-lighting and a sensuous "soft rope of . . . hair" that tosses "from side to side." Even "in places the most hostile to romance," her image stays with him. For instance, in the throngs of street marketers he imagines he is carrying a chalice, which brings to mind the Arthurian romance of the search for the Holy Grail as well as religious images of the cup that holds wine for the Eucharist. Note: "Her name sprang to my lips at moments in strange prayers and prais-

es"; the boy pressed his hands together, murmuring "*O love! O love!*" as if he were praying.

3. The boy can't share his feelings with his callow and prosaic friends. Mangan seems unreachable or distant as the "older sister"— who waits for the boys to come in from their play. He can't tell his aunt because she is religious and would disapprove; she may even have hopes he'll become a priest.

4. The uncle is the uncomprehending adult who is oblivious to the boy's anxieties and frustrations. He comes home late under the influence (the boy "could interpret these signs") and has forgotten his promise to give the boy money for the bazaar. He is one of the obstacles a prosaic world puts in the way of the boy's romantic yearnings.

5. The bazaar has associations of glamor and promises special excitement—but it is really a place for cheap goods and shallow, superficial sales clerks.

6. For example, this sensual description of Mangan suggests the boy's erotic feelings, without his expressing them explicitly: "The light from the lamp opposite our door caught the white curve of her neck, lit up her hair that rested there and, falling, lit up the hand upon the railing. It fell over one side of her dress and caught the white border of a petticoat, just visible as she stood at ease."

THE PERSONAL RESPONSE

Here is a *journal entry* recording one student's personal involvement with the story:

At times I was impatient with the boy's self-indulgent attitude, but my impatience made me think about how we slowly become less romantic, less impassioned, or more cynical as we grow older. We are still experiencing romance, but it becomes a more adult version. The boy experiences it completely. It figures in his every waking moment. He hardly knows anything about the girl; he hardly speaks to her. He doesn't have to; the emotions fill his whole being. At the end of the story, the boy is disappointed, disillusioned. He will never experience love in the same way again.

Bobbie Ann Mason, "Shiloh" 45

PERSPECTIVES—THEME AND SETTING IN MASON'S "SHILOH"

Francis King, in "Fantasy Lives" (*The Spectator*, August 20, 1983), describes a typical Mason story as "a recreation of life, in all its quaint, baffling, funny, pathetic inconsequentiality, in one small corner of the world." One of Mason's "constant themes is the manner in which, with no decisive snap of the thread, human relationships become unraveled. In some instances, they remain that way; in others, the fabric knits up again, with no apparent effort by either of the parties." In "Shiloh," for example, "a truck-driver, out of work after an accident, observes, through a haze of marijuana smoke, how his tough independent wife is slowly receding from him, in a new-found interest first in body-building and then in English composition." King sees the battlefield site of the couple's last picnic as particularly apt: When Leroy takes his wife to the Civil War battlefield of Shiloh, "she, in effect, vanishes out of sight, leaving him with the desolating sense that, just as he has never understood the inner workings of history that erupted in so much carnage, so he has never understood the inner workings of the marriage that is now causing his own living death."

DISCUSSION STARTERS:

How "Southern" is this story? How do your students react to the following *journal entry* by a student from the South?

The setting is the South, where women have their place among the menfolk but are not supposed to be better than the men. There is a class system among the people in the South. There are the genteel ladies and gentlemen of the upper class, and there are your working-class couples, bordering on what the South calls PWT (for "poor white trash"). Norma Jean and Leroy fit into the second category, but Norma is not satisfied with her role and sets out to rectify the situation. She is named after Marilyn Monroe, a person of no stature until she changed her name. Norma is changing her life: body building, physical therapy, barbells, English classes. Norma Jean is progressing from being the wife of a common truck driver, and Leroy is unable to adapt and accept the change in her.

THE RECEPTIVE READER

1. The *language* is Southern and working-class: "Great day in the morning!" exclaims Mabel. "I reckon I ought to be right proud," says Leroy. "Like *heck* you are" and "You ain't seen nothing yet," declares Norma Jean. When Norma Jean begins taking an English class at the community college, language becomes an issue. She tells her mother the correct pronunciation of *dachshund*, and she explains to Leroy the organization of a paragraph. Leroy says, "Driving a rig, nobody cared about my English." Is the author sympathetic to both characters? While acknowledging Norma Jean's need for intellectual stimulation, the author sympathizes with Leroy's fears: He's intimidated by Norma Jean's knowledge and is afraid that when she "gets smarter," she will leave him.

2. Most prominent among details that remind outsiders of the Southern setting: Shiloh is a Confederate battle site. When they finally go to Shiloh, Leroy and Norma Jean buy a souvenir Confederate flag for Mabel. There they picnic on "piminto sandwiches, soft drinks, and Yodels."

3 One striking example of trivial *realistic detail* is Norma Jean's explanation of cosmetics, the "three stages of complexion care, involving creams, toners, and moisturizers," which leads Leroy to think "happily of other petroleum products—axle grease, diesel fuel." This makes him happy because "there is a connection between him and Norma Jean." This foreshadows the couple's later sharing at the table—Norma Jean doing her outlining and Leroy looking over his log cabin blueprints: "As he and Norma Jean work together at the kitchen table, Leroy has the hopeful thought that they are sharing something, but he knows he is a fool to think this. Norma Jean is miles away."

4. At the story's beginning, Norma Jean, lifting weights, "reminds Leroy of Wonder Woman." Later, at Shiloh, Norma Jean picks "cake crumbs from the cellophane wrapper, like a fussy bird." At the story's end, the "sky is unusually pale—the color of the dust ruffle Mabel made for their bed."

5. Their lives are relatively ordinary, with a wife who says about her mother, "she won't let me alone." Tragic occurrences such as the death of a child and Leroy's disabling accident are treated without melodrama, as if they happen in the lives of many.

6. "What did I do wrong?" "Nothing." This bit of *dialogue* is one example of the characters' inability to articulate, let alone pour out, their thoughts and feelings.

7. Mabel as a *supporting character* serves as a foil for her more modern daughter: Mabel caught her daughter smoking, lectures her about her use of swear words. She thinks that the trip to Shiloh will bring on a "second honeymoon." At the story's beginning, Leroy perceives Mabel to be somewhat of a pest. But as Norma Jean grows away from him, he turns to his mother-in-law for advice and support?

8. The parked rig symbolizes Leroy's lack of movement, physically and intellectually. The electronic organ initially shows us how smart Norma Jean is; at first touching the keys "tentatively," Norma Jean masters "the organ almost immediately." Then, when she begins to get involved in school—moving further from Leroy—she puts aside the organ, a gift from her husband. The "nondescript" rented house suggests its temporary place in their lives, which is why Leroy wishes to build something more stable and solid, the log cabin. The log cabin represents something traditional and permanent, which is why Leroy longs for it and Norma Jean rejects it? The change in Norma Jean's cooking shows she is learning, growing, and changing, becoming more sophisticated. Does the trip to the battlefield represent the irrelevance of the

past, with its memories of dash and glamor? Or does it symbolize conflict—or the death of their marriage?

9. Perhaps the conversation about the log cabin ("I don't want to live in any log cabin") is the first strong hint that the two are definitely moving apart.

10. Norma Jean is a vital woman, unsatisfied with stagnation and status quo. She is moving toward the future. Leroy seems a kind but simple man, unable to articulate his feelings and needs. He uses drugs to anesthetize himself, to keep himself from thinking. He is mired in the past.

THE PERSONAL RESPONSE

One student wrote: "Leroy on his dope projects an aura of mellowed apathy, and he is no match for the goal-oriented Norma Jean." Do the responses in your class split along male/female lines? along generational lines?

FOLLOW-UP—THE CREATIVE DIMENSION

Here is one student's rewrite of the ending of the "Shiloh" story:

Shiloh Continued . . .

After the visit to Shiloh, Leroy and Norma Jean tried to work out their problems, but too much in the past had come between them. They tried counseling for a little while. Norma Jean agreed to go after Leroy pleaded for one more chance. It wouldn't hurt, and everybody seemed to be seeing a counselor for one thing or another.

During the sessions, Norma Jean would say little, but she did comment on how she felt lonely and trapped in the marriage. She yearned for something more from her life, and this was not what Leroy could give her. Leroy, meanwhile, sat next to her at a distance and did not say much. Many different thoughts were going through his mind, yet he could not bring them to words. He had all of these ideas in his mind before he came for the appointment. Yet when his time came to speak and respond, every ounce of determination and urgency to get these feelings out died suddenly. After several months, the sessions came to an end, and plans for the divorce were made. Leroy, who was very sorry to see the marriage end, packed up his old dusty rig and drove away for a while.

Norma Jean stayed in town. A year after the divorce, she became a personal trainer at the local gym. She had completed all her classes at the junior college after realizing what an important part of her life exercise had become. She married a personal trainer at the club who had just moved to Tennessee from California. She and her husband get along well, using their free time to bike, travel, and experiment with new, low-fat recipes.

Leroy began trucking again, shortly after the divorce. Through physical therapy, his leg is back to normal, except for a dull pain once in a while. He also got remarried, to a waitress at one of the truck stops he used to frequent. They are both simple people with uncomplicated lives. When they are together, they enjoy relaxing at their log cabin home in the hills above Shiloh.

Yukio Mishima, "Swaddling Clothes" 57

PERSPECTIVES—MISHIMA: REASSESSING A REPUTATION

An Associated Press story (November 24, 1995) provided a "literary reappraisal" of a "complex and tormented artist" on the twenty-fifth anniversary of Mishima's spectacular ritual suicide ("a classically Japanese act"). Twenty-five years earlier, Mishima had plunged a samurai sword into his belly after delivering a "harangue against Japan's no-war constitution, urging soldiers to rise up and revolt." The unsigned article described Mishima, hugely popular abroad but belittled as a minor figure at home, as a continuing embarrassment in his native Japan. "Although his books remain in print and sell steadily, his showy style, dark homoeroticism, macho posturing and right-wing nationalism cause unease even today." Cultural critic Donald Richie is quoted as saying that even though Mishima "became taboo in his own country," he is "a strong influence, and a troubling one. He's like a bad conscience." According to the AP article, Mishima was the pale sickly child of a government bureaucrat and was rejected by the military as too weak. He "became a fitness fanatic, taking up boxing, kendo and body-building, affecting a buzzcut and posing for photos in a loincloth." Although most Japanese reject Mishima's fanaticism and militarism, many "can identify with his belief that Japan's prosperity is destroying its soul." The writer's "love-hate relationship with the West—he embraced its literature and aesthetics while denouncing it as a cancer on Japanese culture"— remains a familiar dilemma in today's Japan.

DISCUSSION STARTERS

What assumptions about Japan and Japanese culture are your students bringing to this story? (Have their ideas about Japan been influenced by war movies, for instance? How do your students feel about the Japanese as economic competition for the United States?) Have them brainstorm or cluster first "traditional Japan" and then "modern Japan." Have them compare the results—what is the connection between the two sets of images, stereotypes, or associations?

THE RECEPTIVE READER

1. Do you have students of Japanese ancestry or with firsthand knowledge of Japan? Is the author's portrait of the husband an expression of familiar anti-American feeling or suspicion of Western ways?

2. The Americanized or Westernized husband is brash and loud (he wears a garish tweed coat and puffs on cigarettes); he thinks of the sordid birth of the illegitimate baby as a kind of crude joke. Toshiko is "oversensitive" ("that was her nature"); her "delicacy of spirit" is evident to everyone. It is the sensitive person who carries the burden of shame and guilt in this story and is in the end destroyed by it.

3. The wife feels horror at the neglect and squalor surrounding the baby's birth; above all she feels a nightmarish guilt that makes her anticipate retribution directed at her own child or at herself. This seems paradoxical, since she is the least Westernized of the two spouses. Although presumably more "Japanese" than her husband, she does not share the moralistic attitude of the traditional culture, which treats illegitimate children as outcasts or pariahs. (Students may have had some exposure to earlier American and European literature dealing with the ostracizing of unwed mothers and their children, from *The Scarlet Letter* to *Adam Bede*.)

4. One student wrote: "You know that something is going to go wrong, and yet the ending of the story was for me terribly disappointing. It seems to be as if the author started with the image of seeing someone on a park bench covered in newspaper and worked his way backward." Do your students find the story contrived, or are they carried away by it, as if by a nightmarish dream?

5. The newspapers—first used to wrap the unwanted baby—are the connecting link between the beginning and the end. When we see the dirty newspapers blown around the park and the papers covering the figure on the bench, we subliminally sense that the story that started in Toshiko's living room is approaching its nightmarish conclusion.

6. Is Toshiko playing a Christlike role in assuming the burden of shame and guilt of a prejudiced society?

THE PERSONAL RESPONSE

You may want to ask students to explain and defend the entry under "The Range of Interpretation" that comes closest to their own personal response to the story.

Chapter 3 CHARACTER The Buried Self 68

How curious are your students about other people? You may want to ask them questions inviting them to explore the "mystery of personality":

- What makes you like people?
- What makes you dislike people?
- Have you ever gone beyond surface impressions to understand a person better?
- Have you ever liked or disliked someone at first but then changed your mind?
- Have you ever been puzzled—unable to understand someone's actions or motives?

You may want to give your students the following questions as a guide to an understanding of character in fiction:

1 Who are these people?
2 How do you get to know them?
3 How does what they say reveal character?
4 How does what they do reveal character?
5 What incidents or challenges put them to the test?
6 What motives do you recognize?
7 How do the characters look to other people in the story?
8 Does what others say about them tend to inform you or mislead you?
9 How do they interact with other people?
10 Do they live up to your estimate of them, or do they surprise you?
11 Does the author directly or indirectly steer your reactions?

First Reading: Tim O'Brien, "Stockings" 70

PERSPECTIVES—O'BRIEN: WRITERS AND THE VIETNAM WAR

Editors of literature anthologies have been faulted for colluding with a collective national amnesia about the Vietnam War by including little or no material about the conflict. A collection intended to correct this situation is H. Bruce Franklin's *The Vietnam War in American Stories, Songs, and Poems* (Boston: Bedford, 1996). Among writers who have written about the war from the perspective of the grunt or raw recruit ("the F___g New Guy"), two stand out: Larry Heinemann, who had served as an infantry sergeant, published his Vietnam novel *Close Quarters* in 1977. In 1985, writing about interviews he conducted with other veterans, he said: "Tens of thousands of GIs got chewed up in Vietnam, and there are tens of thousands on whom the war still chews." He said, "I have been thinking and talking and reading about the war since I came back in 1968." Tim O'Brien, drafted out of college, went to Vietnam convinced that the war was "wrongly conceived and poorly justified." He first wrote about his war experience in magazine pieces that became part of his autobiographical *If I Die in a Combat Zone, Box Me Up and Ship Me Home* (1973). In his novel *Going after Cacciato* (1976), he told the story of a GI who decides to call it quits, striking out across the jungle in the general direction of Paris, and is hunted down by his buddies as a deserter. In this volume, poems by Alberto Rios and Jeffrey Harrison (in Chapter 14) and by Denise Levertov (in Chapter 21) address the Vietnam experience.

DISCUSSION STARTERS

Is it obsolete or sexist for men in jail, in dangerous occupations, or life-threatening situations (read: war) to have pinups or articles of feminine clothing?

THE RECEPTIVE READER

O'Brien says Dobbins is "like America itself" because he is ponderous, heavy, well-meaning, and naive. Dobbins is "big and strong, full of good intentions, a roll of fat jiggling at his belly, slow of foot but always plodding along, always there when you needed him, a believer in the virtues of simplicity and directness and hard labor." The stereotype of America and Americans here is that of a large and strong country populated by overweight people who are optimistic and not overly thoughtful. Dobbins is a sentimentalist who does not let the truth interfere with his love for his girlfriend. His feelings of love for her are undiminished, despite the fact that she has written him a letter and "dumped him." Is it this sort of emotional idealism that he transfers to the girlfriend's stockings? It is not surprising that Dobbins reacts the way he does at the end of the story. The stockings are a "good-luck charm," "a talisman," and he believes "firmly and absolutely in the protective power." Even the platoon was delighted when Dobbins continued to wear his protective stockings: "It was a relief for all of us." The men of the platoon do not challenge or ridicule O'Brien—although some readers might?

The Range of Characterization

Raymond Carver, "The Third Thing That Killed My Father Off" 72

PERSPECTIVES—CARVER: CHRONICLING ORDINARY NIGHTMARES

Reviewers of Carver's collections of stories were struck by his capacity for being a keen observer of ordinary people while treating them without either condescension or sentimentality, and without letting them self-destruct "with easy irony" or dark humor. Thomas R. Edwards, in *The New York Review of Books* (April 1, 1976), said that Carver's characters "are waitresses, mechanics, postmen, high school teachers, factory workers, door-to-door salesmen. They live in the Pacific Northwest, not for them a still unspoiled scenic wonderland but a place where making a living is as hard, and the texture of life as drab, for those without money as anywhere else." We see characters in a domestic, familial setting, getting by, accommodating themselves. However, "their problems come when their marginal lives are intruded upon by mystery, a sense of something larger and more elemental than they are used to feeling, possibilities that either frighten them or elude their intellectual categories."

Gary L. Fisketjon, in a review titled "Normal Nightmares" in the *Village Voice* (September 18, 1978), described Carver's characters as "down-the-block" people who do not "hold forth on intellectual subjects" but are probably thinking "about the weather, or bass and geese, or some everyday sort of thing." The men "play poker, bowl, and fish together." However, under the surface of "Normal Life," we are likely to discover something "complicated and tortured" in human relationships; we may sense something desperately gone wrong. Carver's characters may at times be pathetic, but he neither patronizes nor sentimentalizes them. Although understated and simple on the surface, Carver's fiction "is full of the emotion that starts in the stomach and moves upward, choking, to the chest and the throat."

DISCUSSION STARTERS

Attitudes toward people who used to be called retarded have changed over the years. How, or why? What provisions are made in today's schools? How is the topic treated in the media? (Would your students call Dummy "retarded"?)

THE RECEPTIVE READER

1. We learn about Dummy through the *naive narrator*, Jack. Jack's father works at a sawmill where Dummy works as the cleanup man. Jack is an observer rather than a participant: He goes to the sawmill occasionally and sees and hears some of the action firsthand; he listens to his father and the small-town gossip of others. We see the events in the story from the vantage point of a boy who is young and naive enough not to bring preconceptions or stereotypes to what he sees, allowing us to take a fresh, unprejudiced look at Dummy's story as we puzzle over missing links or apparent contradictions.

2. Dummy cannot talk, but he's apparently not deaf. He comes to life through the narrator's description: "He was a little wrinkled man, baldheaded, short but very powerful in the arms and legs. If he grinned, which was seldom, his lips folded back over brown, broken teeth." He wore a khaki

workshirt, a denim jacket and coveralls. He carried around rolls of toilet paper and lots of tools—he could thus pretend that he was needed and important?

3. Dummy's coworkers are different from the narrator and from his father in that they find Dummy's limitations a source of amusement. They tease him: "Carl Lowe, Ted Slade, Johnny Wait, they were the worst kidders of . . . Dummy." The coworkers are bullies, teasing an unfortunate soul.

4. Jack's father never teases Dummy the way the others do. The father is the closest thing Dummy has to a friend. The true central character in the story may well be the father; by telling this story, Jack tries to make sense of what "killed" his "father off."

5. Because Dummy doesn't speak in the story, we need to puzzle over his personality. He seems basically good-natured (or long-suffering?), since for much of the story he never seems to get angry at the people teasing him. He "took it all in stride." It seems as though the fish are the only things he has. He is an outsider working a menial job, and his wife, apparently, is unfaithful to him. The fish take him into a world where he is not automatically an inferior and the butt of the joke. They give him a purpose; they make him feel he is accomplishing something. He is raising the fish not really for practical purposes, but as a symbolic affirmation of self-worth?

6. Dummy's wife represents *terra incognita* to the boy and his friends. There are rumors about her, but no one really knows much about her. When Jack and his friend stop by her house one day, her behavior puzzles them. Women in the story are on the fringes. Even Jack's mother is enigmatic: "I wonder if she ever went around back in those happy days, or what she ever really did."

7. Dummy communicates through body language: "Dummy jerked his head back and forth. He moved his weight from one leg to the other and looked at the ground and then at us. His tongue rested on his lower lip, and he began working his foot into the dirt." When he chases Carl Lowe "with a two-by-four stud after Carl tipped Dummy's hat off," Dummy seems to be saying that he's had enough teasing and disrespect. He seems to be saying, "I'm a human being." His major statement may be his refusal to let the others intrude upon his private world—his refusal to let other fish in his pond.

8. Carver tells Dummy's story with amused and bemused affection, managing to make us smile at Dummy's limitations without contempt? There is something sad and comical about the father's ineffectual good will?

THE PERSONAL RESPONSE

Many people are impatient with disability and like to put it out of their minds. (Others make it the target of sick jokes.) Do students see the fear of ridicule and incapacity as Dummy's particular, personal problem or as part of the human condition generally?

FOLLOW-UP—THE CREATIVE DIMENSION

Do your students enjoy doing rewrites, updates, sequels, prequels, or alternative endings for stories? The following alternative ending was written by a student for whom Carver's bittersweet humorous story had led to too downbeat a conclusion. How well did the student get into the spirit of Carver's story?

The Second to Last Time We Heard about Dummy

After the attendants had loaded the partly decomposed body of the drowned man into the ambulance and driven off, Dad and I headed back through the pasture towards the car. By this time, the rain had started up again. "Looks like we're in for another one," Dad said. "I hope they can keep the river from flooding this time."

The next day began just like any other. I went downstairs and joined Dad at the table. We sat in our regular seats, Dad at the head of the table, I to his left, and Mother, if she did sit down, to his right. Dad read the *Daily Gazette* out loud. "They found more mountain lion tracks over in Ponderosa Park."

Just then a pickup pulled up to the house and honked its horn. Dad got up from the table, and as soon as he opened the door Carl Lowe from the sawmill was standing on the other side of the screen. Out of breath Carl said: "Did you hear? That drowned man they pulled outta the pond, that wasn't Dummy. It was a Mexican fella."

Dad said, "What are you talking about?"

"It wasn't him. Dummy musta skipped town."

I was still sitting at the table, but I could hear everything. Dad shut the door. Without saying a word, he grabbed his coat and left for work.

That was the second to last time we heard about Dummy. It wasn't until fall the next year, after the river had flooded, that Dad and I were raking the leaves in the yard when we heard about him for the last time. Ed the mailman walked up the sidewalk and handed Dad the mail.

"How's it goin', Ed?"

"Fine, Del, and you?"

Dad sat on the front step and began browsing through his October issue of *Field and Stream.* He usually flipped to the back first to look through the ads. And that's when he saw it, with bright colors and bold print. It read across the top, "DUMMY'S LIVE BLACK BASS SHIPPED ANYWHERE IN THE U.S."

Dad said, "It couldn't be." But we both knew it was.

Alice Munro, "Boys and Girls" 81

DISCUSSION STARTERS

How familiar are your students with the "only a girl" mentality? This story dramatizes gender roles in a way that cuts across stereotypes and expectations. You may want to start by having students write or talk briefly about who their strongest role model was—father? mother? other?

THE RECEPTIVE READER

1. Many striking specific *details* create an authentic real setting, such as the cellar "whitewashed and lit by a hundred-watt bulb" and the "calendars to hang, one on each side of the kitchen door." The author re-creates in loving detail the "medieval town" where the foxes prowl in their pens, with "their delicate legs and heavy aristocratic tails . . . their faces, drawn exquisitely sharp in pure hostility, and their golden eyes." Readers are likely to be both repelled and fascinated (as the children are) by the gruesome details about the killing and skinning of the animals. The author's description of the outdoors includes vivid imaginative details—for instance, "snowdrifts curled around our house like sleeping whales."

2. The girl's *father* is emotionally distant: "My father did not talk to me unless it was about the job we were doing. . . . Whatever thoughts and stories my father had were private, and I was shy of him and would never ask him questions." However, she reveres him, and the work she does with him in his "service" is "ritualistically important." After growing a bit and then seeing her father shoot Mack, she feels "a little ashamed." She begins to feel "a new wariness, a sense of holding-off" in her attitude toward her father and his work.

3. The *mother* works indoors, not coming out of the house unless it is to do something domestic, like handwash or garden. To her daughter, the mother represents constraint: "Work in the house was endless, dreary and peculiarly depressing. . . . she was also my enemy . . . plotting how to get me to stay in the house more." The girl does not have the same reverence for her mother that she does for her father; she feels her mother is "not to be trusted." However, unlike the father, the mother sometimes opens up, telling "all sorts of things—the name of a dog she had had when she was a girl" and other details about her past, as well as her feelings. "She was kinder" than the father and "more easily fooled, but you could not depend on her, and the real reasons for the things she said and did were not to be known." In an ironic foreshadowing, the girl says she is certain her mother knows very little "about the way things really" are.

4. The obtuse salesman deflates the girl's pride in being her father's helper by his "I thought it was only a girl." The mother says to the father, "Wait till Laird gets a little bigger, then you'll have a real help . . . and then I can use her more in the house." The mother is a constant reminder to the girl

of how girls must follow prescribed roles: "I just get my back turned and she runs off. It's not like I had a girl in the family at all."

5. In a *climactic episode*, the girl identifies with the high-spirited Flora and helps her in a last desperate attempt at escape—going against her loyalty to her father for the first time. She passes from childlike admiration for her father to adolescent rebellion. The closed gate and Flora's impending fate symbolize the restrictions of adulthood closing in on the girl?

6. Among the *minor characters*, the grandmother reinforces the mother's conception of male/female roles, constantly reminding the girl of what girls *don't* do (slam doors, keep knees apart when sitting down, ask questions that are "none of girls' business"). The younger brother, at first condescended to and manipulated by his older sister, has the "inside track" merely by virtue of being male—he will be accepted into the male world represented by the father and Henry.

7. In this story of *initiation*, the girl is moving from naive pride and conformity to a realization of the limits and complexities of the adult world?

THE PERSONAL RESPONSE

You may want to use the following candid personal response to trigger class discussion of some of the central issues:

> I suspect I am in the minority in considering this story a triumph for women. The girl realizes what is wrong with the callousness of her father and his male friends toward the foxes, the horses, and everything else. I think her changes toward becoming a female are beautiful. There's a certain amount of femininity that's in us—just born into everyone and especially into women. There are of course sad and sorry outcomes from the reception of these feminine traits by a scared and male-dominated society, but to become a woman is an amazing thing. It seems to me obvious that the compassion and nurture and instinct of women is what the world and humanity need. Imagine being afraid of realizing these traits in favor of being more—manlike!

Louise Erdrich, "The Red Convertible" 93

DISCUSSION STARTERS

What do your students know about reservation life? What assumptions about or personal observations of reservation life do they bring to the reading of this story? What personal contacts have they had with Native Americans?

THE RECEPTIVE READER

1. Lyman and Henry are Chippewas and have grown up on a reservation in the northern United States. Lyman, the younger brother, has a great deal of initiative ("I went on managing. I soon became part owner, and of course there was no stopping me then"); he has charm ("I was the only kid they let in the American Legion Hall to shine shoes, for example, and one Christmas I sold spiritual bouquets for the mission door to door"); and he thinks of himself as lucky ("I always had good luck with numbers, and never worried about the draft myself. I never even had to think about what my number was"). Lyman has a talent, "unusual in a Chippewa," for making money. As a result he is able to buy the convertible with Henry. The two of them are inseparable and drive everywhere together, spending an entire summer traveling all over the northern United States, Canada, and Alaska in an idyll of seeing places and meeting people. Lyman and Henry not only do not look alike; Lyman is a far more dynamic character who has a faintly sardonic yet whimsically amusing voice.

2. Henry had enlisted and actually served in the Marine Corps. In 1970, Henry is "stationed up in the northern hill country" in Vietnam. Henry is not a prolific letter writer and he only manages to get two letters to Lyman "before the enemy caught him." "It was at least three years before Henry came home," Lyman says, so Henry spent most of his time in Vietnam as a prisoner of war. When Henry finally returned home, he "was very different, and I'll say this: the change was no good." After Vietnam Henry is "jumpy and mean," and "quiet, so quiet, and never comfortable sitting still anywhere." Before, Henry had been a great teller of jokes, "and now you couldn't get him to laugh, or when he did it was more like the sound of a man choking, a sound that stopped up the throats of other people around him." The reader learns all of this in bits and pieces probably in part because that is how Lyman learned it. Lyman's tone is deceptively casual, without a great deal of detail.

3. The *red convertible* comes into the boys' lives at a critical juncture. For the last time, Lyman and Henry will spend a summer together as unfettered travelers, as unscathed adolescents. The car calls to mind the time when the boys were free to travel anywhere they chose, were out of reach of the U.S. Army, and were psychologically untroubled. Life, at this stage, is the freedom of the road, and the road appears to stretch out endlessly before them. "We went places in that car, me and Henry," Lyman says. "We took off driving all one whole summer." For Lyman, then, the car comes to represent his youth, his happy relationship with Henry, his joy at being free and behind the wheel of the classic fantasy car, the red convertible. Behind that wheel, Lyman is in control and able to dictate speed, direction, and course. Once Henry drowns, Lyman rolls the car into the river. It has no meaning for him anymore. It is merely a bitter reminder of youth and times forever lost.

4. There are three *minor characters* in this story, all female. The mother makes a brief appearance after Henry, so obviously troubled, returns home. She confirms that there is very little the family can do to help Henry. Another, more significant, role is played by Susy, the girl the brothers meet during their summer on the road. Susy is hitchhiking and on her way home to "Chicken." It turns out that Chicken is in Alaska, that the brothers drive Susy back there, and that their time in Chicken was the highlight of that extraordinary summer. Lyman says, "We got up there and never wanted to leave." However, the "season was changing. It was getting darker by that time, and the cold was even getting just a little mean." Winter, metaphorically, is about to enter the lives of the brothers as well. Just before they leave Susy stands upon a chair, and, Rapunzel-like, lets her hair down for the brothers to see. At this, Henry tells Susy to jump on his shoulders. She does and her hair reaches past Henry's waist. He "started twirling, this way and that, so her hair was flung out from side to side." Until his dance by the river at the end of the story, this is the last spontaneous burst of joy from Henry. This fact is confirmed by the picture taken by the third minor character, eleven-year-old Bonita. As Bonita snaps the picture, Henry "might have drawn back, because the shadows on his face are deep as holes. There are two shadows curved like little hooks around the ends of his smile, as if to frame it and try to keep it there—that one, first smile that looked like it might have hurt his face." Henry, who is dressed in "his field jacket" and "the worn-in clothes" he returned from Vietnam wearing, has never rejoined his former life.

5. At the end of the story, as Henry sleeps by the river, Lyman vicariously feels what Henry is enduring: "I felt something squeezing inside me and tightening and trying to let go all at the same time. I knew I was not just feeling it myself; I knew I was feeling what Henry was going through at that moment." When Henry awakens, he is aware of what has happened, and he says, "I know it. I can't help it. It's no use." A few minutes later, the brothers have a fist-fight ostensibly over the red convertible. After the fight, they have a poignant and hilarious exchange about Lyman taking care of the car and Lyman giving Henry "Hoof-and-mouth disease." But the fight and the hilarity are typical responses to an extremely emotional situation. Henry has been permanently psychologically scarred by his experiences in Vietnam, and all the beer and all the "Kashpaw girls" and all the red convertibles in this world cannot right what is wrong with him. The "wild" dance Henry does (Lyman says, "no kind of dance I ever saw before, but neither has anyone else on all this green growing earth") echoes the joyous dance Henry did with Susy on his shoulders, but this dance at the river ends abruptly when Henry "all of a sudden" runs over to the river and leaps in.

6. The *reservation* is located near some areas of wild natural beauty like the high running Red River and Little Knife River and Montana, and, especially, the place where the willow trees bent down so protectively around the brothers ("I do remember this one place with willows. I remember I laid under those trees and it was comfortable. So comfortable"). On the negative side, we get glimpses of a life marked by deprivation and by things

in a state of disrepair. After Lyman takes a hammer to the red convertible, he describes the result: "By the time I was done with the car it looked worse than any typical Indian car that has been driven all its life on reservation roads, which they always say are like government promises—full of holes." Health care is lacking: "While Henry was not around we talked about what was going to happen to him. There were no Indian doctors on the reservation, and my mom was afraid of trusting the old man Moses Pillager, because he courted her long ago and was jealous of her husbands. He might try to take revenge through her son." There is no care for Henry, as a recovering prisoner of war and a Marine veteran, on the reservation, and a "regular hospital" will simply drug him into quietude.

THE PERSONAL RESPONSE

On the one hand it appears as though no one in the family is willing to acknowledge the truth about Henry (when Henry bites through his lip, supper goes on: "There was still blood going down Henry's chin, but he didn't notice it and no one said anything"). On the other hand Lyman did manage to come up with a sort of therapy that did work, however briefly.

THE CREATIVE DIMENSION

Returning veterans often feel that telling their story would be futile, and their bottled-up feelings may make them seem bitter and hostile. Have any of your students had the opportunity to get beyond the communication barrier?

Juxtapositions: Capsule Portraits

Sherwood Anderson, "Paper Pills" 102

DISCUSSION STARTERS

What makes us label people as eccentrics or cranks? How do we decide whether someone is "normal" or "different"? How much do surface appearances (dress, hair, manners) have to do with our estimate? Do different people seem weird to different people?

THE RECEPTIVE READER

1. Both his appearance and his habits make the doctor seem strange. His white beard, huge nose, and knuckles (like "walnuts fastened together by steel rods") help make him one of Anderson's "grotesques." He sits all day by an unopened, cobwebbed window. He writes messages to himself on scraps of paper and then rolls them up into paper balls. But Anderson wants to make us see the humanity behind the weird, grotesque exterior. He says that in "Doctor Reefy there were the seeds of something very fine" but suggests that, until the "tall dark girl" came along, no one bothered to get to know him. This is why the doctor had to write his feelings and thoughts down on

scraps of paper? After marrying, the doctor had someone with whom to share his "scribblings." Unfortunately, in this bittersweet story, he was soon alone again after her sudden death.

2. Unlike the doctor, the woman has had many people in her life, but none who cared about her as a person rather than as a rich unmarried woman or a sex object. She is like the doctor (and like central characters in Anderson stories such as "Unlighted Lamps") in that she needs human contact and human warmth, but no one really seems to know her, listen to her, take a real interest in her. The suitor who talks all the time in an obsessed way about virginity (but seems to her more intrusively concerned with her body than the others) is one of Anderson's studies in the twisted byways of human motivation.

3. Like Dr. Reefy, the gnarled "twisted apples" look uninviting on the outside, but those who look beyond appearances discover their sweetness. And the twisted apples, like the doctor, don't come from the sophisticated city but from the goodness of sweet country life.

Jamaica Kincaid, "Girl" 105

PERSPECTIVES—THE DOMINANT VOICE IN KINCAID'S "GIRL"

In her discussion of "Girl" in *Jamaica Kincaid* (Twayne, 1994), Dione Simmons offers a cautionary reading of the story, sternly critical of the domineering mother. Simmons analyzes the "whipsaw effect" of the mother's voice—"the all-powerful voice of maternal nurture and knowledge" which is at the same time the "voice of condemnation and threat." This voice is not one "to which one effectively speaks back" (the daughter offers only two feeble comments). In what the mother says, "the positive and negative currents are so intermixed that it is nearly impossible to detect the moment at which one merges into the other." Well-meant advice on how to buy material for a blouse or cook fish slides without warning into admonitions against singing disreputable native songs in Sunday school, speaking to "wharf-rat boys," or having disgusting table manners, not to mention "the ugly accusation" about seemingly being bent on turning into a slut. "Nurture and attack here are inseparable"; intermingled are pointers on "how to control and manipulate"—managing your smiles in talking to people you don't like too much or not at all. Finally, the mother's advice deals with matters "veering into the dangerously magical," reminding us of the world of West Indian obeah magic, as she instructs her daughter about "medicine to throw away a child before it even becomes a child." According to Simmons, "what is finally taught in this maternal litany is that the world is full of masked dangers and that one of these dangers is the maternal voice itself." If the girl in the story is to mature, she must cease to be a child "paralyzed by the mesmerizing maternal voice"; she must find a voice of her own "beyond the faint squeak of self-defense heard here."

DISCUSSION STARTERS

How do your students feel about being nagged, lectured, admonished, criticized, corrected? You may want to have your students write for a few minutes on the topic: "Who criticizes you, and for what?"

THE RECEPTIVE READER

1. The person talking in the story is judgmental and didactic—the kind of moralistic, self-righteous, nosy elder that has frustrated and antagonized countless rebellious adolescents. The range of her favorite topics covers poor manners, neglect of household duties, immoral music, and the danger of acting like a "slut" in relationships with men. (Are these still the main topics in the lectures young people today receive from moralistic elders?)

2. The two times the listener speaks, her statements begin with "but . . ." This suggests she is taking exception to much of what the speaker says. If she had a chance, she might ask questions and defend herself.

THE PERSONAL RESPONSE

Does *anyone* in your class—old or young—have something good to say about the older woman in the story? (If not, why does she seem such a familiar if not ubiquitous type?)

Chapter 4 PLOT
The Chain of Events 111

We have many terms for an "unplotted" record of events—a recording of what happened without a strong story line. Ask your students to explain the difference between a story and, on the other hand, a chronicle, annals, a log, a diary, a police report. You may want to ask your students to offer a preliminary definition of terms useful in a discussion of plot: *protagonist, antagonist, external action, climax, flashback, suspense, irony.*

First Reading: Doris Lessing, "Homage for Isaac Babel" 113

There is little external action in this "short short": Two young people go to a movie. (The girl is shaken up by the sad tale told by the movie, and her sensitivity about capital punishment contrasts with the doorman's callous self-righteousness.) The girl discusses the book she is reading with the adult telling the story. The final letter ties these strands together by offering a kind of "last word" on both the film and the book and by reiterating the girl's interest in the boy. There is, however, a connection between the superficially uneventful happenings: A basic motive or tension provides the mainspring of the story. The thirteen-year-old girl aspires to be as sophisticated as the older boy. We smile at her attempt to be knowing and grown-up (repeating almost verbatim what the adult had told her about Babel). This attempt to seem grown-up creates an ironic contrast with the girl's interest in the other sex (she may "just die" if the boy doesn't come to her party).

Plotting the Story

Bernard Malamud, "The Magic Barrel" 116

PERSPECTIVES—MALAMUD AND JEWISH TRADITION

American Jewish writers, reminiscent of criticism leveled at other writers allied with a tradition in the American multicultural spectrum, have at times been criticized for being too eager to leave their Jewishness behind and at other times for the surface use of Jewish trappings. Bernard Malamud, representing what has been called the "renaissance of American Jewish writing," reminds critics and reviewers in both essential and peripheral ways of his Jewish roots, of the Jewish New York City setting, and especially of Jewish humor. Reviewing *Talking Horse*—a collection of Malamud's letters, lectures, and unpublished papers (Columbia UP, 1996)—in the *Boston Globe*, Robert Taylor says: "Malamud's stories are often tragicomedies, and they read wonderfully aloud. The Jewish expressions have a strongly patterned aural element, and the direst circumstances are punctuated by soaring bursts of comic invention." Malamud said that "The Magic Barrel," about a Jewish marriage broker and a young rabbinical student, originated in a Yiddish anecdote. From a list of prospects he received from a New York City matrimonial agency, Malamud remembered the phrases: "well Americanized," "owns Dodge car," and "her father is a dentist." Malamud also said that the imagery at the end of the story, where "violins and lit candles revolved in the sky" as Finkle rushed toward Stella with "flowers outthrust," was inspired by the colorful surreal dream imagery of the Russian Jewish painter Marc Chagall.

Sanford Pinsker, in "Bernard Malamud's Ironic Heroes" (in *The Schlemiel as Metaphor*, Southern Illinois UP, 1971) linked Finkle to a classic figure of Jewish folklore, the schlemiel, who hatches schemes for advancement but constantly falls flat on his face. To Pinsker, Finkle is a "moral schlemiel"—"a moral bungler, a character whose estimate of the situation, coupled with an overriding desire for 'commitment,' " invariably causes comic defeats. He desires to "change the essential conditions" of his life, but he "is inadequate to the task." He finally makes "a tortured attempt to achieve spiritual regeneration" or redemption in turning to Stella, the matchmaker's daughter.

A less sardonic reading of the story focuses on the *schadchan*, the matchmaker. In a literal interpretation of the story, Salzman might be seen as the designing, if not pimping, manipulator, palming off his daughter on the naive victim. A more spiritual interpretation of the story might see the "uncanny" Salzman—who has no real, literal worldly office or place of business—as an "improbable but intentionally redeeming angel." He serves the function of a spirit "placed on earth to bring Leo Finkle from an arid knowledge of the law to the perception that he can fulfill the spirit of the law only by loving in this world." (In "The Short Fiction: An Essay," in *Bernard Malamud: A Study of the Short Fiction* [Twayne, 1989].)

DISCUSSION STARTERS

How do people find marriage partners in traditional cultures and in our modern society? Do any of your students remember or know about arranged marriages or about matchmakers (*bishakunin* in Japanese)? Do your students have friends who try to "fix up" single people with eligible counterparts? How do your students feel about the use of personal columns as a way of finding a marriage partner? What about dating services, computerized or otherwise, and other kinds of commercial Cupids?

THE RECEPTIVE READER

1. As in a fairy tale, the hero of this story encounters obstacles and detours on his way to finding true love. In the words of one student reader,

On the surface, the plot finds a young rabbinical student, Leo Finkle, at a stage in his life where he needs a wife. Prosaically, he needs a wife to further his career. However, on a deeper level, there is a taste of fairy tale woven in among the literal thoughts. The title first pricks the imagination because, in a sense, Leo reaches into the "magic barrel" and pulls out the answer to his dreams. He finds Stella and can dream of a life where he lives "happily ever after."

2. The traditional view puts practical considerations first and then hopes that "love comes later." The romantic view that the story ultimately endorses is that there is one person who is the right one, who is often separated from the other by barriers of custom or social status, but who will transform the other person's life. This conflict is central to the plot; after "realism" has the upper hand during much of the story, the surprise ending tilts the story toward the romantic view.

3. Salzman, like a person selling used cars, embellishes the qualifications of his clients (including those of Leo). Leo's conversation with Lily Hirschorn is an example of a conversation where much of what both people think and feel remains unsaid.

4. Finkle is ashamed of himself for needing the services of the disreputable Salzman. But Salzman is the catalyst (the master magician in a shabby disguise) that transforms Leo's life.

5. Salzman, the "trickster," is full of subterfuges and excuses—and he gets caught (for instance, when he gives contradictory information about the age of his aging prospects). He is given to expostulation. ("Jewish children, what can I say to somebody that he is not interested in high-school teachers?") His shoestring operation is sad and funny, as is his cadging for food and drink.

6. Underlying the fairy-tale plot is Leo's journey toward self-realization. One student called him "a hollow dead soul," who buries himself in books and study. In the course of the story, he realizes that "he had never loved anyone." ("He saw himself, for the first time, as he truly was—unloved and loveless.") What gives the story its emotional power is the aching reality and intensity of Finkle's need.

7. Is the ending the traditional fairy-tale triumph of desire over reality? Or is it an affirmation of the belief that in drab ordinary lives marvelous things can and do happen? Or is it an ironic comment on the human tendency toward self-delusion?

THE PERSONAL RESPONSE

Is the combination of dolefulness (of anticipating adversity, of living on the fringes of poverty) with finding rich humor everywhere in the events of daily life a particularly distinguishing trait of the Jewish tradition? (Do other ethnic groups have it? Is it a stereotype?)

Shirley Jackson, "The Lottery" 130

PERSPECTIVES—A MARXIST READING OF "THE LOTTERY"

In "A Marxist/Feminist Reading of Shirley Jackson's 'The Lottery' " (*The New Orleans Review*, Spring 1985, Peter Kosenko examines the social hierarchy and ruling ideology of Jackson's village from a Marxist perspective. Although there are hints of a redeeming humanity in the children and some of the adults, the story as a whole presents a "pessimistic vision of the possibility of social transformation." A look at the social stratification of the village shows that "those who control the village economically and politically also administer the lottery." Mr. Summers is "the most powerful man in town." From a Marxist point of view, the question is: "What relationship is there between his interests as the town's wealthiest businessman and his officiating the lottery?" The lottery "reinforces a village work ethic which distracts the villagers' attention from the division of labor that keeps women powerless in their homes and Mr. Summers powerful in his coal company office." At one level, the lottery "seems to be a modern version of a planting ritual that might once have prepared the villagers for the collective work necessary to produce a harvest." Old Man Warner becomes the voice (the "ideologist") of a work ethic that "encourages villagers to work without pointing out to them that part of their labor goes to support the leisure and power of a business class." The village children "have been socialized into the ideology that victimizes Tessie." They are not "proof of the innate depravity" of human beings; they have learned their callous behavior from their parents.

DISCUSSION STARTERS

How aware are your students of rival ways of looking at evil? We may imagine evil as being perpetrated by forces taking heinous, frightening shape—booted, helmeted robotlike oppressors; nightmarish aliens; witches who sleep with the devil. (We might call this the *devil theory* or monster theory of evil?) Or we might assume that horrendous evil is often perpetrated by people who look ordinary, wear suits, make a to-do about their families and children, and love dogs. (Hannah Arendt, in her book about the Eichmann trial in Jerusalem, talked about the *banality of evil.*) Have your students encountered either perspective? Can they think of examples or test cases for both? To which version do they personally incline?

THE RECEPTIVE READER

1. On the surface, everything that is happening is ordinary and reassuring—but we are never told the purpose of the "lottery" or what the winners gain. We never really get to understand the deeper motives or rationale

of what goes on. We slowly and gradually discover the horrible truth for ourselves as horrified, helpless bystanders. The author does not warn us or preach or denounce. Her style is the opposite of the style of moralists and writers of "letters-to-the-editors" who vent their outrage and indignation. Jackson writes as if she wants to leave it all up to *our* collective consciences.

2. All the details about the box and its history highlight the strong roots of the ritual and the mindless adherence of people to tradition long after its original purposes have become blurred or forgotten. They also make it hard for us to write this story off as a nightmare vision. The fact that "so much of the ritual had been forgotten or discarded" seems natural for modern people. That Mr. Summers was able to substitute paper slips for wood chips is the kind of updating of familiar routines that seems eminently normal.

3. Details like the heap of stones the boys have piled up and guard are the first ominous hints. The ominous black box does not seem to hold good fortune. And the names of the two organizers—Mr. Summers and Mr. Graves—represent youth and death?

4. The mindless inertia of tradition seems to be the major force keeping the lottery going? Old Man Warner says, "There's *always* been a lottery," lambasting those against it. Mrs. Adams questions the tradition: "Some places have already quit lotteries." "Nothing but trouble in *that*," retorts Old Man Warner.

5. Mr. Summers, a "round-faced, jovial man," has the "time and energy to devote to civic activities." He sounds like any well-meaning, somewhat pedantic busybody that people rely on to keep organizations and activities going. It is ironic that Jackson would call such a horror a "civic activity"—just like the "square dances, the teenage club," and "the Halloween program." Mr. Summers takes his role seriously, seeming "very proper and important" in his position. His name is ironic, too, for summer usually connotes youth and freedom, but he perpetuates a deathly ritual.

6. The story has made us well aware of Mrs. Hutchinson, who unbeknownst to us and to her is the destined victim. The story has already focused on the victim when we still thought of her as a spectator concerned not to miss the event. She'd been finishing up the dishes, so she jokes, "Wouldn't have me leave m'dishes in the sink, now, would you, Joe?" The second drawing draws out the horror and gives us an opportunity to see how the Hutchinson family reacts to knowing one of them will be "it."

7. After opening their papers and seeing they were not chosen, the crowd immediately wants to know who "got it." When Mrs. Hutchinson begins to protest, the others show no sympathy. They do breathe a collective sigh of relief when they realize they will not have to stone a little boy, the Hutchinsons' young son. And Nancy's school friends hope Nancy is not chosen. When everyone realizes Tessie is the chosen one, they waste no time in

picking up stones from the pile. The villagers do not consider Tessie's retorts; they're just glad they're not the ones about to be stoned to death.

8. Like everyone else, Tessie goes along with the ritual. It's only when she has been chosen that she screams, "It isn't fair; it isn't right." Our sense of justice is not activated until we are the victim of injustice?

9. Would woman readers identify more strongly than men with the woman who is the victim in a ritual instigated by men? The only one who questions the tradition is a woman (Mrs. Adams), and its most vehement supporter is a man (Old Man Warner).

FOLLOW-UP—A COLLABORATIVE PROJECT

Some years later, Shirley Jackson wrote *The Witchcraft of Salem Village*, a book for adolescents on the trial and execution of the Salem witches in seventeenth-century Massachusetts. (She had a private collection of over five hundred books on witchcraft and demonology from many countries.) This history of persecution and mass hysteria may already have been in Jackson's mind when she wrote "The Lottery." You may want to ask your students to research the Salem witchcraft trials. What are parallels and differences between them and the events of this story?

William Faulkner, "A Rose for Emily" 139

PERSPECTIVES—FAULKNER: PARADOXES OF A LITERARY REPUTATION

In "The South and the Fury" (*The New Republic*, August 23 and 30, 1993), C. Vann Woodward reviews Joel Williamson's *William Faulkner and Southern History*. Woodward uses the review to highlight the paradoxes in Faulkner's role as a towering figure in twentieth-century literature. Why was Faulkner's stature appreciated widely abroad before it was recognized at home? Faulkner's greatest novels were published between 1929 and 1936, and yet by 1945 all his books except *Sanctuary* were out of print. At the same time, "at the peak of his anti-Americanism, Sartre declared Faulkner to be a god for French youth; and Faulkner already had a devoted public in Italy and Japan."

How are we to reconcile the writer's life with his literary achievement? Faulkner was a "furious worker." However, he was a "seventh-grade dropout, . . . virtually without formal education, and well along in his youth without a penny or a job." He "became a pathological drinker, a consumer of bootleg booze in huge quantities over incredible spells and with disastrous results. Periodically confined to institutions to dry out, he eventually died in one. His wife, Estelle, shared his addiction, which was more a consequence than a cause of their unhappy and tumultuous marriage, as were her attempts at suicide." Faulkner "stuck to (or was stuck with)" an extended family of several generations of relatives, with "proliferating nieces, nephews, in-laws and first, second, and third cousins once, twice or thrice removed. Many of them, along with 'connections' black and white, became his dependents, and he went to any length to help them out, to bail them out, or bury them. . . . This helps to explain why he was so often near bankruptcy, no matter how many Hollywood bonanzas, literary prizes, or publishers' advances came his way."

What was Faulkner's relationship with the South? For Faulkner, as for James Joyce, "his native culture, tradition and history provided the subject matter of his fiction." Both "were conscious of the provinciality of their culture and of its subordinate relation to a dominant one." Woodward says that Faulkner did not romanticize the South. "Commenting on his Nobel Prize in 1950, *The New York Times* complained that his South was 'too often vicious, depraved, decadent, corrupt,' and added primly that 'incest and rape may be common pastimes in Faulkner's "Jefferson, Miss." but they are not elsewhere in the United States.' " Faulkner himself told a publisher that he just happened to know the South well enough to write about it. He said, "Man stinks the same stink no matter where in time." Woodward concludes that what "was often taken as an apology for the South was really an indictment not only of the South, but of America."

DISCUSSION STARTERS

Critics have discussed this story as an especially concentrated example of Faulkner's ambivalence toward the *Old South*. Which of two conflicting strands is for your students uppermost in the story as a whole? On the one hand, are we supposed to feel a paradoxical admiration for the gallant, defiant Emily? Does she represent the pride and aristocratic tradition of the South—as "a woman of indomitable spirit"? Or, on the other hand, are we supposed to be revolted by Emily as morbid, haughty, and irrational? Is she the representative of "an aging and impotent culture"?

THE RECEPTIVE READER

1. A lock of hair has often been a symbol or pledge of love. The single strand of hair on the pillow becomes a dominant symbol or memento of love aborted. Also, the single strand of hair represents Miss Emily's isolation and loneliness?

2. The story begins with the narrator telling us Emily has died. The sharing, next, of Emily's refusal to pay taxes introduces us to her stubborn

personality, as well as to the conflict between her traditional background and the modern life emerging in the town. We are beginning to take in plot elements essential to our understanding of the story, with the bad smell of the house, the gossip about her romance with Homer Barron, and—for most readers, the central clue—her purchase of the arsenic ("For rats").

3. The description of her house could also be a description of Emily, with its "stubborn and coquettish decay." The old-fashioned house is a haunting (and haunted?) relic of the past in a modern town.

4. Colonel Sartoris has old-fashioned notions of respect for family status or the family name and disrespect for blacks ("he who fathered the edict that no Negro woman should appear on the streets without an apron"). *Noblesse oblige*, French for "high rank imposes obligations," means that people with high social status have special responsibilities. For instance, riffraff should not presume to court or marry a young woman from a respected family.

5. Miss Emily has a stubborn, vindictive pride and an automatic assumption of superiority, which she inherited from her father? She represents the Old South, with her china painting lessons, the black servant, and a kind of Southern mansion. She is a creature of an era in which a father could turn away (and threaten to horsewhip?) all suitors. The townspeople at first are envious of her money and stature, but when those things go, they pity her. She has become an anachronism, like much of the vaunted chivalry and culture of the Old South.

6. *Coquettish* (flirtatious), *macabre* (gruesome), *impervious* (incapable of being affected), *perverse* (perverted; stubborn; contradictory) could all define elements of Miss Emily's personality. Like an "idol in a niche," Miss Emily is the revered enigma, untouchable in the isolated recesses of her house and traditions.

7. The story does start very close to the final revelation—but then fills in the context and the many clues before the climactic ending. Are your students ready to appreciate the special effects Faulkner achieves by this departure from conventional storytelling?

THE PERSONAL RESPONSE

The chief difficulty with trying to imagine this story told in chronological fashion is that the pivotal event—the murder of Homer Barron—would take place early in the story. There could be no climactic revelation at the end. Whatever fascination Emily's character has for us would wear off long before the anticlimatic end of a more traditional story?

Chapter 5 POINT OF VIEW Windows on the World 153

The modern critic's emphasis on point of view in fiction mirrors a basic assumption in the modern consciousness: Reality exists as it is *perceived* by someone. What we call reality is a construct. For students, on the other hand, the idea that a story makes them look at the world through a particular lens, at a characteristic angle of refraction, may be a new concept. To help students become sensitive to point of view, ask them to look back over the stories they have read to find examples for narrative points of view that they have already encountered:

Omniscient Author: Bernard Malamud
Third Person Objective: Ernest Hemingway
First Person Protagonist: Alice Munro
First Person Observer: Doris Lessing
Naive Narrator: Raymond Carver

First Reading: Anton Chekhov, "Vanka" 156

PERSPECTIVES—CHEKHOV'S "VANKA" AND AUTHOR BIOGRAPHY

Anton Chekhov (1860–1904) was one of a generation of prerevolutionary Russian intellectuals trying to rise above their peasant origins and struggling ineffectually against a legacy of political impotence and religious obscurantism. Chekhov wrote hundreds of stories and still frequently performed plays—*The Seagull, Uncle Vanya, Three Sisters, The Cherry Orchard.* One reviewer called the keynote of Chekhov's writing a "melancholy skepticism."

Chekhov was born of peasant stock in an obscure provincial town, went to Moscow to become a medical student, and eventually became a spectacularly successful playwright for the Moscow stage. He died of tuberculosis at age forty-four, after leaving Moscow because of his illness for Yalta on the Crimea and eventually a German spa. The tragicomic view of childhood in "Vanka" mirrors Chekhov's own experience, as chronicled in Henri Troyat's *Chekhov* (1986, transl. by Michael Henry Heim). The father, who wound up as a bankrupt and a drunk, has been described as "an incompetent grocer and religious fanatic who spent most of his time praying, preaching, and beating his six children." The young children had to work in the father's unheated shop. On Sundays, they stood up for hours in church. Chekhov said, "When I was a child, I had no childhood."

DISCUSSION STARTERS

In introducing Chekhov's stories, one of his editors said:

> He is no teller of fairy-tales, no dispenser of illusory solaces or promises. He does not tailor his material to fit our sense of poetic justice or to satisfy our desire for a happy ending. In his mature years he clung to the conviction that a writer was not an entertainer, not a confectioner, not a beautician, but . . . bound by his conscience to tell the whole truth with the objectivity and the indifference to bad smells of a chemist.
>
> —Avrahm Yarmolinsky

Does this story fit the editor's description?

THE RECEPTIVE READER

1. *A possible capsule portrait:* Vanka is a young, poor, orphaned shoemaker's apprentice. He has been traumatized by being taken from his happy childhood world in the country to the dog-eat-dog world of the big city, where he is starved and beaten by his abusive master and mistress. Like many people who find themselves in a harsh, hostile world, he dreams about the childhood days when he was the favorite of the land owner's "young lady" (the daughter?) who taught him—although he was only the chambermaid's son—to read, write, count, and dance. His eccentric grandfather, a watchman, is for Vanka the symbol of the sheltered village life, where sneaky or thieving dogs were one of the few dangers to guard against.

2. We come to know Vanka as a lovable, loving, vulnerable orphan first—which is likely to rouse our indignation against his callous, abusive new employers?

3. Vanka sees everything from the perspective of a servant's child, as when he hopes to be taken back on at the estate as a boot cleaner or shepherd boy. He knows what goes on in the kitchen (where his grandfather sleeps) but not much about the larger world. His perspective is that of a peasant who has no clue as to how the mail works or what the post office needs to deliver a letter. Like the child he still is, he asks for a special gift for Christmas (which he is not likely to be there to receive).

4. The *limited point of view* in this story enables us to identify directly with Vanka's sad and comic predicament. No one comes between us and the boy to explain, to lecture, or to appeal overtly to our sympathy. At the same time, the author's affection for the boy and the grandfather, the author's sense of humor, and his sense of irony show in the selection of details and in the ironic contrast between the boy's naiveté and our more knowing adult perspective.

THE PERSONAL RESPONSE

Is the idyllic village world of the ignorant lower classes of czarist Russia remote for our worldly wise, city-bred students? Or is the experience of being yanked from a sheltered, affectionate childhood world to face the "cruel world" on one's own archetypal enough to maintain its appeal for today's young reader?

Worlds of Thought and Feeling

Joyce Carol Oates, "Stalking" 160

PERSPECTIVES—OATES AND THE AMERICAN EXPERIENCE

Greg Johnson, in *Understanding Joyce Carol Oates* (U of South Carolina, 1987) describes Oates, as a writer "understanding the violent and frequently ironic terms of the American experience." She "has conceived her primary role as an artist who must dramatize the nightmarish conditions of the present, with all its anxiety, paranoia, dislocation, and explosive conflict." She has her "distinct ways" of focusing "upon the intense conflict between the individual" and the "individual's social environment." Among her "representative" recurrent "bewildered, inarticulate" characters is the adolescent girl from an affluent home, with a compulsion to shoplift, who may serve as the sardonic narrator or through whose eyes, as in "Stalking," we see the world of the story. Many of Oates' stories have in common "both a riveting psychological intensity and an authoritative, all-inclusive vision of 'what American experience is really like' for people who suffer various kinds of emotional turmoil" and who "become emblematic of America as a whole." Johnson credits Oates, adhering throughout her career "to the mode of psychological realism," with impressive "subtlety of individual characterization" but also with "increasingly bold and resourceful experiments in fiction." Johnson calls her "notable as an industrious chronicler of America's personal and collective nightmares."

DISCUSSION STARTERS

Reactions to Oates' fiction vary widely—from admiration to outright hostility. Gretchen is the kind of Oates character that tends to play to very mixed reactions. Are we supposed to judge or dislike her? Does Gretchen have what today we call an "attitude"? Is she a weird individual—a strange person? Or is the story a plea for understanding? Does Gretchen represent alienated American youth? Is she kin to hostile adolescents who rebel against a plastic society by writing graffiti, vandalizing schools and stores, joining gangs, and engaging in looting sprees?

THE RECEPTIVE READER

1. Everything in this tightly controlled story helps create Gretchen's world. Gretchen's boots "cost her mother forty dollars not long ago"; they are new and expensive, but she has ruined them already. In a world of artificiality and materialism, Gretchen has no respect for things. Also, her mother seems to value shopping above a relationship with her daughter, so Gretchen rebels by ruining the boots. The car coming into view as she crosses the street gives Gretchen a chance to demonstrate her disregard for all ordinary cautions and ordinary rules—her refusal to recognize anyone else's authority or rights. Walking out into the street in front of cars, like her vandalism, gives her a sense of power: "*Slow down*, Gretchen thinks; and like magic he does."

2. Gretchen's attitude toward school and gym is defensive and pseudo-aloof: "She could be good at gym, if she bothered." When playing basketball, she "bumps into other girls, hurting them." This may be her way of getting back at those who hurt her with unkind words or actions, like the boys who laugh and call her "babe" when she runs into a trash can. This angry, isolating behavior is her shield. When she sees some kids her own age, she thinks they "might be classmates of hers." She doesn't know her classmates; she has no friends. Her attitude is a way of bearing her isolation.

3. One of the *connecting threads* in the description of the suburban landscape is the unfinished nature of the buildings, such as the gas station and the office building. Everywhere one sees "a jumbled, bulldozed field of mud and thistles and debris that is mainly rocks and chunks of grass." All the construction represents helter-skelter change and a lack of rootedness and belonging. Another connecting thread is the artificiality everywhere, such as the "blue pavement," "cedar siding with deep simulated shadow lines," homes on "artificial hills," the "flimsy plastic hanger," and the artificial rooms in the furniture store. Even faces are artificial, such as the makeup-filled face of the salesgirl, whose eyes are "penciled to show a permanent exclamatory interest."

4. Gretchen does not seem to steal anything she wants for herself. She steals for the thrill of adventure and defying the powers that be; as she leaves the store, a "small smile tugs at her mouth." And the things she steals she enjoys destroying. She has no sense that anything she does matters; perhaps she is trying to make her small mark in the world. Living in a plastic society, Gretchen has no sense of anything being important or permanent. Her mother buys her forty-dollar boots, but buying things cannot substitute for parenting. Her father travels, her mother shops, the family just moved to town six months ago; this lack of belonging and stability has helped shape Gretchen's solipsistic universe.

5. The narrator says Gretchen's "face is attractive," but the description highlights Gretchen's deepset eyes and heavy, dark eyebrows, and her "stern, staring look, like an adult man." This does not sound like society's descrip-

tion of physical beauty. And her face is "blank, neutral, withdrawn . . . detached."

6. We know her mother bought her expensive leather boots; that the family has lived in this town only six months; that Gretchen's not sure what her mother's car looks like; that she sees her mother in the mall and evades her; that furniture in a mall store reminds her of her family's furniture; and that when she gets home to their upper-middle-class suburban home, no one is there. "Her mother is probably still shopping, her father is out of town for the weekend." Weighty *key line*: "The house is empty." Gretchen does not seem to belong in her family. No one takes much interest in her beyond buying her "nice things."

7. The *imaginary adversary* represents the fantasy life that adds a touch of drama in her otherwise empty existence. (This is the same function that movies, TV, and rock concerts have in the popular culture of the young?) The adversary is the only being that interacts with or takes an interest in Gretchen. Physically he is the opposite of Gretchen; she has "solid legs," he has "long spiky legs brisk as colts' legs." However, like her, he enjoys challenges and risks. He runs, teases, taunts her—but ultimately he is under her power? (One student wrote that the adversary is the imaginary entity that Gretchen creates for "the chip she carries on her shoulder.")

THE PERSONAL RESPONSE

Note that this story is somewhat of a litmus test for the reader's own affirmative or negative view of life in modern society, and especially of the direction or lack of it of American youth. (Some readers intensely dislike Oates' fiction—because it often comes very close to painful truths?)

Tillie Olsen, "I Stand Here Ironing" 168

PERSPECTIVES—OLSEN: WOMEN AS VICTIMS AND SURVIVORS

Writing in the *Village Voice* (May 23, 1974) about Tillie Olsen's work editing and compiling bibliographies of working-class women's literature, Bell Gale Chevigny said that Olsen "disdains her role of culture-bearer, of preserving man's culture, and salvages instead the work, the thought, the dream nearly buried beneath it because it belongs to the poor and forgotten, especially women." Olsen's best-known stories pose "the paradox confronting women: that children, who most identify and confirm the values women want to bring to the transformation of the world, most surely bind them away from such action."

Olsen has said about "I Stand Here Ironing" that the story, while not autobiographical, is "somewhat close to my own life." In an interview, she said that she has "always been interested in the hardest job of all in society—having to raise kids on your own." In *Tillie Olsen* (Twayne, 1991), Mickey Pearlman and Abby H. Werlock review critical reactions to "I Stand Here Ironing": In the story, a mother who was young and inexperienced recounts with "almost painful" honesty her forced neglect of her oldest child in a depression era when poverty was unrelieved by the now much maligned welfare state. In the story, the mother is called a child "of depression, of war, of fear." The mother is haunted by her memories of Emily's cries and weeping; she has wrenching memories of Emily's unhappiness in loveless institutions. The critics note the cost to Emily, as we observe "her stiffness, her quietness, her trouble at school." We see her suffering nightmares and "long periods of silent solitude," feeling unloved during the dark days. The mother-daughter relationship even now has an element of coldness; it "even now lacks overt involvement and warmth." However, some critics see a silver lining: Emily has discovered her gift for bringing happiness "to strangers who need the humor, the entertainment, the warmth she is able to provide them." In some ways, "the mother's strength has been handed down to her daughter." Emily "illustrates the enigma of human life: it contains poverty and tragedy and pain but also some fulfilling of potential, a desire to survive." The "feminine image" of the dress "coupled with that of the iron" suggests "the harsh oppressive molding reality of society and circumstance and its effect on women. Yet neither the mother nor Emily has succumbed."

DISCUSSION STARTERS

What preconceptions about poverty and poor people do your students bring to this story? Do any of them think of the poor as shiftless and irresponsible (people who, as in ex-President Reagan's anecdote, cash their welfare checks to buy vodka)? Or do your students think of poor people as helpless victims of the system? Or have your students bought into the current fashionable talk about poor people as a "culture of dependency"? How is the perspective in this story different from these or other familiar notions? What about the perspective on poverty in this story is different, new, or disturbing?

THE RECEPTIVE READER

1. The story is addressed to one of several well-meaning persons (a teacher?) who nudge the mother with implied criticism (she doesn't take enough time; she doesn't smile enough at Emily). But the larger implied *you* is people in general, including us as readers, whose disapproving, uncomprehending looks make her try to explain, to justify herself, to come to terms with the past.

2. By the age of eighteen the narrator had married, had a child, been deserted by the father, and forced into a succession of menial jobs forcing her to thwart the child's need for security and affection. There is the sour smell

of poverty. There is a strong sense of being trapped, of being helpless while bitterly aware that the economic plight of the parent is stunting the child's development. A sense of guilt (remembering the "clogged weeping" of a child abandoned during the day by her working mother) struggles with the sense of having done the best under the circumstances.

3. Ironically, the well-meaning teacher and old man are of no real help, any more than the irresponsible absconding father.

4. The mother is bitter toward *institutions* that are insensitive to the real needs of those they serve. The mother calls nursery schools "parking places for children" where they suffer "the fatigue of the long day, and the laceration of group life." Children who are victimized by other children are ridiculed by the teachers. The convalescent home is superficially in good order, with well-tended grounds, children wearing bright bows, and "sleek young women" from the society pages holding festive fund-raisers. However, the reality behind the façade is that of a prison: Rules are rigidly enforced. Children see their parents from a high balcony; they are allowed no personal belongings (not even letters); the poor food makes them lose weight. Emily changes radically there: "I used to try to hold and love her after she came back, but her body would stay stiff, and after a while she'd push away. . . . Food sickened her, and I think much of life too." The schools Emily attends later reward "the glib and quick," and since Emily is neither, the "overworked and exasperated" teachers label (and neglect) her as a "slow learner."

5. Emily was "thin and dark and foreign-looking when every little girl was supposed to look or thought she should look" like Shirley Temple. She grows up with deep-seated fears and with an inability to make friends. She has been branded a "slow learner" and tries to escape the trauma of school by feigning illness. She bears a "corroding resentment" toward her sister Susan who "is everything in appearance and manner Emily is not." Her gifts show when on the stage she experiences for a time the recognition and approval she has long been denied. The mother recognizes and blames herself for her natural preference for the more attractive, more outgoing younger child.

6. The resentment against harsh, unfeeling, repressive institutions and the feeling of bitterness at being forced to seem lacking in love give the story a strong emotional force.

7. The attitude is one of acceptance of lowered expectations rather than of militancy and rebellion. The child has been denied her full potential (like many others); the mother's hope is that Emily will make the best of what she has. The attitude of resignation is one that the story has led up to with many minor and major defeats and disappointments?

8. This story is an example of tightly defined *limited point of view*. During most of the story, we seem to be limited to the mother's perceptions and

explanations. For example, the representatives of the institutions never have a chance to present their side of the story or to defend themselves against the mother's charges?

THE PERSONAL RESPONSE

The following *journal entry* represents one student's reaction to the story:

So many of the media images we see of women glorify youthful beauty, frivolous pursuits, and managers of tidy homes. This intense story focuses on the reality of an impoverished single mother trying to support a family. The speaker, the mother, has an aura of grey around her, a seemingly intangible presence of despair laden with the burden of struggle and exhaustion. For Olsen, even the brief moment of her daughter's success as a high school comedienne is overshadowed by a kind of cautious doom, a shadow of trepidation. The mother's chronic anxiety never allows her to get too comfortable with signs of apparent progress. If good things happen, she accepts them stoically and is thankful. She is the ultimate example of someone who never wants to rise too high because she knows how hard the ground is.

Katherine Anne Porter, "The Jilting of Granny Weatherall" 175

PERSPECTIVES—PORTER'S "JILTING" AND THE RANGE OF READER RESPONSE

"The Jilting of Granny Weatherall" is one of the most widely anthologized short stories of modern times, used widely in textbooks and bringing the author hundreds of letters from students and teachers. The story has been read from points of view representing the whole critical spectrum, not counting the lunatic fringe. (The story was banned in high schools because at the end Granny, in saying "God, give a sign," allegedly took the name of God in vain. As Porter said, "She's an old woman dying. She was an old-fashioned lady who used that kind of strong but perfectly solid language.")

Dealing with the subject of death, the story invites analysis from a philosophical or religious point of view. Willene and George Hendrick, in *Katherine Anne Porter* (Twayne, 1988), quote a critic positing as the moral lesson of the story "that the universe has no order, the proper bridegroom never comes—to expect him will inevitably lead to cruel disillusionment." The Hendricks see the story as offering "a bitter and grimly determined" truth: At the end, Granny, in a panic "begins to think of all the unfinished things she wanted done. She asks God for a sign, but there is none." Again, as on the day she was jilted many years ago, "there is a priest in the house but no bridegroom—in this second jilting, the absent bridegroom is Jesus of Matthew 25:1–13." She cannot forgive being jilted again. In the words of the story: "She stretched herself with a deep breath and blew out the light."

A Freudian reading of the story might stress the puritanical climate of repression that shaped the central character's attitude toward men. William L. Lance, in *Katherine Anne Porter and the Art of Rejection* (U of North Carolina, 1963), found that Granny represented "the puritanical fear of sex instilled into her by her religious and moral tradition. Among the women of the old order . . . this fear was an impediment to satisfying spiritual intimacy with their husbands. This in turn gave the men many of the faults which led women to scorn them, in an unconscious defense reaction, and to stand alone with hardened hearts." Granny's "first apparent love has been simply a romantic dream, never in any danger of becoming real. The jilting provides a perfect escape from marriage and an ideal excuse for hating men."

DISCUSSION STARTERS

Are your students willing to track perhaps five or ten minutes of their actual "stream of consciousness"—the jumbled stream of observations, thoughts, and memories that passes through their minds at any give time?

THE RECEPTIVE READER

1. We essentially see the world from Granny's point of view. Most of the story is stream of consciousness, interrupted by the voices and faces of people at Granny's sickbed in the present. This alternative strand of things happening that Granny does not take in represents the perspectives of the doctor, the priest, and Cornelia, Granny's daughter. They try to talk to her, but she rarely connects with them. The alternation of the two points of view sets up a contrast between the rich inner *subjective* world of memories, emotions, and regrets and the outer *objective* linear world of practical concerns.

2. Memories of her past with her first love, her husband, and her children take up the early pages of the story. When she thinks of her grown daughter, Cornelia, Granny imagines spanking her "and making a fine job of it." The pillow pressing against her reminds her of the feeling in her heart when she was jilted. Cornelia connects her to memories of Hapsy "standing with a baby on her arm. She seemed to herself to be Hapsy also, and the baby on Hapsy's arm was Hapsy and himself and herself, all at once, and there was no surprise in the meeting."

3. The first allusion to the jilting occurs when Granny thinks about "George's and John's letters and her letters to them both." Later we see that as a young woman Granny had been left at the altar by George. Granny still is emotionally involved with the event, as well as defensive about it. She thinks, "I want you to find George. Find him and be sure to tell him I forgot

him. I want him to know I had my husband just the same and my children and my house like any other woman. . . . Tell him I was given back everything he took away and more." Then she realizes that he took away something she did not get back, perhaps an innocence or sense of security or hope.

4. Ask students to compare Granny's relating differently to the two daughters to the mother's relationship with two very different daughters in Tillie Olsen's story?

5. The surface plot line of the story takes place in one day, with the ill Granny getting worse, her children and the priest gathering around her, and her dying. Parallel to this surface story line is Granny's last reckoning and settling of accounts with the lover who jilted her. Death in the story becomes an abandonment parallel to the jilting, with "again no bridegroom and the priest in the house."

6. Have students share, and discuss the merits of, their suggested summings up.

THE PERSONAL RESPONSE

Do your students respond to the theme of strength in adversity in this story? Or is the feeling of disappointment and bitterness uppermost for them in the story?

Chapter 6 SYMBOL The Eloquent Image 189

You may want to explore with your students the range of associations of recurrent symbols. Ask them to pool images, ideas, and associations that are brought to mind by symbols anchored in universal human experience:

- water (life-saving and life-giving for plants and other living things? fertility? drowning? cleansing?)
- desert (absence of life? drying up of emotions?)
- light (light of knowledge versus darkness of ignorance? God manifesting Himself? blinding through excessive light?)
- rock (strength? insensitivity? lasting through the ages and a symbol of permanence?)
- dawn (hope? new beginning?)

First Reading: Ann Beattie, "Snow" 191

PERSPECTIVES—BEATTIE AND THE END OF INNOCENCE

One editor has identified Beattie's characters with a generation that came of age during the Vietnam War. Idealistic young people emerged from the experience "bewildered and sensitive" and "haunted by missed connections and suspended convictions." For Beattie's characters, the Vietnam War often represented the end of childlike innocence, and they seem unable to find meaning and direction in the postwar phase. They are alienated from the goal-oriented materialistic society around them. They often seem isolated (like a statue or a rock that, in the words of the song, "feels no pain"). They may seem to be hankering for the world of adolescence—exploratory, open-ended, not beholden to deadening adult expectations. In Ann Beattie's story "Shifting," the husband from the beginning seems unfunny, serious, goal-oriented, self-centered—"wrong" for a young woman who seems spontaneous, drifting, at loose ends. The in-laws equally seem confining with their "perfect timing" and "careful smiles"—and with their nagging criticism of her for not being the stereotypical wife. A keynote is struck in the story when the main character has an argument with her husband over the inventory of "possessions" needed for the insurance man. "What's worth anything?" she says. The husband's compulsively neat car —vacuumed every weekend, with "not even a sweater or a lost glove in the back seat"—gives the young woman a vague feeling of unease, of not being able to be herself in these almost oppressively tidy surroundings. Another car, inherited from a dead uncle, has "character"—it is not impersonal and sterile like the husband's.

DISCUSSION STARTERS

For your students, do rain, snow, lightning, clouds, or other weather phenomena have symbolic associations?

THE RECEPTIVE READER

The snow seems to mean different things to the man and the woman? For her, snow seems to represent the relationship she had that winter in the country, before the couple separated. When she remembers that time, snow figures prominently. She remembers the man "like a crazy king of snow," wearing a white turban and shoveling the walk. She remembers looking up at the sky as the snow streamed down: "It seemed that the world had been turned upside down, and we were looking into an enormous field of Queen Anne's lace." Because this was a happy and optimistic time for the woman, she views the snow as an integral part of a joyous experience. Her response to the snow is an enthusiastic one, and she doubtless loved being secure in her warm country house while the snow fell all around. For the man, that winter was not such a lark. The woman says of him: "You remember it differently." He would not look back upon the time with such nostalgia. He views it as cold, moonless, repetitive, and grim. One night he tells her: "Any life will seem dramatic if you omit mention of most of it." To the man, in ironic and complete contrast to the woman, snow represents all that was wrong with that winter in the country. While she remembers him as Snow King, does he remember what a tedious chore it was to shovel and re-shovel the walks? The chipmunk, which appears in the opening sentence, leaps into the house as if it belongs there, despite the fact that it obviously does not; one could perhaps say the same thing of the couple? The pool, covered with a black shroud of plastic, under a torrent of rain, may hint at the death of the couple's relationship?

John Steinbeck, "The Chrysanthemums" 193

DISCUSSION STARTERS

How do your students react to the following journal entry by a student? Are they likewise disappointed by the ending of the story? (You may want to ask your students to write a different ending for the story.)

I cannot say that I liked the ending. It was much too anticlimactic. It's not so much that Elisa learns that she cannot trust the smooth talk of a traveling man. (The darned tinker! I couldn't believe he blatantly deceived both her and myself.) She realized her desire to break out of the mold when she met the tinker. She became aware of a different part of herself. The anticlimax is not that the tinker deceived her—it's a cruel, mean world. The anticlimax is that Elisa returns to her original subservient mode by the end of the story. The husband is a fool who cannot fathom her intelligence or her potential, but he certainly finds ways to criticize her.

THE RECEPTIVE READER

1. The chrysanthemums give Elisa's life meaning. They are a symbol of strong, burgeoning life. She can grow them beautiful and strong; they give her a chance to be competent, effective, in charge. Nevertheless, in the practical world, they are ornamental; they are not of "real" importance like growing apples in the orchard—a man's job. When the man in the wagon arrives, he humors Elisa's strong emotional commitment to the flowers in order to get a job from her. The flowers he tossed in the road symbolize the insignificance of the flowers in a "man's world"; they say that the man was too narrow and selfish to take her seriously as a human being.

2. Flowers are often felt to be beautiful but ephemeral—they wilt soon. They may connote romance (which also has a way of not lasting). In this story, however, they are symbolic of vitality, of strong suppressed vital impulses instead?

3. Elisa wears a man's hat, "clodhopper shoes," and "heavy leather gloves" while she works in the garden; she is described as "handsome." Looking like a man, she does the work that makes her feel important. When she dresses up femininely for dinner, Henry tells her she looks "nice." When she challenges him, he says, "I mean you look different, strong and happy." But she doesn't feel strong when she sees the flowers in the road; it's like seeing herself discarded. The weather is described as smothering "high gray-flannel fog," which could connect to men in suits doing "important business," from which she is isolated. The fog sits "like a lid on the mountains," making the "great valley a closed pot." Again, the image of being closed off—in a pot of domesticity—connects to Elisa's smothered life. Her interest in boxing symbolizes her fascination with an instinctual, violent, animalistic side of life from which she is shut off?

4. Sexual imagery pervades the meeting between Elisa and the tinker, particularly when she describes "planting hands": "It's when you're picking off the buds you don't want. Everything goes right down into your fingertips. You watch your fingers work. They do it themselves. You can feel how it is. They pick and pick the buds. . . . They're one with the plant. Do you see? Your fingers and the plant. You can feel that, right up your arm?" She builds to a crescendo, "kneeling on the ground looking up at him," her breast swelling "passionately." Her voice grows "husky": "Why, you rise up and up! Every pointed star gets driven into your body. It's like that. Hot and sharp and—lovely." Paradoxically, the shabby tinker, scrounging for a living, becomes a kind of Pan, a fertility spirit, a symbol of tabooed vital forces.

5. Her husband is dense and uncomprehending (and at times diffident around her), but he plays the stereotypical dominant male role. He is the one who makes important business deals with men in suits. He makes the decisions, "takes her" to dinner and the movies. When she first hears his voice, she "starts." The first thing he says to her is, "At it again." He seems to admire her way with the flowers, but he does not consider her work important: "I

wish you'd work out in the orchard and raise some apples that big." She counters with, "Maybe I could do it, too." She is often on the defensive with him, stiffening up and making forthright statements about her value, as though she has to remind him of it—and reassure herself. He takes care of "important business"; she gardens and tends to the house. She must ask him questions about his work affairs, such as, "Who were those men you were talking to?" She also must ask his "permission," such as, "Could we have wine at dinner?"

6. Is Elisa "androgynous"? She is capable of man's work but has strong female instincts, and she can also be feminine in appearance?

7. For many readers, the sight of the discarded flowers in the road is the climax. Perhaps Elisa had known deep down the man in the wagon didn't really need the chrysanthemums, but it had felt so good to be needed, even if it was a lie. But seeing the flowers in the road highlighted at a conscious level that someone taking her seriously was a lie. After that, Elisa is injured, no longer able to feign strength and happiness. She just wants to drink some wine, perhaps to anesthetize her feelings. And she no longer feels strong and youthful; she cries "weakly—like an old woman."

8. Steinbeck is indebted to the naturalistic tradition in his concern with frustrated desire and our thwarted instinctual nature. Is this naturalistic (and Freudian) view of women, like the earlier stereotype of the "angel in the house," also a perspective conceived and perpetuated by males?

THE PERSONAL RESPONSE:

Do your students' responses vary along male/female or younger/older lines? Do students from different ethnic or cultural traditions respond differently to Elisa?

Juxtapositions: The Range of Interpretation

Stanley Renner, "The Real Woman in 'The Chrysanthemums' " **202**

Marilyn H. Mitchell, "Steinbeck's Strong Women and 'The Chrysanthemums' " **203**

THE RECEPTIVE READER

Both critics focus on women's sexual frustration or lack of emotional fulfillment. However, Renner sees a root cause of frustration in women's tendency toward romantic fantasy—romanticizing shabby and unpromising reality (the tinker) and thus dooming themselves to disappointment. Mitchell, on the other hand, blames the limited possibilities and narrow range available to women in a male-dominated world, with males focusing on women's physical bodies while showing little interest in their personalities.

Charlotte Perkins Gilman, "The Yellow Wallpaper" 204

PERSPECTIVES—GILMAN AND REVISIONIST RECENT CRITICISM

Julie Bates Dock in " 'But One Expects That': Charlotte Perkins Gilman's 'The Yellow Wallpaper and the Shifting Light of Scholarship" (*PMLA*, 1996) says that in the last two decades leaving out "The Yellow Wallpaper" from an American literature anthology has become almost as unthinkable as cutting out "The Raven" or "Civil Disobedience." She quotes Susan S. Lanser, writing in *Feminist Studies*, as saying that from the 1960s until the mid-1980s feminist criticism proceeded as if "men's writings were ideological sign systems and women's writings were representation of truth, reading men's or masculinist texts with resistance and women's or feminist texts with empathy."

With Lanser, Dock believes it is time to "revisit" the accepted feminist readings of "The Yellow Wallpaper." Many familiar background "facts" do "not hold up well under scrutiny." These include Gilman's struggle against a male editorial establishment to get her story into print. (There is still debate over an apparent claim by the eminent contemporary editor and "man of letters" William Dean Howells that he helped get the story printed.) There are questions about the alleged tendency of insensitive contemporary readers to see "The Yellow Wallpaper" as a mere ghost story. Gilman's claims concerning the angry reception of the story by the medical community may be based mainly on a single letter to the editor by a person not clearly identified.

Dock takes a leaf from scholars who warn against subjectivity in autobiography, saying that memoirs should never be taken at face value. Some biographical facts may become embellished in the retelling, while others may be forgotten or overlooked. The story "of a heroic woman author fighting valiantly in defiance of a thwarting male editorial presence makes for great drama," but it rests largely on Gilman's own personal accounts, not confirmed and sometimes contradicted by contemporary evidence. For instance, there is no independent confirmation that Weir Mitchell, the neurologist mentioned in the story, did indeed change his rest cure treatment as the result of the story; evidence indicates he was still practicing his brand of therapy at a much later date.

DISCUSSION STARTERS

Who is the woman in the wallpaper? How does your perspective on the wallpaper shift and evolve? Is the narrator mad? Did she start out sane? Where and why does she go over the edge?

THE RECEPTIVE READER

1. They're the traditional professional married couple. He's a doctor. She's a mother, having just given birth. She offers an excited, stereotypically

feminine description of the house with the "*delicious* garden." Her husband dotes on her, and he is concerned about her well-being like a model husband. The first hint of a possibly "haunted house" comes when the narrator is still bubbling about reaching "the height of romantic felicity" there. Very gradually we sense something extraordinary about the house: "There is something strange about the house—I can feel it."

2. We learn that she feels "nervous"; she cannot be with her newborn. Her husband directs her to rest and have "proper self-control" so that her imagination does not get the best of her. The "cure" for her nervous condition is to cut her off from healthy activity and from people whose company she might find stimulating. The "worst for a nervous patient," she has been told, is to give in to morbid fancies stimulated by her overactive imagination. While she officially goes along with her husband's cheer-me-up attitude ("I am glad my case is not serious"), we as readers are in her confidence ("John does not know how much I really suffer").

3. At the beginning of the story, she is sure her paternalistic, smug husband is right; "he is so wise." He is the authority figure, and when she gets angry with him or deceives him by secretly writing, she feels guilty and is sure she's being "unreasonable." As the story progresses, she moves from feeling "a little afraid of John" to enjoying deceiving him: "He laughed a little the other day, and said I seemed to be flourishing in spite of my wallpaper. I turned it off with a laugh. I had no intention of telling him it was *because* of the wallpaper."

4. In this story, the *central symbol* shifts and evolves and grows on the reader until it totally takes over what started as a fairly realistic-sounding story. The "horrid" wallpaper starts off as just ugly, "committing every artistic sin." But it increasingly becomes more ominous and hallucinatory as we see faces and a "broken neck" and "bulbous eyes" in the pattern. Next, "the interminable grotesques seem to form around a common center," which leads her to see a "woman stooping down and creeping about behind that pattern."

5. The woman is trapped, looking out from behind bars. Ultimately, there are many women, and when they get out, they must creep and hide. The compulsive creeping, leaving a smudge along the wall, is a symbol of an oppressive trapped existence with no exit? The narrator becomes the woman who was trapped behind the pattern? She is a woman trapped in her life and has freed herself by going where her husband has forbidden her to go—into the world of her hallucinatory imagination?

6. The *contrast* between the green world outdoors and the yellow world of the sickroom becomes strong toward the end of the story. The garden is the outside; it is beauty and freedom. The enclosed room is inside; it is ugly and confining. However, the outside also could represent society—the place where one must be proper? The inside, then, could represent the

recesses of one's mind, where one can escape the pressures of society. By throwing the key away, the woman has claimed herself?

7. The *ending* could be read as a kind of liberation. The woman has defied her husband by moving into the recesses of her mind, perhaps the only place she can be free. However, an opposite reading might claim that the woman has locked herself into the prison of her own mind—that the truly sad or tragic thing about the story is that the patient has fully accepted her insanity and walls herself off from the outside world of the sane.

8. *Writing* here, as in much current feminist biography and criticism, is an act of self-assertion, of defying obtuse male authority that infantilizes women. It is also, for the author if not for the woman in the story, therapy and a way of exorcising the private demons of the self?

THE PERSONAL RESPONSE

How up-to-date are today's students on the questions raised by this story? Seismic shifts have occurred in our view of mental illness, making this story perhaps more topical and thought-provoking than it was at the time it was written. From William Blake to Sigmund Freud, mental illness has been seen as the manifestation of festering repressed desire. The British psychiatrist Laing and his followers saw mental illness as a retreat from an insane society. Current biochemistry makes us see mental illness as the result of chemical imbalance in the brain, which can be corrected, like diabetes, by the correct dosage of compensatory drugs.

Gabriel García Márquez, "The Handsomest Drowned Man in the World" 217

PERSPECTIVES—GARCÍA MÁRQUEZ AND STUDENT RESPONSE

Will the surreal and macabre elements of García Márquez' story be a barrier between the story and our student readers? The following is a sample student reaction:

I think that this story was a like a folktale that teaches a moral—although the moral is not spelled out. I think the story tells us that we should appreciate life and everything in our lives. We should give praise and be thankful for all that we have in our lives. There are many people who are physically alive but spiritually and emotionally dead. They need to realize that there is something to live for and that we need to take advantage of everything available to us. Have you ever stopped to wonder how much parents or other people close to you have meant in your life? If you were to lose them tomorrow, would you feel there were many things that you needed to tell them? We should not take anything for granted, and we should learn from the villagers and start to change and be appreciative of everything that we have in our lives.

DISCUSSION STARTERS

Do cultures or ethnic traditions differ in prevailing attitudes toward death? For instance, what is the difference between an Irish wake and other kinds of funerals? Is it true that death plays a special role in the folklore and festivals of Mexico and other Latin American countries? Have your students encountered parallels to the situation in this story, where death is less frightening than usual and in fact has humorous overtones? Is it significant that the villagers responding most fully and spontaneously to the influence of the dead man are women?

THE RECEPTIVE READER

1. This island setting is no ordinary prosaic location—it is a strange *fantasy* world that has left more than one student reader "utterly clueless as to what is going on here." We find ourselves on a strange island—with a few wooden houses on the edge of a barren cape and with so little land that mothers were afraid "the wind would carry off their children" and with dead villagers thrown off the cliffs for lack of ground to bury them. The corpse washed up on the beach weighed "almost as much as a horse," with the villagers thinking "that maybe the ability to keep on growing after death was part of the nature of certain drowned men." The body washed up on the beach "wore his death with pride." And so on.

2. The tale has a deceptive surface simplicity reminiscent of a folktale, with the kind of wonderment and naive explanations that we might expect in a tale told to children. The children help us get into the spirit of innocent, playful wonder that we need if we are not going to reject the story as strange or preposterous.

3. The people live in a small, isolated fishing village, with desolate streets, barren courtyards, and narrow dreams. Their island is surrounded by a shark-infested ocean, and men feel "the bitterness of endless nights at sea."

4. The *miracle* is that such a beautiful, larger-than-life person would come to such a desolate, cramped place and transform the outlook and lives of the villagers. Alternately, the miracle is that a dead man brings the village to life, bringing the people excitement, adventure, and ultimately hope.

5. In the face of the "splendor and beauty" of the drowned man, the villagers become "aware for the first time of the desolation of their streets, the dryness of their courtyards," and "the narrowness of their dreams." The corpse is a symbol of a fuller life—with a richer environment, more spacious buildings, and abundant flowers. The villagers "knew that everything would be different from then on." The central transformation is a change in attitude, a change in expectations. The dead man inspires a change toward a more affirmative and joyful attitude toward life.

6. Passengers on ocean liners passing by in the future will marvel at the rich fragrance of the flowers and at the bright sun bathing the island. What happened here is not going to be a localized epiphany; the spiritual regeneration experienced by the villagers will spread beyond the island?

7. It is paradoxical that a dead, bloated body would inspire fantasy, adventure, excitement, and hope.

Chapter 7 THEME
The Search for Meaning 231

This chapter will bring students face to face with a basic paradox of the modern tradition in literary criticism: We claim that imaginative literature is fraught with human meaning. However, we are reluctant to spell out the meaning of a story or a poem in prosy abstract terms. You may want to explore with your students key terms like abstraction vs. concrete detail, static vs. dynamic (in a great story, meanings take shape as the story develops); clichés or ready-made phrases vs. an authentic individual response.

First Reading: Luisa Valenzuela, "The Censors" 233

DISCUSSION STARTERS

Have your students have had any first-hand experience with censorship?

THE RECEPTIVE READER

This spooky political parable is about how totalitarian or other repressive regimes blur the distinction between the oppressor and the victim. Juan signs on as a censor in order to intercept a thoughtless letter he himself wrote, but he becomes absorbed in the work and in the mission of his agency. He zealously censors his own letter and informs on himself, and he is executed as an enemy of the regime. Among the possible "morals":

> Oppressors cannot ply their trade without the cooperation of their victims.
>
> In one way or another, hostile or reluctant people are nevertheless sucked into the "system."
>
> In a truly paranoid society, today's oppressor is tomorrow's victim.
>
> (This last version is likely to appeal to our sense of irony and poetic justice.)

The Thinking Reader

Alice Walker, "Everyday Use" 236

PERSPECTIVES—"EVERYDAY USE" AND THE RANGE OF RESPONSE

In an unpublished paper ("Alice Walker's 'Everyday Use': The Black Woman's Search for Identity," Santa Clara University, 1996), Kathryn Harrison compares critical perspectives on Alice Walker's relation to the three key characters in "Everyday Use." While many critics are extremely negative toward Dee, the sophisticated urbanized daughter in the story, at least one comes to her defense. Mary Helen Washington in "An Essay on Alice Walker" (*Alice Walker: "Everyday Use,"* ed. Barbara T. Christian, Rutgers UP, 1994) refers readers to a 1973 interview where Walker says that she sees the story as a reflection of her own struggles as an artist. The three characters really represent three parts of herself. The mother and Maggie are parts of herself that are able to "stay, sustain, abide, and love," whereas Dee represents that part of her that wants to "go out into the world to see change and be changed." Walker says, "I do in fact have an African name that was given to me, and I love it and use it when I want to, and I love my Kenyan gowns . . . it's all part of me. But, on the other hand, my parents and grandparents were part of it, and they take precedence." Washington sees Walker as most connected with the "bad daughter," because, like Dee, Walker "left her community, appropriating the oral tradition in order to turn it into a written artifact, which will no longer be available for 'everyday use' by its orginators."

Among critics hostile to Dee, Nancy Tuten (in "Alice Walker's 'Everyday Use,' " *Explicator*, Winter 1993 focuses on Dee's using language "to oppress and manipulate others and to isolate herself" rather than using it as "a medium for newfound awareness and for community." Tuten quotes the narrator's description of Dee as reading to her mother and sister "without pity; forcing words, lies, other folks' habits, whole lives upon us, sitting trapped and ignorant underneath her voice." Tuten stresses "the vast difference between Dee's aggressive, oppressive, self-seeking use of words and Maggie's calm, selective, community-building use of language." In the end, "Mama's actions, not her words, silence the daughter who has, up to this point, used language to control other and separate herself from the community."

Many critics agree on the central symbolism of quilt making—not so much the final artifact (as valued by Dee) as the process of making it. Houston A. Baker, Jr., and Charlotte Pierce-Baker, in "Patches: Quilts and Community in Alice Walker's 'Everyday Use' " (*The Southern Review*, Summer 1985), say that "a patchwork quilt, laboriously and affectionately crafted from bits of worn overalls, shredded uniforms, tattered petticoats, and outgrown dresses stands as a signal instance of a patterned wholeness in the African diaspora." Finally "it is the 'self,' or a version of humanness" that will be the African American self, that "must in fact be crafted from fragments on the basis of wisdom gained from preceding generations."

DISCUSSION STARTERS

Why do people change their names? And from what to what? (Do your students know of any celebrities or prominent people who at some point in their careers changed their names?) Do families anymore hand on heirlooms or items of sentimental value from generation to generation? (What kinds of items, for instance?) Is there a generation gap in this story? If so, how is it different from more familiar or stereotypical gaps between the generations?

THE RECEPTIVE READER

1. The mother daydreams about weighing a hundred pounds less, having much lighter skin, having a quick wit, and shining on television in witty banter with Johnny Carson. In her daydreams, she is much more the sophisticate that her oldest daughter could be proud of. But in real life, she accepts her down-to-earth existence and unpretentious ways. She is independent, is good at "a man's job," and likes sitting on the porch and enjoying a pinch of snuff.

2. Serving as a *foil* to the ambitious Dee, Maggie is the homely, homebody counterpart of her determined, sophisticated, outgoing, politically aware sister. Maggie bears the scars of a disastrous fire that left her physically and emotionally impaired—"chin on chest, eyes on ground, feet in shuffle."

3. Little touches like the sunglasses that hide "everything above the tip of her nose and her chin" make Dee seem an artificial, plastic person who gives herself airs. She is determined to "educate" her mother and sister, forcing on them "words, lies, other folks' habits."

4. The central *conflict* in the story is over two opposed ways of looking at folk art (and indeed art in general): One view sees art as an artifact to be displayed, taken out of its original context. The opposite view prefers art that is part of people's living, that serves a living purpose—whether as an object of worship in a church that is not a museum, or as objects of daily use that carry a rich freight of memories and associations. The mother has more of a living sense of her heritage than her oldest daughter—whose views and slogans seem to the mother more the product of academic learning or ideology than of firsthand experience.

5. Possible wording of the *theme*: Things of everyday use, cherished by real people, are more precious than art taken out of a living context?

6. The quilts as a central symbol keep the conflict from being an abstract confrontation. The simple rural home and Maggie's shy, embarrassed ways dramatize the contrast between Dee's citified ways and her true "heritage."

THE PERSONAL RESPONSE

You may want to discuss with your students the following sympathetic account of Dee's role in the story:

Dee fairly accurately mirrors how many young people today feel about their heritage. There is a resurgence of ethnic thinking going on right now, and African Americans, along with other minorities, are trying to establish who they are by understanding their past. Since blacks are the only group that did not migrate here, for many blacks today their dominant feeling is anger. They, like Dee and her friend, are denouncing their slave names and giving themselves African names instead. They are also choosing religions like Islam and Rastafarianism rather than branches of the Christianity whose missionaries tried to "civilize" them. Dee is learning new things about the history of her people and exploring new ideas. She wants the quilts because to her they are a symbol of her heritage rather than just something you throw on to keep warm. When my great-grandmother died, the only thing my mother wanted was a butter knife that my great-grandmother had used daily. The knife looks old and rusty, and the wooden handle is split down both sides. When the knife first arrived, I couldn't understand why my mother would want something so old and used. But as I have gotten older, the significance of the knife has changed. It did not just spread butter for sixty years, but it is part of my history. The butter was eaten by people in my family while they sat discussing their thoughts, feelings, and lives.

Stephen Crane, "The Open Boat" 244

PERSPECTIVES—ABSURDITY AND MORAL PURPOSE IN "THE OPEN BOAT"

Jean-Paul Sartre once said that the human mind cannot accept the idea of a universe without purpose. In Crane's story, the death or survival of the shipwrecked sailors is a matter of happenstance—it serves no higher purpose; it has no redeeming significance. The sea—nature, the universe—does not care one way or another. In fact, in the strict naturalistic interpretation, even the Darwinian concept of the "survival of the fittest" is a human attempt to find some kind of rhyme or reason in the accidental twists and turns of evolution. In this story, it is the *un*fittest who survive: the badly injured captain, the cook comically paddling himself on his back like a canoe, the correspondent untrained for the rigors of a sailor's life. Crane found the answer to the ultimate absurdity and meaninglessness of existence in human solidarity—in the feeling of human brotherhood the four shipwrecked and possibly doomed men experience as they find themselves in the same boat.

However, critics have understandably been looking in the story for a more definite affirmation of moral purpose. Thus, Eric Solomon, in *Stephen Crane: From Parody to Realism* (Howard U, 1966), found an affirmative moral meaning in the fate of the four men in the boat. "Only the oiler goes it alone, secure in his own strength"—and he drowns. Each of the other three has "grasped tightly to his person, a part of the boat, a relic of their fellowship." The captain calls to the correspondent by name, asking him to rejoin the group: "Come to the boat! Come to the boat!" As he rejoins the group, trusting not himself but his fellows, the correspondent "receives help from the sea" and is flung toward the shore. This is "the true miracle of the sea."

DISCUSSION STARTERS

What is meant by the term "male bonding"? Where and how is it used—for instance, in reference to Hollywood movies? What kind of male bonding goes on in this story? What, for the modern reader, are the ideas and associations that cluster around the term *nature*? (Have your students cluster the term.) Does Crane look at nature from a different perspective than your students do? Do we today tend to romanticize nature more than Crane does?

THE RECEPTIVE READER

1. From the beginning, the reader is impressed with the *mismatch* between the puny little boat that represents human effort and the mighty ocean with its "wrongfully and barbarously abrupt and tall" waves. The grueling experience becomes real for the reader through Crane's unrelenting reiteration of recurrent motifs: "A singular disadvantage of the sea lies in the fact that after successfully surmounting one wave you discover there is another behind it just as important." "In the meantime the oiler and the correspondent rowed." "They rowed, and they rowed, and they rowed." They sleep for a short spell, only to be awakened too soon for another turn at rowing.

2. The *dialogue* is devoid of melodramatic outbursts or heroics. The men are strangely courteous and considerate toward one another. ("Will you spell me?" "Sure, Billie.") But the talk, in an understated, strangely businesslike way, circles back to the desperate life-and-death issues: whether or not there are manned life-saving stations along the coast; the prospects for favorable wind and for making it through the surf.

3. Possible readings of *key symbols*: The sea symbolizes nature seen in the light of the naturalistic tradition—indifferent to our petty human hopes and fears. The boat symbolizes the laughable inadequacy of human invention and technology when pitted against the atavistic destructive forces of nature (whether epidemics, volcanoes, hurricanes, or desertification). The seabirds symbolize the animal creation—better adapted than we are to life in an alien setting? The shark symbolizes nature "red in tooth and claw" (Tennyson) in the Darwinian vein: "Eat or be eaten; kill or be killed." The unmanned life-saving station could represent the vanity of human hopes—dashed hopes, illusions shattered. The tourists on the beach are obtuse fellow humans unable to understand and sympathize with the suffering of others.

4. The *intruding author* takes us beyond surface appearances: The injured captain, while appearing calm and brave to the other men on the boat, feels "profound dejection" because the ship went down. The author editorializes about the "subtle brotherhood of men that was here established on

the seas"—the "comradeship" that made the grueling experience for the correspondent "the best experience of his life." The intruding, omniscient author knows more than his characters: "It is fair to say here that there was not a life-saving station within twenty miles in either direction; but the men did not know this fact."

5. As we would expect in similar situations, some of the crew espouse the hopeful hypothesis: Rescuers will come from a house of refuge. The captain, who probably knows better, says that the lighthouse keeper will spot them and "notify the life-saving people." (The oiler does not seem to be one of the optimists.) In very human fashion, the crew goes through a stage where it denounces the "incompetence and blindness and, indeed, cowardice" of "the nation's life-savers." The correspondent moves from thinking that fate cannot drown him because of all the hard work he's done to get that far, to thinking—in his complete exhaustion—that letting go of life "must really be a comfortable arrangement" (moving from rebellion to resignation?)

6. Optimistic readers believing in the indomitable human spirit will root for the shipwrecked sailors? Pessimistic readers will expect them all to be drowned?

7. The word *indifferent* echoes throughout the story. The correspondent, for instance, calls the wind-tower "flatly indifferent." He is "impressed with the unconcern of the universe." Crane seems to be saying that nature is indifferent to human struggle, that to nature life and death are insignificant. The ocean did not care that the oiler did not survive. We cannot expect sympathy or succor from an inscrutable, indifferent universe—which does not even care enough about us to be hostile. As a result, the only support and comfort we can find is in our solidarity with other human beings. The "subtle brotherhood of men" is our human antidote to the indifference of a world in which we find ourselves an on an alien planet. "A high cold star on a winter's night" is the symbol of nature's indifference to human hopes and fears and to the rebellion of human beings against their fate.

8. A central *irony* of the story is that nature is sublimely beautiful when we can view it in a detached manner—while not fighting desperately for survival: "Viewed from a balcony, the whole thing would doubtless have been weirdly picturesque." There is a "terrible grace" in the movement of the waves. Even the shark has "speed and power . . . greatly to be admired." An ultimate irony is that the oiler, who seems to be the strongest and therefore should illustrate the concept of the survival of the fittest, is the one who drowns. Ironically, it is the weak and the wounded who survive.

Nathaniel Hawthorne, "Young Goodman Brown" 262

DISCUSSION STARTERS

The attempt to come to terms with the Puritan past has been a recurrent theme in American cultural history. What ideas and associations (pilgrims, Salem witch hunts, Jonathan Edwards) does the term *Puritanism* bring to mind for today's students? How do your students react to the following journal entry about Hawthorne's story?

The Puritan universe is truly a polarized either-or world. For the Puritans, if true goodness cannot be achieved, then the only alternative is pure evil. You are either with God or with the devil. You are either eternally blessed or forever damned. Once Young Goodman Brown realizes that goodness is a mirage and that everyone around him has been corrupted by evil, he sees no choice but to embrace evil himself: "Come witch, come wizard, come Indian powwow, come devil himself, and here comes Goodman Brown."

THE RECEPTIVE READER

1. It is after sunset when Young Goodman Brown says goodbye to Faith and heads into the darkening forest, bent on a mysterious "evil purpose." The meeting with the dignified elderly personage on the "dreary" road among gloomy trees causes a "tremor" in the young traveler's voice. The curiously carved stick of the older traveler at times seems to twist and wriggle "like a living serpent"— the first overt symbol of the omnipresence of sin among Brown's "race of honest men and good Christians." Ironically, the devil is not a horned monster but has "the undescribable air of someone who knew the world" and would not feel out of place at the governor's or the king's table. In fact, the devil turns out to have been close to Brown's own family, helping the grandfather and the father with such pious enterprises as having a Quaker woman lashed for her faith or setting fire to an Indian village. The exposure of false piety makes for sardonic humor when Brown with naive amazement discovers that the most pious people of the village are traveling through the forest to the same evil destination. He says about Goody Cloyse: " 'That old woman taught me my catechism,' said the young man; and there was a world of meaning in this simple comment."

2. At the story's opening, Faith seems to Brown a "blessed angel on earth," who tries—in vain, however—to keep him from embarking on his journey into the dark forest of sin and devil worship. Faith both literally and allegorically is his last defense against the rising tide of sin and corruption: "With heaven above and Faith below, I will yet stand firm against the devil!" He leaves her behind as he journeys into the "heathen wilderness"—yet her pink ribbon fluttering down on the path seems to signify that his pure young wife is headed to the same destination he is—she is no more immune to the universal corruption of sin than he. He finds himself next to her at the Witches' Sabbath and cries out to her to "resist the wicked one." There is no joyful reunion with his wife upon his return—he passes Faith without a greeting. (Has he lost his faith in a merciful God, being left only with an overpowering sense of guilt and sin?)

3. The witches' sabbath is a blasphemous *parody* of church services—note terms like *hymn*, *organ*, *convert*, *congregation*, *proselytes*, *communion*,

worship, *altar*, and *baptism*. The devil serves as the minister preaching to the worshippers, and the reddish liquid—blood?—serves for baptism of the new converts. Brown's anguished cry asking Faith to resist the devil makes the ceremony end like an evil dream. But the overwhelming sense of universal sin that Brown has acquired does not vanish with the hallucinatory vision.

4. Is the discovery of corruption behind the façade of goodness still an archetypal experience for readers today? Are we expected to agree with Brown with a knowing wink? Or are we supposed to be frightened and appalled by his paranoid vision of universal evil?

5. Some possible ways of stating the central *theme*:

Evil is not perpetrated by "others"; it lurks in everyone's heart.

Superficial righteousness is often only a thin veneer covering corruption.

Preoccupation with sin or corruption alienates people from humankind.

THE RANGE OF INTERPRETATION

You may want to discuss with your students terms like *ambiguity* and *ambivalence*. (What's the difference between being ambivalent and being two-faced? What's the difference between having mixed emotions and being wishy-washy?)

Chapter 8 STYLE The Writer's Voice 277

Style here is treated as more than decoration or surface fashion. Style is typically more than a matter of style. (It "makes a statement.") The selections in this chapter show that outward style mirrors or reflects a view of oneself and a perspective on people and the world. You may want to explore with your students pairs of opposite terms that help us chart a writer's style:

- understatement and hyperbole
- abstract and concrete
- denotation and connotation
- literal and figurative
- formal and informal
- seriousness and irony

Ask your students: What do these differences have to do with the kind of person the author—or the narrator in a story—is? What *kind of person* tends toward overstatement, exaggeration, dramatizing, hyperbole? (And what would make that kind of person easy or difficult to live with?)

PERSPECTIVES—CONVENTION AND POPULAR CULTURE

Style can often be defined in relation to an established convention. Writers conform to a style, adapt it to their own purposes, depart from it in significant ways, or rebel against it (sometimes going to an opposite extreme). How much thought have your students given to the role of convention in shaping both serious literature and popular entertainment? For instance, do they recognize the conventions of the traditional Western? How many of the features enumerated in the following excerpt do they recognize? What examples or evidence can they cite from Westerns they remember?

> More than any other genre, the Western is enveloped by rituals and conventions. We are at home in any frontier town. The main street, the cemetery (often called "boot hill"), the saloon, the general store, the stable, the bank, the railway terminal, and the sheriff's office enclosing a jail are all immediately recognizable places. We also know the people who inhabit these towns: the sheriff, the doctor, the dance-hall girl, the telegrapher, the saloon keeper, and the quiet mysterious stranger who wanders in and may be the fastest gun alive. We recognize the hired killer, the ranching baron, the cardsharp. . . . We know the role of women in this society, and we understand the rituals of the posse, the hanging party, the cavalry rescue, the Indian attack (and massacre), the poker

game, the cattle roundup, the cattle drive, and the shootout on the main street.

—William Bayer, *The Great Movies*

THE CREATIVE DIMENSION

You may want to encourage your students to play with convention by preparing a journal entry along the following lines:

- Write a synopsis for a totally stereotypical Western.
- Write a scenario for a new-style Western incorporating the conventions of the sadistic-killer movie à la *Natural Born Killers.*
- Write a miniscript for a movie transposing the conventions of the Western to the era of the samurai or of Puritan New England.
- Script a soap opera or sitcom set in a small Western town of gold rush days.

First Reading: David Michael Kaplan, "Love, Your Only Mother" 281

DISCUSSION STARTERS

These days we hear much about emotionally absent parents. What experience have your students had with physically absent parents?

THE RECEPTIVE READER

In 1959, when the narrator was seven, her mother left. She has never seen her mother since, but there has been contact of a sort: "Sixty-three postcards, four hundred-odd lines of scrawl: our life together." Perhaps when she was seven the speaker developed the habit of talking to her mother as if her mother were still present. Talking to her mother cuts right to the heart of the matter, without wasting explanatory words on an assumed reader: "I received another postcard from you today, Mother, and I see by the blurred postmark that you're in Manning, North Dakota now and that you've dated the card 1961."

The speaker's attitude toward her mother is very ambivalent. At times she has responded to the mother's messages with hate: "And I've always read them, even when my husband said not to, even if they've driven me to tears or rage or a blankness when I've no longer cared if you were dead or anyone were dead, including myself." On the other hand, the speaker acknowledges that her absent mother has, in a ironically unique way, always been faithful. "And it's true: somehow, you've always found me." Sometimes the speaker's tone is one of wry amusement: "You were down among the trees in the mountain panorama, or just out of frame on that street in downtown Tupelo, or already through the door to The World's Greatest Reptile Farm." At the end of the story the speaker says, "But on summer evenings, when the windows are open to the dusk, I sometimes smell cities . . . wheat fields . . . oceans — strange smells from far away — all the places you've been to that

John Cheever, "The Enormous Radio" 287

PERSPECTIVES—DISILLUSIONMENT AND AWAKENING IN "THE ENORMOUS RADIO"

Bypassing much of the story's zany humor and satirical byplay, Samuel Coale, in *John Cheever* (Ungar, 1977), focuses on the personal journey into disillusionment and toward "the beginnings of understanding" of Irene as the central character in "The Enormous Radio." "What is unexpected and unsettling in the story is the change" that by the end of the story "Irene has undergone in her outlook on life. At the beginning she is no more than a statistic, the sum total of the bits and pieces of information that make up 'that satisfactory average' of her social class." However, the radio, compared in the story to "an aggressive intruder" with "a malevolent green light," intrudes "upon the happy life that the Westcotts appear to be leading. The radio reveals to Irene, who listens to it furtively and obsessively, the seamier side of life"—in the words of the story, "indigestion, carnal love, abysmal vanity, faith, and despair." Jim, who finally fixes the radio and shuts off the flow of disturbing eavesdropping, acts "as if infected by the discord of the radio." He starts railing against his wife, denouncing her for stealing her mother's jewelry and callously having an abortion—"exploding her fond illusions that their life is as pleasant and decent as any life should be." The radio in the meantime has returned to its "normal" suave and noncommittal voice, reporting twenty-nine dead in a railroad disaster and the day's temperature "in almost the same disinterested and calmly carefree manner that Irene once possessed." She is "left suddenly aware of the discord and illusion upon which much of her own life has been built, while the voice of the enormous radio calmly chatters on." We as readers, too, have "become aware through Irene's 'conversion' of the pain and discord of life, but the radio has now 'returned' to that serene and careless objectivity that we have come to despise."

DISCUSSION STARTERS

A classic strategy of science fiction is to take us to a deceptively normal setting. Everything seems ordinary or even boring. The writer then lets the strange or irrational *gradually*, slowly erupt into everyday reality. All the while, our skeptical, rational selves deny it or explain it away for a time as best we can. How does this story fit this pattern?

THE RECEPTIVE READER

1. We soon realize we are in for a scathing satire of upwardly mobile people with no real commitment or purpose in life? This couple lives a comfortable, nonquestioning life, with their "two young children" and their the-

atre attendance of "10.3 times a year." Their main hope for the future is to "someday live in Westchester," an affluent suburb. In his irreverent listing of the details in their lives, Cheever portrays people without substance, people concerned mainly with surface upward mobility. Irene is "pleasant," "rather plain," and empty with her "wide, fine forehead upon which nothing at all had been written." She wears fake mink. Jim is wearing prep school clothes after the time has passed and is earnest and "intentionally naive."

2. There is something ugly, "aggressive," intrusive, and violent about the radio from the beginning. The thread that begins to connect the snatches of conversation or fragments of people's lives is that of conflict, dissatisfaction, and anguish under the plastic surface of ordinary lives?

3. Our dismay at the *dissonance* between surface normalcy and subsurface turmoil and confusion may well find an outlet in the absurdist's zany humor—"comic relief" from disturbing reality?

4. At the beginning of the story the couple is portrayed as an average, normal couple, differing "from their friends, their classmates, and their neighbors only in an interest they shared in serious music." Listening in on the disturbing lives of their neighbors, they console themselves that they are different—not petty or "hypercritical" or "dishonest." But by the end of the story we see that they are, indeed, average and normal—since average and normal is to be petty, hypercritical, and dishonest. As with their fellow tenants, their outward piety and virtue too are a thin cover for grasping selfishness (keeping a fair share of the inheritance from a sister) or for self-centered vindictiveness and recrimination ("all of my energies, all of my youth, wasted in fur coats").

THE PERSONAL RESPONSE

Here is a serious reading of the story by a student reader:

I first encountered this story when a friend read it to me over the phone. At the time, I was not as aware as I am now of how many Irene Wescotts there are out there. Irene, with her fake fur coat and the clothes bill she cannot pay, lives in a fantasy world where pain and injustices do not exist. Her complacency is shattered when a glitch in the strange radio provides her and her husband with a fly-on-the-wall view of their neighbors' hidden lives. Cheever's statement about our society as a whole is that it is not wise to live under a rock and come out only when there is a sale.

Franz Kafka, "The Country Doctor" 296

PERSPECTIVES—THE MULTIFACETED KAFKA

What makes Kafka a great modern classic? What made Kafka for many readers (and for many who have never read him) a prophet of the modern consciousness? As in reading Shakespeare's *Hamlet*, readers of widely differing critical persuasions look in the mirror of Kafka's fiction to see their own faces. With its dreamlike lack of surface logic, Kafka's fiction at the same time has the intensity of a dream vision that seems fraught with weighty but tantalizingly obscure meanings. It therefore can become a test case (a Rorschach test) for a whole range of modern critical approaches.

- "The Country Doctor" provides an ideal opportunity for the *symbol*-hunting that is a legacy of both the New Criticism and the myth critics. What is the symbolism of the horses, the groom, the maid, the wound in the patient's side?

- Kafka's feverish anxiety-ridden prose is an open invitation to *psychoanalytic* probing. How does this story illustrate the pervasive neurotic *angst* that Kafka made a household word? What makes the doctor totally insecure if not impotent, in his calling and in his human relationships?

- Kafka's closeness to orthodox Jewish tradition (while seeing it through an intellectual early modern consciousness) encourages a search for *religious* themes and symbols. Is the wound in the patient's side the wound in the side of Christ?

- To critics stressing the *historical* context of literature, Kafka is the great prophet of the totalitarian mentality, with its pervasive subtext of the impotence and irrelevance of the individual.

- *Feminist* critics, reexamining sex roles in much modern fiction, point to the totally subordinate role of the maid in "The Country Doctor." Admirers of Kafka, on the other hand, see in his hypersensitive heroes the antithesis of the traditional macho bully (represented by the groom in this story) and an expression of the androgynous side in Kafka's personality.

Important dimensions of Kafka not always recognized in current critical discussions include the following:

THE EXISTENTIALIST KAKFA Modern intellectuals have tried to come to terms with the hypothesis that life is "absurd." Did life on our planet evolve by accident? Does our existence on this earth have no higher meaning? Modern existentialism asks us to create our own human meaning in a meaningless universe. The French existentialist writer Albert Camus claimed Kafka as one of the "existentialist novelists and philosophers." Camus said that in Kafka's work "the absurd is recognized, accepted, and humanity is resigned to it." Perhaps we should modify this statement to say that Kafka's characters recognize but typically *refuse* to accept the underlying absurdity of human existence. They gallantly struggle to keep their five wits about them, "calmly putting everything in its place."

In "The Country Doctor," preoccupation with his own inadequacy is not uppermost in the doctor's mind. Only intermittently does he face his recurrent inability to solve the puzzle, to cut the knot: "What was I doing there in that endless winter!" More often he employs a tone reminiscent of other Kafka heroes—a paradoxical gallantry, becoming at times a pathetic bravado: "I was altogether composed and equal to the situation." The driver whose horses are out of control, the doctor whose patients threaten and humiliate him, pictures himself as thoroughly composed and in charge of events.

KAFKA'S HUMOR Kafka's "apprehensive clowning" (Thomas Mann) dramatizes the tragicomic discrepancy between human purposes or efforts and the laughably incongruous results. The task confronting the doctor is urgent (the seriously ill patient is waiting), but the means of reaching him are missing (no horse). When horses suddenly materialize, they appear as the result of action that is absent-minded and random (kicking the door of the sty); as the groom readies them for the journey, the doctor is a passive, nonplussed spectator. When the groom attacks the doctor's maid, the doctor's protests are cut short, as he is "swept away" on the journey that a little earlier he had given up as impossible.

Much of the zany humor is in the refusal of Kafka's characters to learn from experience. Instead, we laugh and weep at the untiring ingenuity, the imperturbable officiousness, of the human mind in coming to terms with reality. Each irruption of the incongruous is a new challenge to the human genius for putting a rational façade on the irrational, for finding a mental formula for things that are intolerable and yet must somehow be accommodated.

DISCUSSION STARTERS

As one student said, this is a "truly bizarre" story. You may want to get some solid footing for class discussion by asking: "At the most basic level, what actually *happens* in the story?" Would your students agree with the following student-written bare-bones summary? Has anything important been left out?

A doctor is called away on a house call. His horse has died. He is looking for a stand-in to get him to his patient. He finds muscular horses in his pigsty. The groom is going to rape the doctor's maid. The doctor is helpless to help her because the horses whisk him away towards the patient. He is instantly there. There is nothing wrong with the boy in the bed. The doctor is going to leave, but the family isn't going to have any of that. The doctor checks the boy again and finds a gaping wound in the boy's side. The family and a chorus of helpers strip the doctor of his clothes and put him in the bed next to the dying boy. The boy is crowded by the doctor's presence in the bed. The doctor finally makes his getaway but is unable to put on his clothes. His horses drag along like snails. He is alone in the cold night, abandoned and betrayed.

THE RECEPTIVE READER

1. Being stranded in a snowstorm, knowing that the ordinary means of transportation have broken down, and sending an employee out for help without success—all these may make us think of the country doctor as a beleaguered fellow human being. (For a very short spell, we might read the story as if it were realistic fiction.) It is the kick at the door of the abandoned pigsty that triggers the archetypically Kafkaesque eruption of the *irrational.* (The Freudian horses and animalistic groom burst forth from the subterranean subconscious?)

2. Who is the *groom*? From the beginning, the doctor experiences the characteristic Kafkaesque feeling that reality is out of control. The world around us defies our best efforts to be effective, patient, and reasonable. (We live in an absurd universe that defies our best efforts to manage it and to understand it.) The "brute" groom and his "buttocking" horses are the first emissaries in this story of that tantalizing absurd reality that always threatens to defeat us. The groom arrogantly defies his master's orders. While the doctor has some absent-minded concern with the servant, Rose (and is probably unable to find fulfillment for his sexual desires), the groom turns into a rapist battering down doors. And yet, in typical Kafkaesque fashion, the doctor makes allowances for the "brute"—he was a stranger "and of his own free will he was helping me." We must not admit the brute destructive nature of reality lest it drive us mad!

The doctor's motto is: "I must with improvised ingenuity somehow straighten things out in my head." He has the saving genius for extenuation that enables him to rationalize noncommitment when direct confrontation with bestial, destructive evil (as in the person of the groom) would seem to call for energetic action:

> "You brute," I yelled in fury, "do you want a whipping?" but in the same moment reflected that the man was a stranger; that I did not know where he came from, and that of his own free will he was helping me out when everyone else had failed me.

3. Note the doctor's determination to treat the ominous and surreal as if it were normal—to give due acknowledgment to the satisfactory or "correct" aspects of experience: "A magnificent pair of horses, I observed, such as I had never sat behind, and I climbed in happily." Even the unthinkable is treated as if it were part of a familiar story: "I had to get my team out of the pigsty; if they hadn't chanced to be horses I should have had to travel with swine. That was how it was." Possible *symbolic* readings: The horses might be suppressed sexual desire that batters down the restraints imposed by the

conscious, rationalizing self? The pigsty—a warm, confined, cozy place—might be the womb?

4. Although Rose plays a peripheral role in the doctor's male-centered spiritual odyssey, she is obviously of special interest to both Freudian and feminist critics.

5. Whatever the specific *diagnosis* of the patient, like all human beings, he is doomed to be cut down eventually as by the "strokes of the ax" that cut down the doomed trees? The maggots foreshadow the inevitability of putrefaction?

6. Communication with the *patient's family* fails completely ("from their confused ejaculations I gathered not a word"). The air of the sickroom is stifling, oppressive. The patient (a bony, empty-eyed, shirtless boy) pleads with the doctor, not to save him, but to let him die. Diagnosed as a malingerer, the patient on second sight is found to suffer from an incurable wound. The spectators turn against the doctor (stripping him and putting him in bed with the patient); his attempt to escape leaves him stranded in the waste of winter, unable ever again to reach his home and office—naked, exposed to the elements, drifting aimlessly—lost, deserted, betrayed.

7. Note that Kafka himself died young, a victim of the impotence of early modern medical science.

8. The *parson* (or other man of the cloth), like the physician-healer, has no miracle cure or "silver bullet" for the spiritual malaise of the modern consciousness. The alienated modern individual is essentially alone—with neither sex, religion, nor medicine providing the magic cure for our alienation?

9. Clichés give people the reassuring feeling that they live in a familiar, understandable world. ("That's how it is" the doctor will say at the most preposterous junctions in the story.) He is not averse to the pompous self-congratulatory phrase: "Take the word of honor of an official doctor." "I . . . did my duty to the uttermost." Only once in the story does the doctor verge on the direct expression of rage ("You brute!"), abandoning the laborious effort to maintain a civilized surface.

JUXTAPOSITIONS:Playing the Role 302

DISCUSSION STARTERS

How do your students feel about the world of conspicuous consumption—designer jeans, Dior shirts, leather skirts priced at two thousand dollars, toys for a rich kid that cost a month's wage? To what kind of people does the world of high fashion and expensive jewelry cater?

Dorothy Parker, "The Standard of Living" 302

THE RECEPTIVE READER

1. The girls come from lower-income backgrounds; they each pay half their salaries to help support their families. They gorge on cheap starchy, sugary, and fatty food; they dress the opposite of classy or conservative, with their excessive makeup, bleached hair, and tight clothes. However, they like to pretend they are high class, stepping "over the necks of peasants." They each have found in the other an understanding friend—a person to confide in and connive with.

2. The game takes the young women into a *fantasy world* that helps them transcend or escape from the drab reality of their office work. In the game they must spend all the inherited money on themselves, whereas in the real world, half of their hard-earned money must go to their families.

3. Parker reveals her *wit* in many understated ironic touches: When talking about boyfriends that come and go, she comments that the newcomers are "scarcely distinguishable from their predecessors." Describing the girls' airs, she says they carry "themselves tall" and walk "a straight line, as befitted young heiresses." When the girls enter the jewelry store they wear "expressions of bitter disdain, as if they stood in a sty."

4. The author seems to have a paradoxical *sympathy* for her spunky, albeit "conspicuous and cheap" characters, with their simulated haughtiness and "icy" superior airs. In their own way, with a rough populism or egalitarianism, they provide a comment on the conspicuous consumption of the socially irresponsible rich, with their quarter-of-a-million necklaces and the sycophants who sell them. At the end, when the girls' game loses its charm and they are for a moment their wearied true selves, we may sympathize with them and admire their spirit when Midge reinvents the game.

THE PERSONAL RESPONSE

It is true that the story is set in the long-vanished twenties. But a vast cosmetics, fashion, fitness, and entertainment industry is built on people's hankering to transcend the limitations of their drab ordinary existence? And the impulse of underprivileged young people to taunt representatives of wealth and status beyond their reach is as strong as ever?

Toni Cade Bambara, "The Lesson" 306

DISCUSSION STARTERS

What do the young people in Parker's and in Bambara's stories have in common? What difference does it make that Parker's characters are white and Bambara's black? How is the attitude of each author toward her characters similar or different? Do the two stories have a similar point, message, or theme?

THE RECEPTIVE READER

1. What is the kids' *style*—what is their characteristic way of acting and talking? They are jauntily defiant and in rebellion against "proper" adult authority trying to make them conform to standards of genteel behavior. "Surly" is Miss Moore's word for them. They are used to fending for themselves: The narrator, along with "Sugar" and "Junior," has been parked with an aunt while "our mothers were in the la-de-da apartment up the block having a good ole time." Their humor is crude and aggressive: Old people are funny and ugly; fat kids pigging out are funny. People wearing fur coats on Fifth Avenue in the heat to flaunt their wealth demonstrate that "White folks crazy."

2. The tough *street language* mirrors disrespect for adult authority and an assertive, defiant "don't-step-on-me" attitude. Used to being put down and insulted, the kids adopt a kind of *preemptive* stance—insulting others before the others have a chance to do the same to them. (Note for instance Rosie Giraffe "shifting from one hip to the other waiting for somebody to step on her foot or ask her if she from Georgia so she can kick ass").

(NOTE: You may or may not want to look at the English spoken in this story from a linguist's point of view—looking at deleted auxiliaries for instance: "*We* all *walking* on tiptoe." Note that the characteristic ways the narrator's language works is not a matter of "errors"—her language follows the *rules* of "Black English.")

3. The schoolmarmish "very black," very plain, and very proper Miss Moore at first annoys the narrator with her "goddamn college degree" and her schemes for the educational improvement of the uneducated. ("She was always planning these boring-ass things for us to do.") But it turns out in the end she has something valuable to teach.

4. The sobering *contrast* between poverty and ostentatious, obscene wealth becomes a focal point of the story: "Who are these people that spend that much for performing clowns and $1000 for toy sailboats?" (The story becomes a parable of an America once committed to egalitarian ideals but splitting up into what Disraeli, at the height of predatory nineteenth-century *laissez-faire* capitalism, called "two nations"?)

5. Sylvia, the smartass narrator, tries to maintain her blasé façade (slouching around the store being "very bored" and priding herself on cheating Miss Moore of four dollars from the taxi ride). But it is not really a sufficient defense against the sobering, serious thoughts that the experience has left everyone with (including the reader)?

6. While the author fully understands and sympathizes with the tough kids, does she perhaps just as fully understand Miss Moore's mission to teach alienated youth some sense of responsibility and give them the week's "lesson on brotherhood"?

The long-dominant formalist critical perspective stressed the autonomy of each work of literature, treating it as a self-contained whole creating its own world. In practice, however, we read fiction or poetry by a favorite writer almost as installments of the writer's work. We recognize familiar themes, savor familiar features of style—while at the same time being intrigued by new developments or departures.

PERSPECTIVES—RECURRENT THEMES IN O'CONNOR'S FICTION

You may want to focus your students' attention on recurrent themes in O'Connor's fiction and on recurrent conundrums in critical discussions of her work. Do the following comments and excerpts become meaningful to them as they read and ponder the stories in this chapter? Can they cite evidence from the stories to explain, support, or question the points made here or the perspectives suggested?

- O'Connor on the creative process:

> I often ask myself what makes a story work, and what makes it hold up as a story, and I have decided that it is probably some action, some gesture of a character that is unlike any other in the story, one which indicates where the real heart of the story lies. This would have to be an action or gesture which was both totally right and totally unexpected; it would have to be one that was both in character and beyond character; it would have to suggest both the world and eternity. . . . It would be a gesture that transcended any neat allegory that might be intended or any pat moral categories a reader could make. It would be a gesture which somehow made contact with mystery.
>
> —Flannery O'Connor, *Mystery and Manners*

- O'Connor on the dualism of *good and evil*:

> Most of us have learned to be dispassionate about evil, to look it in the face and find, as often as not, our own grinning reflections with which we do not argue, but good is another matter. Few have stared at that long enough to accept the fact that its face too is grotesque, that in us the good is something under construction. The modes of evil usually receive worthy expression. The modes of good have to be satisfied with a cliché or a smoothing-down that will soften their real look.
>
> —Flannery O'Connor, *Mystery and Manners*

- On O'Connor's relation to the *rural South*:

  O'Connor was fascinated with people who "are sort of halfway between poor white trash and good country people." In one of her letters, she described a family that came to live on her mother's place: They had two children "with leaky noses and no shoes" and owned "nothing but a red automobile and one suitcase." (They made another family living there—"displaced persons," or refugees from Eastern Europe—"look like John D. Rockefellers.") Some critics see O'Connor as part of a Southern tradition that pokes fun at the naiveté and crudeness of the plain folk, but that "seldom finally demeans the rural at the expense of more cultivated or wealthy city people. The country man may be discomfited, embarrassed, ridiculed, but the element of integrity is usually his and not the city-dweller's."

  —(Louis D. Rubin, "The Comic Imagination in American Literature"

- On O'Connor's predilection for the freakish or *grotesque*:

  For O'Connor, the freak is the image of both the author and the reader—and of all human beings. The freak in his distortion is able to reveal what ordinary people carefully hide. The wounds and needs manifest in the freak will point up the deficiencies carefully hidden by most ordinary people. The freak's very distortions allow the author to present some image of the whole person.

  —Brian A. Ragen, *A Wreck on the Road to Damascus*

- On O'Connor and *religion*:

  Human dereliction sets O'Connor's narratives in motion and directs their course and outcome. What we need to look for is the gift of grace, the exultant salute to the eternal that she avows in her lectures and correspondence and that brings her anguished conflicts to a higher resolution. . . . To the undiscerning or the psychologically oriented, O'Connor's unrelenting exposure of human fault might seem like obsession or preacherly harangue; for O'Connor, however, the sight of inner wretchedness precedes the experience of love. . . . The guilt and punishment that her characters bring upon themselves have no independent reality of their own, but are the dark shadows of the grace and life that O'Connor finds in existence. . . . Her strange choices for heroes—nihilists, petty tyrants, and killers—turn out to be wanderers in love. . . . Her fundamental understanding of this mysterious incursion is that love is not a human right or a mental deduction but a divine revelation, a gift of plenitude found within the human heart.

—Richard Giannone, *Flannery O'Connor and the Mystery of Love*

- On the *automobile as* an icon or a symbol in O'Connor's fiction:

Critics have noted the special role of the automobile in her fiction—often "beat-up cars, either traveling on into the sunset or wrecked behind a country road." For some critics, the automobile becomes a symbol of the American myth of innocence, with the American Adam, like Huck Finn on his raft, setting out for new territory—"without Eve . . . with no obligations and responsibilities" (Jill Baumgartner).

What might be the symbolic meaning of the automobile in "A Good Man Is Hard to Find"?

- On the role of *women* in O"Connor's world:

Though O'Connor's attack on the American Adam figure is at root theological, it also takes aim at the treatment of women in that tradition. In much American literature, women only appear as threats to the man who wants to move ever onward, and the hero's triumph is to escape the woman's attempts to entrap and domesticate him. . . . O'Connor shows how cruelly this tradition treats women, who become nothing more than objects men manipulate in order to prove their illusory freedom.

—Brian A. Ragen, *A Wreck on the Road to Damascus*

DISCUSSION STARTERS

Is the South a different country? What stereotypes about the Old South do your students remember? Do they associate the South with traditional assumptions about race, womanhood, secession, emancipation, reconstruction, Yankees? How is the New South different?

"A Good Man Is Hard to Find" 319

THE RECEPTIVE READER

1. The grandmother—one of O'Connor's *grotesques*—from the very beginning plays the bird of ill omen—garrulous, self-righteous, limited, and wrong-headed. Ironically, it is she who sounds the prophetic warning about The Misfit loose in the countryside: "I wouldn't take my children in any direction with a criminal like that aloose in it." She is a constant pest, lecturing her son about police officers lurking in hiding to trap speeders and lecturing the

bratty children about the need for respect. She tells a brainless racist watermelon joke. It is her misguided search for a tourist attraction (a mansion actually located in a different state) that causes the family to take the fateful and fatal turn in the road that sets them on a collision course with The Misfit. It is her benighted cat that causes the accident leaving the family a helpless target for the killers. Although she and her family become victims of a barbarous crime, exasperated critics and student readers often seem to feel that "she deserved what she got."

2. *Minor characters*: The mother with a "face as broad and innocent as a cabbage" and the children excited by the adventure of having an accident are innocent bystanders, but perhaps they are too intentionally boring or callous to arouse our sympathy?

3. The *interlude* at the fat man's barbecue is an acerbic *vignette* of Americana: It features nostalgia for a safer, less crime-ridden past; blatant advertising ("A VETERAN!"); the sentimentalist's determination to find children "cute" no matter how sassy and deplorable they might be; and a grotesque owner whose stomach hangs over his trousers "like a sack of meal."

4. Ask your students to trace these tourists' road to the fateful encounter: Is this all mere happenstance, or are they all the while on their way to their appointment with destiny?

5. Are these people the American Everyman and Everywoman, mired in banality and destroyed by monsters of their own making?

6. The grandmother and The Misfit, headed for their climactic confrontation from the beginning of the story, make a kind of cosmic "odd couple." In the words of one critic, "The Misfit flaunts every deviation and evil that the grandmother conceals beneath prim hat and gloves." The Misfit's story can be read as grim parable on the futility of society's ways of administering "justice." A half-remembered crime triggers an impersonal, relentless mechanism of retribution that in turn leaves the criminal totally devoid of all human fellow feeling or compassion. ("Sooner or later you're going to forget what it was you done and just be punished for it.") Paradoxically, at the same time, The Misfit—an escaped convict who coolly orchestrates the murder of a helpless family—has a strange perverted religious awareness. "Whereas most people ignore the ultimate matters that the Incarnation and the Resurrection present, The Misfit is wracked by these concerns, his life in utter disarray because he cannot finally bring himself to believe in Christ. Too much the literalist, The Misfit says that for him to have given his life to Christ, he would have had to see Christ perform his miracles; and so unable to open himself to Christ, he has closed himself off from him and has embraced a life that is completely without him—a life of waste and destruction, a life embodied, in his own words, of 'no pleasure but meanness' " (Brinkmeyer). The grandmother's attempt to reach him by claiming him as a man of good blood may seem to many readers a final climactic demonstration of her narrow-mindedness and irrelevance. However, it has been seen by some critics as a

demonstration of love that transcends anger and the desire for revenge. (Could her claiming The Misfit as one of her children be a Christlike gesture to touch The Misfit?)

7. The story is a masterpiece of *dark humor*. The constant squawking by the grandmother and the bratty children creates an atmosphere of sinister farce. The business about the shirt, The Misfit's strange courtesy and businesslike demeanor in scenes of ultimate horror, and the final bloody silencing of the loquacious grandmother ("She was a talker, wasn't she?") fuel a strange, half-choked hilarity.

8. O'Connor makes the climactic eruption of violence seem not so much "senseless" as an inevitable, logical conclusion?

THE PERSONAL RESPONSE

Does the very name or label of the "Misfit" tend to intrigue students? One wrote: "The very name conjures up images that delight my mind and invigorate my passion for this story. He sees himself as an avenger; he is as self-righteous as he is violent."

THE CREATIVE DIMENSION

Striking, unforgettable images include, for instance, the overturned car in the ditch, the children being led to their execution, The Misfit shooting the grandmother pointblank.

"Everything that Rises Must Converge" 331

PERSPECTIVES—MULTIPLE IRONY IN "EVERYTHING THAT RISES"

In " 'Everything That Rises Must Converge': O'Connor's Seven-Story Cycle" (*Renascence: Essays on Values in Literature*, Summer 1990, Harbour Winn traces multiple irony in O'Connor's treatment of the "parasitic relationship" between Julian and his mother in "Everything That Rises Must Converge," the opening story of the cycle. The story illustrates "some of the basic trademarks of O'Connor's fiction," including especially "the vivid use of color in the description of Julian's mother's hat to emphasize the grotesque quality of a character" and the "relentless use of verbal, dramatic, and situational irony to tear apart the protagonist's façade of pious respectability." Julian "prides himself on his cultural sophistication, racial liberalism, and ability to perceive his mother's genteel affectation and racial paternalism." He realizes that "the governing principle of his mother's fantasy world 'was to sacrifice herself for him after she had first created the necessity to do so by making a mess of things.' " However, Julian himself becomes the target of the author's relentless irony. The mother's "suffocating love contributes to her son's immaturity." His "pompous assumptions" about being liberated from his mother's small-mindedness and prejudices "prove to be only self-deceptions, for his every action reflects his dependence on his mother." He is living with his mother who partly supports him until he can be successful as a writer. He "fabricates a martyr role" for himself as he puts up with his mother's ways while thinking of himself as emancipated. He "is consumed by the petty need to annoy her"—for instance, taking a seat next to a black passenger on the bus. While priding himself on his advanced liberal views on race, he "reveals his own deep-rooted racism" as he daydreams about integrationist gestures to torment his segregationist mother—having her treated by a black doctor, bringing a black woman to her house as a prospective daughter-in-law. Rather than achieving maturity and knowledge, "Julian will always be weighted down in a life tormented by guilt and horror."

THE RECEPTIVE READER

1. From the beginning, does Julian's mother seem of the same tribe as the grandmother in "A Good Man Is Hard to Find"? She is trying to hold on to the faded glory of better days in the South (the neighborhood where she lives was fashionable forty years ago). She is obtuse, self-centered, and self-righteous, constantly hectoring her son. She is prejudiced (she will not ride alone in the recently integrated buses). She is the kind of person that constantly demands special attention and consideration for her petty needs and concerns. As one critic observed, she has the "martyr's genius" for deriving perverse pleasure from the "sacrifices" she makes for others. The hideous gaudy hat is a symbol of the grotesque lack of taste and sophistication that drives her son crazy. Her high blood pressure is like a time bomb.

2. *Julian* fights a constant losing battle to keep from being engulfed by his mother's banality and bigotry. Is he perhaps an American type—an American intellectual educated beyond his means and station, constantly annoyed and frustrated by the shortcomings of his environment? (Are we supposed to fault him for his chafing impatience and his lack of charity toward his mother?)

3. The *black people* in this story, as often in American culture, serve as touchstones of white prejudice and white guilt. It's not overt white malevolence that triggers the rage of the black mother, but the condescension that treats the black child as someone inferior enough to have to be thankful for an insulting, worthless handout.

4. Make sure to have students *read* key passages aloud.

5. In the end, with the kind of cruel cosmic irony of which O'Connor is fond, Julian's cool, disdainful posture crumbles as catastrophe overtakes him and his mother. In true martyr style, her collapse (stroke?) is her final trump card, which aces out his bitter lectures about a "new world" of changing realities. Critics looking for a religious epiphany are likely to see in the

ending a conversion of Julian from intellectual pride to love and to a "world of guilt and sorrow." ("At the moment of death, Julian's mother finally mothers her son into love"—Giannone.)

6. The story plays off the son's understanding of shifts in racial sensibilities against the mother's racist condescension. At the same time, the black mother does turn violent (and she is also gaudy, like Julian's mother); the kid is "wide-eyed" and naive. O'Connor does not romanticize black people—but then we wouldn't *expect* her to romanticize her characters, black *or* white.

THE PERSONAL RESPONSE

Allow students to vent contradictory reactions that would attest to the ambivalence of the O'Connor story.

"Enoch and the Gorilla" 343

DISCUSSION STARTERS;

You may want to list and explore with your students hallmarks of O'Connor's fiction that play a role in this lesser-known (and more light-hearted?) O'Connor story. Key features that your students might recognize might include:

- an ambivalent love-hate of American *popular culture* (are the moviegoers shaking hands with a fake gorilla idiots—or are they people with a healthy capacity for fantasy and a sense of humor?)
- a *bizarre character* whose motives, though perhaps seeming crazy to literal-minded people, make perfect sense from his own perspective (the gorilla job provides a chance for meeting people and being looked upon with friendly smiles missing in many other occupations?)
- *violence* erupting in banal ordinary settings and perpetrated by banal people (as if it were a natural or inevitable part of our existence)
- a zany kind of *dark humor*
- ambiguous, puzzling *thematic implications* (is this a parable on the frustrated need for love and a sense of belonging that many atomistic individuals experience in our fragmented, uprooted society?)

Juxtapositions:A Range of Sources 349

What kind of background or backup material do your students find most helpful? Do they feel they learn something from author testimony? (What do they make of O'Connor's comments on the basic or central Christian assumptions underlying her work?) How much do your students profit from the informal author's letters, a fellow writer's perspective, a critical analysis? You may want to farm out these selections to small groups for class presentations.

Chapter 10 PERSPECTIVES The Reader's Response 360

Critics offering to guide our reading and interpretation come to a piece of literature from differing perspectives. They are likely to focus on different corners of the communication triangle: An *author* (sender) writes a *text* (message) that will be read by a *reader* (receiver). Critics may focus attention on the author—on the creative individual shaped by personal experience and working in the context of a specific time and place. They may focus on the internal workings of a story—its structure, its internal dynamics. Or they may focus on what happens in the reader's mind—in the area of reader response.

Juxtapositions:The Range of Interpretation 367

You may want to farm out study of the critical excerpts to small groups. Ask each group to explain and critique a major critical perspective for the class.

James McGlathery, "The Psychoanalytic Kafka" 367

THE RECEPTIVE READER

In the story, Rose, the maid (here Rosa, as in the German original) plays a limited and somewhat stereotypical servant's role. She is sent on errands; her master thinks about her intermittently at best; and she arouses the lust of the more brutish members of the household—with fewer protections against sexual abuse than women with more social status. In the Freudian analysis, which predictably plays up the sexual overtones of the story, her role is magnified: She becomes the clue to the doctor's journey, which turns into a Freudian guilt trip as the male devotes his time and energy to a profession rather than to his biological destiny of relating to the female of the species. Although the narrator on the conscious level deplores the brutish groom, on the subconscious level he identifies with him and is also a latent rapist.

Ernst Fischer, "The Marxist Kafka" 368

THE RECEPTIVE READER

If for the Freudian critic the basic category of interpretation is the repressed libido, or frustrated sexual energy, for the Marxist critic the basic category providing the key to everything is the individual's role in a dysfunctional capitalistic society. The country doctor is anxiety-ridden because his idealism as a health care provider is not honored or privileged in a cutthroat capitalistic system (leaving him with totally inadequate means in his profession as a healer). The basic human need for relating to other people in a humane fashion is nowhere recognized in a society worshipping the bottom line.

Evelyn Torton Beck, "Kafka: A Feminist Perspective" 369

THE RECEPTIVE READER

From a feminist perspective, the salient point about Kafka's story is the totally subordinate, peripheral, disempowered role of the maid. She is a mere object, a mere pawn, as Kafka's males act out their parables of power and impotence. Kafka becomes merely another representative of an androcentric, male-oriented perspective, with no credit for the sensitive, vulnerable, caring androgynous side of Kafka that made him a bête noire to both Nazi and Stalinist censors.

Contexts for Reading

Shirley Jackson, "Biography of a Story" 370

DISCUSSION STARTERS

Do your students know people who respond to what they read or view with strong emotional reactions, ranging from enthusiasm to outrage? What recent examples can they cite? Have they seen letters to the editors or reviews that express strong positive or negative reactions to books, plays, movies?

THE RECEPTIVE READER

When in June 1948, Shirley Jackson wrote and *The New Yorker* magazine published "The Lottery," neither the writer nor the magazine were prepared for the volume and tone of reader response. As Jackson says, "I had written the story three weeks before, on a bright June morning when summer seemed to have come at last, with blue skies and warm sun and no heavenly signs to warn me that my morning's work was anything but just another story." What is ironic about the setting in which the story was written is that it is reminiscent of the seemingly pastoral and benign setting of the story itself. Initially, Jackson's little Vermont village, where she chats with the postmaster and pushes her daughter's stroller and the day's groceries up the village hill, is as innocuous and timeless and unexciting as is the village in the story.

Although Jackson says somewhat tongue-in-cheek that she had "dwelt lovingly upon the thought of the millions and millions of people who were going to be uplifted and enriched and delighted by the stories I wrote," she had not anticipated an entirely opposite reaction. "It had simply never occurred" to Jackson that her readers "might be so far from being uplifted that they would sit down and write me letters I was downright scared to open." Writer and magazine received an immense amount of mail in response to

"The Lottery" (the magazine "did issue one publicity release saying that the story had received more mail than any piece of fiction they had ever published"), and Jackson concludes: "Judging from these letters, people who read stories are gullible, rude, frequently illiterate, and horribly afraid of being laughed at." She identified the three themes which dominated the letters as "bewilderment, speculation, and plain old-fashioned abuse." A *capsule portrait* of an ideal Jackson reader might describe a reader with an open and critical mind who combines a vivid sense of humanity's recent record of brutality and of the darker side of human nature with a wicked sense of humor.

Toni Cade Bambara, "Trying to Stay Centered" 373

DISCUSSION STARTERS

Have your students had the opportunity to listen to a writer in person? Where or when? What impression did they carry away of the writer and the person?

THE RECEPTIVE READER

Although sounding somewhat ironic about people who analyze literature and writers, Bambara finds that the critics have gleaned some of her larger purpose: "That sense of caring and celebration is certainly reflected in the body of my work and has been consistently picked up by other writers, reviewers, critics, teachers, students." The connection between being black and being a woman is that this society is "systematically orchestrated to oppress each and both." Such oppressed groups have a "special contribution to make to the collective intelligence."

The special challenge Bambara faces as a woman writer is to devote sufficient attention to the daughter she is apparently raising alone while dedicating herself to the writing profession. Like many writers, Bambara is subject to "that mad fit that gets hold of me and makes me prefer working all night and morning at the typewriter to playing poker or going dancing." Not surprisingly, such devotion to the craft of writing is very hard on interpersonal relationships. Once the fit has passed, Bambara tries "to apply the poultices and patch up the holes I've left in relationships around me."

Although Bambara does not think that literature is "*the* primary instrument for social transformation," she does believe that literature has "potency." One way to effect social change is to confound stereotypical thinking: "to bring to center stage all those characters, just ordinary folks on the block, who've been waiting in the wings, characters we thought we had to ignore because they weren't pimp-flashy or hustler-slick or because they didn't fit easily into previously acceptable modes or stock types."

However, "first and foremost," Bambara says, "I write for myself." She has used writing as a tool for "self-instruction and self-development." Even without publishing outlets for her writing, without markets or presses, Bambara would still write. For her the process is akin to building a nation: "the inner nation needs building, too," she says.

Stanley Kozikowski, "Symbolism in 'Hills like White Elephants' " 376

PERSPECTIVES—A CLOSE READING FOR SECONDARY SYMBOLS

Samuel Coleridge, chief literary theorist among Romantic poets, developed the criterion of "organic unity," which stipulated that in a great poem or play (and especially a Shakespeare play) there was no such thing as a minor casual or insignificant detail. Everything was deliberate; every detail contributed to the grand design and overall impact of the work. Apparently peripheral details—a gesture, a utensil—could foreshadow or echo the major theme of the work. The New Critics (now often labeled formalists) subscribed to Coleridge's theory and made it a practice to search for the symbolic parallels or correspondences missed by more casual readers. Kozikowski implements this critical perspective in a close reading of the Hemingway story, finding unsuspected symbolic meaning in many apparently peripheral details.

THE RECEPTIVE READER

In the hot train station a man and a woman wait for the Barcelona Express. The woman is pregnant, and their cryptic conversation reveals that the man wants her to have an abortion. At the end of the story, the woman has made the decision to keep the child and to end her relationship with the man. This underlying agenda is mirrored by the hills, the breeze, the curtain, and the drinks. The hills are like white elephants for the woman because "they carry ambivalent evocations of the child within her—like a white elephant, an unwanted gift, a seemingly remote but immense problem." The color of the hills further mirrors the woman's ambivalence. On the one hand, "They ominously suggest the pallid skin tone of a stillborn infant," but on the other hand the luminous tone is "beautiful with the promise of life, and intrinsically of value, as was the highly esteemed Siamese white elephant."

Just as the man has responded only casually to the woman's comments about the hills, his response to the breeze is antithetical to hers. Kozikowski says: "To this bimodal breeze, the American man and Jig respond differently: He feels it as a simple, quick remedy to a removable annoyance. She experiences it, in her ambivalence, as a 'lovely' invigoration, at the very moment that she has looked upon the 'lovely hills' which are like white elephants—fearfully unwanted but precious." For the man, the breeze "simply defines casually and literally what an abortion is," and this leads him to explain to the woman that "They just let the air in and then it's perfectly natural." It is testament to their imminent disunion that the woman experiences the warm breeze as oddly invigorating while the man uses it to help persuade the woman to take the course of action he wants her to take.

As the woman holds two strands of the beaded curtain, the heart of the story is reached, what Kozikowski calls its "culminating design." In a sequence of action that mirrors the actual abortion procedure, the man, not the child, is aborted from the woman's life. "Conveyed out from the barroom, through the breezy doorway, through which the 'air' gets 'let in' from the other side, 'the man' (appropriately nameless, mere reiterated 'seed' from 'bull'—Anis del Toro—but now like an aerated fetus himself) is ironically terminated, expelled—in her (now triumphantly ironic figural) consciousness—from any further relationship with Jig." These events are summed up as the man "metaphorically" going "out through the bead curtain"; indeed, "out of their [the woman and unborn child's] lives."

The great gulf between "the figurative consciousness" of the woman and "the literal awareness" of the man is illustrated again with the "Anis del Toro." Kozikowski observes: "The breeze, the moving beaded curtain, and the evocative drink—like hills like white elephants—connote to Jig the sweet promise of seeding and the bitter termination of birthing. The same objects convey to the man an easy sense of exit, excision, and getting on with other things."

Sandra M. Gilbert and Susan Gubar, "Enclosure and Escape: Gilman's 'The Yellow Wallpaper' " 378

DISCUSSION STARTERS

Do the students in your class identify most strongly with the view of woman as victim in a male-dominated society? Or do they identify most strongly with the view of woman as a source of strength and wisdom? Is either of these views the true feminist position?

THE RECEPTIVE READER

1. *Patriarchal* and *paternalistic* both derive from the Latin *pater*, which means "father." In a patriarchal society, the father reigns supreme in the family. Wives and children are legally dependent upon the father. Authority and inheritance in succeeding generations are reckoned only through the male line. In the Old Testament, Abraham, Isaac, Jacob, and the sons of Jacob were the patriarchs or founders of the ancient families; thus there is a biblical connotation to the word that is not present in *paternalistic*. In a paternalistic society, the male authorities take care of and monitor those under their control in a manner similar to the way fathers take care of and monitor their children. On the surface, a paternalistic society has softer edges and authority appears to be more flexible, but the end result of both societies is total dominance of women and children by the males.

2. The common strand in how women are traditionally treated in texts by male authors, in how they are treated in the home, and in how their lives are defined by "maternal female bodies" is "confinement." The authors write of "parallel confinements in texts, houses, and maternal female bodies." This

parallel is traced in Charlotte Perkins Gilman's story "The Yellow Wallpaper," where an unnamed woman is suffering postpartum distress following her confinement for childbirth. As part of the cure the woman is forbidden from writing and confined to what is apparently a children's nursery. Within the nursery are all types of instruments of confinement like "rings and things" and "the gate at the head of the stairs." Worse, the room is papered in a ghastly wallpaper: "Ancient, smoldering, 'unclean' as the oppressive structures of the society in which she finds herself, this paper surrounds the narrator like an inexplicable text, censorious and overwhelming as her physician husband, haunting as the 'hereditary estate' in which she is trying to survive."

3. Imprisonment and escape are presented as yet another parallel between the actual woman who is confined to the nursery and the mysterious figure skulking behind the wallpaper. As fellow prisoners, the woman and the figure help each other to escape: "I pulled and she shook, I shook and she pulled, and before morning we had peeled off yards of that paper." The woman tears the wallpaper to bits and allows the figure to creep away. The critics help to illuminate the complex relationship between the women: "Eventually it becomes obvious to both reader and narrator that the figure creeping through and behind the wallpaper is both the narrator and the narrator's double."

MAKING CONNECTIONS—FOR DISCUSSION AND WRITING

Bambara says that her "responsibility" is "to try to tell the truth," and that this truth is particularly precious because it comes from an often silent or unheeded voice. Gilbert and Gubar, too, are making the point that Gilman's fictitious characters, Gilman, and the vast majority of women before and after Gilman have all been silenced, their truths unspoken, because of the multilayered confinement imposed upon them by those in power.

Wilfred L. Guerin, " 'Young Goodman Brown': Id versus Superego" 381

DISCUSSION STARTERS

H. L. Mencken defined Puritanism as "the terrible nagging suspicion that somebody somewhere might be happy." Do your students associate Puritanism and Puritan New England with repression, sexual dysfunction, and similar Freudian categories? Is Puritan New England to them, in the words of one reader of Hawthorne, "the veritable birthplace of repression"?

THE RECEPTIVE READER

The synopsis includes most of the critical points. It does not make clear that Young Goodman Brown does not want to go into the forest, has to be continually coaxed to go further when he gets there, and has been preceded on the journey by his father and grandfather. The clues for symbolic, nonliteral meanings include the "light and order" of Salem village as representing consciousness, while the "dark recesses" of the forest are seen as representing the unconscious. Goodman Brown's journey must be undertaken at night, also symbolic of the unconscious, rather than during the day, which signifies consciousness. Furthermore, Goodman Brown is not merely leaving Faith behind, he is also at least temporarily abandoning faith.

Guerin uses the village, "a place of social and moral order (and inhibition)" as an analogue to Freud's "superego, conscience, the morally inhibiting agent of the psyche." The "Freudian id" is compared with the "wild, untamed passions and terrors" of the forest. Finally, "as mediator between these opposing forces, Brown himself resembles the poor ego, which tries to effect a healthy balance and is shattered because it is unable to do so." Guerin interprets the story as insisting that "sooner or later, we must all confront Satan" because Hawthorne's version of Satan is Goodman Brown's alter ego. Thus, Satan is in all of us, and we cannot always remain safe in the village. Guerin asks, is Goodman Brown's "predicament that of all human beings, as is indicated by his common, nondistinctive surname?" Goodman (Everyman) Brown "projects" the evil part of his psyche onto the devil. Guerin describes Faith "as the projection of another part of his psyche." A wife of three months, Faith is the pinnacle of goodness, piety, and purity, and it is her presence at the meeting that finally inspires Goodman Brown to reject baptism into evil.

Hawthorne presents Goodman Brown as a "tragic victim of a society that has shut its eyes to the inevitable 'naturalness' of sex as part of humankind's physical and mental constitution, a society whose moral system would suppress too severely natural human impulses." All of the Puritan prohibitions lend glamour to the vices so vigorously condemned; as a result, Goodman Brown has "developed a morbid compulsion to taste of them. He is not necessarily evil; he is, like most young people, curious." Such curiosity, in Puritan society, understandably leads to "Brown's gloomy destiny."

Chapter 11 OTHER VOICES/OTHER VISIONS A World of Stories 394

In the student text, these stories for further reading appear with only brief headnotes and with no questions for discussion or writing. You may want to use these stories for open, exploratory reading, without editorial or critical guidance. Or you may want to draw on the additional background material and the suggested questions provided here.

Donald Barthelme, "The School" 394

Barthelme was writing award-winning poems and stories while still a high school student. He became prominent among postmodern writers who are introspective and "self-conscious" about language and the writer's craft, playing sophisticated word games with literary conventions and critical categories. Lois Gordon, in *Donald Barthelme* (Twayne, 1981), calls "The School" an "upbeat Kafkaesque fable." In the end, as the teacher and Helen embrace and the new gerbil walks in cheered wildly by the children, the children have come to understand: "Live gives meaning to life; love, not philosophy, produces gerbils."

SUGGESTED QUESTIONS

1. How long might readers fool themselves, thinking that this is a story about a real classroom with real children? What are the first hints that there is something zany or surreal about this teacher's story? What are some of the many details that in a different context might be accepted as ordinary or believable? In this context, what makes them funny?

2. How do you react to the story's macabre humor—jesting about death? The grotesque as a genre mixes the comical and the horrifying. Does this story tilt in one direction or the other?

3. Would you give this story an R rating for the episode at the end dealing with sex? Can it be read as a parody of sex education?

4. Are the teacher and the students in this story in some ways like real teachers and real children? In what way? Where do you think the similarity ends?

5. Would you call the author of this story pessimistic? disillusioned? cynical? What label would *you* choose, and why?

Kate Chopin, "The Story of an Hour" 396

PERSPECTIVES—CHOPIN AND THE CHANGING CANON

Joyce Dyer says in *The Awakening: A Novel of Beginnings* (Twayne, 1993) that Chopin has gone from obscurity to canonization "in less than one generation." She quotes the editor of *American Literature* as saying, "It is a rare month that goes by without a submission on Chopin and an unusual issue that does not contain an article, note, book review, or allusion to Chopin's work." For Barbara C. Ewell (*Kate Chopin*, Ungar, 1986), "one index of Chopin's experimentalism" is the delays or resistance she encountered in originally placing some of her stories. *Century* magazine, "Chopin's usual first choice for her better work, rejected 'The Story of an Hour.' " In the story, according to Ewell, Chopin "exposes Louise's complicity" in Mallard's, her husband's, "subtle oppression. Her submission to his 'blind persistence' has been in the guise of Love, that self-sacrificing Victorian ideal. Glorified in fiction Chopin had often decried, this love has been, for Louise and others, the primary purpose of life. But through her new perspective, she comprehends that 'love, the unsolved mystery' counts for very little 'in face of the possession of self-assertion which she suddenly recognized as the strongest impulse of her being!' As Chopin often insists, love is not a substitute for selfhood; indeed, selfhood is love's precondition." R. W. Gilder, the editor of *Century* magazine at the time, "had zealously guarded the feminine ideal of self-denying love, and was that very summer publishing editorials against women's suffrage as a threat to family and home."

Kate Chopin became widely known, as the result of the feminist reexamination and redefinition of the traditional canon. Her characters are soulmates of Ibsen's Nora in *A Doll's House*, rebelling against what Chopin called "the soul's slavery."

SUGGESTED QUESTIONS

1. What do you learn in the story about the central character's marriage? What was her attitude toward the marriage and toward her husband? Was hers a "loveless marriage"?

2. How does this story treat the theme of a woman's liberation or self-assertion? Do you think the story would have been shocking to Chopin's late-nineteenth-century readers? Do you think there are people who might find it shocking today?

3. In Chopin's time psychologists were just barely beginning to explore women's unacknowledged or repressed emotions or desires. Which of the

central character's feelings or thoughts do you feel you understand? Do you find any of them hard to explain?

4. Earlier readers of short stories liked "O. Henry" endings—sudden unexpected twists or coincidences to wind up the plot. Does the ending seem like a trick ending to you?

5. (The Creative Dimension) You may want to rewrite the ending of the story for the modern reader.

Paul Laurence Dunbar, "The Ingrate" 398

Dunbar wrote during a period in American history when, in the words of his fellow writer Charles Chesnutt, "a literary work by an American of acknowledged color was a doubtful experiment, both for the writer and for the publisher." Dunbar's story harks back to a time when it was illegal to teach slaves to read and write, since slaveholders correctly assumed that education would in the long run become a means to break the chains of slavery. In this story, a literate slave turns the tables on his avaricious master.

SUGGESTED QUESTIONS

1. In African American folklore, as in the folklore of many other cultures, the trickster, making a living by his wits, is a familiar figure. Often the trickster stories appeal to our desire to see the rich and powerful bested. For you, does this story make a good trickster story?

2. What do you know about the "underground railroad"?

3. Current treatments of slavery often paint its injustices and brutalities in vivid colors. Do you think Dunbar's treatment of slavery is too low-key and "civilized"?

4. Have you seen evidence that some or much of today's African American humor is at the expense of white people?

Ralph Ellison, "Mister Toussan" 404

PERSPECTIVES—"MISTER TOUSSAN": A COUNTRY WITHOUT SLAVES

The "Mister Toussan" of the title is Toussaint L'Ouverture (1743–1803), a self-educated former slave who led the people of Haiti in their fight against both English and French colonial rule. Napoleon was rising to power as emperor of post-revolutionary France at the time. For a time, Toussaint liberated both Haiti and Santo Domingo, the two parts of the island of Hispaniola. Toussaint was taken by Napoleon's forces and shortly after died in a dungeon in France. Robert G. O'Meally, in *The Craft of Ralph Ellison* (Harvard UP, 1980), says that "at the time of the actual Haitian revolt, the tale of the black revolutionary grew into a kind of folktale and spread like wildfire among American slaves." ntozake shange's "lady in brown" in her *for colored girls who have considered suicide / when the rainbow is enuf* (1976) talks about her girlhood fantasies about Toussaint, a black man "who refused to be a slave."

Ralph Ellison became famous for his novel *Invisible Man* (1952). It traced the spiritual odyssey of a Southern black male who comes to New York and at each waystation discovers that he is identified as a member of his racial group and "invisible" as a person. Employers and coworkers, white radicals, and black nationalists alike are unable to see him as an individual in his own right. In "Mr. Toussan," two black Southern boys are learning pride in their history and in who they are.

SUGGESTED QUESTIONS

1. For you, does this story counteract racial stereotypes? (What kind of stereotypes do you bring to the story? How does this story deal with them?)

2. What kind of word play has a role in the story—what kind of language games do the boys play?

3. The boys claim that the Toussaint story and others like it are not found in their schoolbooks. To judge from your own experience, has this situation changed? How?

4. Does a group you identify with have unsung heroes or heroines? Could you tell the story of one of them?

Ursula K. Le Guin, "The Ones Who Walk Away from Omelas" 410

Much early science fiction sketched a future utopia in which age-old human dreams —of unlimited power, of perpetual happiness—were coming true. But gradually, the vision of an ideal future darkened, and many wrote the opposite—*dystopias*, or visions of future worlds that made our nightmares come true. Where on the spectrum ranging from utopia to dystopia would you place Le Guin's story? (The William James alluded to in the subtitle of the story lived from 1842 to 1910 and was a pioneering American psychologist who wrote a famous book on the range of religious experience.)

SUGGESTED QUESTIONS

1. How does the author create the "joyous" setting of the opening paragraphs? What striking details help create a beckoning world?

2. Why do you think the author lets each reader fill in his or her own details to complete the description of Omelas? In her own specifications, what does the author explicitly exclude from her imaginary world, and why?

3. When do you first suspect that the joyous, happy surface of Omelas might be deceptive? What is the role of the imprisoned child in the world of the people of Omelas? For what in their world or yours is the child a *symbol*?

4. Do you think the author meant to suggest that the world of Omelas was fatally flawed—or that it was nearly perfect except for one serious flaw?

5. (Personal Response) Do you think you would have been among those who "walked away from Omelas"? Or would you have been one of those who stayed behind? Justify your choice.

6. (Creative Dimension) Science fiction has a special way of stimulating the imagination. Does it stimulate yours? Write down what your *first impressions* would be if you suddenly found yourself walking the streets of Omelas (or the streets of another imaginary location in a story you have read). Would your impressions be similar to or different from those in the following student-written sample?

Walking in Omelas

I am walking down the crowded streets of Omelas. It would be a lovely day except that the sunlight is too bright, the weather is too warm, and the noise of the crowd is too loud. It is not easy walking down the street; people bump into me, and sometimes I have to disentangle myself from their welcoming embraces. This celebration of which I am a part reminds me of Mardi Gras in New Orleans, which suggests that I do have memories of a time before Omelas. The people of Omelas are all smiling, but their smiles are only on their lips and do not reach their eyes. Those smiling faces are too perfect, and they remind me of masks. I wonder what is behind those smiling faces. The people all talk to me, but although I understand their words, I do not understand their meaning. As the crowd presses against me, I feel as though I might suffocate. Will I ever be able to walk away from Omelas?

Toni Morrison, "1920" 414

PERSPECTIVES—FEMINISM AND ETHNICITY IN MORRISON'S FICTION

In her article "The Convergence of Feminism and Ethnicity in the Fiction of Toni Morrison" (*Critical Essays on Toni Morrison*, ed. Nellie

Y. McKay, G. K. Hall, 1988), Carolyn Denard focuses on Morrison's treatment of two major components of the sexist and racist oppression of African American women. In her first novel, *The Bluest Eye*, Morrison had explored the oppressive effect on black women of society's maintaining the white Anglo-Saxon standard of physical beauty "as a measurement of self-worth." Morrison's special target was the black community's own acceptance of the standards of feminine beauty glamorized by the white culture—with blacks valuing light brown skin, straight hair, "sharply chiseled features." In Morrison's words, "The concept of physical beauty as a virtue is one of the dumbest, most pernicious and destructive ideals of the Western world, and we should have nothing to do with it."

In later novels—including *Sula*, of which "1920" is a part—Morrison focused on women oppressed by and rejecting "the subservient roles that black women generally play in society." Some of her major characters cross the traditional boundaries "at the risk of distancing themselves from other black women." The women who escape from the narrow confines of the traditional roles—and become models, performers, singers, dancers—find themselves cut off from their "ethnic cultural connection" with the black community and may find themselves leading "free-spirited" and superficially glamorous but ultimately empty and meaningless lives. "For black women, Morrison suggests, and perhaps for all women whose ethnic group and culture has been discriminated against by the larger society, 'liberation' must not bring with it alienation from the ethnic community." Morrison "validates the traditional beauty and strengths of black women." She honors black women who "have had 'the ability to be the *ship* and the safe harbor,' to build the houses and raise the children, to be complete human beings who did not allow education to keep them from their nurturing abilities."

A reviewer has called Toni Morrison the quintessential African-American writer, accomplishing the feat of "being both academically and popularly canonized: Her books claim a high place on college reading lists as well as on best-seller lists; she holds a prestigious professorship at Princeton, and she is a prominent spokeswoman on racial questions, large and small" (Ann Hulbert). Morrison has aggressively criticized "whitemale" culture. She edited a book focused on the workings of sexism in the controversy precipitated by charges of sexual harassment lodged by Supreme Court nominee Clarence Thomas by another African American, Anita Hill.

SUGGESTED QUESTIONS

1. What is Helene Wright's life in the North? What does she remember about the South?

2. How does the trip to the South for Helene become a journey into the past? Why does she say at a crucial point: "So soon?" Why does the conductor play a crucial role?

3. Why does the smile Helene gives the conductor at the end of their encounter become an issue in the story? What is its symbolic significance?

4. What are Helene's "extremely mixed emotions" about the trip and the people and places she revisits?

5. What role does Helene's daughter Nel play in the story?

6. Have you ever come back to a setting or to people you used to know with heavy "misgiving" or "mixed emotions"?

Bharati Mukherjee, "A Wife's Story" 421

PERSPECTIVES—MUKHERJEE'S NEW AMERICANS

American popular opinion in an age of backlash politics tends to see the new non-European immigrants of recent decades through the prism of two opposed stereotypical views. A conservative position views the new immigrants with hostility or suspicion, thinking of them as aliens, as the unassimilable other. A liberal tradition presents the immigrant as victim—victim of prejudice, racism, economic exploitation. Liew-Geok Leong in "Bharati Mukherjee" (*International Literature in English*, ed. Robert L. Ross, Garland, 1991), sees Bharati Mukherjee as presenting a more differentiated, empathetic view of the new Americans. Mukherjee sees immigrants as positioned between two poles of the immigrant experience. At one end of the spectrum are people who are temperamentally expatriates, who cling to their own ethnicity, who resist adaptation and assimilation. In an essay on immigrant writing, Mukherjee says that the mind-set of the expatriate or exile can lead to isolation, for the native society of the country of origin "marches onward and perhaps downward; the exiled writer preserves her image of it in prose increasingly mannered and self-referential." The "deeply rooted" exile, "lacking a country, avoiding all the messiness of rebirth as an immigrant," may wind up "talking only to herself and her biographer."

At the other end of the spectrum, according to Leong, Mukherjee sees immigrants who "in their determination to see America as their home, exuberantly will themselves to become Americans over and above their original nationalities." Mukherjee has said, "There are people born to be Americans. By American I mean an intensity of spirit and a quality of desire. I feel American in a very fundamental way, whether Americans see me that way or not." Leong concludes by saying that Mukherjee's "abundant imagination brings the tensions and forces within the multicultural and multiethnic spheres of her new Americans to vivid life." Her immigrants may more often than not be "relegated to marginal status by mainstream North America." But they live in a world "throbbing, exuberant, and dynamic with the energy and passions of 'aliens' determined to survive, succeed, and, ultimately, belong."

Bharati Mukherjee is a writer of fiction (*The Tiger's Daughter*, 1972; *Wife*, 1975) and nonfiction (*Calcutta*, 1986; *The Sorrow and the Terror*, 1987). Her second collection of short stories, *The Middleman and Other Stories* (1988), won the National Book Critics Circle Award. She was born in India and now lives in the United States. Her writing draws on the contradictory, disorienting experience of the wanderer between two worlds. Drawing on her memories of India, she dramatizes the contrast between the lifestyle of the privileged Brahmin class and the poverty and squalor of Indian cities like Calcutta, with their "militant hordes of the destitute" (Martin Levin). She challenges the deep-seated traditions of passivity and dependence defining the woman's role in her native country. Drawing on her experiences in Canada and the United States, she chronicles the discrimination and racism encountered by Third World immigrants. The protagonist in her fiction is often a woman who is faced with the task of constructing a new identity, building a new life. In the words of one critic, "In Mukherjee's books, everyone is living in a new world, even those who never left home. As traditions break down, the characters must try to make lives out of the pieces" (Polly Shulman).

SUGGESTED QUESTIONS

1. How can you tell that the narrator comes from an upper-class background in India? What has she kept of the lifestyle or customs of her native country?

2. How Americanized has the narrator become? Do her ethnic past and her new American identity clash? Where, or how?

3. At the theater, why does the narrator take the "Patel jokes" so personally? Do you think she is oversensitive? What is her theory about stages immigrants from India go through? Is it true that in this country insult "is a kind of acceptance"?

4. What role do other immigrants—the Hungarian friend, the Chinese roommate—play in the story?

5. What is the story of the narrator's marriage? What is her relationship with her husband? What happens during the husband's visit to America?

6. Mukherjee's characters move in a multi-ethnic world—a world with people from many backgrounds and cultures. Does this world seem familiar or strange to you?

Lesléa Newman, "A Letter to Harvey Milk" 431

Half a century after, the holocaust remains an unmet challenge to any optimistic theories of human history or human nature. Books by a new generation of historians document the complicity of German army personnel and of German officials far beyond a small hard core of SS in the genocide. A visit to the Holocaust Museum in Washington, D.C.; studying the documentation at the rebuilt New Synagogue in the former East Berlin; or the pilgrimage to the Auschwitz site in Poland becomes a shattering experience for untold thousands of visitors. Newman's story establishes a bond between Jewish and gay victims of murderous bigotry.

SUGGESTED QUESTIONS

1. What is the role of the shared Jewish background in this story? How familiar is the world of Jewish culture and history to you as the reader? Are both teacher and student "Jewish" in the same sense? Does it make a difference that they represent different generations?

2. What do you know about Harvey Milk or the gay community in San Francisco? How does a gay or lesbian perspective help shape the story?

3. What do you know about the Nazi death camps? How does this story confirm or change your assumptions?

4. For the author of this story, what is the link between the concentration camp experience and the story of Harvey Milk?

5. Have you read other literature where you could imagine the author or a character saying: "I remember too much, the pen is like a knife twisting in my heart"?

Edgar Allan Poe, "The Black Cat" 442

Poe (1809–1849) was one of the great early masters of the American short story. His stories—"The Gold Bug," "The Murders in the Rue Morgue," "The Fall of the House of Usher," "The Tell-Tale Heart," "The Cask of Amontillado"—have been read by millions around the world. In spite of the immense popularity of his poems ("The Raven," "Ulalume") and stories, he enjoyed only fitful material reward, working for a time as a magazine editor and critic and dying under scandalous circumstances. Poe had an uncanny gift for activating the hidden terrors of the human heart and mesmerizing or hypnotizing his audiences, giving outlandish horrors a hallucinatory reality.

SUGGESTED QUESTIONS:

1. Poe has often been put down as a writer creating wildly implausible situations for sensational effects. Does he make this "tale of household

events" believable or real for you? Why, or why not? Can you understand the narrator's thoughts and emotions, or are they totally outlandish for you?

2. Poe was a precursor of writers of detective fiction. Does the story follow a formula that includes suspense, crucial coincidences, an intriguing beginning, a climactic ending?

3. Poe has often been considered a writer cultivating spine-tingling horror for its own sake. Do you think this is more than a horror story? Does it have a theme or human significance?

4. What is the fascination of horror movies, horror comics, or other forms of entertainment that make horror their stock in trade? How do you explain their appeal? Does it work for you? Why, or why not?

5. The modern short story has often cultivated a deliberately understated if not minimalist style. What is the effect of Poe's hyperformal style and rhetorical flourishes on the modern reader? Is it totally obsolete, or does it work for the purposes of this story?

Amy Tan, "Two Kinds" 449

Amy Tan is a native of Oakland, California, who has an M.A. in linguistics from San Jose State University. She first received national attention with her best-selling *The Joy Luck Club* and published *The Kitchen God's Wife* in 1991. Reviewers have praised her for her faithful chronicling of Chinese life and tradition; her creating of a "brilliant desperate world made magic by superstition and old wives' tales and the pure drama of hard times"; and her probing of a world of traditional repression of women that she indicts with a "survivor's vinegar wit."

SUGGESTED QUESTIONS

1. Many thousands from China came to America, the land of the "Gold Mountains." What role does the siren song of America as the land of promise play in this story?

2. What role does the clash of two cultures, experienced by many children of immigrants, play in this story?

3. Is the mother-daughter conflict in this story specific to the historical context and cultural tradition, or does it seem to you archetypal and universal?

4. Do you take sides in this story? Which side, and why?

5. The Chinese are sometimes stereotyped as having a particularly lively, wicked sense of humor. What kind of humor plays a role in this story?

6. (The Personal Response) Psychologists claim that childhood experiences can affect a child's personality in basic ways or mark a person for life. Do you remember early experiences that may have had much to do with who or what you are?

Guadalupe Valdés, "Recuerdo" 457

Guadalupe Valdés is a Chicana—a Mexican American woman—from the American Southwest, where the two worlds of the affluent North Americans and their often poor Spanish-speaking neighbors meet. El Paso, where she was born, is a border town, across the river from Juárez, one of the largest cities in Mexico. Her story gives a human face to the harsh realities of Third World poverty, exploitation, and prostitution that people from the other side of the border see only as tourists or try to wall off.

SUGGESTED QUESTIONS

1. How does the setting of the story shape the people's lives? Poverty and overpopulation often remain sociological abstractions. How does the author make poverty real for you? What details are especially telling or revealing?

2. What kind of people are the mother and the daughter? What choices do they confront? Do you understand what they think and feel?

3. What is the role of men in these women's world? Are the men all alike?

4. Everything in this story is seen from a woman's point of view. How would a male reader have to adjust his view of the world?

5. How does the author expect you to judge the mother?

Eudora Welty, "A Visit of Charity" 462

Eudora Welty (born 1909) prided herself on what a fellow writer called her "blistering humor" and "just cruelty." In "A Visit of Charity" (1941), Welty looks at both youth and age without sentimentality—without the rosy glow that comes from making reality more innocent, more heart-warming, or more reassuring than it is. She once said, "What alone can instruct the heart is the experience of living, experience which can be vile; but what can never do it any good, what harms it more than vileness, are those tales, those legends . . . , those universal false dreams, the hopes, sentimental and ubiquitous, which are not on any account to be gone by."

SUGGESTED QUESTIONS

1. What striking details early in the story help establish the mood? How do they make you feel about the institution? How do they guide your expectations?

2. What telling details shape your reaction to the nurse?

3. How does the author bring the two old women to life? (What are striking images?) How do the two women fit the setting in which they live?

4. What are the motives and feelings of the girl as the major character? Why is she there? How does she respond to finding herself transplanted to a strange new setting? How does she react to being "out of her element"?

5. Is the apple at the end of the story a *symbol*? What might it stand for or symbolize?

6. (Personal Response) How do you think the author expects you to feel toward the girl? toward the old women? How do *you* feel towards them? Do you think the girl should have acted more "mature"? Do you think the old women should be shown more compassion?

Part Two POETRY

THOUGHT STARTERS

What makes poets different from people using language in more ordinary ways? Poets are more responsive, more sensitive to experience—they *take in more* or register more of what we see and hear and feel. They *use more* of language—exploiting the full range of words, meanings, overtones, and implications. Language is what makes us human, and poets make the fullest, richest use of it. Finally, poetry is one manifestation of the human impulse to impose *a shape, a pattern*, on the chaotic flow of our lives. A poem is a finished whole, an affirmation of our ability to bring order out of chaos.

What has been your students' previous experience with or exposure to poetry? You may want to ask starter questions like the following:

- Do you remember any nursery rhymes or childhood jingles?
- Do you remember a poem you particularly liked? What do you remember about it?
- Do you remember a poem you particularly disliked? What was wrong with it?
- Have you ever memorized a poem—do you remember any of it now? Can you recite all or part of it for the class?
- Have you ever written a poem? What was the occasion? What was the poem about? Have you shared it with anyone?

Overview

This introduction to poetry explores the major dimensions of poetry, ranging from metaphor to myth, from image to theme. The formal features of poetry—image, metaphor, symbol, irony— are not treated as ends in themselves. Instead, the emphasis is on how they work in the poem as a whole and on how they serve its human meaning. The treatment throughout aims at an organic blend of form and content. The sequence of chapters combines formal and thematic considerations: *How* a poem and *what* a poem means are closely intertwined.

The introduction to poetry here aims at the right balance of promoting close, careful reading; of recognizing the personal connection that makes poems meaningful for the reader; and of stimulating the creative participation that brings the reader's own imagination into play.

Guide to Contents

12 PREVIEW: THE VOICE OF POETRY The opening chapter sketches out a preliminary definition of poetry. Poems including Robert Frost's classic

"Stopping by Woods," Emily Dickinson's "Presentiment," and Walt Whitman's "A Noiseless Patient Spider" appear in a preview of key features from image, metaphor, and symbol to traditional rhyme and meter or more modern variable rhythm and open form. Students are encouraged to develop the habit of close reading, personal response, and creative participation.

13 PATTERN: THE WHOLE POEM This chapter focuses on the shaping or pattern-making that is at the heart of the poet's art. Wendell Berry's beautifully finished and self-contained "The Peace of Wild Things" helps students experience the sense of the whole that gives meaning to the parts. A range of poems helps students develop their sense of shape, of pattern, by alerting them to recurrent features that help organize a poem: focus on a central image or situation, purposeful repetition, the playing off of polarities, climactic order, closure. A juxtaposition of poems by N. Scott Momaday and John Donne helps students see how poets relate to or play variations on the basic rhythms of human experience.

14 IMAGE: THE OPEN EYE Poets do not so much translate ideas into vivid imagery as they think in images. In this chapter, poems from Peter Meinke's exuberant "Sunday at the Apple Market" to John Keats' richly sensuous "To Autumn" show the range of visual, auditory, and tactile images that make the language of poetry concrete. Key poems by William Stafford, Mary Oliver, and Theodore Roethke show the power of the striking image to call up and channel our emotions; they show the hold the memorable central image has on the imagination.

15 METAPHOR: MAKING CONNECTIONS This chapter focuses on metaphor as central to the poet's ability to transcend the limits of ordinary language. Key poems by Emily Dickinson and May Swenson allow the teacher to demonstrate how metaphor extends the reach of language by the imaginative leap. Other poems show metaphor to be a close cousin to other kinds of figurative language, such as simile and personification. The elaborate Petrarchan conceit organizing a poem by Sir Thomas Wyatt contrasts with the bold, rapidly shifting or evolving metaphors of Shakespeare and of the metaphysical poet John Donne.

16 SYMBOL: A WORLD OF MEANINGS We often sense that what we see in a poem has a larger symbolic meaning beyond itself. Key poems by David Wagoner, Denise Levertov, and Li-Young Lee (among others) show the power of central symbols to focus our attention and to shape our emotional response. Poems by William Blake, Adrienne Rich, and William Butler Yeats show how poets go beyond the shared language of public symbols to develop a rich symbolic language of their own. Poems by Christina Rossetti and William Blake show how symbols play their role as parts of a pattern in allegory.

17 WORDS: THE WEB OF LANGUAGE Poets are in love with words as words—their sound, their shades of meaning, their emotional associations and implications. Poems by Maya Angelou, William Carlos Williams, and others remind readers of the sheer delight of language exuberantly used. Key poems by William Carlos Williams and others show poets exploiting to the full the resources of language—using the word with exactly the right shade of meaning, drawing on words with a rich range of connotation. Poets like Gerard Manley Hopkins, Dylan Thomas, and e. e. cummings reach the limits of language—punning, yoking words together in new combinations.

18 FORM: RHYME, METER, AND STANZA This chapter begins by exploring the role of traditional formal features and the resources of variety that keep them from becoming mechanical. The treatment here demonstrates the uses to which poets put full rhyme, alliteration, and slant rhyme or the range of traditional meters. Stanza forms discussed include the ballad stanza, the sonnet, and the villanelle. Poems by Anne Sexton, Sharon Olds, and others help students explore the different effects and appeal of traditional form and open form.

19 PERSONA: MASKS AND FACES This chapter asks students to listen attentively to the voice speaking to them in a poem. Who is speaking—the poet? in what role? assuming what identity? assuming what relation to the reader? Poems by Rita Dove, Sappho, Louise Erdrich, and Gwendolyn Brooks among others play variations on the autobiographical "I." In poems by Dylan Thomas, Walt Whitman, and Audre Lorde, the poet assumes a public persona. In poems from Louise Bogan's "Cassandra" to Robert Browning's dramatic monologue ("My Last Duchess"), the speaker is a fictitious, imagined character. Throughout, the question is: What is the distance between the poet as a person and the persona assumed in the poem?

20 TONE: THE LANGUAGE OF THE EMOTIONS A Shakespearean sonnet and William Stafford's "Traveling through the Dark" highlight the contrast between the passionate, hyperbolical tone of much earlier poetry and the understated, "cool" tone predominating in the modern tradition. Masters of the ironic mode range from Stephen Crane and W. H. Auden to Sylvia Plath and Anne Sexton. Masters of a paradoxical style range from Petrarch and Shakespeare to the metaphysicals (Herbert, Donne, Marvell). A pair of poems juxtaposes the bold permutation of the *carpe diem* theme in Andrew Marvell's "To His Coy Mistress" and a woman troubadour, the Countess of Dia, turning the tables on the traditional "plaint" of the male lover.

21 THEME: THE MAKING OF MEANING This chapter focuses on a key concern of twentieth-century criticism and literary theory: What is the difference between poetry on the one hand and editorializing on the other? How do we become sensitive to the issues a poem raises and the answers it seems to suggest—without reducing the poem to a simple message, to a vehicle for ready-made ideas? Poems by committed poets from Wilfred Owen and Robert Hayden to Denise Levertov and Czeslaw Milosz make us ask: What is the relation between a poet's political commitments or social conscience and our estimate of the poet as poet?

22 MYTH AND ALLUSION: RECOVERED MEMORIES This chapter explores the close link between myth and poetry, both rooted in the prehistoric past. The chapter examines mythology as a rich source of inspiration and allusion for poets through the ages. It shows the myth-making faculty alive in contemporary culture in the myth of the cowboy (e. e. cummings, "Buffalo Bill's") or the Hollywood sex goddess (Sharon Olds, "The Death of Marilyn Monroe").

23 THREE POETS IN DEPTH: DICKINSON, FROST, BROOKS This chapter probes the way our knowledge of the poet shapes our response to poetry. Each featured poet is introduced to the student reader with a tribute drawing on recent biography and current critical perspectives; each poet is represented by a rich sampling of major poems. The chapter puts special emphasis on the poet's distinctive voice (Dickinson), on the poet's life and public persona (Frost), and on the poet's commitment (Brooks). The Writing Workshop includes suggestions for library papers that require students to explore a range of biographical materials and critical reaction.

24 PERSPECTIVES: THE AGE OF THEORY This chapter looks at the symbiotic relationship between poetry and criticism. It discusses and illustrates critical approaches including biographical, historical, formalist, psychoanalytic, political, feminist, and deconstructionist. The chapter presents a range of commentary on poems by Sylvia Plath and features poets writing about poetry.

25 OTHER VOICES/OTHER VISIONS: A Gathering of Poets This mini-anthology for further reading includes classics and readers' favorites from George Herbert's "The Collar" and John Keats' "Ode to a Nightingale" to T. S. Eliot's "Love Song of J. Alfred Prufrock" and Robert Lowell's "Skunk Hour." It features poems by women from Aphra Behn and Louise Bogan to Rita Dove, Linda Pastan, and Sylvia Plath. It features poems by writers from culturally diverse backgrounds, from Nikki Giovanni and Etheridge Knight to Audre Lorde, Mitsuye Yamada, and Chitra Divakaruni.

POETRY
Teaching Suggestions and Answers to Questions

Chapter 12 PREVIEW The Voice of Poetry 469

> *I wrote—and I write today—because I conceive of literature as a dialogue with the world, with the reader, and with myself, and dialogue is the opposite of the noise that denies us and the silence that ignores us.*
>
> OCTAVIO PAZ

Poets and critics often make large claims for poetry. They honor it as our most intense, concentrated way of responding to our world, coming to know it, and giving it shape. Poetry gives us a way of expressing the unsayable: It gives us a language of the emotions; it puts us in touch with the subconscious or the hidden recesses of ourselves. Our students, however, live in a world in which poetry is very much on the periphery. To give them an inkling of what poetry can do for the reader, you may want to stress three key considerations:

What does the poet give us to see? Poets take in more than ordinary people. They notice things that people with more blunted senses overlook. They can make us feel more alive by involving us more fully in the world of sense experience.

What does the poet invite us to feel? A recurrent theme of much twentieth-century literature has been the inability of people in the modern world to give voice to their feelings. Does a poem make us experience twinges of remorse, nostalgic yearnings, outbursts of anger? Love, the fear of death, loneliness, a pervading sense of alienation—these are some of the basic emotions that we may find hard to put into words but for which a poem may give us a language.

Does the poem make us think? The spider in a poem by Walt Whitman or the dead deer in the road in a poem by William Stafford does not represent an isolated image or an isolated incident. It makes us think about something that matters in our lives and the lives of others.

W. S. Merwin, "Separation" 470

DISCUSSION STARTERS

Separation is an abstract noun. The dictionary defines *separation* as the act, state, or instance of being parted. The poet makes us experience the feeling of being separated through a metaphoric leap to stitchery to describe the pattern the feeling of absence makes in the speaker's life. A needle is a sharp object, able to pierce, suggestive of pain.

Audre Lorde, "Coping" 471

DISCUSSION STARTERS

Let students, in small groups, cluster the difference between coping and thriving. Associations such as the following might emerge:

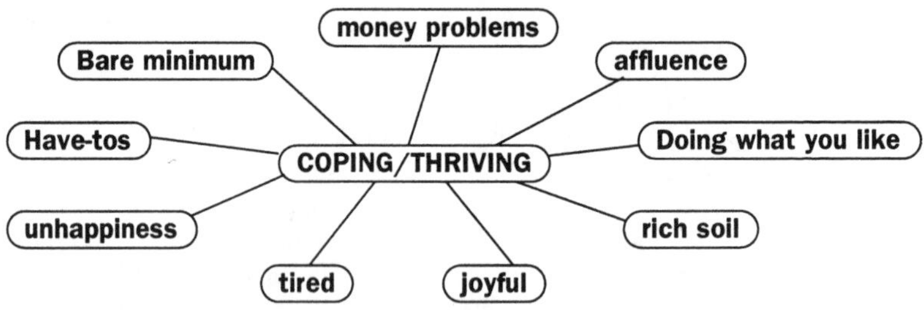

They may feel that "coping" means hanging on, struggling; that one needs help to cope—the young boy bails water from his flower patch; that it is easy to forget how it feels to thrive in the sunlight; that, if you only know rain, it is easy to drown.

THE RECEPTIVE READER

1. The rain coming down "for five days running" may seem an ordinary experience in many parts of the country, with streets or fields partially flooded at times.

2. The poet gives the experience a special imaginative spin by making us see the "small islands" of land as struggling to stay dry. We begin to sense the dread of drowning, of being washed out or washed away. The seeds that "have not seen sun" become symbols of endangered, struggling life. The "young seeds" of human potential are in danger of being destroyed; they are at risk, denied their chance to sprout and grow in the nurturing sun.

3. The title of the poem, "Coping," is its key word, as all the images have to do with the struggle to exist amidst a state in which one must simply "cope" to stay afloat. The word is highlighted in the title and repeated midpoint in the poem, set off for emphasis: "beginning / to cope." Lorde, a black woman poet, here mirrors the essence of the black experience in America since the 1960s. In 1968, the Civil Rights Movement contained only a few "small islands" that were only beginning "to cope" with the "sunless water" of racism.

FOLLOW-UP—THE CREATIVE DIMENSION

You may want to ask students to write their own vignettes, or snapshots, of a situation "after the rain" or "after the storm." Student sample:

The homeless man organizes his windswept belongings.
The rain has melted his cardboard box to a
pulp of despair.

The Poet's Language

(image) Emily Dickinson, "Presentiment" 472

DISCUSSION STARTERS

A *presentiment* is a foreboding—the feeling that something is about to happen, especially something dire or evil. In these four brief lines, we can discover several dimensions of meaning: At the literal level, we become aware of the cycle of day and night. At the level of emotions, we become aware that even our lightest moments may alternate with inevitable grief. At the deepest level, the "long shadow," an image carrying a sense of threat, hints at death and those flickering moments when we are startled into realization of our own mortality. Most people have had presentiments—those eery feelings that something isn't quite right in the universe: A door is left ajar. A car is absent when it's normally there. Sounds aren't quite right, or there is too much silence. Ask students to talk or write about a presentiment of their own?

(metaphor) Countee Cullen, "For My Grandmother" 473

DISCUSSION STARTERS

Have students spell out in their own words everything that relates to the extended central metaphor in this poem. When a flower dies, it falls to "seed"; yet without a seed there can be no renewed cycle of growth. The poet addresses "sun and rain," asking them to "work gently." Note that the poet isn't necessarily the one who believes "that she would grow again"; rather it is the grandmother who "held it as her dying creed." Do your students expect the grandson to have lost the certainty of the grandmother's "dying creed"?

THE RECEPTIVE READER

1. The sun and rain here appear to be both literal and metaphorical. The sun and rain are going to fall on the grave, literally. But they also provide a natural bridge to the growth metaphor that promises rebirth and renewed life.

2. The word *creed* might indicate that the poet was thinking of religious beliefs concerning resurrection and eternal life. But the word *seed* also has traditional associations with the idea of future generations.

(symbol) Robert Frost, "Stopping by Woods on a Snowy Evening" 474

DISCUSSION STARTERS

How would the feeling of the poem differ if the title were "Stopping by Woods on a Summer Evening"? Ask students to cluster all words or phrases in the poem that refer to winter in some way. Here is an example:

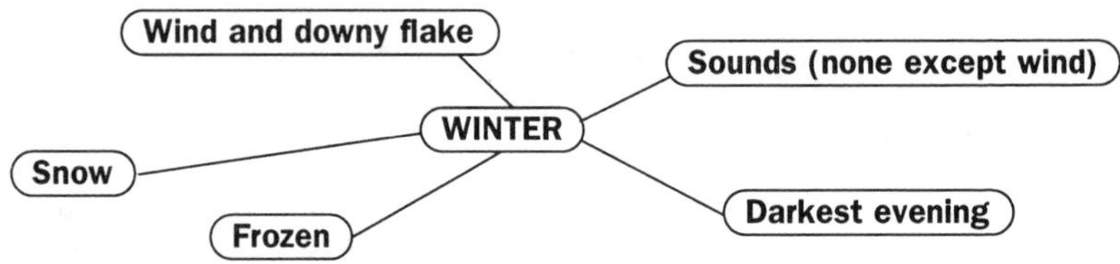

You may want to ask students to write freely for a few minutes about their own "winter feelings." Or ask them to write about a pause or thoughtful interval in a trip undertaken during spring or summer.

THE RECEPTIVE READER

1. What obligations or responsibilities do your students feel the pressure to come back to at the end of a day—cooking, children, pets, taking care of the sick? (When are the "promises" we need to keep made explicit, and when do they remain unspoken?)

2. The evening is "the darkest evening of the year," winter solstice. It is also the shortest, in a period of cold and darkness. The images of the frozen lake, the dark, the deep, could be used to argue that Frost is thinking of death. Death here is beckoning, an escape from care. (Compare Keats: "Now more than ever were it rich to die / To cease upon the midnight with no pain.") Often death is spoken of as a long slumber? Note also "Rest in peace."

3. The repeated lines at the end seem to reinforce the heavy sense of obligation? They make the "promises" seem more weighty, inescapable?

(rhyme) William Cowper, "The Snail" 476

DISCUSSION STARTERS

Cowper's discerning eye *notices* the snail, and he magnifies a creature that he probably encountered every day to human proportions. Read his poem aloud, and then ask students to pick out a comparable creature—

preferably one that's small, undomesticated, and virtually unnoticed (ants? cockroaches?). Have them dwell on it, try to magnify its significance. Readers of Cowper's day most likely saw snails differently before and after reading his poem. Perhaps your students can produce a similar heightening of awareness.

THE RECEPTIVE READER

1. The ending lines of each stanza give it a "constrictive" form, contracting the normal iambic pentameter to three syllables. This contraction mirrors the action of a snail pulling inward, thus matching form to content.

2. The poet extends the more common two-line rhyme to a third. This echoing effect intensifies the disunity the fourth line causes by ending so abruptly and with a different rhyme sound. All of the fourth lines rhyme. This heightens the sense that when this "snail" pulls in he truly comes to his own "treasure." The rhyme for the last line of each stanza remains unchanged even though the triple rhyme within each stanza "travels."

3. This creature has "self-collective power," a house, chattel (goods), and tends to be hermit-like (is happily single). This could describe some human beings. Even if this poem weren't titled, readers would know this creature isn't human, however. It has horns, and is permanently attached (in the most literal sense) to its house.

4. Like some human beings, this creature "feeds / The faster" when someone else threatens to share in what food is available. As for a serious point, the poem invokes an eighteenth-century ideal of a self-sufficient genteel English country life?

(meter) Alfred, Lord Tennyson, "The Eagle" 477

DISCUSSION STARTERS

Why did many nations use the eagle as the symbol of national glory or imperial might? Is the eagle for today's generation still a symbol of fierceness, grandeur, and power? Or does our culture have a special talent for cutting people and ideas "down to size"?

THE RECEPTIVE READER

1 Do your students tend to accentuate a metrical beat mechanically—or do they read with natural expression, with meter merely accentuating the natural rhythms of the language? You may want to have students work together in small groups to mark each *foot* and each *accent* or beat (heavy or soft) for the entire poem. (The first two lines are marked in the text).

He CLASPS | the CRAG | with CROOK | ed HANDS;
CLOSE to | the SUN | in LONE | ly LANDS,
RINGED with | the A | zure WORLD | he STANDS.

The WRIN | kled SEA | beNEATH | him CRAWLS;
He WATCH | es FROM | his MOUN | tain *walls*,
And LIKE | a THUN | derBOLT | he FALLS.

Each group may want to select someone to read the poem to the entire class, asking the others to judge whether the reading feels stiff and mechanical or whether it adds the life of the human voice to the written text.

2 The eagle has both the power to seize unsuspecting prey and to soar above the mundane concerns of the earth. The bird became a symbol of a fiercely independent, militant nationalism. Tennyson presents the eagle as a powerful figure, able to reside "close to the sun" with the "azure" world at his feet. (The sea, itself an awesome natural power, seems to have become almost dwarfed through the poet's use of words like *wrinkled* and *crawls*?) Like Zeus' thunderbolt, the eagle strikes to kill?

(rhythm) Walt Whitman, "A Noiseless Patient Spider" 478

PERSPECTIVES—WHITMAN, BARD AND MYSTIC, AND THE MODERN CRITIC

Whitman's spider poem is widely considered the most successful of his shorter poems. Although to many readers, at home and especially abroad, Whitman has often seemed the most quintessentially American of American poets, twentieth-century critics have not had an easy time relating to Whitman's rhapsodic celebration of a new continent and a "new nation of nations." Whitman was a child of the age of Emerson's transcendentalism. Like Emerson, he was the expansive mystic seeking for communion with some spiritual center of the universe, communing with "the whole." Like Whitman, Emerson, in "The Poet," could see the "factory village and the railway," the "beehive or the spider's geometrical web," all as part of the "great order" of being that it was the poet's mission to celebrate. Critics today have a hard time reconciling Whitman's celebration of the almost narcissistic individual with his glorifying of "Nationality"—of a "real Union," which will produce a "larger, saner brood of female, male." Suspicious of the biographical "I" that seems to speak in many of Whitman's poems, critics today tend to read the poems conscious of a persona that speaks in a dramatic context rather than of a larger-than-life national bard.

DISCUSSION STARTERS

Ask students to compare the compactness of Tennyson's "The Eagle" with the flowing lines of Whitman's "A Noiseless Patient Spider." Have them check one indicator: How many words are one-syllable or two-syllable words? (In Tennyson's poem, the only word containing three syllables is *thunderbolt.*) How many words are multisyllabic words? (In Whitman's poem, note *promontory, filament, measureless.*)

THE RECEPTIVE READER

1. As suggested for the Tennyson poem, students might find working in groups enjoyable and productive. Students are likely to disagree on which syllables should carry emphasis. Ask each group to reach a consensus and then select a reader to read the poem to the rest of the class.

2. Spiders are usually considered repulsive? They are often seen as irritants, something to be swept away or sprayed. However, different cultures may see them differently, as in the Spider-woman myths that see this insect in spiritual terms. Whitman does here also, comparing the aspirations of his soul to the workings of a spider.

3. Whitman compares his soul to a spider. Like the spider, it hangs out in space, suspended by a thin filament until it can find a place to catch, or land. This filament, or bridge, is not like a suspension bridge, but rather like a thin thread that holds until firm footing can be found. It is gossamer, thin and light; it is the poet's soul, or musings that ceaselessly venture, throw out exploratory lines, and seek spheres to connect with. Both spider and soul have a tireless, unceasing vital energy that keeps them striving in the face of uncertainty and the abyss of the unknown?

4: Whitman and his transcendentalist contemporaries did not bring spirituality ready-made into a material world from the outside in the form of dogma or ideology. Rather, they found intense spiritual significance in this world. Spirituality or transcendent significance is anchored in this world and is an integral part of reality. (The world as we know it is "shot through" with profound meanings.)

(open form) Gwendolyn Brooks, "Truth" 480

DISCUSSION STARTERS

A student said about Brooks' poem, "Because the truth hurts, it has 'firm knuckles.' " Another wrote: "Because the darkness of the inside is 'dear' and 'sweet,' perhaps there is some truth to the saying 'Ignorance is bliss.' " Can students think of truths from which they might try to hide or which they might prefer to avoid—the truth about a failing relationship, a deteriorating car, serious illness, unreliable friends, an endangered job, or our endangered planet?

THE RECEPTIVE READER

1. The repetitive lines beginning "Shall we not" and "Though we have" and "Sweet is it" are almost hymnlike. These set up an almost chanting rhythm to guide the reader. The words *shimmering*, *morning*, and *hammering* all within two lines create an echoing effect. The line breaks, too, support the images presented—one can almost hear the "hammering / . . . knuckles / Hard on the door." The jolting effect of this noise is softened with the lulling sounds of escape "sweet . . . sweet / . . . sleep . . . / . . . snug," lulling us into unawareness.

2. Pararhyme—repetition of the final *him*—appears in lines 2 through 4 and again in line 7—keeping the "sun" and its light in front of readers, confronting them with the initial question that the poem presents. We find repetition of *un*accented final syllables in the words *shimmering*, *morning*, and *hammering* and in the third stanza's *shudder* and two occurrences of *shelter*.

Consonance (identity of consonants with different main vowels) occurs in the first stanza with the multiple "s" and "sh" sounds; in the "w" sounds of the second; and again the "s" sounds of the fourth stanza. The last stanza's "h"s truly "hang heavy" helped by this device.

Assonance (identity of vowels with different consonants) appears in the first stanza's "e" sounds, both long and short (*we*, *greet/dread*, *length*, *session*). In the next to the last stanza, note "sweet . . . sweet . . . sleep."

3. The sun usually calls up good associations: light, brightness, and warmth. And darkness usually is associated with the fearsome in life. Brooks reverses these images ironically: we tend to hide in the sheltering dark, hugging our ignorance.

4. Brooks may have been thinking of personal truths or of "truths" associated with the shared experience of African Americans. These were the common experiences of "night-years," those spent in servitude in a seemingly free nation. People who fool themselves about the harsh realities of prejudice and discrimination may be said to hide from the truth?

(theme) Juana Inés de la Cruz, from "A Satirical Romance" 481

DISCUSSION STARTERS

What does the term *misogyny* mean to your students? Are men today used to being accused of being insensitive and prejudiced toward women? Does it bother them?

THE RECEPTIVE READER

1. The poem leads up to its central message by opening with an accusation against men, indicting the double standard that plagues women to this day. On the one hand, the men pursue the women, and lament that the women are aloof and disdainful and refuse to encourage amorous advances.

On the other hand, should the woman encourage such advances, the pursuit would end and the woman would be condemned for having yielded. This sort of dichotomizing results in the Madonna/whore categorizing of women, and is reflected in the poet's mirror image. An economical choice of words helps to make this image effective: "What humour can be so rare / that carelessly will blur / a mirror, and then aver / that it's not clear?" This question—what kind of a man would consort with a woman and then allege that she is not pure—leads to the heart of the matter. In this world "no woman can win." Resist, and she is condemned: "keep you out, and she's too tight." Yield, and she is also condemned: "she's too loose if you get in."

2. Despite advances in education and women's equality, in most of the world women remain second-class citizens? Even in the countries of the world where women have made the greatest strides, a double standard persists: A sexually active young woman who has known many partners is condemned, while a sexually active young man who has known many partners is, if not lauded, deemed to be doing the things that young men do. Therefore, de la Cruz's poem should speak to the modern reader? In the courtship rituals of this poem, both men and women play out preassigned and preordained roles. However, since the men indisputably ran such a world, and, more particularly, controlled the churches that monitored that world, they are the inevitable targets of the poet's indictment.

3. Female poets from the Countess of Dia to Aphra Behn have spoken out frankly, although until recently their poems may not have been represented in conventional anthologies. Frank criticism of traditional male roles in courtship is common today?

4. The poem's indictment is ostensibly addressed to men. The poem's lament, however—"no woman can win"—is addressed to women? The poem's description of the pervasive bias against women and of the hypocrisy of the actions of the men would find an appreciative audience in the women of de la Cruz's time as well as the present?

5. Have students share their responses with the class?

MAKING CONNECTIONS—FOR DISCUSSION AND WRITING

You may want to have students *read and discuss* a favorite poem.

Close Reading and the Personal Response

Linda Pastan, "Sometimes in Winter" 483

DISCUSSION STARTERS

Do your students ever puzzle over a poem line by line, word by word? Have they ever felt stymied by sections of a poem or a whole poem?

THE RECEPTIVE READER

The student reader stresses the idea of the skaters' skimming the surface, not "getting in too deep," not getting involved. There is less emphasis on the emotional coldness of the ice-skaters' world? The startling use of the word *fragile* makes us think of something that breaks easily. We might imagine a delicate wine glass slipping from the hands, shattering. The word dramatizes the heart-breaking vulnerability of the human beings we love. The people dancing over the surface of life do not dance in joyful abandon but in tense, chilled fear of painful commitments?

Seamus Heaney, "Valediction" 485

DISCUSSION STARTERS

A "valediction" is an utterance made in bidding farewell or taking leave. In this poem, it is not the one "taking leave" who speaks; instead, it is the one left behind. The speaker is "bidding farewell" from the point at which he's been left. It might be interesting to have the "Lady with the frilled blouse and simple tartan skirt" speak her "valediction." (Some psychologists say that writing a letter to a departed lover helps one to move through the grief of loss.) You may want to ask students to write the woman's "valediction," imagining the situation from the absent lover's point of view.

THE RECEPTIVE READER (CLOSE READING)

Notice how this close-reading response stays caught up in the dominant metaphor. The few lines before the turning point, the opening word *rocked* in the eighth line, recall a feeling of calm. As the student writer mentions, the boat was "anchored" secure in its mooring. "Time rode easy," suggesting the placid setting and the speaker's peaceful state of mind. The word *rocked*, however, sets in motion a completely different state of affairs. The speaker is "unmoored" and the days "buck and bound," having been "pitched" there by the memory of his love's voice (or perhaps by rejection). The phrase "resume command" does seem surprising—since, nonstereotypically, it is the woman and not the man who seems to have been in control.

THE RECEPTIVE READER (PERSONAL RESPONSE)

In this response, the same student writer makes the personal connection. The tie-in with the student's dream makes overt the universality of the poem's appeal, dramatizing its human meaning. The recurrent image of the "ship at sea" connects both experiences. As the student says, "It is easy to identify with the poem" because of its central metaphor.

Alice Walker, "New Face" 487

DISCUSSION STARTERS

Do your students think of love as a source of hassles and worry? Do they remember having been lectured or nagged about the need to beware of the "rush of feelings"?

THE RECEPTIVE READER

1. The poem takes off from the usual worries and apprehensions about love and the speaker's decision to leave these behind. The focus is on love as a powerful, heedless, driving force, welling up from the depths of one's being.

2. One of the strongest images is that of these feelings being compared to swirling, swiftly flowing, heedless blood. There are also images of a spring that is inexhaustible and the concept of a rich multilayered personality ("twin or triple / selves").

3. The face that no one else on earth has ever seen before means that the speaker is coming to this new love with a fresh uniqueness and, regardless of how many times she has loved before, innocence?

The Creative Dimension

Wallace Stevens, "Disillusionment of Ten O'Clock" 488

PERSPECTIVES—WALLACE STEVENS: THE BUSINESSPERSON AS POET

Reviewing a new Wallace Stevens biography in *The New Republic* (December 19, 1988), Michael Levenson discusses the "rich confusion" of a "quietly complicated existence." According to Levenson, it's not true that "too much has been made of the split between the poet and the insurance lawyer." On the contrary, "too little has been made of it. Stevens himself was acutely sensitive to the discontinuities of his life. He refused to poeticize his business world, and he refused to make a business of his poetry. And yet it's clear that he was stimulated by the rub of the incongruities." In fact, "poetry and business were only two terms in a life composed of clefts and fissures. Struggling for so long with obesity, he could abruptly release himself in big-bellied satisfaction. At the office he was a man of correct and sober deportment, but if the luncheon company were right or the Christmas atmosphere convivial, he could drink his way into memorable intoxication. In the midst of his constrained Northeastern domesticity, he would leave his wife and daughter for high-spirited body-indulging trips to Florida with Arthur Powell, judge and bon vivant." Stevens was raised in a "late Victorian patriarchal family that upheld the sanctity of work but also enjoyed the sweet fruits of labor. Self-reliance was one good thing; piano-playing was another. His father stood for the first, his mother for the second; and the young Stevens liked to cast his parents in the contending roles of reason and imagination."

DISCUSSION STARTERS

This poem indicts people lacking imagination and creativity; they wear "white night-gowns." They not only lack originality; their dreams are plain dreams, not dreams of "baboons and periwinkles." Ironically, the only fantasizing that takes place is induced not by the imagination but by the sailor's drinking. You might want to ask students: "Are your dreams fear dreams or fantasy dreams? Do you dream in color or in black and white?" "Disillusionment," wrote a student, "comes only when we forget to dream playfully and wildly, instead dreaming in the antiseptic monochrome of white, of white nightgowns which are distressingly reminiscent of hospital gowns, suggesting a sterile setting in which all is uniform and correct—and bland instead of vibrant with 'tigers / In red weather.' "

THE RECEPTIVE READER

1. The poet seems to be disillusioned by the tedium of life without color or excitement.

2. The houses aren't haunted by lurking ghosts but by "white night-gowns." The color white here does not suggest purity but the absence of color and life—being unimaginative, empty of thought or imagination, simply routine and sterile. "Haunted" suggests there is something spooky about the emotional deadness of these people who, unlike the "old sailor" catching "tigers / In red weather," are not "strange."

3. We often expect dreams to be an escape valve for buried subconscious urges, but in this poem, ironically, even people's dreams are permeated by the ordinariness and colorlessness of their waking hours?

4. Stevens doesn't see the drunk as irresponsible; instead he is an "old sailor," a voyager in life? Not happy with the mundane, he dreams of storms or adventures in "red weather."

THE RANGE OF INTERPRETATION

In Irving Howe's discussion, how or why could the "drunken sailor" become a symbol of rebellion against an "impersonal and recalcitrant age"?

William Carlos Williams, "This Is Just to Say" 491

DISCUSSION STARTERS

This is one of the best-known and best-loved of modern poems—for many people, one of the few they know by heart. Make sure students hear the poem read aloud to students. Ask them to think of a brief but intense moment in time that has stayed in their memory: images of color or light or taste or smell; a moment of pleasure, a moment of pain. Ask them to re-create such a moment. These don't have to be "big events."

THE CREATIVE DIMENSION

Students who try to follow or imitate the pattern of the original poem will discover that a poem without rhyme, meter, or pre-packaged stanza form nevertheless has its own organic form. It has its own rhythm and characteristic pauses; it is laid out in a characteristic pattern. It has its own unmistakable shape. (Help students see that the sample imitation in the text "dances out" a pattern whose development and pauses are very similar to that of the original.)

Donald Justice, "Men at Forty" 492

DISCUSSION STARTERS

What birthday or anniversary do students remember as a milestone?

THE RECEPTIVE READER

1. The doors can be seen as representing the caution and world weariness of men at forty. Whereas a man at twenty might slam the door with all his strength or leave it entirely open, at forty, men "learn to close softly / The doors." By forty men are quietly closing these metaphorical openings and acknowledging that Robert Frost's "Road Not Taken" is no longer an option. As the men rest on the landing, a thing they have perhaps only recently begun to do, they can feel beneath their feet the gentle movement of the ocean across which their ship is inexorably traversing. The mirror reminds them of their own role in the cycle of replacement, as the boy practices to be the man that will replace the father ("The face of the boy as he practices tying / His father's tie there in secret"). Crickets, "Filling the woods at the foot of the slope," announce the arrival of twilight; the bright sun of twenty or thirty has been replaced with the lengthening shadows of dusk to be followed inevitably by darkness.

2. The connecting thread in the five stanzas are the metaphorical depictions of time passing. Youthful passion has been replaced by wiser discretion; doors are shut quietly and life's direction choices are carefully winnowed down. The poem is not overtly anxious about the inexorably finite

aspect of life, but there is a somber edge to the observations: "They are more fathers than sons themselves now."

Maurya Simon, "Women at Thirty" 492

DISCUSSION STARTERS

Where do students most clearly see the poet's following the pattern of Justice's poem while playing her own variations on it?

THE RECEPTIVE READER

1. At thirty, Simon says, women "Learn to swing slightly / In the hinges of their steps / As they ascend." Does Simon mean that by the age of thirty women have learned to be comfortable with their femaleness? (The remainder of the poem suggests a woman coming into her own). The women are comfortable—("At ease") on the carpeting; indeed, it is like an "air-borne sail." And even though "its speed is slowed down," the carpeting hints at a very magic carpet ride, gliding gently aloft? Women "recover" their girlish faces in the mirrors, seeing themselves as in the transition from adolescent gawkiness they started experimentally imitating their mothers' smiles and kisses, "warmed by the mystery of father." By thirty, "They are more and more women now," comfortable at last in their identities as women. Indicative of this slightly exalted state is the halo-like glow of the sun that illuminates them: "something / That is like the sun's brush / Of white light." The sun also assists in "Unfurling the ferns at the base of the yard / Beyond their children's windows." The ferns, reminders of wild and lush tropical undergrowth, and their location, "at the base of the yard," "beyond" the windows of the children, hint at a still unfolding sexual blooming?

2. Simon's thirty-year-old woman is a more positive creature than is Justice's forty-year-old man? Justice's men must take a quick rest on the stair landing; their mirrors reveal their status inevitably as fathers, not sons; and everything, including the coming of twilight and the chirping of crickets, conspires to remind them that "Time's winged chariot" is "hurrying near." Simon's women have yet to peak. They step briskly past the stair landing with their hips slightly swinging; their mirrors reveal them to be "more and more women now"; and the limitless possibilities of life are everywhere visible.

Juxtapositions: Reading and Writing Haiku 493

The re-creation of the Wallace Stevens poem and the formal and informal haiku are designed to help wean students away from the "passive observer" stance in their relation to poetry. Creativity is everyone's birthright. Informal publication or sharing of student responses and student re-creations can help break down the barrier between poetry and the student reader. (If you can, have someone who knows Japanese read the sample haiku for your students.)

Chapter 13 PATTERN
The Whole Poem

The dream of the human heart, however much we may distrust and resent it, is that life may complete itself in significant pattern.

SAUL BELLOW

Explore with your students words that suggest a *whole*—in which parts have become part of an overall pattern. How are the following different—and what do they have in common: the web, a fabric, a design, a skyline, a signature, a grid? What does the word *pattern* bring to the students' minds? Have them cluster or write about the term: What distinctive patterns do they spontaneously remember? Where or when do they become especially aware of things or details that fall into a pattern? What patterns made a special impression on their minds?

Ecclesiastes (3:1–8), "To Every Thing There Is A Season" 503

DISCUSSION STARTERS

Many of the paired opposites here are universal and timeless. Being born/dying, planting/plucking up, killing/healing, weeping/laughing, mourning/dancing are all polarities that students will probably find play a major role in their lives. Casting stones to punish offenders may seem archaic, but we still warn people not "to cast the first stone." "Rend" and "sew" may seem outmoded in our department-store society, though students should be able to relate to their figurative meaning—tearing something apart or breaking it up versus trying to stitch it back together.

Archibald MacLeish, "The Genius" 503

DISCUSSION STARTERS

The cock is wakened by a "pale pink/Intimation" (soft colors rather than vivid add to the opening "slow" feeling). He is the passive "prey of every beast." But by the fourth line, this rooster (the poem as well) begins to move. The verbs get stronger: "takes breath . . . leans . . . shrieks." Dramatic adjectives heighten the building excitement: *fiery*, *brazen*, *uncontrollable*. The last lines build toward the *climactic* two crows, "He first! He first!" It is often said that recent years have been the era of the "Me first!" generation. You may want to ask students to write a passage or short poem that culminates in "Me first!"

Wendell Berry, "The Peace of Wild Things" 504

DISCUSSION STARTERS

What images and associations are triggered in your students' minds by the term *nature*? For some, the word may call up images similar to those in Berry's poem—nights of calm, lakes of calm, wildlife peacefully resting. Others may think about the awesome power of natural forces, from thunderstorms to volcanoes and storms at sea. (Is it true that the media turn attention to nature mainly when it turns destructive?) Some students may have had bad or life-threatening experiences in nature—from mosquitoes to getting lost in the wilderness?

THE RECEPTIVE READER

1. Stress and anxiety keep the speaker in the poem awake at night. But the serenity and peace of nature calm the speaker in this poem: the "peace of wild things," "still water," and the "day-blind stars." Human beings often attempt to escape their consciousness of the future: drugs, alcohol, suicide are all ways to blot out our fears.

2. In this poem, "the wild things" are not seen as wild, fear-ridden, locked in the struggle for survival. They "feed" quietly or rest on the water. Fear, the poet suggests, is the effect of "forethought," our ability to imagine our future and its possible griefs, which can engender "despair."

3. The phrase "day-blind" might be seen from the point of view of the speaker (he cannot see these stars during the day) or from the stars' point of view (these stars, coming out only at night, are "blind" to the day, and hence, to the daily realities that disturb the speaker)? In either case, it is clear that the feeling of calm in the poem resides in the nighttime images, the sight of stars bringing peace from the day's "despair."

4. "*Grace*" as used here might blend both meanings? There is something sacred or divine about the serene, supreme beauty of nature that offers us a respite or redemption from the despair of our troubled existence. ("Grace" can also mean "favor shown in granting a delay or temporary immunity." This definition might fit as well—the world grants the speaker temporary immunity from his chains of fear and his "taxing" forethoughts of grief.)

THE PERSONAL RESPONSE

These fears could be everyday fears much like those we all encounter: Will we be able to make our mortgage payments or find the money to pay back taxes? Will an illness turn out to be serious, and will I lose my health insurance? Will my children do well enough to be admitted to this or that college? Will they be happy?

The Power of Attention

William Carlos Williams, "Between Walls" 505

DISCUSSION STARTERS

Can the ordinary and bleak be "poetic"? Poet and critic Babette Deutsch said about Williams' poetry: "There is no effort to flatter, to cajole, to enchant the reader. Williams seems to be content with the clear line, the pure color. Or the mangy line, the dirty color, if he is looking at the uglier details." The four two-line stanzas describing a drab setting that is not traditionally poetic culminate in a single line illuminating "pieces of a green bottle." Williams referred to these small moments of awareness as "radiant gists" or significant moments. A student observed:

> "Between Walls" is like a skeleton, the flesh is absent and all that remains is a stark outline to give the reader a few powerful clues. Only the words "shine" and "green" bring life to this skeleton. Green brings connotations of living organisms and nature, newness and birth. Shine, the sign of health, is a contrast to the sterile hospital sprayed with Lysol.

THE RECEPTIVE READER

1. Williams was a physician who wrote poetry in between seeing patients and performing other hospital duties. The bleakness of the cinders and the sole touch of green (as a symbol of hope?) may have summed up for the poet the struggle between despair and hope that is central to the struggle against sickness? Or he may have felt the futility of trying to heal in a place that "between the walls" contains "cinders" and "broken / pieces of a green / bottle"?

2. The first stanza is merely a prelude to the word *hospital.* As students read the opening words "the back wings / of the . . ." they will be looking for place or setting, and the word *hospital* gains emphasis because it answers the reader's unspoken question, "Where?" The words *nothing* and *cinders* are placed at end-line and end-stanza—the end positioning a natural place of emphasis.

3. The lone touch of green is a paradox in this poem. It is true that some bottles are green, but the color, normally associated with growth and new life, is a contradiction to the scene.

4. The lines seem as bare or stark as the scene? Hospitals normally have stark white walls, and here nothing grows. To have lush lines "growing" from this experience would seem inappropriate?

Sharon Olds, "The Possessive" 506

DISCUSSION STARTERS

Ask students to think about what they are possessive about in their lives. They may want to jot down thoughts or images that cluster around the word *possessive.* Do they ever feel possessive about other people? What are possible problems with that?

THE RECEPTIVE READER

1. The barber, it appears, bobbed the girl's hair—perhaps into a severe hairdo that the mother didn't like. The hair at first was "wispy as a frayed bellpull." This brings up an image of free, gentle innocence. Later, the hair is "sharpened" and the bangs are boldly confrontative, like "carbon steel." The barber, "that knife grinder," gives the girl weaponry of her own in the form of her hair. The poet says "all the little / spliced ropes are sliced"—like the ties that connected the mother and daughter up to this point. The hair becomes a "helmet" ready for defiance and defense.

2. A military metaphor governs this finely honed poem. The daughter's first haircut heralds the inevitable battle between parents and adolescents. Words associated with cutting or slashing, weaponry, and war are abundant: "knife grinder," "hair sharpened," "each strand now cuts," "carbon steel," "helmet," "watch fires," the "enemy," and at last, "war."

3. The poet is well aware of the impact of the small possessive word *my.* She wrestles with it at the beginning of stanza 5, reevaluating its validity. She comes to the conclusion that "I'll have to find / another word."

THE PERSONAL RESPONSE

Hair is a powerful symbol of the tug-of-war between the generations, as this personal response illustrates:

When my friend, Sheryl, cut her almost knee-length hair into a 1920's style bob, all hell broke loose. Her parents said her hair was a blatant example of rebellion, and it was. Hair is usually handled by our mothers until we are old enough to start thinking how we want it, usually at around age eleven. That's when we realize we might be different from our parents. Olds illuminated this in-between moment with great precision.

THE CREATIVE DIMENSION

The re-creation shown in the text centers on the image of the helmet, which protects the girl enough to "prepare for battle." Here is another example:

What war begins without
something being clung to?
A wispy desire sharpens,
a curtain drops,
a line is divided unawares;
a thin line
turns into a hard line,
leaving us on separate sides.

Leroy V. Quintana, "Legacy II" 507

DISCUSSION STARTERS

Is it true that ours is the country of youth? Is it true that we no longer believe in the wisdom of age?

THE RECEPTIVE READER

1. The four directions are laid out in a pattern that is basic to the way we orient ourselves in our world. Our sense of direction helps turn an uncharted, confusing world in which it is easy to get lost into a world in which we know where we are. Had the poet lined these words up in linear fashion, the sense of place, of orienting ourselves in our world, would have been lost. Here all the words mirror a basic dimension of our sense of the world; they confront the reader at the same time, and the eye is directed toward the center.

2. The opening lines give the reader details regarding the grandfather: he never went to school and he spoke only a few words of English. These details might ordinarily mean "illiterate," or "semi-illiterate." However, the image of the grandfather only speaking a few words doesn't make him either. He is, instead, a "quiet man." This sets up the reader to appreciate his simple life and message.

3. Sharon Olds' poem talks about distancing—the rift that she knows is coming between mother and daughter. The Quintana poem, however, is about connection. Perhaps a better word is re-connection.

THE PERSONAL RESPONSE

You might want to help students clarify their thoughts by having them explore the relations and differences between words like *legacy*, *heritage*, *inheritance*, *roots*.

Thomas Hardy, "The Darkling Thrush" 509

DISCUSSION STARTERS

Was the poet's pessimism at the turn of the century justified? What "hoped for" things has the twentieth century produced? What did it bring that justified "gloom"?

THE RECEPTIVE READER

1. The "weakening eye of day" is the pale weak sun of winter. The "cloudy canopy" is an oppressive cloud cover reminiscent perhaps of the grey covering over a crypt. The "ancient pulse of germ and birth" is the rhythm of germination and renewal that brings back spring. The bird's plumage is ruffled by the cold blast of the wintery wind.

2. The mournful *opening lines* seem to set us up for a dirge for the dying century, with words like *specter-gray*, *dregs*, and *desolate*. All mankind is "haunted," the century is a "corpse outleant," and the wind is singing a "death-lament." Most readers will expect this poem to continue with thoughts of death and decay?

3. The poem, instead of ending in death, finishes with the hope of new life. Though the thrush is "aged . . . frail, gaunt, and small," he nevertheless is able to transcend the wintery setting, letting us hear the voice of life and hope.

4. The bird's first notes are an "evensong," a prayer. He flings his "soul" upon the growing gloom. The sounds he makes are "carolings" and "ecstatic" though there is little cause to be joyful. These are all songs one might hear in a church or ceremonial celebration. Hope is not only personified, it is also "blessed." Hardy called himself a "meliorist," one who believes that the world may be made better by human effort. In spite of the religious overtones, the joyful certainty of firm religious belief seems to be missing?

THE CREATIVE DIMENSION

In this poem, the speaker who is composing an epitaph for the nineteenth century is leaning against a gate leading to a bleak grove of small trees. Ask your students what might be an appropriate setting or location for their own epitaph for the twentieth century.

Sylvia Plath, "Frog Autumn" 510

DISCUSSION STARTERS

Keats described autumn as "season of mists and mellow fruitfulness / Close bosom-friend of the maturing sun." Ask students to compare the mood of Keats' opening lines with the mood of Plath's poem. You might ask students to look at other contrasting perspectives on the seasons, for instance, winter in Pastan, Hardy, Frost, and Shakespeare.

THE RECEPTIVE READER

1. We usually view a swamp or bog from the *outside*, without empathy for its creatures (especially if they are clammy or slithery reptiles or amphibians). This poem drastically changes our point of view by having these creatures speak to us as sentient, suffering fellow creatures, uttering a lament about the dearth of food and the "genius of plenitude" who "houses himself" somewhere else. (Humans who might see this bog most likely wouldn't notice that the insects had grown "scant, skinny," nor that there were no more spiders about; nor would they realize that the frogs were bordering on starvation.) At the same time, these are real frogs, croaking among the reeds.

2. Striking examples of sparse statements, fitting for the bleak scene, include "Summer grows old," "Flies fail us," and "The fen sickens."

3. The word *lamentably* appears on a line by itself at the end of the entire poem, subsuming and reiterating the note of mourning This is what it all adds up to—the frost, the cold, the failing food supply. At the same time, this "last word" reminds us that these are living creatures, capable of suffering.

THE PERSONAL RESPONSE

Students may feel that this poem, unlike the Hardy poem, leaves little hope, indicating the frogs will die and that's that. There is no hope, however muted or distant, of renewal, rebirth. Some may want the poem to continue, giving the reader (and the frogs) a sense of a cyclical return to "plenitude." Others might like the poet's way of accepting, without varnish, the grim truth?

The Shape of the Poem

Dorothy Parker, "Solace" 511

DISCUSSION STARTERS

How often do events in real life fall into this kind of pattern? Can any of your students describe several related incidents that "spoke for themselves," telling the same story? Can they recount several observations that all pointed in the same direction? Can they point to a spate of recent news stories that all "told the same story"?

THE RECEPTIVE READER

1. The basic story: Someone has suffered a loss and others say "don't worry about it—there are other fish in the sea." The speaker doesn't answer the "them" in the poem, the people that didn't experience the loss and so make light of it. The speaker's attitude shows when, after hearing the same unfeeling, glib reaction twice, she doesn't wait around to hear it the third time.

2. Each mini-event is conjured up in a short concise statement—"There was a bird, brought down to die"— that immediately presents a subject that is going to experience loss. The second half of the statement is specific about the loss. The "they" or "others"—those unaffected—then give their advice, or solace. But their solace shows a lack of empathy. (They distance themselves from the event by not referring to the specific individual but to "roses budding everywhere," to the "hundred," to the "many"?)

THE PERSONAL RESPONSE

Ask students to give some personal examples of what parents or friends have said after a loss. What kind of "solace" did they offer? (Do different cultural traditions have different ways of consoling the disappointed or the bereaved?)

William Meredith, "A Major Work" 512

DISCUSSION STARTERS

To make students appreciate the effect of *cumulative repetition,* you may want to ask them to write several consecutive parallel sentences (parallel in both sentence structure and meaning) that fill in one of following sentence frames:

__________ are hard to ___________.
__________ are easy to ___________.
__________ are confusing to ___________.

THE RECEPTIVE READER

1. Love is an ambivalent emotion: It might be rooted in "brute" physical need—or it might be inspired by a divine or spiritual impulse. (But either way it does move the "great sloth heart.")

2. What might move the "great sloth heart"—a sudden revelation? a traumatic incident? a slow learning to appreciate the other?

Anne Bradstreet, from "The Vanity of All Worldly Things" 513

DISCUSSION STARTERS

How has the language of religion changed from Bradstreet's time? Has our religious vocabulary moved away from terms like *stern, austere, righteous, vice,* and *conscience*? How, and why?

THE RECEPTIVE READER

1. Each segment of this tightly structured poem starts with a similarly worded rhetorical question (one to which the speaker already knows the answer). The question is then followed by the predictable nay-saying response, which often culminates in a pithy, epigrammatic clincher: "He's now a captive that was king of late." "It's his today, but who's his heir tomorrow?" Honor, wealth, pleasure, beauty, and youth are all in turn found wanting.

2. Some of the many polarities that help organize the Bradstreet poem: captive/king, poverty/wealth, riches/sorrow, today/tomorrow, pleasure/guilt, youth/age, vice/virtue, beauty/foulness.

3. Students may find the fervor of this piece strange, along with its dogmatic rejection of the rewards and blessings of this life? The tightly parallel organization of the poem is a fitting expression for the kind of orthodox

thinking it embodies, which allows no personal deviations or detours, no spontaneous departures from the straight and narrow.

Kay Boyle, "October 1954" 515

DISCUSSION STARTERS

October, November, December. Late autumn and early winter. For a child, dead and dying leaves were a plaything; for the adult they produce a sense of grieving. The poet was fifty-one when she wrote this poem. What if the poem's title were April 1954 or July 1954? What images might the poet have focused on at her stage in life?

THE RECEPTIVE READER

1. The poet presents the image of leaves in the first line of the poem, immediately presenting this image as a focus-point for the reader. Boyle then elaborates. These aren't any old leaves. It's time for them to burn. They also remind her of the kind she used to run through as a young girl. She presents the image of leaves, burning, mid-point in the poem, as the speaker stands alone, and again at the end, when the speaker reveals how she would like to run through them again as she used to as a young girl.

2. There are many polarities here that highlight the ideas of youth and age: the woman's grief/the girl's singing, the burning leaves/the heart "light as a leaf," red mouth/red (turning) sumac; bell-like singing/clang of blue-jays.

3. The wind in October and the harsh blue-jay cackles seem to give the air a harsh metallic feel. October intensifies the speaker's pain and sense of loss—all that is ahead now is the dead of winter.

THE PERSONAL RESPONSE

Some students (especially those who live in environments that have drastic changes of season) will be quite aware of the changing seasons—one can't ignore sixteen feet of snow or a hot-humid summer. What do the seasons mean to today's city dweller—to people who spend time in indoor malls or indoor stadiums?

Juxtapositions: The Daily Cycle

N. Scott Momaday, "New World" 516

PERSPECTIVES—MOMADAY AND THE NATIVE AMERICAN HERITAGE

Major themes that critics have explored in discussing Momaday's prose and poetry include the love of the land as the "first truth" of the

Native American, the interplay of "racial memory" and the individual imagination, and Momaday's closeness to the spirit of the oral tradition. Kenneth C. Mason in "Beautyway: The Poetry of N. Scott Momaday" (*The South Dakota Review*, Summer 1980) describes "New World" as offering "an integral vision of a sacred natural richness before the advent of the course of empire." In his widely reprinted memoir *The Way to Rainy Mountain* (1967), Momaday paid tribute to the history and the spirit of his Kiowa ancestors, and to members of his family who were his link with the "sacred songs" and "old stories" of his people. He said about his grandmother: "My grandmother had a reverence for the sun, a holy regard that now is all but gone out of mankind. There was a wariness in her, and an ancient awe. She was a Christian in her later years, but she had come a long way about, and she never forgot her birthright. . . . She was about seven when the last Kiowa sun dance was held in 1887 on the Washita River above Rainy Mountain Creek. The buffalo were gone. In order to consummate the ancient sacrifice—to impale the head of a buffalo bull upon the Tai-me tree—a delegation of old men journeyed into Texas, there to beg and barter for an animal from the Goodnight herd. She was ten when the Kiowas came together for the last time as a living sun-dance culture. They could find no buffalo; they had to hang an old hide from the sacred tree. Before the dance could begin, a company of soldiers rode out from Fort Sill under orders to disperse the tribe. Forbidden without cause the essential act of their faith, having seen the wild herds slaughtered and left to rot upon the ground, the Kiowas backed away forever from the tree."

DISCUSSION STARTERS

You may want to divide the class into four groups, each group focusing on one section of the poem. Ask each group to pull out and discuss images and phrases that cluster around the key word: *earth*, *dawn*, *noon*, or *dusk*. Then have the groups pool their findings.

THE RECEPTIVE READER

1. There is a light, airy feeling to the dawn? The eagles "hie and / hover" and "light / gathers / in pools." The grasses "shimmer / and shine." The high noon feels different. It is slower, hotter, more intense. The turtles smudge into the "warm / dark loam." The bees "hold / the swarm" and "meadows / recede" under the heat. All moisture is evaporating into a "pure / distance." Dusk frames the world. Everything slows down or "freezes" (the birds are fixed; the foxes stiffen) into silhouettes (gray foxes and blackbirds). The "white track / of the / full moon" seems cold and lifeless, although the rivers continue to flow.

2. The flow of the daily cycle will continue to another dawn? We get a sense of basic security—of belonging and rootedness—from the age-old pat-

terns that shape life on our planet? The poem leaves us with a renewed sense of wonder as we look at the daily cycle as if for the first time, like the first human beings on earth?

THE CREATIVE DIMENSION

As students divide up their day into stages, ask them to bring in specific images from their lives. For instance, what do they see when they awaken? A flickering streetlight, rustling curtains, screen-saver swirls on a computer, dew-drops on an herb patch?

John Donne, "A Lecture upon the Shadow" 452

PERSPECTIVES—JOHN DONNE AND THE WOMAN READER

Traditional love poetry before Donne, with its hyperbolical praise of the unattainable stereotypically beautiful lady, laid itself wide open to charges of insincerity and artificiality. Donne has been praised by women readers for his truth-seeking and his recognition of women as equal partners in the love relationship. In *The Common Reader 2* (Hogarth, 1986), Virginia Woolf said about Donne, "An obstinate interest in the nature of his own sensations . . . made him the most vigorous of satirists and the most passionate of lovers." Falling in love "meant, to Donne, a thousand things; it meant being tormented and disgusted, disillusioned and enraptured; but it also meant speaking the truth." His "determination to record not the likenesses which go to compose a rounded and seemly whole, but the inconsistencies that break up semblances, the power to make us feel the different emotions of love and hate and laughter at the same time"—these set Donne apart from other poets of his time. Donne's poems do not show a lady with a conventional register of simple predictable emotions; instead, "she was as various and complex as Donne himself."

Joan Bennet said in *Five Metaphysical Poets* (Cambridge UP, 1964), "Donne had enough experience to realize love's many moods, from the most brutally cynical to the most idealistic. . . . That he scorned, hated, lusted after, loved, worshipped, there can be little doubt for anyone who has read his poetry." He "could handle sensual love in all its aspects, from the bitterness of desire thwarted, to the fleeting paradise of desire fulfilled. But he was to do more than this. There are a number of poems which celebrate that rarer love in which the senses are but vehicles and mating is a 'marriage of true minds.' " Donne "never, even in his religious poetry, belittled physical love; no poet has paid more consistent homage to a complete human relationship."

Janet Mueller, in "Women among the Metaphysicals: A Case, Mostly of Being Donne For" (*Modern Philology* 1989), discusses women as subjects of metaphysical poetry and as readers of it. (Her article is reprinted in *Critical Essays on John Donne*, ed. Arthur F. Marotti, G. K.

Hall, 1994.) For Mueller, Donne is "the last English poet to sustain the force of the great, centuries-old Continental tradition of love lyrics that had celebrated femininity for offering the male poet a privileged access to ideality and divinity as well as a means of grounding his selfhood through intimacy with a person figured to and by this self as other." Donne outgoes almost every precedent "in focusing a number of his lyrics on fulfilled rather than thwarted love, as Lu Emily Pearson was quick to note early in this century's critical vogue of the metaphysicals." Thus, we are not prepared "to encounter the Donnean male speaker who discourses analytically in these lyrics on the joys of fully reciprocated sexual love to his female counterpart. The yield is an astonishingly exact articulation of what man in Western culture has tended to make of woman and of himself in relation to her." The onset of love "unsettles and even shatters a man by destroying all illusion that he can live in self- containment and self-sufficiency; instead, he discovers that he is contingent, vulnerable, without a center." On the evidence of Donne's poetry, "the Donnean male speaker can love a woman much more easily than he can God in a dominating role. Most interesting of all are the reflections offered on femininity. They complete what the love poetry leaves implicit or undeveloped in the Donnean representation of woman as they push to a vanishing point in her the distinction between the human and the divine."

DISCUSSION STARTERS

Everything in life casts a shadow (as long as there is a source of light). How many uses, references, and associations—literal or metaphorical—connected with shadows can your students think of?

THE RECEPTIVE READER

1. The "cares" were fears and uncertainties; the "disguises" were the pretenses that the lovers put on so that others wouldn't know they were in love. They are diligent in this, with love "still diligent lest others see." These fears disappear the way shadows disappear under their feet under the hot clarity of the noonday sun. The new shadows (fears) that appear in the afternoon are different from those experienced in the morning. The morning shadows stand for fears about others knowing of their love; the afternoon shadows stand for fears about the other's loyalty and sincerity. ("these which come behind / Will work upon ourselves, and blind our eyes.")

2. The last line of the poem says that the "first minute after noon is night." While the morning's fears are short-lived, the afternoon shadows would normally grow longer throughout the day. If the lovers allow these to exist and their love to "decay," their day will turn to night quickly? This perspective clips the usual cycle morning—noon—afternoon—night; it becomes morning—noon—night.

THE PERSONAL RESPONSE

One student responded to a discussion of this poem as follows:

I see this less as a statement about "all love fades" and more as an argument that the shadows created in the afternoon—i.e., doubts and fears about each other—make for a very short love life. This is Love's philosophy: "Love is a growing or full constant light, / And his first minute after noon is night." In other words love can exist with fears about whether others will find out (morning shadows) or without any fear (noon) but it can't exist when lovers doubt each other. (The long shadows of the afternoon might as well be night.) However, Donne says, "love's day is short, if love decay."—Donne isn't saying it must. Some readers feel he was saying that all love must end— but there's an IF here.

Poems for Further Study

Marge Piercy, "Simple Song" 519

DISCUSSION STARTERS

You may want to ask students to do a re-creation of this poem after hearing it read aloud. Sample re-creations:

Two trains roar toward each
other,
pass, and all is silent.
The grass by the tracks

Marriage:
two people, alike, different,
independent, dependent,
agreeing, disagreeing,
leaving the door at least ajar—
always leaving the door at least ajar.

Ask your students what they learn about the poem from responses such as this.

THE RECEPTIVE READER

1. The initial focus on the opposed feeling of meeting and departure gives the poem at the start a deceptive simplicity, reminiscent of a sad folk song about love. We start with simple alternatives, presented in closely parallel form: "how easy to be together / how hard . . . to be together."

2. Brothers ideally communicate and think alike. Ideally, a brother's reactions and preferences are familiar; we are comfortable with them. "Word matches word" as one brother gives responsive, empathetic answers to the other. The leather and skin images emphasize the thick, tough boundaries we

set up by having a "tough hide." We are caught up or imprisoned within our own skins. The open door invites communication; it beckons to us to enter into another's world of thought and feeling.

3. In pairs like "we cannot communicate / we can never agree," parallel sentence structure bonds parallel thoughts. However, in other pairs ("When we are going toward" / "When we are leaving") parallel structure lines up opposites for a more dramatic contrast.

4. The poem starts with a simple playing off of opposites. However, the third stanza opens up a more complex perspective, focusing on the paradox of being "sealed in" and needing to be "open."

THE CREATIVE DIMENSION

Look for student contributions that show a sensitivity to pattern—to overall movement, development, shape; to the play of opposites; to cumulative or climactic progression.

Arna Bontemps, "A Black Man Talks of Reaping" 520

DISCUSSION STARTERS

How does the poem deny or invert the biblical "As ye sow, so shall ye reap"? Remind students that the title of the poem is significant, especially with respect to the distinction between "my brother's sons" who are doing the reaping and "my children" who are doing the gleaning. (Jean-François Millet's famous painting *The Gleaners* gives us a strong image of the difference between gleaning and reaping.)

THE RECEPTIVE READER

1. Insistent repetition, or *reiteration*, helps set the solemn tone. Notice parallel sentence structure: "I have sown . . . I planted deep . . . I planted safe . . ."

2. The *turning point* occurs in the second part of the second stanza: "But for my reaping . . ."

3. The planting metaphor becomes the central organizing metaphor that would logically lead to the reward of the harvest, when human effort comes to fruition. But the insistent counterpoint of disappointed hope and thwarted effort leads to the powerful climactic conclusion—the garnering of "bitter fruit."

4. Planting and harvesting and family relationships are among the basic constants in human experience. The facts of exploitation are an ironic inversion of the biblical "As ye sow, so shall ye reap." (As ye sow, so shall

others reap.) The tone of the poem is the more bitter because the people denying the speaker the fruit of his labor are supposedly his "brothers" in the sight of God.

Gary Soto, "Oranges" 521

DISCUSSION STARTERS

Ask students to select a key phrase, crucial element, or striking contrast that stands out for them in this poem: "The first time . . ." in someone's life; the lack of money that prevents a twelve-year-old from being truly suave; the wisdom of the saleswoman who knew the worth of a nickel *plus* an orange; the contrast between the succulence of oranges and the deathly cold of December; the oranges the twelve-year-old brought intuitively because he had nothing else to bring; the connection between the special moment of holding hands for the first time and the chocolate that was "making a fire in my hands."

THE RECEPTIVE READER

1. Ask: What is exceptionally visual and apt or accurate about images like the following: "the candies / Tiered like bleachers," "weighted down / With two oranges in my pockets," "Fog hanging like old / Coats between the trees."

2. The poem is written as a story—with an exposition of the situation, a problem (the lack of money and the risk of deathly embarrassment), suspense (as we look at the nickel and the orange on the counter), a happy resolution of the problem (thanks to the understanding woman behind the counter), all leading to the climactic "fire in my hands."

3. A would-be sophisticate might have considered the events and the emotions in this poem too embarrassing, too kidlike, too trivial? Re understatement: Neither what the boy nor what the saleswoman thought is spelled out—the silent gestures speak for themselves. The human quality of the poem results in part from our being in on what went on in the minds of these two actors in the mini-drama?

James Laughlin, "Junk Mail" 522

DISCUSSION STARTERS

Ask your students to make up some unique, extremely important or extremely irrelevant, ambitious, judicious, or just plain astounding examples of junk mail?

THE RECEPTIVE READER

1. Most students will agree that this short poem takes a new look at the value of "junk mail." It *is* a communication from people who care enough to

pay the postage. And for some people, like the old man in the poem, junk mail is better than no mail at all?

2. The poem moves from the stereotypical view of old people being "out of it" ("drift / ing into irreality") to a view of them as human beings who, like the rest of us, have a need to communicate—they have a need for being wanted as an audience or listener. They are capable of exercising "care" and of feeling "delight." Sadly, junk mail (or for many, television?) is the only means left of filling these needs.

Robert Frost, "Fire and Ice" 523

DISCUSSION STARTERS

There is something grimly jesting in the poet's understatement, the mode of one of Frost's characteristic personas. Babette Deutsch notes that some of his poems "fulfill his own formula by beginning in delight and ending in wisdom. There are others that begin in anguish and come, it may be riding on a jest, to the same luminous end."

THE RECEPTIVE READER

1. Playing off these seemingly contradictory "ways to go," Frost's understated message is that either will "suffice." The poet ties "fire" to desire —whether love or lust or passion. Whatever it is, it has great destructive power: It overpowers reason; it breaks all restraint; it carries all before it. Hatred is the cold, stiff, and rigid "ice" that freezes all fellow feeling and humanity.

2. The rhyme scheme helps us focus on the great destructive elements: *fire/desire/fire*, *ice/twice/suffice*, and *hate/great*.

THE PERSONAL RESPONSE

What imaginative reenactment of the destructive power of desire or passion have your students encountered? *Anna Karenina*, *Madame Bovary*, *Othello*, *Romeo and Juliet*? Shakespeare wrote, "Love is a devil: there is no evil angel but Love." Sir Walter Raleigh wrote, "Hatreds are the cinders of affection," and Congreve observed, "Heaven has no rage like love to hatred turned."

Adrienne Rich, "Novella" 523

DISCUSSION STARTERS

The brief, stark, laconic statements in this poem may leave us with the bleak feeling that this is what happens between couples, is being reenacted in households all over the world even as we read this poem, can happen, does happen. This is just the way it is. There is no comment, no interpretation; there are no suggested remedies. Does this mean the poet is unfeeling—merely recording the grim facts without getting emotionally involved? Does the poet care?

THE RECEPTIVE READER

1. The vantage point is that of the outside observer who reports disinterestedly— seemingly impartially (but only seemingly). What goes on in the minds of the actors in this scene—the history of their quarrels and relationship—seems beyond our ken.

2. The poem is filled with succinct factual statements, two of which are in parentheses. Others include the initial line that sets up the scene, "Two people in a room, speaking harshly" and "It gets dark outside." The fact that the poet distances herself from both characters suggests a familiar reluctance to seem oversentimental, to do a sensational tear-jerking treatment. In the tradition of modern understatement, the poet lets her images largely speak for themselves. However, we are also hit by a few lines that carry powerful feeling—perhaps the stronger for not being part of effusive shows of emotion or a flood of complaints: "She has no blood left in her heart." He "hears sobbing on the stairs."

3. The fact that the two people have no names (and no faces) makes them seem a kind of Everyman and Everywoman, acting out an age-old pattern.

4. The movement in the last two lines from the separate minds in the household to the distant, cold stars that "come alight" at night reinforces the dominant feelings of coldness, separation, and distance? Just as stars are light-years apart, so are the man and woman?

Chapter 14 IMAGE The Open Eye 530

John Dewey (in *Art as Experience*) distinguished between the practical and the aesthetic person by saying that the practical person on seeing rain clouds goes back into the house to get an umbrella, whereas the aesthetically sensitive person walks on saying: "Look at those clouds!" How visual or visually oriented are your students? How attuned are they to the image making (or image capturing) of the poet? Ask them whether they ever pause to look at or to marvel at some sight that catches the eye. Ask them to write a *capsule sketch* of something memorable they saw or noticed, including striking details that will bring it to life for the reader.

First Reading: Peter Meinke, "Sunday at the Apple Market" 531

DISCUSSION STARTERS

Where do people in our society go so that they can feel "free and happy"— a flea market? a parade? a country fair? a blues festival? Ask students to jot down images—visual and other kinds—that would help others to share in their feelings at a favorite festive occasion.

THE RECEPTIVE READER

1. This poem is alive with sights and sounds and smells. It is loaded with *concrete* noninterchangeable, nonroutine images, from the weathering old cider presses and the old ladders tilting at empty branches to "the cool applechunks" people are rolling in their mouths and the "dogs barking at children in the appletrees."

2. The *keynote* is one of abundance? There is "apple-smell everywhere," with boxes and bins and bags and bushels of apples of every kind. They are "piled crazy" in "miraculous profusion."

THE PERSONAL RESPONSE

Apples, unlike packaged homogenized artificially flavored, additive-ridden foods, actually grow and ripen in the great outdoors and carry their own 100 percent natural smells and flavors. Buying them by the bushel or box gives the buyer a pleasing sense of money well spent and a pleasurable anticipation of a fall or winter where every so often we take time out to eat an apple?

Visual and Other Images

Nan Fry, "The Plum" 533

DISCUSSION STARTERS

In a journal entry or in a three-minute or five-minute writing in class, what kind of tribute would students pen to their favorite kind of fruit (or vegetable)?

THE RECEPTIVE READER

1. The plum's looks, color, and taste are brought to life with phrases such as "Dark globe," "your swelling, / your purple shading to rose," "the color of garnets, rubies, wounds," and "It is bitter just under the skin." A striking extended metaphor occurs immediately: "Dark globe that fits easily into the palm, / your skin is speckled with pale galaxies, / an endless scattering." The plum as earth expands until the plum's skin is seen as space, with its infinite variety of stars. The taste of the plum is "all the world's waters and all its sweetness / rolled into fruit that explodes / on the tongue." The poet is a careful observer and recorder of sense data: what she sees and tastes are recorded in precise and inventive detail.

2. When the poet looks at the plum's skin and sees the universe, she thinks of the vast number of places where The Fall could be occurring: "Everywhere Adam and Eve are leaving / the Garden." Then the Adam and Eve image is read into the everyday actions on this planet: "You are the fruit we pluck / and eat." To eat a plum requires no tempting serpent; the fruit itself is lure enough: "We need no serpent to urge us, / drawn as we are to your swelling, / your purple shading to rose, your skin / that yields to the touch, to the teeth." Fry's ruminations on the fall of Adam and Eve have shrunk from the unimaginable number of places in the universe where expulsion from the Garden could be occurring to the palm-sized, no-serpent-required temptation of the plum itself.

William Stafford, "At the Bomb Testing Site" 533

DISCUSSION STARTERS

Whatever the momentous questions or apocalyptic visions ultimately suggested by this poem, the lizard is first of all a live, panting lizard. How alert is your students' visual imagination? Ask students what they have noticed about lizards, either from direct observation or from television nature programs. Jot their observations on the board. Sooner or later someone will note that the front legs of lizards are held in such a way (with the "elbows" jutting out at the sides) that they seem to be doing push-ups, giving the impression of tenseness, struggle. Lizards have strangely human yet at the same time alien-looking "hands"—so that they can seem to be bracing themselves, holding on. Lizards "pant," as if in state of tense apprehension.

THE RECEPTIVE READER

1. Noon is the time when the sun is at its highest point—at "high noon" morning drowsiness has worn off and afternoon sluggishness has not yet set in. Now is the time for major confrontations—with the full glare of the sun clearing away any shadows that might have served as disguises for the truth? Perhaps, with the nuclear technology tested at the testing site, our civilization has also reached its "high noon," making us wonder whether human life on this planet will make it past its apparent high point—or exterminate itself. A curve in the road should alert us to the unexpected—something might suddenly come around the bend, or we might happen upon danger as we come around the bend. Literally, creatures like the lizard might be the "little selves." Figuratively, we as human beings, with all our grandiose plans and self-glorification, will be dwarfed by the far-off apocalyptic event.

2. Some possibilities: Our civilization is on the brink of wiping out millions of years of evolution? Or, when we are through self-destructing, only creatures like the lizard may survive?

3. Some students may be repelled by the lizard. The lizard may seem too snakelike and alien. If so, they can perhaps come up with another creature toward which they feel more empathy. However, the lizard is one of the oldest creatures on earth, dramatizing for us our human capacity for wantonly undoing what has taken millions and millions of years to evolve. We are endangering not merely our own species but life on this planet.

Mary Oliver, "The Black Snake" 534

DISCUSSION STARTERS

Re-creations (sometimes written in a few minutes) are a way students can get *inside* a poem—relating to some central image, pattern, or theme. What did the student author of the following response relate to most strongly in the poem?

> The snake, propelled by life,
> meets death on the road.
> Death: sudden, heavy, certain.
> Life: light, energy, propelling
> us all toward
> the end of the
> road.

THE RECEPTIVE READER

1. The living snake was "coiling and flowing forward." This same movement is seen as a "flash" in the opening lines as the snake meets death. Afterwards, he lies "looped and useless / as an old bicycle tire." The narrator in the poem carries the dead snake off the side of the road. Through her eyes,

we see that the snake is "gleaming as a braided whip . . . beautiful and quiet." Through her hands, we can sense the "cool" feel of the dead reptilian body.

2. Most people, like the speaker as she drives away, know about death in the rational, "thinking," and frightening sense: "its suddenness, / its terrible weight, its certain coming." However, at a level beyond reason, in her "bones," the speaker shares the elementary life-sustaining belief in our being special and exempt that burns fiercely in us like a "brighter fire."

3. A cell can be visualized as a miniature solar system, with its nucleus as its vital center, similar to the light-giving sun that is the source of all vital energy?

THE PERSONAL RESPONSE

In our culture, reptilian creatures tend to be seen as an extreme of what is alien, nonhuman in life. And in the Judeo-Christian tradition, the devil takes a reptilian form in the garden of Eden, becoming a symbol of sin and guile. Eastern and other cultures, however, view the reptile differently, seeing the snake, particularly, as the symbol of eternity. Representations of snakes with their tails in their mouths symbolize life, with the continuity of no beginning. For both poets, the reptiles seem archetypal, representative of life on this planet—which dates back far beyond our puny human history?

Theodore Roethke, "My Papa's Waltz" 536

PERSPECTIVES—ROETHKE ON THE RECEPTIVE READER

In *On the Poet and His Craft* (U of Washington, 1965), Theodore Roethke talked about the ideal receptive attitude for the reading of poetry, including the willingness to let the poem bring the reader's emotions into play. He said, "A student of mine once wrote in an examination: 'I greet a poem, now, like a living person: with curiosity and respect.' I suggest that if this attitude became habitual with the ordinary reader . . . there would be little trouble understanding most modern poetry. For curiosity brings a certain heightening of the attention, an extra awareness of the senses, particularly the eye and ear, an expectancy; and 'respect' means, as I take it, that the work will not be cast aside with irritation, or spurned with fear or contempt." For such a reader, the poet will be someone "who has felt and thought deeply and intensely, or seen something freshly, and who may be lucky enough, on occasion, to create a complete reality in a single poem. . . . Most important of all, such a reader will not be afraid of a reality that is slightly different from his own: he will be willing to step into another world, even if at times it brings him close to the abyss. He will not be afraid of feeling—and this in spite of the deep-rooted fear of emotion existing today, particularly among the half-alive, for whom emotion, even when incorporated into form, becomes a danger, a madness." Poetry is written for the whole person; "it sometimes scares those who want to hide from the terrors of existence, from themselves."

DISCUSSION STARTERS

Critics have discussed the father-son relationship as a central theme in Roethke's poetry. They have talked about the "mixture of love and fear" or the "complexity" and "duality" of the son's relation to the father. One critic said that there is a "sense of awesome, godlike power" in many accounts of the father-son relationship. Is the authoritarian, "godlike" father a thing of the past?

THE RECEPTIVE READER

1. The poem makes the reader visualize a kitchen, with pots and pans sliding from their shelf as the young boy, who "hung on like death," and his father "waltz" around the room. The boy's mother is standing on the sidelines frowning disapprovingly at the spectacle (with a "countenance" that, even though she might have felt she should try, "could not unfrown itself"). The father, as they dance, beats time to the music on the boy's head, with dirt-caked hands. However, we do not merely *see* the scene, but share in rough physical sensations: the hanging on and clinging of the dizzied boy; the wrist being grabbed by the father's rough, battered workingman's hand; the ear scraped by the belt buckle. And the whole scene is permeated by the *smell* of whiskey on the father's breath.

2. There is a sense of being overpowered, of being carried away, holding on for dear life. We are reminded how small the boy is—his ears at the level of the father's belt?

THE RANGE OF INTERPRETATION

In his biography of Roethke, *The Glass House* (1968), Alan Seager quotes from a memoir Roethke wrote after his father's death. In the memoir (written in the third person) an incident similar to that in "My Papa's Waltz" occurs: "Sometimes he dreamed about Papa. Once it seemed Papa came in and danced around with him. John put his feet on top of Papa's and they'd waltz. Hei-dee-dei-dei. Rump-tee-tump. Only babies expected dreams to come true." Some students may find that the father seems alcoholic, out of control—the mother passive and weak. Is this a case of child abuse? Others may view this as a happy poem, a bit of horseplay after a long week's work (the father's hands are dirty). Finally, the key to the poem may be the boy's *mixed* emotions: fear mingling with wild excitement, love mingling with revulsion?

Images and Feelings

Ursula K. Le Guin, "The Old Falling Down" 537

DISCUSSION STARTERS

Childhood memories, implies Le Guin, are often terrifying. Ask students to share a childhood experience that made a big impact. Which childhood memories were predominant—the scary or the joyful?

THE RECEPTIVE READER

1. Is the dominant emotion one of fear and apprehension? Or is it the sense of being lost, of being cut off from what is dear and comforting? As in many a fear dream, the dreamer is in urgent search of a place that once meant safety and protection (the "high room" upstairs that the speaker lived in as a child), but there is no way to get there. The stairs have disappeared, leaving the speaker clambering precariously in a perilous void—only to find when finally reaching the room that everything that made it cozy and welcoming (the bed, the chair) has vanished. There is no way to go back to the warm, protected world of childhood?

2. Clambering is a form of climbing with difficulty and perhaps danger; the word suggests hectic activity?

3. Each of the divided words emphasizes direction in a poem that ultimately is about the loss of direction, about a sense of being lost. The first divided word at the end of a line is the word *down-/stairs*. This gives readers the sense of dropping, as though the footing fell out from beneath them or there was a deeper dropoff than expected before the foot found the first stair. The next divided word (in the very next line) is *out-/side*, which leaves us outside the house proper under the stars. The next and final divided word is *up-/stairs*. The break helps suggest that this is not going to be a simple routine going upstairs—this is going to be a struggle.

THE CREATIVE DIMENSION

Many people have dreamed of being in an uncontrollable "free-fall" down a cliff, or off a building, or into some dark unknown. Others have recurrent dreams about the same enigmatic incident. From obscurest antiquity to Freudian psychiatry, the "interpretation of dreams" has been the task of soothsayers and analysts of every kind?

Robert Hayden, "Those Winter Sundays" 538

DISCUSSION STARTERS

Hallmark greeting cards tend to sound syrupy because they do not acknowledge perturbing mixed emotions. You may want to ask students to write down spontaneously their honest and perhaps contradictory feelings about a parent or relative. Here is an example:

My father is unpredictable. He is happy and angry, both. He drives me crazy. He breaks lightbulbs because I don't turn them off. It is an unnatural action, but an action maybe out of love, an action to teach me to improve and change my outlook to try harder. He sits up at night and smokes. When I get up to get a drink, I get scared because he sits there like a vulture waiting to prey on my bad decisions.

THE RECEPTIVE READER

1. Although the poem describes the Sunday morning scene in a fairly factual, low-key fashion, many details from the beginning might steer the reader's sympathy toward the father: his cracked hands are aching from a week of labor in the cold; he is getting up early when others still rest; laboring in the "blueblack cold," he makes the house hospitable for the family; he polishes the shoes for a son who speaks to him only "indifferently," wary of the quarrels that are "chronic" in the house. But at the same time, could the lack of communication in the house be the fault of the "austere" father's inability to put a caring attitude into words?

2. We may expect love to be talky, overtly emotional. But in the poem, the services of a caring father are performed wordlessly and alone, as if holding aloof, in the cold and dark of a Sunday morning. (It is the "chronic angers" in a family such as this that tend to find expression in overt quarreling and hateful words?)

3. The repetition of "What did I know" accentuates the sense of regret that underlies the poem as a whole.

THE CREATIVE DIMENSION

Why is the word *regret* often associated with the idea of futility, as in "futile regrets"? What is the difference between *regret* and *remorse?*

William Stafford, "One Home" 539

DISCUSSION STARTERS

You may want to ask students to complete the opening line "Mine was a __________ home." Ask them to follow up with two or three striking images that make a setting and mentality or dominant feeling real for the reader.

THE RECEPTIVE READER

1. "One Home" recalls the Midwest land of the poet's childhood with great affection: it "would hold us up"—with its "wind," its "buffalo grass," its storms for children to run toward. People live close to the open spaces, with

the strong summer sun "like a blade." The speaker insists "you can keep your world." Although the atmosphere is one of friendship and small-town closeness, these people wear "plain black hats"—they are earnestly religious people living by their code, being friendly toward people whose "cut of a thought" they liked, singing hymns, riding herd on their children's thoughts. The people in this town sang their hymns under roofs "near God"—with no grand churches to come between them and their maker.

2. Here are some possible waystations in the development of the poem: (stanza 1) the plainness of manner and simple piety of the Midwestern tradition; (stanza 2) a simple unpretentious lifestyle with homemade supplies in the prairie setting; (stanza 3) the still remembered dangers of what was until fairly recently untamed open country; (stanza 4) friendliness—without gushiness—toward other people; (stanza 5) closeness to the land with its hot sun and wild storms.

3. The idea of plainness and of conformity to a plain traditional code—shutting out the confusions, insecurities, or frustrations of what the poet calls "your world"—becomes the keynote of the poem?

4. There is a simple rhyme scheme (*aba*) in stanzas 2 and 3. But the other stanzas do without rhyme—as if the poet were trying to keep the poem from sounding too arty or too pat. The line that appears to have the most consistent five-beat rhythm is the last: "WherEVER we LOOKed the LAND would HOLD us UP." The steady, even rhythm well mirrors the sense of security and predictability that the line expresses?

Lorna Dee Cervantes, "Freeway 280" 540

PERSPECTIVES—BILINGUAL POET: THE POLITICS OF LANGUAGE

In a postcolonial or postimperialist setting, the writer's choice of language may be a conscious political act or act of cultural commitment and identification. (In Brian Friel's play *Translations*, the work of British soldiers and surveyors in the Irish countryside, preparing maps where English or Anglicized place names replace traditional Gaelic names, is an act of cultural imperialism. In the postcolonial setting, new names like Zimbabwe for Rhodesia are an affirmation of political and cultural independence.) As Marian Arkin and Barbara Shollar say in the introduction to the *Longman Anthology of World Literature by Women* (1989), the "cultural dominance" of a language—like English and French in many ex-colonial countries—reflects a history of "economic and social domination." Thus the decision not to write in English, or French, or Russian, or Japanese is a "strategy of decolonization." Similarly, in a country with an "official language," using "a dialect or regional language is part of an effort to preserve a particular character, history, and culture." On the other hand, writers may opt to continue to write in one of the "semi-universal" languages that make communication possible in a country like India (perhaps seven hundred languages, not counting dialects). Only this way could writers "reach the audiences . . . who most need to hear their messages." As Arkin and Shollar say, some bilingual or multilingual authors (like Cervantes in this poem?) write "on the linguistic border," using "a macaronic language that combines the different languages of their world like so many strands of spaghetti." Do their texts then "point to differences in what can be said or is said in different languages"?

DISCUSSION STARTERS

How many of your students use English as a second (or third) language? How many grew up in a family where some of the members spoke another language? What names, what words or phrases, came into their own way of talking from different linguistic and cultural roots?

THE RECEPTIVE READER

1. The "raised scar" is an overpass, or raised portion, of Freeway 280 that cuts through what was once an organic, living landscape of small homes and gardens. The "fake windsounds" are the swooshing and whistling of the speeding cars. The freeway seems like a violation of what was once a living community.

2. The poet says, "Once, I wanted out, wanted the rigid lanes / to take me to a place without sun, / without the smell of tomatoes burning / on swing shift in the greasy summer air." As a teenager, she rebelled against her home in a neighborhood dried out by the unrelenting California sun and invaded by the rancid, burnt smell of tomato refuse from the adjoining canneries—which offered some of the few jobs available to her people.

3. At this time in her life, the poet wants to return to her roots. Her descriptions of the place are wistful, nostalgic, affirmative. Even though the houses are gone, the grasses are new and the land yields an abundance of fruits and vegetable greens from the abandoned orchards and herb gardens. The wild mustard is also there, "remembering" a time when this particular place was a valley of orchards and farmland rather than a high-tech freeway mecca.

4. The poet shifts to Spanish naturally when she names the small houses, the trees in the orchards, and the vegetables in the vegetable plots that she remembers from her childhood. Giving them English names might make her feel like an outsider, someone denying her own roots. She calls the old women "viejitas" because the word carries memories and affections that might not translate to her acquired second language. The last example of

code-switching, calling the setting "campos extranos"—strange fields, reinforces the sense of a beckoning heritage that now seems strange in the urbanized (and Anglicized) landscape.

THE PERSONAL RESPONSE

The poet looks for her roots: the part of herself she is looking for is either "like a corpse" or "a loose seed." That she identifies more with the "loose seed" than with a "corpse" is suggested by the growth of new grasses and wild mustard, the "old gardens" coming back "stronger than they were." The grasses sprout, the wild mustard is remembering and blooming again, and the vegetables and trees are bearing enough fruit to feed the "viejitas." The poet's most life-affirming statement is "I scramble over the wire fence / that would have kept me out." Now she wants in, she wants to be connected to the heritage she once tried to escape.

THE CREATIVE DIMENSION

Although there is much sentimental idealizing of an idyllic childhood world, other writers graphically describe the fears, insecurities, and pain of less than ideal childhood experiences.

Juxtapositions: Writing to Commemorate

Alberto Rios, "The Vietnam Wall" 541

DISCUSSION STARTERS

Do we need war memorials? What war memorials have your students seen? How do they feel about them?

THE RECEPTIVE READER

1. Specific details that help to re-create the poet's walk past the monument begin with an observation of how the wall rises slowly from the ground: "The walk is slow at first / Easy, a little black marble wall / Of a dollhouse." Immediately comes the first name—the first of over 58,000—representing the earliest casualty. After this first name, the number of names inexorably builds up: "One name. And then more / Names, long lines, lines of names until / They are the shape of the U.N. Building / Taller than I am."

2. In the opening stanza, the poet uses a most mundane metaphorical object—an onion—to convey the wall's powerful emotional effect. He says the wall works like "magic" on its observers: "The magic, / The way like cutting onions / It brings water out of nowhere." Despite the number of household remedies, there seems to be no way to cut an onion without tears, and, furthermore, the tears are not painless or benign drops of water. Tears caused by onions are bitter, one's eyes burn, and there is no catharsis as they fall.

3. The speaker expected to see the usual sort of war memorial, with an alphabetical list of names, and with a bunch of bored and uninterested children capering around. Instead, he is struck immediately by the different nature of the Vietnam War Memorial. The monument begins "Invisible from one side, a scar / Into the skin of the ground." "And everything I expect has been taken away, like that, quick," the speaker says: "The names are not alphabetized. / They are in the order of dying, / An alphabet of—somewhere—screaming." A chronological list of anguish conveys the horror of the names far more effectively than could a straightforward alphabetical listing. "Little kids do not make the same noise / Here," the poet notices. "Junior high school boys don't run / Or hold each other in headlocks." This somber response is not the result of rules posted somewhere: "No rules, something just persists / Like pinching on St. Patrick's Day / Every year for no green. / No one knows why."

4. The poet uses a matter-of-fact style when he talks about such powerful emotions because he knows such a style is effective on more than one level. Words do not exist in this language or any other that can convey the anguish of war. A matter-of-fact style underscores the huge gap between the thing described and the description itself. The words do not compete with the experience described; they are seemingly innocuous, inconspicuous, and mundane.

5. The poet has conjured up a number of powerful images that are easily remembered. Among them are the onion metaphor ("It brings water out of nowhere"), the rise of the wall from dollhouse size to the size of the United Nations Building, the chronological list ("An alphabet of—somewhere—screaming"), and the strangely subdued young people.

Jeffrey Harrison, "Reflections on the Vietnam War Memorial" 543

DISCUSSION STARTERS

Is one of these two poems more emotional, less detached than the other?

THE RECEPTIVE READER

1. At the beginning of the poem, the wall is almost transparent. "You can see them milling around in there," the poet says, "screened in by their own names." And from inside the wall, the dead are "looking at us in the same / vague and serious way we look at them." The wall calls to mind an "underground house" with "a roof of grass." The wall is the "back porch of the dead." It is as if the poet is trying to assume a detached, everyday voice that will carry him through the emotions the wall inspires. However, at the last, he is unable to continue to mask his grief. The wall is again solid, unrevealing, and cold to the touch: "And yet we feel it as a wall / and realize the dead are all / just names now, the separation final."

2. The first mention of names calls to mind the unusual image of the names screening in the milling crowd of the dead. This suggests that the memory of the dead is obscured by their being reduced to a name carved upon a black wall. If it were not for the names on the wall, perhaps these dead could rest in peace without being constantly reminded of the grief their deaths cause in their survivors. By the second mention of names, the grim image caused by the first is dispersed as the speaker compares the name list to a telephone book. The speaker ironically comments that this name list "seems to claim / some contact can be made / through the simple act of finding a name." At the end, though, the speaker finally acknowledges what the carved names represent. The carved names are not screening in the dead, and they are not merely a representation of the names in the location book. The carved names are a terribly long list of young people who have been reduced to names on a wall.

Poetry and Paraphrase

Edna St. Vincent Millay, "Childhood Is the Kingdom Where Nobody Dies" 544

DISCUSSION STARTERS

When does childhood end? Is it true that it is not a matter of reaching a "certain age"? When do we put away "childish things"?

THE RECEPTIVE READER

The relatives become real because of the poet's use of small but authentic *details*: They give small bits of candy in a "pink-and-green striped bag, or a jack-knife" to the child. The cats are not anonymous dead pets but real creatures that "die on the floor and lash their tails." Grimmer still is the picture of the little girl not being able to fit the stiff cat's body into a shoebox: "She won't curl up now: / So you find a bigger box." But the griefs and losses of childhood, although they alert us to the reality of death, are only a prelude to the loss of people who really "matter." The fourth stanza moves beyond any routine or generalized expressions of grief as the speaker wakes up at night screaming, "Oh, God!" with knuckles in her mouth. She hears the voices of dead relatives and friends, trying in vain to make them respond as she offers them the tea that "was such a comfort" or "the last jar of raspberries" that they would have found tempting when alive. Much as she wants to shake them and yell at them, they "slide back into their chairs." "Your tea is cold now. / You drink it standing up, / And leave the house."

THE PERSONAL RESPONSE

Are there different styles of grieving and of mourning? Are some more subdued than others? Are we today more callous or our feelings more blunted? Has death become commonplace in the society around us?

Poems for Further Study

Dana Gioia, "California Hills in August" 546

DISCUSSION STARTERS

We are often told that America is becoming more and more homogenized, with the same MacDonalds and shopping malls and domed-in stadiums everywhere. Ask your students: Can you pinpoint one striking feature that makes your city or state or region different from others?

THE RECEPTIVE READER

1. The poet "is talking back" to the outsider or casual visitor who does not appreciate the "gentleness" of a landscape beloved by those who have grown up there and know it well. (When we are on the defensive, we may wax eloquent in defense of what we love?) The poem turns the tables on the uncomprehending visitor parched by the sun, scorning "the meagreness of summer."

2. There are many, many concrete details that the poet uses to make real this "landscape short of rain": brittle dried-out weeds cracking in the dust underfoot, "dry / twisted shapes of black elm," scrub oak, chaparral, clinging thistle, sparse brown bushes, stillness of noon, and the hungry hawk "suspended / in the blinding sunlit blue." Some students may feel surprised when the turning point is reached and they find themselves in a "gentle" place; others will have sensed the irony at the expense of the Easterner to whom the glorious golden poppies are "just a weed" and who is unable to understand that the dry shrubs and trees are alive and will turn green again with the coming of the winter rains.

3. The land is "short of rain." It is "drained of green." The poem ends with "the wish for water." Many of the images seem to center on drought-like conditions—dryness. In the very first stanza, we find heat, dust, and brittle weeds underfoot, trees and shrubs that seem dead, causing the speaker to wish for more shade. (The thistle, foxtail, and golden poppy, like the trees and shrubs, are all natural California plants—drought-resistant.)

4. How many of your students expect summers to be green and lush, with drenching rains or thunderstorms? How many expect summer to be dry, parched, hot?

FOLLOW-UP—THE CREATIVE DIMENSION

Students may feel defensive about loving a megalopolis like New York or Chicago, about their affection for a small backwater town, or about their being attached to the much-maligned sprawling city of many freeways that is Los Angeles. You may want to stage dialogues in which detractors and defenders present their contrasting visions of such a place.

John Keats, "To Autumn" 547

PERSPECTIVES—IMAGERY IN KEATS' "TO AUTUMN"

John Keats remained a critical favorite even when the New Critical vogue of the fifties and sixties shifted attention from the lush rhythms and overt emotions of the romantic poets to the complexities and ironies of the metaphysical John Donne and his seventeenth-century contemporaries. Critics have reveled in the rich tactile, visual, and auditory imagery of "To Autumn," differing somewhat in the weight they give to the melancholy overtones of the autumnal scene. Douglas Bush, in *John Keats* (Macmillan, 1966), said, "The first two stanzas build up, or appear to build up, a wholly happy picture of summery warmth and bursting ripeness in everything, of vines and trees and fruits and nuts and bees fulfilling their creative destiny." The "personified spirit of autumn becomes a mythic figure, a kind of immortal; although reaping and cider-making are not lifted out of the practical world, they are invested with the dignity and aura of seasonal rites. Yet even in these stanzas there is the overshadowing fact of impermanence. The summer has done its work and is departing; and if autumn comes, winter cannot be far behind. Precise hints are few—the bees 'think warm days will never cease,' the cider reaches its 'last oozings'—but we cannot escape the melancholy implications of exuberant ripeness." In the last stanza, "every item carries an elegiac note. The day is dying and gnats and lambs and crickets and birds all seem to be aware of approaching darkness."

For T. R. Barnes, in *English Verse* (Cambridge UP, 1967), "Autumn brings the fruition of the year, and its death . . . though sad, is inevitable, and a necessary part of the cycle of life. . . . A rich and calm resignation imposes the acceptance of nature's, of life's rhythm." Keats "spreads Autumn's riches in effortless profusion. . . . 'Maturing' and 'ripeness' work together, and lead to the hint of sadness, of mutability, in the bees thinking warm days will never cease, and yet, of course, they will. Ripeness is a moment of perfection, which must, in the nature of things, pass; a climax after which there can only be a decline: yet this ripeness, this perfection, sustains life." The god, or goddesses, "at once mysterious and homely, share in or contemplate the season's tasks. The modern reader must remind himself that threshing with flails, reaping with scythes and sickles, gleaners, and handworked cider-presses were all common country sights." There may be no bird song, "but we are not to regret this because autumn has a music of its own, which is sad but not despairing because autumn is in the harmony of things. . . . The verse rises and falls mournfully with the cloud of gnats, but the lambs bleat loud. They may no longer 'bound as to the tablor's sound' and they are protesting because they have been separated from the ewes, but they will live on; they symbolize life's continuity, like the robin who whistles cheerfully through the winter and the migrating swallows who will return from the 'warm south.' "

DISCUSSION STARTERS

Do your students think of nature as lush and sensuous? Ask them, "Is this poem primarily happy?" Most may say yes, yet some may note wordings that point to a pensive autumnal sadness: the bees innocently "think warm days will never cease"; Autumn watches the last "oozings" from the cider press; the day is "soft-dying"; the small gnats mourn "in a wailful choir"; "gathering swallows twitter." The gathering swallows make us think of their impending migration, a sure sign of the coming winter, even though winter is nowhere mentioned in this pensive, golden moment of praise.

THE RECEPTIVE READER

1. Perhaps older students remembering the rural past can help explain to city dwellers or suburbanites such harvest images as the threshing of the grain in a granary; the gleaner carrying collected leftover grains in a basket on her head; the stubble left in the harvested fields, to be turned by the plow in preparation for the next cycle of seedtime and harvest.

2. "Mellow fruitfulness" and the "maturing sun" are phrases that from the beginning set the prevailing mood of a richly blessed season that conspires to "load and bless" the vines with grapes, causes the trees to bend and sag under the weight of apples, makes the hazelnuts plump around their sweet kernels, and causes the gourds to swell, while the bees in their hives fill the cells brimming over with honey. Stanza 3 focuses on *sound* images: the "wailful choir" of gnats, the bleating of the lambs, the hedge crickets' song, the redbreast's whistling, and, finally, the swallows' twittering.

3. Swallows are migratory birds, so it is probably no coincidence that Keats mentions them in the last line. Their gathering for their flight to a warmer climate is a harbinger of approaching winter?

THE PERSONAL RESPONSE

After a long antiromantic or postromantic interval of preoccupation with a Darwinian view of nature as "red in tooth and claw," is the idealization of nature as the source of physical and mental health again very much part of our cultural milieu? Like the romantics, do we again look to nature as a source of renewal and spiritual rebirth?

T. S. Eliot, "Preludes" 548

PERSPECTIVES—T. S. ELIOT: PUBLIC PERSONA AND PRIVATE PERSON

T. S. Eliot came "A Long Way from St. Louis"—the title of a *Time* piece by Paul Gray (September 26, 1988)—to become one of the most influential literary figures of the modern period. Eliot "not only wrote *The Waste Land*, the single most influential poem in English of the 20th century." He also produced poetry, criticism, and plays that "permanently rearranged the cultural landscapes of his native and adopted lands." Gray comments on the poet's continuing influence and surprising vitality: "By many standards he should have been old news by now. He professed conservatism, elitism and sectarian Christianity at a time when the fashionable tides were running against all three."

As Gray had said in an earlier *Time* article (December 3, 1984), the basic biographical facts about the Midwesterner who became part of the conservative Anglican establishment are well known: Born in St. Louis, offspring of a prominent American family, he studied English literature at Harvard and then "pursued, with diminishing zeal, a Ph.D. in philosophy. He settled in London and worked in a bank to support himself and his English wife. . . . He took up British citizenship and abandoned the Unitarianism of his parents to become a convert to the Anglican Church. He spent the last four decades of his life more or less in the public eye, a polite, carefully tailored lecturer ministering to the declining health of Western culture." His plays, including *Murder in the Cathedral*, *The Cocktail Party*, and *The Confidential Clerk*, gained him increasing stature, as did his Nobel Prize for Literature in 1948. In 1956, fourteen thousand people heard him speak in Minneapolis on "The Frontiers of Criticism."

For many years, exploration of Eliot's vulnerabilities—his anti-Semitism, his acquired Oxford accent, his distancing himself from his roots—was pretty much taboo within the American literary establishment. Perhaps inevitably, however, probing and irreverent current literary biography began to catch up with the poet-sage's public image. Gray says, "Behind the lectures and public appearances of the latter decades—the tall, stooped figure in the three-piece suits, issuing pronouncements—was concealed a soul in torment, trying to purge itself of sin and of the world that lavished so much praise on what he considered his unworthiness before God." *The Waste Land* "is not simply an impersonal, jazz-age jeremiad. It is also a nerve racking portrait of Eliot's emotional disintegration during his 20s; his emigration, against his family's wishes, from the U.S. to England and, once there, his disastrous marriage to Vivien Haigh-Wood, a vivacious but increasingly unstable partner whom Virginia Woolf once described as a 'bag of ferrets' around Eliot's neck. To read *The Waste Land*'s overwhelming catalog of cultural decay is also to eavesdrop on a typical evening with Mr. and Mrs. Eliot. The wife is overheard: 'My nerves are bad tonight. Yes, bad. Stay with me. / Speak to me. Why do you never speak. Speak.' "

DISCUSSION STARTERS

A prelude is a musical term for a piece that precedes a more important movement; thus, a prelude suggests the preliminaries before any major action. The preludes in this poem are a series of observations of a grimy winter evening, leading to a similar set of observations of the next morning, not glorious and rejuvenating, but sad and dingy. You may want to ask: To what is this poem a prelude? "The conscience of a blackened street" is "Impatient to assume the world." But nothing of the kind happens in this poem? (Is this the kind of T. S. Eliot poem that is all preamble and no action—suggesting the paralysis of will of the alienated, disoriented modern individual?)

THE RECEPTIVE READER

1. Students are likely to agree that most of Eliot's images move in the opposite direction of the conventionally beautiful. Labels like *burn-out*, *grimy*, *withered*, and *broken* occur in the first few lines. Stale beer smells, muddy feet, and dingy shades provide a setting for people whose souls are made up of a "thousand sordid images." The sparrows aren't in the trees; they're "in the gutters." The showers don't cleanse; they "beat." The newspapers don't inform; they're strewn in vacant lots. Are your students simply repelled by these images, or can they sense the strange fascination they had for the poet? One student noted the paradox of beauty in ugliness, writing: "The images of the 'Preludes' are sometimes hard to bear, but their striking realism and Eliot's love of language make even the most sordid images seem gorgeous: 'His soul stretched tight across the skies / That fade behind a city block / Or trampled by insistent feet.' "

2. Let students explore and try to interpret the fragmentary clues to the role the three people play in the poem. The "you" in the poem (a woman taking out the papers that she uses at night to curl her hair?) seems to be caught up in the sordid images that constitute her soul. In a characteristic gesture, she can be expected to wipe her hand across her mouth, and laugh. Another person, a man, finds himself "trampled by insistent feet" rushing through the city at busy hours? The "I" speaking in the poem is "moved by fancies that are curled / Around these images, and cling." But the speaker's reaction is unexpected and paradoxical? The sordid images that dominate the poem suggest to him the "notion of some infinitely gentle / Infinitely suffering thing." Is our reaction to sordid ordinary people in a sordid ordinary setting perhaps the true test of our ability to feel sympathy and tenderness for others?

THE CREATIVE DIMENSION

As a prelude to this assignment, you may want to ask students to wander through the city or town with pad and pencil, acting as the "camera eye," jotting down characteristic, provocative, or intriguing sights and sounds.

Ann Darr, "Advice I Wish Someone Had Given Me" 550

DISCUSSION STARTERS

Ask students if they ever respond negatively or defensively to advice. Advice is often given in self-righteous tones. It often sounds old-fashioned; it is often in the imperative, which seems to order people around: "Do this"; "don't do that." Is the imaginary advice given in this poem different? Does it seem particularly modern or up-to-date? How do your students react to it?

THE RECEPTIVE READER

1. It would be a protection against not only hints and innuendos but also against outright hurtful attacks if we could "thicken our skins." By putting truth and people in "their right- / ful angle in the sun," we would make sure they are seen in the right light—neither obscured by failing light nor overexposed to a glare. However, we should also face the shadows in our lives.

2. The "heel marks on your head," ugly to see and painful to feel, would result from being stomped on or harshly abused; they would be a result of letting someone "walk all over you"? Advisers, counselors, or psychiatrists might be said to be "scraping" layers of alleged disguises or rationalizations from our souls in order to lay bare our real selves. The image makes their attentions seem like a barbaric, presumptuous, and intrusive procedure? At the same time, we would smart, feel raw?

3. Although we should "care" about other people, we should "take care" to do so with due caution—not losing our heads, not exposing ourselves to exploitation or to dependency? Have your students had experience with over-caring, with caring too much, with not knowing when to let go?

4. *Head* and *bed* in lines 3 and 5 serve as occasional rhymes that do not lock the poet or the reader into a rigid pattern. *Light* and *right- / ful* serve to highlight the light metaphor at the center of the poem. At the same time, the break in the second word helps continue the syncopating counterrhythm started by the echoing of the initial *be* at the end of the first line ("*Be* strange if it is necessary, *be*").

Chapter 15 METAPHOR Making Connections 554

Metaphor is at the heart of the poet's art. Metaphor requires the gift of seeing similarity in dissimilarity. It is a way of making fresh connections, of seeing unexpected relationships. It is the antidote to the blinkered literal-mindedness that stifles our imagination. It has a way of illuminating what was opaque or obscure. To show that metaphor is alive in common speech as well as in poetry, ask your students to find the metaphors (and discuss their workings) in a student-written sentence: "Photosynthesis is nature's alchemist transmuting the gold of sunlight into living matter." (You may want to ask your students to be on the lookout for striking fresh metaphors in their current reading or listening.)

For a preliminary exploration of metaphor, write some striking metaphors on the board:

> We drive the same highways
> in the dark, not seeing each other,
> only the lights.
>
> —Diane Wakoski

> Like any other man
> I was born with a knife
> in one hand
> and a wound in the other.
>
> —Gregory Orr

First Reading: Linda Pastan, "The Seven Deadly Sins: Anger" 555

DISCUSSION STARTERS

Can your students visualize the person holding forth and gesturing in this poem? Should it be read diffidently or assertively, doubtfully or assuredly? You might want to have students chart the basic rhetorical pattern:

> You tell me . . .
> You say . . .
> But!
> Ah, you think . . .
> But . . .
> And . . .

THE RECEPTIVE READER

1. The speaker's anger is compared to a "rabid thing," a wild untamed animal, representing a key part of our animal heritage. This beast that naive people would release needs a cage; it claws and bites; it may turn on its

owner, mauling her and drawing blood. It is rabid, and it "sharpens its teeth" on her bones.

2. The other side of the basic animal metaphor contrasts the true wild beast of anger with the civilized, attenuated emotions of wimpy domesticated "pet dogs" whose canines are "dull with disuse."

3. Some people think it healthy to release anger, even though it might prove to some extent destructive. But the speaker is afraid of the destructive and self-lacerating power of that emotion once it is released. Should we be afraid of the raw and ferocious quality of emotions that turn us into clawing, mauling animals, escaping from the civilized restraints that make us human?

THE PERSONAL RESPONSE

Are students aware of pop culture trends encouraging people to "act out" hostile emotions?

THE CREATIVE DIMENSION

What might be a metaphor for healthy anger or for righteous anger? What might be a metaphor for meekness, tenderness, shame, guilt, or diffidence? You might want to ask students to try their hand at a haiku like the following student-written example:

My anger:
the burning acid
of slow tears.

Reading for Metaphor

May Swenson, "Question" 558

DISCUSSION STARTERS

Ask students to explore the implications and connotations of familiar common-language phrases and sayings clustering around our bodies, such as "the Body Beautiful," "body building," "body language"; "body and soul"; "the spirit is willing, but the flesh is weak."

THE RECEPTIVE READER

1. Traditionally, the body has often been seen as a source of corruption or temptation, as something to escape, as something that weighs us down or slows us down, as something that does battle with the soul. Swenson, though, sees it as a home, a place to come to for protection and to sleep. She views it as the mount "eager and quick" that enables us to "ride" and to "hunt." It is the trusty hound, sniffing out "danger or treasure."

2. The three intermeshing body metaphors in this poem seem to converge on a positive, affirming view of the body as a trusted ally, offering us security and allowing us to deal competently with the vicissitudes of life?

3. The title points forward to the final existential question: "How will I fare when the body that has been my security, my means of vital motion, and my means of scouting treasure and danger is gone?" Instead of the firm faith in an afterlife in the Countee Cullen poem, we here have a much more modern sense of fear and apprehension of a state when wind and cloud take the place of our alert eyes and our protective garments, when there is no place to hide and be safe from final disintegration.

THE CREATIVE DIMENSION

Before having students write their body poems, you may wish to discuss with them possible evocative metaphors. The body as bird—what kind of bird? what kind of animal—the "heavy bear"? the body as a worm? the body as cocoon? the body as a coat of armor?

Emily Dickinson, " 'Hope' is the thing with feathers" 559

DISCUSSION STARTERS

What might be an abstract dictionary definition of *hope*? ("The feeling that what is desired is also possible, or that events may turn out for the best.") Metaphorically, in this poem, hope is a bird: it is feathered, it perches, it sings, it brings pleasure—and it asks for nothing in return. The abstract concept, hope, is illuminated and brought to life by the extended bird metaphor whose ramifications prove marvelously apt for the role hope plays in our lives.

THE RECEPTIVE READER

1. A bird, like hope, can rise above the problems of our weighted-down, earthbound existence. Its song does not need specific words or a specific message to give us an uplifting or cheering hopeful feeling. It is not niggardly or bound to a limited schedule—we hear it off and on at unexpected times so that it never seems to stop.

2. The song would seem "sweetest—in the Gale" because glimpses of hope are most welcome in stormy weather, in rough times? The bird of hope warms many people's spirits—it is needed by all to fend off despondency or despair. And the fact that the bird never "asked a crumb" means it is available to anyone, rich or poor, never demanding repayment in any form. It's free.

THE CREATIVE DIMENSION

Hope might for some be associated with the notion of foolish or disappointed hopes—of "raising false hopes"? For others it might be what keeps us going? Some people might "hope against hope"?

Rita Dove, "Silos" 560

PERSPECTIVES—RITA DOVE ON POETRY AND ELITISM

Rita Dove, U.S. Poet Laureate (a position that used to be called Consultant in Poetry to the Library of Congress) "has always liked to approach any subject from a variety of perspectives" (Helen Vendler). She has suffered from a "literary restlessness" that has made her, for instance, devote a recent volume of poetry, *Mother Love*, to a modern rewrite of the mother-daughter myth of Demeter and her daughter Persephone, raped and abducted by Hades. At the same time, Dove had been called "perhaps the most disciplined and technically accomplished black poet to arrive since Gwendolyn Brooks began her remarkable career in the nineteen forties" (Arnold Rampersad). "Called a subtle and penetrating new voice in our midst," Dove is a perceptive observer of apparently minor events and details of African American life and of the larger patterns of history. She says, "I found historical events fascinating for looking underneath—not for what we always see or what's always said about a historical event, but for the things that can't be related in a dry historical sense."

Although Dove has been praised for her subtle and challenging poetry, she has been fighting the widespread negative popular attitude toward poetry as elitist, inaccessible to the ordinary reader, cut off from real life. In her article "Who's Afraid of Poetry?" in *Writer's Digest* (February 1995), Dove says, "I am always astonished when people claim that poetry is 'intellectual' or 'elitist,' that it has to do with 'books and flowers and stuff.' To me, a poem is so firmly rooted in the world—or rather, the juncture between the world and the individual spirit—that I find poems more useful for negotiating the terms of our identities, more efficacious in providing a stay against extinction than the mass media. Mass media can provide us with the news, but they can't tell us what to do with it. Of course, it is not the task of the news media to crank out solutions; but with no instructions on how to incorporate what's happening close to home or far away—how to locate our private emotions in the public sentiment—we feel helpless and betrayed." Dove puts part of the blame on the general tendency in our society to regard "the creative arts with some degree of apprehension, even suspicion." Many "do not expect the arts, especially the arts created by their contemporaries, to be accessible, nor do they see any reason to incorporate the arts into their everyday or professional lives." She places another large part of the blame on methods of teaching poetry that leave students with a lifelong aversion to, rather than love of, poetry: "Many of us have suffered a classroom experience where our brave interpretation of a teacher's treasured poem was declared 'wrong.' Poems, then, became coded texts, something you were supposed to decipher, not enjoy."

DISCUSSION STARTERS

Silos, usually tall cylinders in which livestock food is converted, are Rita Dove's starting point for this descriptive poem. Dove, Pulitzer Prize–winning Poet Laureate, grew up in Akron, Ohio, a place she has described as dominated by two smells: the smell of the rubber factories and the smell of burning oats from the Quaker Oats silos.

THE RECEPTIVE READER

1. The imaginative comparisons that call to mind the cylindrical shape of silos plus their particular odor are the most fitting: "they were like cigarettes, the smell chewy and bitter / like a field shorn of milkweed, or beer brewing, or / a fingernail scorched over a flame." The metaphor of silos as "a fresh packet of chalk, / dreading math work," is unexpected and far-reaching. Also unexpected are the ideas of silos as "tall wishes" and as "the ribs of the modern world." A xylophone is a percussion instrument, consisting of gradated wooden slats, which are struck with small mallets; silos are "never xylophones," among other reasons, because the instrument is horizontal and silos are vertical. Pan, a merry, ugly combination of a man with the ears, horns, and legs of a goat, played the syrinx. Named after the Arcadian maiden who was changed by river nymphs into a reed-bed in order that she might cross the River Ladon as she fled from the amorous Pan, the syrinx consists of a varying number of reeds, with the open ends forming a horizontal line and the closed ends (closed by knots in the reeds) gradually decreasing in length from left to right. Because of the stopped ends, the notes produced are almost an octave lower then notes produced by an open pipe of equal length.

2. Silos are neither beautiful nor fragrant, and a number of Dove's descriptions reflect this. Words and expressions like "martial," "the smell chewy and bitter," and "masculine toys" are not playful. With great subtlety, the poet alludes to the masculine, industrialized, and martial world such silos inhabit. "Martial swans" are "paraded against the city sky's / shabby blue." Silos are "masculine toys" as well as "the ribs of the modern world." Obviously phallic in shape, this, plus their size, makes them symbols of the heavily mechanized modern world.

Figurative Language: Metaphor, Simile, Personification

Robert Burns, "A Red, Red Rose" 561

DISCUSSION STARTERS

Often familiar masterpieces become *over*familiar. Has Burns' figurative language—the "red, red rose," the sweet melody, the seas drying out, and the rocks melting—become trite? Has it worn out?

THE RECEPTIVE READER

1. These two opening *similes* seem to complement one another. Both the freshly opening rose and the sweet in-tune melody are largely unearned, unexpected pleasures that come into our lives. Both can become an antidote to the confusions, frustrations, and sense of futility in our ordinary existence. The rose brings rich warm color where all might have been gray and drab; the melody brings sweet harmony where there was grating noise and cacophony. So similarly love brings warmth, color, and harmony into cold, drab, and disjointed lives.

2. The sand is often used as a *metaphor* for infinity (or at least numbers too large to count). How many grains ARE there on the beach? But here the sand is put into an hourglass, where it runs slowly but surely till "time is up." (In spite of the lover's oaths promising eternal devotion, we do sense in the background of the poem the passing of time that will undo all.)

3. There are several instances of *hyperbole* in this poem. The lover will love this young maiden until "the seas gang dry" and the solid age-old "rocks melt," and he intends to come back to her even if it means walking "a thousand mile."

THE PERSONAL RESPONSE

When Burns published his first book, *Poems*, in 1786, he was called a "Heaven-taught plowman" by the literati of Edinburgh because they saw his poems as spontaneous outpourings of native feelings, often written in the rustic dialect of the Scottish countryside. However, Burns' protestations of undying love for his "bonny lass" are part of a venerable literary tradition? He is playing a familiar role here, but perhaps everyone does who plays the role of a lover?

Langston Hughes, "Dream Deferred" 562

DISCUSSION STARTERS

Langston Hughes writes that "books began to happen to me, and I began to believe in nothing but books and the wonderful world in books—where if people suffered, they suffered in beautiful language, not in monosyllables, as we did in Kansas." Do your students consider it a contradiction to "suffer in beautiful language"?

THE RECEPTIVE READER

1. In the past, minorities denied their place in the sun or their share in the American dream may have just sagged as under "a heavy load." But in the minds of many, discrimination festered "like a sore." And today, pent-up resentment and riotous anger are everywhere ready to "explode"?

2. Most of the poem reflects fatalism or resignation—but the ending erupts into a dramatic warning of the "fire next time"?

Howard Nemerov, "The Great Gull" 563

DISCUSSION STARTER

The poem turns on the polarity of wild/civilized. What contrasting images and associations do the two terms bring to your students' minds? Nemerov reverses any conventional assumptions about the superiority of the civilized world of green lawns to the fierce natural world of the "great gull." However, paradoxically, the word *savage* is used twice—what is the difference in meaning, context, or implication? The gull is "savage"—powerful, haughty, untamed. The people of the "poor province" the gull found are "savage" in a different sense? They have nothing grand or inspiring in their lives; they represent the "miserable regimen" of humans who are restless, rising at dawn, and don't know why.

THE RECEPTIVE READER

1. While we might have been conditioned to think of merchants as grubby, prosaic people, the term "merchant prince" here is supposed to make us think of a more adventurous, proud kind of merchant. Like Shakespeare's merchant of Venice, he would outfit ships to sail to distant exotic regions in search of spices and treasure. Coming upon not a legendary Eldorado but upon an ordinary "poor" setting (as Columbus did who was looking for cities of gold but found fishing villages instead), such a person is likely to turn haughty and disdainful. Like a "high priest," the merchant prince would be above the riffraff of ordinary people?

2. The image of the crypt again takes us away from the grubby concerns of ordinary lives—this time to a burial chamber inspiring feelings of awe, of gloomy grandeur.

3. Paradoxically, the similes clustering around the "savage" great bird from the "wild waters" are taken from human civilization—but from those dimensions of it that go beyond ordinary dull existence, that make us break out of the ordinary and make us visualize the awesome, the exotic.

THE PERSONAL RESPONSE

You may want to explore the connotations of wildness and domestication. What is the difference between a wolf and a dog? a gull and a dove? a goldfish and a shark? a buffalo and cattle?

Emily Dickinson, "Apparently with no surprise" 565

DISCUSSION STARTERS

To show the difference between a view of the world animated by metaphor and a literal, one-track factual view of the world, ask students to write a literal account of the incident, such as "The frost killed a flower but then disappeared as the sun came up." What does the factual report miss—the dramatizing of the "execution" of what was a fragile, beautiful living thing? the strange, paradoxical beauty of the "blonde Assassin"? the ironic contrast between the uninvolved sun and the murderous minidrama played out below?

THE RECEPTIVE READER

1. Is the God Dickinson writes about a distant entity that does not care about His creatures, letting the natural laws of His creation take their course? Is the power of the frost "accidental" because it is simply in keeping with the laws of nature and implies no personal malice?

2. The small incidents and disasters of our earthly existence fade into insignificance when compared with the "unmoved" order of the larger cosmic patterns?

3. One student wrote:

There is no such thing as "accidental" power, for all power emanates from God. By virtue of reason, then, no power can ever be "accidental." The Frost, when it decapitates the flower, is acting like a "blonde assassin." Out of a natural innocence similar to that of a towheaded child, it does God's bidding. It kills. And God, watching, approves.

Edward Hirsch, "In the Middle of August" 566

DISCUSSION STARTERS

Some people are elated, frustrated, and oppressed by their area's climate—and others don't seem to care. What about your students?

THE RECEPTIVE READER

1. One imaginative comparison calling to mind the great relief provided by a summer shower is the crash of "trumpets and cymbals," expanding outward to include a parade down Fifth Avenue and "all / The high school drummers in the city / Banging away at once." Unexpected comparisons include "Bottles shattering against a warehouse" and a "bowl of apricots spilling / From a tenth-floor window." To conjure up the terrific crash that often heralds the beginning of a summer squall, Hirsch uses metaphors that are almost wholly urban: the crash of bottles against a warehouse wall or a machine-gun-like "Rat-a-tat-tat on the hot pavement." A truly unexpected extended analogy is the poet's comparison of the change between brutal summer heat and the spirit-affirming arrival of the rain to the change between the woman sleeping, drunk, leaning on a wall in a tavern bathroom and awakening, "shivering, in an orchard / Of lemon trees at dawn, surprised / By the sudden omnipotence of yellows."

2. The poet's opening metaphor should appeal to anyone who enjoys such wholesome civic pursuits as parade watching, baton twirling, and high school marching bands. For the anarchists in the reading audience, the next comparisons would have appeal: the smashing of bottles, things flying out of high windows, and the sound of rain, which is reminiscent of automatic weapons fire. The party crowd will respond to the tavern stories, particularly the one in which a reveler awoke in a place she did not recognize. Gamblers will appreciate the allusions to card playing and the roulette wheel. At the end of the poem, cynics and skeptics are assuaged with the following disclaimer: "Look, I'm not saying that the pretty / Girl in the fairy tale really does / Let down her golden hair for all / The poor kids in the neighborhood." Following this, the believers and optimists are placated: "But still / I am saying that a simple cloud / Bursts over the city in mid-August / And suddenly, in your lifetime, / Everyone believes in his own luck."

3. A metaphor is an implied analogy that identifies one object with another object, and which applies qualities of one object to another. A simile is an explicit comparison; most similes begin with the word *as* or *like*. This poem contains several of both. Among the metaphors: "So think / Of trumpets and cymbals, a young girl / In a sparkling tinsel suit leading / A parade down Fifth Avenue," and "Think of / Bottles shattering against a warehouse, / Or a bowl of apricots spilling / From a tenth-floor window." Among the similes: "Like the answer to a question, / A real summer shower breaks loose," and "it's like / The night she fell asleep standing / In the bathroom of a dank tavern / And woke up shivering in an orchard," and "Someone else says it's like spinning / A huge wheel and winning at roulette."

4. If the wonderful refreshment of a summer shower does not inspire optimism and hope, there are other, countless experiences that are analogous. This poem uses a natural event—a summer rain shower—to lift the heat-oppressed human spirit. Other natural events that bring about the same exultation might be the vistas in the Rocky Mountains or sunset in the high desert or the crash of waves upon a beach. Many other, seemingly more mundane events can bring about similar spontaneous joy: the smell of something good from the kitchen, the arrival of a letter, the affectionate, unfailing greeting delivered by a pet.

Juxtapositions: The Range of Metaphor

Thomas Wyatt, "My Galley Charged with Forgetfulness" 567

PERSPECTIVES—THE SONNET AND PRE-ROMANTIC PERSPECTIVES ON ARTIFICE

Wyatt was one of the first to bring to England the Petrachan sonnet—a fourteen-line poem using an elaborate interlacing rhyme scheme and built around elaborate conceits—that was to influence poetic convention for centuries. *Conceits* ingeniously trace a metaphor into ramifications that branch off from the central image like the branches of a tree. (Poets using bolder, shifting or evolving metaphors might be thought of as making metaphoric leaps from one tree to another.) When using terms like *artifice*, *artificial*, and *conceit* in discussing the sonnet tradition, we should remember that we tend to see these terms through the lens of romantic poetics that polarized art and nature, championing unspoilt nature as the antidote to the artificial manners and stylized poetry of the eighteenth century. In a preromantic tradition indebted to classical precedents, art was more likely to be seen as an ally to and imitation of nature. Poets like Edmund Spenser saw art and nature as engaged in a friendly contest to see which could do most to beautify God's creation. Ingenuity and virtuosity were prized more than in later ages. Artifice was not necessarily the enemy of true feeling but meant something artfully done; it did not necessarily imply something deceptive and insincere.

DISCUSSION STARTERS

Why didn't people write sonnets with eleven, fifteen, or twenty-one lines (as some of Petrach's contemporaries or predecessor had done) ? What explains the force of a convention that sweeps all before it and forces everyone into the same or similar mold?

THE RECEPTIVE READER

1. The central metaphor of the ship in the wintery seas takes us into a region of cold and darkness. It is a metaphor for a profound spiritual or emotional crisis, as in "the dark night of the soul." The troubled relationship is mirrored in the "sharp seas," the "winter nights," and the rocks (the Homeric Scylla and Charybdis in Petrarch's original). All the parts of the ship extend the metaphor (until we fairly groan under the weight of this contrivance?). The cargo is "forgetfulness" (because the beloved is oblivious to the plight of the lover? or because the lover tries in vain to forget?). The oars are anxious, desperate thoughts. The rain stands for the man's tears, the wind for his sighs, the clouds for the haughty woman's "disdain." The stars, which should guide the pilot's celestial navigation, are hidden. The port—the safety and fulfillment of requited love—will, as in most of the sonnets in the Petrarchan tradition, never be reached. Reason has gone overboard and drowned, leaving the speaker in the grip of a desperate irrational passion.

2. The keynote is frustrated desire or disappointed hope; the prevailing emotion is despair? Is there too much self-pity in the poet's traditional stance for today's readers? Or are they perhaps more than other generations attuned to the precariousness and unavoidable pain of emotional involvements?

William Shakespeare, "Sonnet 73" 568

PERSPECTIVES—A CLASSIC CRITICAL READING OF "THAT TIME OF YEAR"

William Empson's famous explication of the choirs metaphor in Sonnet 73 (*Seven Types of Ambiguity*, New Directions, 1947) became one of the most widely read examples of the formalistic New Criticism of the forties and fifties. In their reaction against the simple-minded versified uplift of the Tennyson and Longfellow tradition, the New Critics had established as criteria of great poetry concreteness of imagery; complexity—looking for bold, challenging multilayered metaphors; and inclusiveness—broadening the scope of poetry beyond what was conventionally beautiful to the whole range of disparate, jostling experience. Empson traced the choirs metaphor—"Bare ruined choirs, where late the sweet birds sang"— into its many possible implications and associations—with the open-endedness and ambiguity of these contributing greatly to Shakespeare's "richness and heightening of effect." The sections once reserved for the choir in the ruined monastery churches abandoned in the wake of the Protestant Reformation are like the once richly leafed but now bare trees in many ways: Both "are places in which to sing," "involve sitting in a row," are "made of wood," are "carved into knots and so forth." The choirs "used to be surrounded by a sheltering building crystallized out of the likeness of a forest, and colored with stained glass and painting like flowers and leaves" but "are now abandoned by all but the grey walls colored like the skies of winter." The "cold and Narcissistic charm suggested by the choirboys suits well with Shakespeare's feeling for the object of the Sonnets." Complex sociological and historical associations— "the protestant destruction of the monasteries; fear of puritanism" enter in. All these rich associations—"there is a sort of ambiguity in not knowing which of them to hold most clearly in mind"—combine "to give the line its beauty."

DISCUSSION STARTERS

Shakespeare here dwells on a favorite theme: "envious and calumniating time." The key metaphor of the first quatrain is the tree shedding its leaves; of the second, twilight; of the third, a fading fire. All three reinforce the inevitability of old age—and the bittersweet sadness its contemplation brings.

THE RECEPTIVE READER

1. The *second metaphor* takes us beyond sunset to the fading afterglow in the west that stands for the twilight of life, with night not far behind. This

coming period of "black night" is "Death's second self," which brings on sleep—and points toward death's real self, a very long final sleep that "seals up all in rest."

2. The *fire metaphor* points to embers, not a bonfire in full force. The fire is near the end of its life. The wood, which at one time fed the fire, now suffocates it as the logs become ash. It thus becomes, like the twilight, a gradual but inevitable decline into death. In this third metaphor, students might see parallels like the following with the earlier metaphors of the ruined church and the twilight of the speaker's life:

- All three metaphors describe the inevitable downward spiral of a cycle.
- All three suggest death's coming.
- All three carry the suggestion of their polar opposites: The tree was a haven for "sweet birds"; the brightness of day ends in twilight; the fire was once the blazing fire of youth.

3. The poet makes a strong defiant statement in the *concluding couplet*: Love grows stronger when we know we are going to lose it. The counterpoint lies in the triumph of a love strengthened by the human awareness of old age and imminent loss.

Poems for Further Study

Rosemary Catacalos, "La Casa" 569

DISCUSSION STARTERS

Thomas Wolfe wrote, "You can't go home again." The title brings the key issue in the poem into focus: *la casa* is the home—we "know we belonged there once," but there has been the inevitable severance or separation that is an essential part of growing up. The mothers do not venture out of the house, which is always of "the same adobe," full of the "same lessons" of tradition. The tradition is built on religion—the mothers light candles and pray. Ask students to think about the experience of separating from the parental home or other home base and to share their experience in small groups or with the class as a whole.

THE RECEPTIVE READER

The key metaphor is that of a fishing line thrown far out into the ocean and reeling off as the fish attached at the end speeds away. But this line—whatever ties still bind the children to the "lessons" and the religion of their parents—is "very weak." There is no return for the children to the simple world of their upbringing—no way to reel them in. Whatever contacts continue are like a mere waving as someone passes by—not a real return. That is why the mothers ask for "The Virgin's forgiveness" and why "they are afraid for us."

William Shakespeare, "Sonnet 29" 570

DISCUSSION STARTERS

What do we envy? Do we, like the speaker in this sonnet, envy others their features or appearance, their friends, their skills or artistic accomplishments, their scope of action or thought? Is the capacity for envy, like the capacity for love, one of the perennial features of our human psychology?

THE RECEPTIVE READER

1. The weeping and cursing and wishing to be more like envied others stay close to the level of literal statement. But the lines are shot through with metaphor: The speaker is "in disgrace" with Fortune as if she were a capricious ruler he might have offended. He feels like an outcast. It is as if heaven were "deaf" to his complaints. People who feel more hopeful are "rich" in hope. Fickle and malicious Dame Fortune or Lady Luck, personifying the uncertainty of human prosperity, spins her wheel to throw off former favorites and raise up former unfortunates.

2. The speaker, despising himself for his own dark thoughts, turns to thoughts about the person whose "sweet love" will prove the answer to the speaker's dissatisfaction with his lot. The simile of the lark rising into the morning sky lifts him out of depression and away from the personified "sullen earth" (sullen and cheerless like a person). In midflight, the bird, known for its bright, trilling high-pitched morning song, turns metaphorically into a worshiper who "sings hymns" of praise "at heaven's gate."

3. The pivotal *yet*, bringing in the answer to the speaker's discontent, occurs exactly at the transition from octave to sestet. The final couplet is a final hyperbolical tribute to the power of love to take us from the extreme of utter dejection to the opposite extreme of more than kingly blessings.

Nikki Giovanni, "The Drum" 571

DISCUSSION STARTERS

Why are drums rich in metaphoric and symbolic potential? How many different uses of them can your students think of? What does it mean to drum someone out of an organization? What did Thoreau mean when he said that some "march to a different drummer"?

THE RECEPTIVE READER

1. Students may envision the initial "drum" as stretched taut, rigid, locked into place. What "daddy" apparently had in mind was that people have very little room for moving around or getting out from under. But the poet turns the table on the initial metaphor, since it is up to the drummer to assume control and beat out her "own rhythm."

2. The "i'm gonna" is the informal language of an actual kid who has a "daddy" and is given the usual sage advice by adults. The formal "I shall" would sound too stuffy and inappropriate for the speaker?

Sylvia Plath, "Metaphors" 571

DISCUSSION STARTERS

Teachers often caution against mixing metaphors. Ask students in small groups to come up with thoughts on why the fourteen distinct metaphors in this poem work together. What do elephants, houses, melons, fat purses, and a cow about to calve have in common?

THE RECEPTIVE READER

1. What are the first or best clues, nudging the reader? "This loaf's big"? "a cow in calf"?

2. The gestation period is nine months. The entire poem is a metaphor for gestation?

3. Green apples supposedly bloat the eater. Students will relate to each of these metaphors in a highly personal way. It might be interesting to see if those students who have experienced pregnancy can relate more directly to some of the metaphors than others.

4. The speaker seems to be in a state in which she feels unequivocally huge—like an elephant, a big loaf, a fat purse. Does she feel resigned, fatalistic, about her condition? She's "boarded the train" and "there's no getting off." She has become "a means" to the end of procreation. The speaker generates wry humor at her own expense: "A melon strolling on two tendrils," for example.

THE PERSONAL RESPONSE

Mixed emotions might range from the traditional fear of traumatic births to the belief in "natural childbirth"?

John Donne, "A Valediction: Forbidding Mourning" 572

PERSPECTIVES—JOHN DONNE AND THE NEW CRITICS

John Donne was Exhibit A for mid-twentieth-century critics who were in rebellion against versified sentiment and who were searching for poets intellectually challenging, boldly imaginative, and formally complex. John Donne's poetry—yoking intellect and passion, science and poetry —was made to order for New Critics like Robert Penn Warren, who championed "a scale of excellence based, in part at least, on degree of complication"; who felt that a good poem showed evidence of the poet's having wrestled with and overcome "resistance." Warren said, "a poem is a motion toward a point of rest, but if it is not a resisted motion, it is a motion of no consequence." New Critics praised Donne for extending the boundaries of poetry beyond the ghetto of pretty sights and pleasing emotions. I. A. Richards, another high priest of the new critical dispensation, made reconciling disparate, incongruous, jostling elements one of the key qualities of great poetry. Metaphor—bold, provocative metaphor—for him was one of the poet's chief means for bringing together elements from widely divergent areas of experience. W. K. Wimsatt said that complexity of outward form was merely the most external manifestation of a poem's "maturity or sophistication or richness or depth, and hence its value."

DISCUSSION STARTERS

The emotions of a lover facing a period of necessary absence are at the center of this metaphysical poem. The similes seem strange and remote; surprise follows surprise as the separation is compared to the separation, at death, of good men's souls from their bodies; to the goldsmith's beating a sheet of gold leaf to an "airy thinness"; and to the two legs of the "twin compasses" first separating and then coming together again after creating a perfect circle. How does the poet bring potentially untamed and overpowering emotions of loss and grief under control? Do your students agree that achieving control over our emotions is the subtext of the poem? Critic Fred B. Millet notes:

> The metaphors from other areas of human experience, "roam" and "comes home"—farm and familiar metaphors—serve to emotionalize the geometry of the simile. Such emotionalizing could imperil the main point of the poem were it not so firmly within the unemotional simile. The calm control and certain accuracy expressed in the compass are what the speaker wants his beloved to achieve, and beyond what it is recommending to her he seems to be trying to persuade himself into the same sure control and achieved calm.

THE RECEPTIVE READER

1. For the lovers, the separation is a kind of temporary death—but the poet wants it to be a gentle, mild kind of death. Just as good men die quietly, so the lovers should accept their separation quietly. In the seventeenth century, the assumption of many pious people was that the final hours of virtuous persons, at peace with their consciences and their maker, would be mild and gentle and that the final hours of a sinner would be agonized and writhing.

2. If the outsiders are the "laity," then the two people in love are insiders (or high priests) to the "sacred." The speaker here pleads that the lovers keep their sad emotions contained so as not to "profane" their joys—so as not to share them with the vulgar multitude unable to share the lovers' feeling of quasi-religious exaltation.

3. Just as believers might wonder what an earthquake or tornado or hurricane is trying to tell them, "Trepidation of the spheres" makes people wonder what signal a perfect God is giving to the imperfect world. "Sublunary lovers' love" is imperfect, like everything under the moon on this imperfect earth; the speaker's love and that of his beloved is so "refined" and spiritual as to be closer to perfection. (Direct your students to the Reading Notes and the Model Paper in the Writing Workshop for more insights into this rich poem?)

4. You may want to arrange to have a student bring twin compasses and demonstrate their workings. The stay-at-home lover is "the fixed foot," planted firmly in the center, while the other foot "roams" —not really roaming freely but kept in orbit to describe a perfect circle. Though planted firmly, the fixed foot inclines (or "leans and harkens") toward the other as it proceeds on its journey.

THE PERSONAL RESPONSE

Do we assume that scientists or physicians are less emotional or passionate than poets and artists? Have your students encountered science majors or math majors who are "passionate" about their subjects? Is the separation of our culture into "two cultures"—the one imaginative and emotional, and the other drily factual and objective—a false dichotomy?

16 SYMBOL
A World of Meanings 578

Symbols, like metaphors, powerfully activate the imagination. However, unlike a metaphor, a symbol is both literal and figurative at the same time. When we send flowers or carry a flag in a parade, these objects are literally there, and they carry at the same time a symbolic meaning. However, when we metaphorically "carry a torch" for someone we love or when chauvinists "wave the bloody shirt," there is no literal torch or shirt.

You may want to ask your students:

- What makes the rose a traditional symbol of love? (The red or scarlet can suggest passion; the sweet smell suggests pleasure; the flowering and fading of the rose suggest the volatility or transiency of human love.)
- What makes water a traditional symbol of life?
- What symbolic associations cluster around the fist, the boot, the lamb?

First Reading: Martín Espada, "Colibrí" 579

DISCUSSION STARTERS

What reminders of vanished pre-Columbian people have your students observed or studied at first hand?

THE RECEPTIVE READER

1. The *historical facts* of the Spanish invasion and conquest echo throughout this poem. In the opening stanza "lizards scatter / like a fleet of green canoes / before the invader." The conquerors assign their own names as Spanish drives out the indigenous languages: " 'Taíno' for the people who took life / from the plátanos [bananas] in the trees," and "So the hummingbird / was christened 'colibrí.' " The hummingbird's frantic life pace recalls "a racing Taíno heart / frantic as if hearing / the bellowing god of gunpowder / for the first time." The poet wishes "history / were like your hands." If history were like the hands that rescue the frantic hummingbird from the hacienda and "lift him / through the red shutters / of the window, / where he disappears / into a paradise of sky, / a nightfall of singing frogs," then so too might the Taíno have been lifted from enslavement and set free.

2. Both of these images conjure up pictures of frightened, nervous, and shocked people. If the native people had not been initially afraid of the invaders, subsequent actions by the Spanish would have instilled in the Taíno a well-deserved fear. The Taíno people were worked and starved to death, their chiefs were overthrown, the men murdered and subjected to brutal punishment, and the women raped. Like lizards, then, they would scatter their green canoes out of sight upon seeing the Spanish. Similarly, the "rock carv-

ings / of eyes and mouths / in perfect circles of amazement" reflect the Taínos shock at the complete upheaval precipitated by the arrival of the Spanish.

3. The hummingbird somehow gets trapped inside of a house: it "darts and hangs / between the white walls / of the hacienda." Similarly, the Taíno people were trapped in the embrace of the Spanish culture that overran them. Like the hummingbird's frantic fear at being enclosed, the Taíno would have been desperate to escape enclosure by the Spanish. Despite its speed, the hummingbird is fragility itself: tiny, almost weightless, dwarfed by all the other birds, and required to continually refuel the racing engine that is its heart. The West Indian peoples, in comparison to the armored, armed, heavy-footed Spanish, were the essence of fragility; they never stood a chance.

4. Historians work on the *fait accompli* principle (while science fiction writers, for instance, work on the "what if?" principle). What if the contacts of Native Americans with Europeans had been more like the contacts between the West and countries like China and Japan?

The Language of Symbols

David Wagoner, "The Other House" 581

DISCUSSION STARTERS

This poem turns on polarities, playing off the boy's own "proper house" against the "other house" of the title, or moving from winter to spring. Can your or your students read the poem aloud in such a way that the listener can "hear" the silence of the parents' house and so that the poem "sings out" at the end?

THE RECEPTIVE READER

1. A frog croaks; many frogs croak in a kind of rhythm (much like that of crickets) that might be called music. The speaker calls it "*their* music"; it is a special kind of music that contrasts sharply with the sad silence in the "proper house." (Roger Rosenblatt writes: "Silence fills first a heart, then a house, then history. The freedom children seek is the freedom from silence.") The setting of the abandoned house with its water and its frogs might seem dreary to an adult, but beckoning, fascinating to a child—children find places to hide or to be their own selves without much regard for the niceties of fastidiously repaired and maintained "proper" bourgeois homes?

2. The poet first makes real and absorbing for us the childhood world of the boy drawn to the "abandoned house" with its frog inhabitants and their music. After this picture is fully painted, the contrast with the deadly silence of the parents' marriage hits us with full force.

3. In the natural world the boy's human sound is symbolic of danger. Wild animals run at human noises. The frogs stop singing. But since the boy is found to "sing nothing," they resume their ode to spring in "a green chorus."

4. The fact that the adult poet writes about the experience of silence in the "proper house" indicates his awareness of the neglect in his childhood and his commitment to overcoming the limitations of his upbringing. You may want to ask students to compare the student response in the text and the one that follows:

A pulse is the very essence of humanness, the steady beat affirming our existence. Rhythm, slow, measured, steady, sure. We feel many different rhythms when we are silent or lonely or cut off from warmth. Listening to them becomes like listening to our own heart and confirming our own existence. At these moments we become vividly aware of our small place in the huge orchestra of the world.

THE PERSONAL RESPONSE

Wagoner's father and mother were silent "All day and during dinner and after / And after the radio / With hardly a murmur all the way into sleep." For many current households, the second line would read "after TV"?

Donald Finkel, "They" 583

DISCUSSION STARTERS

Who are "they"? ("They" are the nameless disciples of technological progress who wield noisy chain saws, cart around a tree chipper—a machine into which cut branches are fed to be shredded into chips—or race power mowers over the lawns. "They" approve of cleaning up the dangers and messes of nature: pin-oaks threatening a taxi, an ash falling on a child, a sweet gum dropping seeds to trip the mail carrier. For the poet, the chain saw becomes a symbol of "progress" because there is no gainsaying its brainless power, and it can destroy in a few minutes what took nature years and sometimes centuries to nurture.?

THE RECEPTIVE READER

1. The voices of the tree cutters, heard only indirectly or at one remove in this poem, insist that the trees being cut are dangerous to life, limb, and property. The poet ludicrously exaggerates the dangers, nudging us to recognize the absurdity of the argument—"never again will the pin-oak threaten a taxi / will the ash lie in wait to fall on a child"; never again will droppings from the gum tree "menace the sensible shoes of mailmen." Pursuing the same line of argument, the tree-cutting forces might go berserk and cut down children to forestall the danger of their "falling / on the school and crushing it"?

2. *Personification* in this poem, helping us imagine the trees and shrubs as living things, is pervasive: pin-oaks "threaten," the ash lies "in wait," the plane will not "dance," the sweet gum "trembles," the grass blades "huddle whimpering." However, the machines also come to life as monstrous predatory half-human creatures: the tree-eating machine snarls and chews, the saws laugh. The massacre of the children is symbolic of technology spinning out of control without warning; there is no new stanza because the shift from trees to children is meant to shock us, catch us unawares? The rosebush, whose uprooting we might have taken in stride, comes to life when it is compared to a pathetically helpless kitten struggling against being drowned.

3. The chariots—the war carts of barbarians with killer blades attached to the wheels—make explicit the idea of the war being waged on nature. Spring is traditionally a season of new growth, but here it ironically brings out of hibernation the death-dealing machinery of officious municipal agencies. In spring, people come out to work in their yards to help things bloom—but here they come out not with new seed, but with destructive equipment that makes the new spring grasses "huddle whimpering" because there is no place to go to escape death; the only thing cheerful in the street is "the laughter of saws."

THE PERSONAL RESPONSE

The images presented here conjure up the relentless efficiency of modern technology—"truck after truck" is filled not only with the life cut down, but the dust of that life as well. All traces of life are being extinguished, and the poet "cannot keep up with them." Is the poet exaggerating or presenting a one-sided picture? Or is he sounding a long overdue alarm?

Denise Levertov, "To One Steeped in Bitterness" 584

PERSPECTIVES—LEVERTOV: POET AND CULTURAL HERITAGE

In the introduction to his collection *Denise Levertov: Selected Criticism* (U of Michigan Press, 1993), Albert Gelpi says about Levertov, "There was much in the circumstances of her life to make her feel divided in her affiliations and commitments. She has been acclaimed as an American poet—not just by citizenship but in the quality of poetic eye and ear; but she was born in England in 1923 and spent her formative years there: educated at home as her older sister Olga had been, studying painting and ballet, beginning nurse's training, publishing her first book of poems. *The Double Image* (1946) demonstrates in its metrical forms and neo-Romantic diction how much of the English poetic tradition she had absorbed by her late teens." The "cultural heritage of this English child was dual: a Welsh mother who sang, painted, and wrote; and her father, a Hasidic Jew from Russia who converted to

Christianity before his marriage in 1910 and settled ten years later in England, where he became an Anglican priest and a scholar and preacher dedicated to Jewish-Christian dialogue." In a review reprinted in the Gelpi collection, Kenneth Rexroth, who had included Levertov in his anthology of *The New British Poets* (1949), called her "incomparably the best poet of what is getting to be known as the new avant-garde." He contrasted her with contemporary poets who "know practically nothing, not even French and algebra." That her father "was a learned rabbi, a leading authority on the Kabbalah, who became an Anglo-Catholic priest, may have helped." To Rexroth, Levertov seemed "to have grown up in a household full of mildly Bohemian scholarship" and free-wheeling humanistic learning. Rexroth said, "she may have read Donne from her father's library at the age of ten. Cultured people do not discover him when they go to Harvard and use him to intimidate the yokels back home in St. Louis."

DISCUSSION STARTERS

Students might notice that the "one steeped in bitterness" is never heard in this poem. We never hear the voice of the person being addressed—someone with a "cooped heart, "timid eye," and dry or parched lips. What, if anything, might the silent partner in this one-way conversation have to say?

THE RECEPTIVE READER

1. The nailed rose suggests a stubborn denial of feelings of love. For the emotionally impaired person, an offer of affection or passion may be seen as an insult, a hostile gesture, reminding the person of his or her deprived state.

2. Water is an indispensable life-giving and life-sustaining part of our world. It often becomes symbolic of the ability (endangered in our alienated modern world) to feel human emotions, to empathize with others, to maintain human contact?

Li-Young Lee, "Persimmons" 585

DISCUSSION STARTERS

How hard or how easy is it to communicate with people from other cultures? The persimmons in this poem become symbolic of the meeting of two cultures, two sets of values, two languages. They become a test case for our ability to bridge the gulf that separates us from others. Each experience the speaker remembers brings into play cultural attitudes. Can your students think of some objects or occurrences of daily life that sometimes become test cases for differing cultural attitudes?

THE RECEPTIVE READER

1. The *angle of perception* is that of the bilingual student, who brings to class knowledge and background that his limited command of English does not yet allow him to show. For instance, he knows more about persimmons and the role of scroll paintings in his culture than the teacher does, who treats him as a dunce. The boy may confuse similar-sounding words like *persimmon* and *precision* (or *wren* and *yarn*) but he knows the difference between the concepts, and precision plays a special role in his heritage. The tables are turned when it becomes apparent that the teacher has no idea how to pick out persimmons with precision and how to recognize the unripe fruit that will cause the boy's classmates to screw up their faces.

2. The persimmons (an occasion for exposing the teacher's well-intentioned ignorance) are first introduced when the speaker describes how to choose one and eat it properly with "precision." One must "sniff the bottoms" testing for fragrance. The sweet ones have it. The "ripe ones are soft and brown-spotted." The persimmons become symbolic of the golden glow and warmth of life, each, according to the mother, carrying inside a sun. (The bird on the windowsill seems to sing "*The sun, the sun*"?) But at the same time the persimmons are a symbol of the speaker's intimate relationship with the culture of his parents, playing a central role in the scroll paintings that his now blind father has done with loving precision "*hundreds of times.*"

3. Words are not just neutral counters; they often have rich personal associations and connotations. The other pairs of words that the speaker has trouble with also carry significance in the poem: *fright* and *fight* are both closely intertwined parts of the experience of the "different" student who may be taunted and provoked by his classmates; trying to tell apart *wren* and *yarn* allows the speaker to give us a glimpse of his bonding with the mother. The scroll paintings become symbolic of the devotion, the skill, and the love of tradition that the speaker treasures in his cultural heritage.

4. The speaker seems to feel a strong affection for his cultural roots, which are exemplified by his mother's old country lore, her traditional crafts, his father's painting. "*Some things never leave a person.*" At the same time, the son is experimental (making love to a young white woman under the moon); he has left home; English has become his language, with many Chinese words long since forgotten.

THE PERSONAL RESPONSE

What causes misunderstanding? What triggers tension? What words and attitudes provoke fights? Which of your students have taken a real interest in a cultural tradition other than theirs?

THE CREATIVE DIMENSION

Have any of your students learned to treasure something that might have little practical or monetary value but that is rich in associations?

Percy Bysshe Shelley, "Ozymandias" 588

DISCUSSION STARTERS

The very name, Ozymandias, suggests ancient worlds, the exotic, life patterns that fired the romantic imagination. In our world, is the romantic yearning for the distant in time, place, and culture still alive?

THE RECEPTIVE READER

1. Ozymandias, "king of kings" with the "sneer of cold command" still on his sculpted face, imitated many other strutting and hubris-ridden rulers by commissioning a colossal statue that would be a lasting symbol of his power and bring despair and envy to lesser tyrants. However, the "colossal wreck" is now decayed beyond recognition; the king has been taken down to the level of "lone and level sands." Ironically, the statue carries the opposite of the intended symbolic meaning to future generations. It has become an eloquent symbol of the inexorable power of time to triumph over the puny achievements of presumptuous mortals. Ozymandias' colossus has become symbolic of the sinful pride of all human beings who mistakenly believe they—or their works— will be permanent, as if they could arrest the uncertain, dynamic flow of life.

2. The frowning, sneering, cold face of tyrannical authority is still there, while all the pompous, strutting display of arrogant power and the adulation of sycophants have disappeared. *Sic semper tyrannis!* (May the same fate overtake all tyrants!)

Public and Private Symbols

William Blake, "The Tyger" 589

PERSPECTIVES—"THE TYGER" AND THE ROMANTIC IMAGINATION

Blake was a great precursor or early representative of the romantic mind-set that saw all of creation as imbued with and manifesting the transcendent vital energy at the heart of creation. Romantics never became blasé about the great ongoing miracle of life. "The Tyger," companion piece to "The Lamb" (see Chapter 25), shows us the poet wondering passionately about a creator—be it God or a universal life-force—and his process of creation. In the words of Lionel Trilling,

> The dominant, the single, emotion of the poem is amazement, and perhaps no poem has ever expressed an emotion so fully—it is as if the poem were amazement itself.

> The means by which it achieves this effect is in part very simple: in the course of twenty-four lines it asks fourteen astonished questions.

However, the "astonishment" here is not puzzlement or bewilderment: The poet apparently assumes that the same overwhelmingly powerful God created both the mild or peaceful and the terrifying, destructive aspects of existence. We should not blame an evil force (the devil?) for creating beasts of prey, nor should we belittle their role, eighteenth-century style, in this "best of all possible worlds." But there also is no hint in the poem that fearful creatures like the tiger were created as a "scourge of God" to punish sinful humanity? Critic Roy P. Basler notes:

> The traditional interpretation that the tiger symbolizes the "Wrath of God" does not make sense to me now and did not when I first read the poem years ago. Blake's question, like his questions in other poems, was meant in the eighteenth century to challenge orthodox theology and at the same time the too simply rational deism of the time.

DISCUSSION STARTERS

What "astonishes" your students about this poem?

THE RECEPTIVE READER

1. The tiger creates "dreadful terrors" but at the same time has a fierce beauty: Its gold-and-black, flamelike coat is "burning bright" in the forest of the night. Supreme "art" twisted "the sinews of thy heart." The "immortal hand" that framed the tiger works on a cosmic stage among the stars. The key phrase is "fearful symmetry"—a kind of beauty that is sublimely beautiful but at the same time awe-inspiring and threatening.

2. We see someone using his hands and eyes to "frame," to "twist," using hammer, chain, anvil. Sublime force, like the force needed to shape red-hot iron on an anvil, and a fiery furnace played a role in forging a creature of terror and beauty. (This is not a vision of creation as the magical appearance of living things in a peaceful, idyllic setting.)

3. The lamb is often considered goodness incarnate because it is meek, nonthreatening, helpless, vulnerable. Conventionally, tigers are perceived as evil because they are rapacious, ferocious animals that are a scourge to human beings. Blake's tiger may be terrifying and dreadful, but Blake is too fascinated by its fierce beauty to see him as evil? Rather, he sees him as a powerful, beautiful creature created by a maker who well may

smile at what he has wrought? (On the other hand, the stars wept when the tiger was created?)

4. The questions are *rhetorical*—with the questioner assuming that the answer is self-evident? There is no real hint in the poem that there would be two rival immortal creators, one responsible for predators and the others for their prey?

Adrienne Rich, "Aunt Jennifer's Tigers" 590

DISCUSSION STARTERS

The topaz tigers come alive in Aunt Jennifer's artfully stitched panel in a way that she cannot. In her actual married life, she must undergo "ordeals," she is "terrified," and she is "mastered" by a husband. Help students see the tension between the two key symbols by having them cluster key words or phrases from the poem for each:

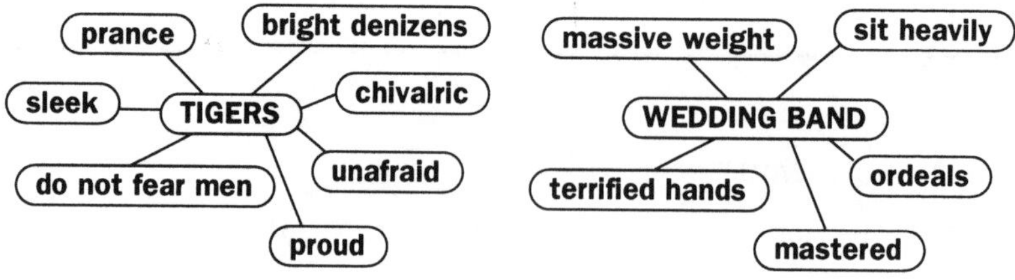

THE RECEPTIVE READER

1. The symbols suggest opposite worlds: the wedding band, constraint and fear; the tigers, the spirit of self-assertion and freedom. Ironically, the wedding band follows her into the grave while her wrought piece stays in the living world to "go on prancing, proud and unafraid."

2. In the context of this poem, *topaz* suggests an exotic and many-colored jewel; *denizen* suggests a natural being in its intended habitat; *chivalric* suggests a bygone time of pride and honor and bright tournaments. *Ordeal*, defined in a dictionary as "a primitive form of trial to determine guilt or innocence by subjecting the accused person to physical danger," suggests the seriousness of this long-suffering subjugation.

3. *Prance* sounds more vainglorious, assertive, strutting? *Stride* sounds more serious, solemn, self-assured, purposeful, independent?

4. For instance, a wedding band conventionally connotes a close bond, lifelong devotion?

William Butler Yeats, "Sailing to Byzantium" 591

PERSPECTIVES—YEATS AND IRELAND

In his introduction to *W. B. Yeats: Selected Poems* (Gramercy Books, 1992), Christopher Moore reminds readers that Yeats is an Irish poet and not an English one. "It is an important distinction which Yeats throughout his career made clear. Although the Yeats family was of English descent, by the time of William's birth—in Dublin on June 13, 1865—they had been in Ireland for more than two hundred years. Yeats grew up in a turbulent era of increasing Irish nationalism and rebellion against English rule, and he became actively involved in the struggle for Irish independence. By the early 1890s he had helped form the Irish Literary Society of London and the National Literary Society in Dublin to promote Irish cultural awareness. In 1896, he became a member of the Irish Republican Brotherhood, an organization which actively sought independence, by violent means if necessary. In 1922, to reward his patriotic efforts, he was made a senator in the newly formed Irish Free State." Yeats helped the new Ireland gain international recognition and visibility. In 1923 he became the first Irish writer to win the Nobel Prize in literature.

DISCUSSION STARTERS

The polarities of youth/age undergird Yeats' rich use of Byzantine art as symbols of permanence played off against symbols of nature, which inevitably moves through the cycles of birth, growth, decay, and death. Byzantium becomes the golden city whose precious artifacts will not follow nature's pattern of decay. Is it true that age has more of a need for and understanding of art than youth has?

THE RECEPTIVE READER

1. Youth is more body-oriented and closer to the unexhausted vital forces of nature than age; conversely, when the body ages, the life of the mind becomes more dominant, making mere physical activity and sensual satisfaction seem "mindless"? The decline of physical vigor makes mere physical satisfaction seem futile and elusive?

2. The three pairs of opposites intermesh: Striking visual images flesh out the underlying polarities: The young are "in one another's arms," caught in "that sensual music." The old are "paltry," petty in comparison, weakened and tattered—until the soul learns to "clap its hands and sing." The birds in the trees and the seas crowded with spawning, growing, and dying mackerel become fitting symbols for the "dying generations" caught up in a merely sensual life without an intellectual or spiritual dimension. Sages or holy men

turning in solemn circles in a gold mosaic are asked to become "the singing masters" who will teach the soul to produce and appreciate art and thought that will transcend the limitations of nature. The bird of "hammered gold and gold enameling," singing (soundlessly) on a golden bough, represents the art that triumphs over decay.

3. Salmon struggling upriver, leaping up waterfalls, are a dramatic symbol for the vital but blind instinctual forces in *nature* that keep life at the animal level going in a cycle of spawning, growth, and decay—without the benefit of "unaging intellect."

4. *Art* here is not an imitation of nature but an attempt to escape from it or triumph over it? Art, like eternity, leaves the restlessness of natural life behind. The poet envisions a perfect, richly formed "art," with such a form as "Grecian goldsmiths make" in order to transcend nature. These artifacts are timeless, disembodied, freed of the turmoil of crowded, ever growing and decaying natural life. The poet claims that once he is "out of nature," he shall never take another "bodily form from any natural thing."

5. The interlaced *ottava rima*, like the sonnet, is a form requiring deliberate, finely crafted artifice (allowing the poet to practice what the poem preaches?). It is at the opposite pole from the spontaneous natural outpourings that might be accommodated by free-flowing free verse.

THE PERSONAL RESPONSE

Do your students believe that art should be "natural"? If so, what do they may make of the abstract or nonrepresentational quality of much twentieth-century art?

Gabriela Mistral, "To Drink" 593

DISCUSSION STARTERS

What images and associations cluster for your students around the names of countries like Chile or Mexico? How much is stereotype; how much is enlightening background knowledge?

THE RECEPTIVE READER

Water is at the center of every stanza, including the refrainlike identical first and last couplets. There is a special intensity in the poet's relationship to the life-giving water—perhaps natural to a poet who has lived in settings where the parching sun is also more intense? The "blessed" water the speaker in the poem drank from a churning, "boiling" waterfall seemed to burn her mouth and make it bleed. The "native" holding her over the well to help her reach the water seems to become one with her ("I drank what he drank")—making her join in a larger human brotherhood beyond the individual self? The milky water of a coconut—drunk by the speaker like a daughter with the palm as the life-giving mother—becomes a living reminder of the mother's love—no "greater sweetness" for body or soul. The thirst for water in this poem becomes symbolic of the thirst for life?

THE CREATIVE DIMENSION

In a successful cluster, there is often a moment when what seemed at first a random branching out of ideas starts to fall into a pattern or to form a web of meaning. You may want to ask one or more students to reenact on the board the way an exceptionally productive or exceptionally centered cluster took shape.

Juxtapositions: Symbol and Allegory

Christina Rossetti, "Uphill" 595

DISCUSSION STARTER

Christina Rossetti's nineteenth-century allegorical vision takes us on an "uphill" spiritual journey that is strenuous and wearying at best. Ask your students about the two speakers in this dialogue: Are we listening to the body questioning the soul? Is it a human being speaking to the spirit of the universe? Is it a fellow mortal speaking to her or his good angel? Is it the fragile, fearful human being imploring God for assurance?

THE RECEPTIVE READER

The one who asks the questions seems to be a searching, striving mortal, for he or she has not yet reached that "resting place." The other speaker's been there, whether it be God, an ex-traveler, an angel, a spirit? It is clear that the second speaker knows about this final resting place at the "inn." Life is a road that takes "the whole long day" to bring us "to the very end." The night is death that awaits us at the end of the journey. That journey, as seen by the earnest Victorians, is "uphill all the way"; it is a struggle to maintain highmindedness that leaves us "travel-sore and weak." But the inn—heaven or immortality—provides rest and comfort. We will there be reunited with those "who have gone before." There will be "beds for all who come"—meaning all those who earnestly seek for spiritual significance in their lives. (Those frivolous souls who spend their time carousing and sleeping off their hangovers are not likely to make it to that promised final "resting place"?)

William Blake, "A Poison Tree" 596

DISCUSSION STARTERS

Blake probed the psychology of repression long before Freud came on the scene. Anger in itself is not bad, Blake suggests, but anger held in, watered in "fears," and repressed grows a poison apple that has the power to do irreparable damage. How much do your students know about modern theories concerning the workings of repression? What have they heard or read about repressed desires that are censored by the conscious mind but fester in the subconscious and find an obscure, tantalizing outlet in dreams?

THE RECEPTIVE READER

1. This poem does not so much warn against wrath as warn against wrath unexpressed, unexplored, unchecked, and remaining hidden. It hides behind a hypocritical surface of smiles and deceit. It festers and turns poisonous, lethal.

2. The *childlike* quality is reinforced by the simple sentences of the first stanza, by the frequent use of a simple *and* instead of a stronger logical link, and by the repetition of the *I* seven times. The gardening symbolism may also seem deceptively simple and childlike—until we sense echoes of the fatal apple in the Garden of Eden and of the first fratricide, the killing of Abel by Cain. (Cain was jealous and wily and secretive, too?)

THE PERSONAL RESPONSE

Students may be aware of pop psychology books that deal with issues of anger, both expressed and repressed. One of these, *When Anger Hurts* by McKay, Rogers, and McKay, dwells in detail on the deleterious effects of chronically "telling one's wrath." Other books deal with the dangers of repressed anger—"telling it not"—and its capacity for triggering depression, alcoholism, and violence.

Poems for Further Study

Lorna Dee Cervantes, "Refugee Ship" 597

DISCUSSION STARTERS

Ships have often provided a stimulus for the imagination. What ships or kind of ships have special symbolic associations for your students—Columbus' caravels, the galleys of antiquity, the *Titanic*, now-vanished other ocean liners, Thor Heyerdahl's reconstituted Polynesian vessels?

THE RECEPTIVE READER

1. Both the cornstarch and the Bible symbolize a world of family tradition that was the enclosed, protected world of the speaker's childhood but from which she has become separated, "orphaned."

2. The speaker was raised without the language of her people, Spanish? (Or perhaps, like many other ethnics, she spoke the language of her parents when very young but was then made to speak English both at home and

at school.) She still carries a Hispanic name but is "orphaned" from the culture it evokes.

3. The mirror confirms her ethnic roots in a world of people with "bronzed skin, black hair."

4. Refugee ships—whether carrying Jews trying to escape from Nazi Germany or carrying boat people from Vietnam—are often unwanted and turned back. Refugees are often considered a burden and considered politically undesirable by both the country that they flee from and the country on whose shores they land. The speaker—alienated from the culture of her family and yet felt to be different and not fully accepted in the Anglo culture—feels like "a captive / aboard the refugee ship." She can't go back, and she can't debark on new shores.

THE CREATIVE DIMENSION

We often empathize or are able to enter vicariously into the perspective and the feelings that shape the imaginative experience of a poem. But sometimes a poem speaks to us more directly—as if it were speaking from one alienated adolescent, or harried parent, or ethnic American to another. Where in their reading so far have students encountered a poet whom they could claim as "one of theirs"?

Matthew Arnold, "Dover Beach" 597

DISCUSSION STARTERS

What is the keynote of this poem—sadness? melancholy? nostalgia? despair? Does this poem about the loss of faith leave us with a pessimistic dead-end view of life? (Or does it end in the affirmation of the need for love and being "true to one another" as the antidote to the spiritual malaise of the approaching modern world?)

THE RECEPTIVE READER

True to nineteenth-century poetic fashion, the meaning of the *central symbol*, the sea, is spelled out—it becomes "The Sea of Faith." The sea is timeless in its constant ebb and flow, long ago in the age of Sophocles as today. It suggests the comings and goings of human life, the "ebb and flow / Of human misery." However, unlike the real sea, the sea of faith, in an age of rising doubt and agnosticism, is only withdrawing, permanently ebbing, leaving us on "a darkling plain" on which "ignorant armies clash by night." The spiritual aftermath of this receding of traditional faith is highlighted in the last stanza: We may have once looked at this world optimistically as a "land of dreams"—"so various, so beautiful, so new"—but the ebbing of faith leaves us disillusioned, high and dry on the barren pebble-strewn beaches of doubt, in a world that has "neither joy, nor love, nor light, / Nor certitude, nor peace, nor help for pain." If the universe no longer has a transcendent spiritual meaning, offering no metaphysical solace or transcendent hope, then the only antidote to alienation and despair is our bonding with other human beings.

John Keats, "Bright Star" 599

DISCUSSION STARTERS

In a letter Keats wrote to Richard Woodhouse in 1818, he compared the poet to a chameleon, who, having no fixed identity of his own, is always identifying with or entering into "some other body—the Sun, the Moon, the Sea." Keats wrote the first draft of this poem in 1819, and it may have been inspired by an observation he made while on a country tour the previous year. In observing the austere natural surroundings, he noted that they "refine one's sensual vision into a sort of north star which can never cease to be open lidded and steadfast over the wonders of the great Power."

THE RECEPTIVE READER

1. The always unchangeably bright star is compared to someone watchful, eternally alert, who never blinks or sleeps—its "eternal lids" are always "apart." Keats personifies and spiritualizes the ebb and tide (a symbol of misery in Arnold's poem), comparing them to a priest who washes the "earth's human shores" clean of their sins with "pure ablution." Even the snow is not merely a cover or a blanket but a "mask"—covering the mountains and the moors as if they were a human face.

2. In the first eight lines, the poet makes the star seem distant, pure, hung over our world in "lone splendor," isolated like a hermit. But what is really admirable for him about the star is not its isolation but its permanence, its steadfastness. Can that immunity to change be transposed to the lover's world of "sweet unrest," where the "soft fall and swell" of the beloved's breast reminds us of the steady pulse (and the constant flux and change) of human life? To be near her would be to "live ever"—and thus come closest to the serene, glorious unchangeable quality of the bright star.

Lucille Clifton, "my mama moved among the days" 599

PERSPECTIVES—CLIFTON: MOVEMENTS AND THE INDIVIDUAL VOICE

Andrea Benton Rushing positions Clifton in the context of the Black Pride movement and the emerging women's movement in "Lucille Clifton: A Changing Voice for Changing Times" (in *Coming to Light: American Women Poets in the Twentieth Century*, ed. Diane Wood Middlebrook and Marilyn Yalom, U of Michigan P, 1985). Many women poets who became widely known during the sixties and seventies "mirrored the strident stance, profane language, and violent imagery of urban, male poetry." Clifton found "her own voice during a turbulent period when so many poets sounded the same chords of outrage and militancy. Rather than merely imitating the sarcasm and fury of male poets, Clifton anticipated the concern with women's issues which is—like opposition to the war in Vietnam, support of homosexuals' rights, and the crusade for environmental protection—in deep, though often unacknowledged, debt" to the strategies and moral commitments of the civil rights struggle. Clifton "anticipated Alex Haley's *Roots* in personalizing history and using her own natal family as a symbol of the anguish and triumph of the African-American experience. Moreover, in an era when many African-American nationalists were harshly critical of their accommodating 'Uncle Tom' and 'Aunt Jemima' elders, the 'opiate' of African-American Christianity," and Anglo-Saxon names considered a legacy of slavery, Clifton "wrote in a different key. While others complained of their elders' failures, she celebrated her ancestors; while others converted to Islam, she wrote about the life-giving power of African-American religion; and, though others assumed African and Arabic names, Clifton justified her own"—which was the name of a grandmother, who as she says in one of her poems, "waited by the crossroads / in Virginia" to shoot a white man off his horse.

DISCUSSION STARTERS

Lucille Clifton is an African American poet. Is she writing about a mother carrying with her the feelings and fears of generations before her, beaten down by an environment hostile to her people? Is this why she is running "right back in, right back on in?"

THE RECEPTIVE READER

"High grass" suggests danger, inability to see far ahead; it suggests being more vulnerable than in a clearing? "My mama" at times seemed to be shepherding her children through difficulties with a dreamwalker's assurance ("what she touched was hers," "what touched her couldn't hold"). However, at times the difficulties did become insurmountable, and she scurried back to the relative safety of lowered expectations. The speaker finds her retreat hard to accept. The repetition in the last two lines, "right back in / right back on in," shows the speaker incredulously or regretfully pondering the situation, as if shaking her head?

Octavio Paz, "Wind and Water and Stone" 600

DISCUSSION STARTERS

Wind, water, and stone—all three are powerful forces that are part of the basic natural substructure of our lives. They are capable of benefiting us as human beings but also of doing much damage. And they are ultimately not separable except by our human tendency for separating closely intermeshing things by intellectual analysis? We as human beings name them different names. But the names, which people have given to these forces to distinguish among them, are "empty"; they all "disappear"; "one is the other." In the words of one student reader, separate and alone "one is nothing" (but together they make our world).

THE RECEPTIVE READER

Water, stone, and wind remind us of the basic givens of our habitat on this planet—givens that antedate all animate, let alone intelligent, life. Water suggests the primeval ocean, the preserver of life, circulating throughout nature in the form of life-giving rain. Wind makes us aware of the thin life-sustaining envelope of air. Like water, it can be destructive, as in hurricanes, or soothing, as in a breeze. Stone is symbolic of strength, solidity, hardness, and durability, outlasting all organic life, which is subject to growth and decay. In Paz' poem, the water hollows the stone, and the wind sculpts the stone—but without basically changing or affecting their role as the elementary "infrastructure" of existence on our planet?

Chapter 17 WORDS
The Web of Language 605

How aware are your students of words as words? You may want to ask: What is the difference in each of the following pairs? What is the difference in the associations and images the paired words bring to mind, the occasions where the words are used, or the people who might use them? Have students discuss pairs like *violin/fiddle, belly/abdomen, animal/beast, gloat/exult, god/deity, accuse/slander, complain/whine.* (A violin makes us imagine a different *setting* from a fiddle—one suggests a concert hall, the other a place for country music? *Belly* and *abdomen* make us visualize different speakers—perhaps an ordinary down-to-earth person and a physician? *Animal* and *beast* are likely to suggest different feelings—we may feel neutral about animals, but the word *beast* reminds us of their potential beastliness?)

First Reading: Jeffrey Harrison, "Bathtubs, Three Varieties" 607

DISCUSSION STARTERS

Which is the preferred tub? Is it the third and last? (It is "deep"; we are "relaxed and yet attentive to the moment.") However, the speaker certainly doesn't bathe in his "old-fashioned" tubs since they are full of walnuts in the fall, snow in the winter.

THE RECEPTIVE READER

1. *Flock* may suggest a more active aggregation, while *herd* may connote a faceless mass of dumb animals?

2. *Tomb* sounds more gloomy, solemn, and ceremonious? A very "theatrical" performance is marked by acting out and spectacular special effects? A "sarcophagus" is weighty, solid, and ancient and contains an important person? "Meditation" shuts out distracting noises and thoughts and puts us in touch with our spiritual selves?

3. A student wrote, "What a cool idea, having a flock of bathtubs under a walnut tree, especially the old-fashioned kind with paws. I'd soak in a cool bubble bath on a hot day, sipping lemonade, the birds singing. A much better idea than the disciplined bathing of a Zen monk."

The Willing Ear

Reuel Denney, "Fixer of Midnight" 609

DISCUSSION STARTERS

This poem needs to be *heard*. It is playful, with its internal rhymes of *awning/yawning*—yet there is a serious undertone of confused, apprehensive listening and nightmare? Students need to hear how the sounds of a poem like this act out and dance out what was inert letters on the printed page.

William Carlos Williams, "The Dance" 610

DISCUSSION STARTERS

Pieter Breughel the Elder is famed for his vivid portrayals of rustic life. (His nickname was "Peasant Breughel.") In addition to the *The Kermess*, see if students can bring copies of his other pictures to class, such as his *Peasant Wedding Feast*.

THE RECEPTIVE READER

1. *Emphatic repetition* should help set up the basic rhythm as "the dancers go ROUND, they go ROUND and / AROUND." The same "rollicking" rhythm is picked up and reinforced by "the SQUEAL and the BLARE and the / TWEEDLE of bagpipes, a BUGLE and FIDDLES." There is a strong echo effect in the parallel string of *ing*-forms (present participles) like

> *tipping* their bellies
> *kicking* and *rolling* about The Fair Grounds
> *swinging* their butts

Internal rhyme accentuates the rhythm in "PRANCE as they DANCE." The last line slows down and comes to a rest on the name of the picture—as if the dancers themselves were tiring, with the dance winding down and the music coming to a stop?

2. Blaring trumpets or loudspeakers have an ear-drum-piercing, blatant quality? *Fiddles* (suggestive of country music?) and *bellies* are simple, down-to-earth words, befitting the peasant dance, while *violin* and *abdomen* are Latinate and have a more refined and formal sound.

3. Williams knows formal language when he wants to use it: *impound*, *rollicking measures*, and *prance*?

THE PERSONAL RESPONSE

People who try hard to become refined, sophisticated, or genteel might have trouble getting into the spirit of rustic merriment in this poem? Others, who delight in the humble peasant origins that all but a small upper crust of aristocrats share, might chuckle and prefer the genuine, authentic mirth of these rustics to more arty and pretentious entertainments?

Maya Angelou, "Phenomenal Woman" 611

PERSPECTIVES—ANGELOU: PERSONA AND SELF-PORTRAIT

Maya Angelou is a much-sought-after speaker and performer whose performances combine exhortation, poetry, chant, and story, and her poems have a strong aural dimension. Angelou, who acted in *Roots*, has had a phenomenal career as writer, singer, dancer, actor, and writer-producer. She became widely known through her autobiographical volumes, starting with *I Know Why the Caged Bird Sings* (1969), about her childhood in Stamps, Arkansas, telling a story of hardship and the brutalities of segregation but also of indomitable pride and aspiration. She said that many of the people in her small rural Southern town knew only to "chop cotton, pick cotton, and hoe potatoes," all the while dreaming of being "free, free from this town, and crackers, and farming, and yes-sirring and no-sirring." They all "needed to believe that a land existed somewhere, even beyond the Northern star, where Negroes were treated as people." In a later volume, *The Heart of a Woman* (1981), she carried the story forward into the era of the Civil Rights movement. Bill Ott said in a review of the book in *Booklist* (September 1, 1981): "Her recollections of encounters with Martin Luther King, James Baldwin, and other activists capture all the fire and idealism of the era." As reviewers have noted, Angelou's "phenomenal" woman—in this and other poems obviously and assertively female and explicit about sex—does not easily fit the established categories of either fashionably ironic and detached male critics or of feminist critics conflicted about female sexuality.

DISCUSSION STARTERS

Will the next generation of women decide it's all right not to be "cute or built to suit a fashion model's size"? Or will many still be brainwashed by the "beauty myth"?

THE RECEPTIVE READER

1. All four stanzas of the poem end with the same four lines: "I'm a woman / Phenomenally. / Phenomenal woman, / That's me" (the last stanza introduces the quatrain with "'Cause"). In approximately the middle of each stanza, the poet introduces the lines that identify her as a phenomenon with "I say," and the lines that follow (e.g., "It's the fire in my eyes, / And the flash of my teeth, / The swing in my waist, / And the joy in my feet") are similarly structured throughout the four stanzas. When read aloud, this poem should be delivered with gusto, and the rhythm and rhyme should be accentuated.

2. The poet uses the features and movements of the human body as the outward signs of a happy and generous human soul. "The fire in my

eyes," "And the flash of my teeth," "The stride of my step," "The curl of my lips," and "The sun of my smile" all point toward a woman who is living life with zest. There is a hint of maternal love ("The span of my hips"), sensuality ("The ride of my breasts, / The grace of my style"), and tender care ("The palm of my hand, / The need for my care"). "The reach of my arms," "And the joy in my feet," and "the arch of my back" all point toward a woman who is earthbound, hard-working, and certainly no shrinking violet.

3. Something phenomenal is highly remarkable, extremely unusual, extraordinary. A person who is a phenomenon has exceptional qualities, aptitudes, abilities. The speaker in this poem is a phenomenal woman because she is so clearly herself. She likes who she is, she is aware of her own "inner mystery," and she is without artifice, pretense, or self-consciousness. Phenomenal, the poet says, can be as mundane as the daily chores as long as they are done with "joy" in the feet and a "flash" in the teeth.

4. This woman's self-image is strong and confident. She is pleased with herself for what she is, and does not waste time lamenting what she is not. Looks are no measure of the essence of a person: "Pretty women wonder where my secret lies. / I'm not cute or built to suit a fashion model's size." This is a woman who enjoys being precisely who she is. The poem makes fun of the shallowness of model-size pretty women who can't seem to fathom that beauty is not a guarantee that one will be happy or loved. It further pokes fun at the speaker's effect on the men around her: "I walk into a room / Just as cool as you please, / And to a man, / The fellows stand or / Fall down on their knees." The speaker rejects garnering attention for any other reason than being oneself: "Now you understand / Just why my head's not bowed. / I don't shout or jump about / Or have to talk real loud."

THE PERSONAL RESPONSE

Are responses to people who "come on too strong" reflective of gender? Is a woman who "comes on too strong" considered more objectionable than a man who does so?

Al Young, "For Poets" 613

DISCUSSION STARTERS

How would someone "stay underground too long" and "turn into a mole"? What is the difference between turning into "a stone" and breathing in trees? Why would anyone want to "knock out mountains" or "commune with snakes"?

THE RECEPTIVE READER

1. Part of the appeal of this poem is in its several cumulative series of related parallel elements, each delightfully more unexpected or imaginative than the last: "Dont turn into a *mole* / or a *worm* / or a *root* / or a *stone*."

Should there be a slight pause between each item—to let the last one sink in and to let us pause in pleasurable anticipation before the next? The whole second stanza is a similar series, cumulating in "& and be the very hero of birds." Although there is no regular end rhyme except for the playfully truncated *blink/think*, there are sound echoes in *mole* and *stone* and in *trees* and *birds*?

2. The truncated, syncopating *blink/think* sets up a counterrhythm very different from iambic pentameter! Many of the instructions or exhortations aimed at the listener go from the reassuringly reasonable ("Come on out into the sunlight") to provocative, mind-stretching metaphors: "Breathe in trees / Knock out mountains / Commune with snakes."

The Right Word

William Carlos Williams, "The Red Wheelbarrow" 614

DISCUSSION STARTERS

Why does so much depend on the red wheel barrow glazed with rain in this wonderful, puzzling, Zen-like poem?

THE CREATIVE DIMENSION

Help students see the pattern danced out in this poem by having them look at examples like the following:

So much depends
upon

driving
a sleek

'64 Mustang
instead of

a boxy
'78 Toyota.

Elizabeth Bishop, "The Fish" 615

DISCUSSION STARTERS

The expert, the insider, has a word for it (and so does the poet). Let different students be the insider explaining to the class what the following are: gills, barnacles, rosettes, peonies, irises, swivels.

THE RECEPTIVE READER

1. The *special language* of a trade, occupation, or hobby can make us feel like insiders. Here it helps us feel as though we were right there with the speaker on the boat? Students are likely to have to look up *thwart*—a seat across a boat; *oarlocks*—a device providing a pivot for an oar; *gunnel*—the upper edge of the side of a vessel.

2. Some students may see the *speaker's feelings* revealed only at the end when she decides to let the fish go. However, others may notice hints earlier throughout the poem. For instance, we become aware of the fish as a fellow creature when the eyes of the "grunting" and "venerable" fish "shifted a little." The speaker in the poem "admired his sullen face." The lines and hooks hanging from the fish's mouth were "like medals with their ribbons frayed and wavering." The details in this poem that make the fish near-human include the "five-haired beard of wisdom," and its "aching jaw." But the fish *is* a fish—with gills (breathing in "the terrible oxygen" when pulled out of the water that is its natural habitat), with a pink swim bladder, and with barnacles and sea-lice.

3. The rainbow, literally created by the oil on the water at the bottom of the boat, suggests the metaphoric glory of the venerable fish who has managed to survive so many entrapments? Like a prism when it tips toward light, the oil slick suggests the larger rainbow of life of which the fish is a part?

4. The speaker in the poem "stared and stared." The prolonged contemplation and the sensitivity to the suffering of the creature prepare us for the ending?

Gerard Manley Hopkins, "Pied Beauty" 617

PERSPECTIVES—HOPKINS: PRECURSOR OF MODERNISM

In "Wings That Spell" (*The New Republic*, October 7, 1991), Richard Jenkyns reviews three books on Hopkins (*Gerard Manley Hopkins: A Very Private Life* by Robert Bernard Martin; *Gerard Manley Hopkins: Selected Letters*, edited by Catherine Phillips; and *The Poetical Works of Gerard Manley Hopkins*, edited by Norman H. MacKenzie). For thirty years after his death Hopkins "remained unknown, but once published, he stood revealed, despite the strangeness of his idiom, as the greatest poet of his generation." Like Emily Dickinson's, his work remained hidden in his lifetime—perhaps not surprisingly, since "modernism was still some way in the future." The "old order was beginning to break down, and we should not be very much surprised if some of the most vital work of the age was the product of odd, quirky minds, not easily accessible to their contemporaries."

For Jenkyns, Hopkins' life is a story of moving from "brilliant promise" to personal anguish and disappointment. Hopkins was born in 1844 into a prosperous merchant family and grew up "on the edge of north London. At Highgate School he shone academically. Spirited, and undemonstratively pious, he also developed a wide culture: he drew delightfully, he was keenly musical, he wrote some poetry. At the age of 18 he won an award to Balliol College, Oxford — at that time easily the most distinguished college in the university. Oxford was an enchantment; in the exuberant letters that Hopkins wrote to his parents. . . . Though too small and slight to be a sporting hero, he was immediately popular." Hopkins "thrived on the study of classics and philosophy, but equally he flung himself gaily into the social whirl, and yet found the time to discover that drifting in a canoe on the River Cherwell beneath the willow trees was a taste of paradise."

In 1866 Hopkins was converted to the Roman Catholic Church, and two years later he joined the Society of Jesus. Bridges, Hopkins' lifelong friend and posthumous editor, "believed that the Jesuits wrecked his life, and even hastened his death." For fifteen years, Hopkins was never long in one place, being sent "by the Society to schools in the north of England, to St. Beuno's in rural Wales (where he was indeed happy and in a few months wrote many of his most famous poems in a burst of joyful creativity), to a curacy in Oxford (where he failed to recapture the happiness of his youth), back north to the parishes of industrial Lancashire." Finally, in 1884, Hopkins' superiors sent him to Dublin as professor of Greek and Latin at the Royal University of Ireland. Jenkyns considers this a disastrous move: "It is evident from his letters that he was already suffering from depression before he left England; and this was made much worse by the drudgery of endless examining and by his isolation in a new and partly hostile land (with his simple English patriotism, he found Irish nationalism peculiarly painful). In his letters, and in the few, terrible poems that he wrote at this time—now often known as the Dark Sonnets, or the Sonnets of Desolation—we see a man disintegrating in the throes of nervous breakdown." Sick with what was probably typhoid, Hopkins died in June 1889, at the age of forty-four.

DISCUSSION STARTERS

Hopkins was fascinated with diversity (what he called "individuation" or "thisness"). He said that it is the virtue of design or pattern to be "distinctive." He admitted that in cultivating distinctiveness "my poetry errs on the side of oddness . . . it is the vice of distinctiveness to become queer. This vice I cannot have escaped." You may want to read the poem aloud to students and ask them to listen for striking unusual words and phrases. Then invite them to do a re-creation that in some way relates to or responds to the rich and joyous multiplicity of the "pied beauty" of our world. Here is an example you may want to read to your students:

Dapped Beauty

I am dazzled by the glimmering
sequins of the rainbow trout,
dappled sun on flickering leaves,
the hovering hawk sweeping the land.
The frog squats, the crickets crinkle, and
wandering, whispering clouds travel in the skies.

THE RECEPTIVE READER

1. Hopkins, in his first few words, praises God for all things "dappled," which means "having spots of a different shade, tone, or color from the background; mottled." (*Mottled*, a close cousin to *dappled*, means "to diversify with spots or blotches of a different color or shade.") Assure your students that they do not need a phrase-for-phrase translation to enjoy this poem. Like much of Hopkins' poetry, it pleases the ear and teases (or just plain puzzles) the mind. Even when explained, the "fire-coal chestnut-falls" may make sense mostly to students who grew up in an area where chestnut trees are common. They may have seen the chestnuts dropping to the ground in their thick green wrappings that burst open to reveal the rich glowing red-brown color—like that of glowing coals—of the chestnuts inside. The "couple-color" of the skies could be any variation of two colors quilting the sky like a "landscape plotted and pieced"? The compressed phrase "fathers-forth" may make us think of a paternal God who begets and thus helps bring forth the rich quirky beauty that is the subject of the poem.

2. Have any of your students taken pleasure in the kind of tool set where screwdrivers or wrenches are laid out in order from large to small? Do they like the feel of a garage or workshop full of the "tackle and trim" of the mechanic's or carpenter's trade?

3. It is true that religious writers traditionally ask us to think of God as unchanged, eternal, immutable. But the glory of his creation, both in Genesis and in many non-Christian accounts, is in its abundant, varied, burgeoning life?

4. The poet delights in the rich diversity and distinctiveness of related words like *dappled*, *stippled*, *freckled* and in the antithetical play of synonym and antonym in pairs like "swift, slow; sweet, sour; adazzle, dim." His frequent use of alliteration—"Fresh firecoal chestnut falls; finches' wings"—goes "counter" to the usual use of end rhyme. The phrasing throughout is fresh, "original," provocative.

THE PERSONAL RESPONSE

Much art moves between two poles: the classical ideal of "smooth" symmetry and harmony on the one hand and a dynamic, vital richness and "quirkiness" on the other. Ask your students: Would they rather worship in a church with columns like a Greek temple or in one that borrows its pointed arches from a Gothic cathedral? Would they rather have an office in a "modern" glass-and-steel office tower or in a "postmodern" office building with gables and curlicues?

Richard Wilbur, "Reading Hopkins' 'Pied Beauty' 618

Wilbur explores a central paradox: Hopkins' love of earthy, material things in all their rich diversity while always seeing them as a reason to remember God, to praise God.

Charles Simic, "Poem" 619

DISCUSSION STARTERS

To highlight the polarity on which this poem hinges, ask students to cluster UP/DOWN and find words and phrases that reflect upward or downward movement?

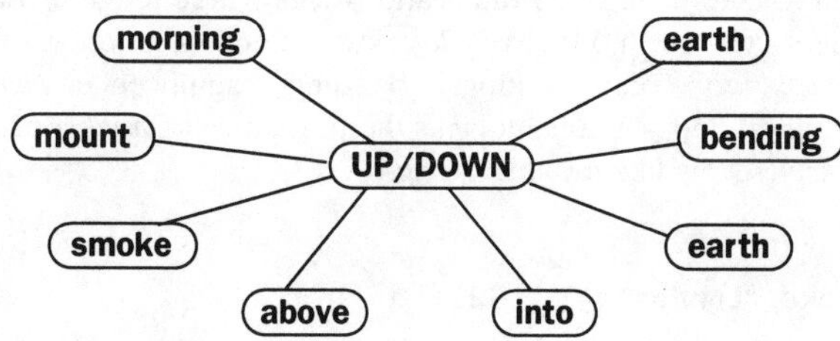

THE RECEPTIVE READER

1. Earth—the fruitful earth, Mother Earth; the earth is the rich substratum needed for planting and growth. It keeps us in touch with reality—"down to earth." But it also weighs us down, as suggested in terms like *earthbound*, *earthy*. We shovel earth into a fresh grave; we "unearth" something that has been buried.

2. "I belong to no one" can sound like a cry for help; "I forget how it is" could suggest how *bad* it is, this free-floating existence. "I watch" implies spectatorship, not participation in life. If we read the first stanza as the negative pole of the polarity, the second is reassuring with its "shoes," its routine of putting them on, its connection to the life-giving soil and its down-to-earth connection with life.

THE PERSONAL RESPONSE

This poem is a good test for the assumptions of reader-response theory? What we bring to the poem has much to do with how we read or interpret it?

Juxtapositions: Cityscapes

William Wordsworth, "Composed upon Westminster Bridge" 620

DISCUSSION STARTERS

What is inspirational about some of the great bridges? What feelings are inspired by the skyline of a great city? Is there something special about a "morning feeling" in a big city?

THE RECEPTIVE READER

Wordsworth—whom we usually associate with romantic nature worship—suffuses the city scene with the worshipful, elated emotions others might feel in seeing the sun "steep / In his first splendor" a natural scene—"valley, rock, or hill." *Brain* suggests the coolly reasoning, clever, practical intellect; *soul* suggests the immortal human spirit, capable of exultation and despondency, of deep-seated yearnings and aspirations. A down-to-earth word like *coat* would suit neither the mood nor the iambic rhythm. *Garment* suggests special ceremonial attire different from and more interesting than the garb of every day? *Churches* suggests familiar places of worship; *temples* and *domes* seem to take us to other times and places where religious ritual and a sense of the sacred are more alive? *Rays* are a literal description of what the sun emits; *splendor* connotes kingly, dazzling magnificence. *Nerve center* sounds biological and scientific; it lacks the resonance of *mighty heart*, which makes the city seems like a living being.

William Blake, "London" 621

DISCUSSION STARTERS

Blake's poem shows a dramatically different London from Wordsworth's. Everywhere he turns, he sees human suffering and sadness. Can your students speculate about *why* there is such a difference in point of view in these two poems?

THE RECEPTIVE READER

1. In Blake's poem, a network of emotionally charged terms like *woe, cry, fear, appalls, hapless, sigh, blood, curse, blasts, blight,* and *hearse* projects the poet's sense of horror at the squalor and degradation experienced by suffering fellow humanity in the big city. Human beings are "marked," almost as if scarred or stigmatized with a curse. "Mind-forged manacles" were not just made routinely like ordinary handcuffs but were "forged" (with the effort needed to shape hot iron) as shackles not easily broken or removed. A "blight" is a rapidly spreading and worsening condition, ending in ruin or death, as is a plague.

2. A palace should inspire feelings of admiration, but the blood shed in senseless imperial wars seems to run down its walls in this poem? Against

a background of prostitution and venereal disease, marriage, which should inspire joyful feelings, seems doomed and tainted, the "kiss of death"?

3. Wordsworth contemplates the city as if it were a painting, looking at the sublime lasting monuments of human effort as if from a distance. We do not, in this serene contemplative moment, see or empathize with the human beings that populate this crowded metropolis. Blake's drastically different perspective makes the buildings only an ironic backdrop to the misery of the city's inhabitants. He takes us from the vantage point of the spectator on the bridge to that of the close-up observer, taking us inside the city as he wanders "through each chartered street" and sees misery piled on misery. Would Wordsworth consider Blake to be "dull of soul" for passing by a "sight so touching in its majesty"?

THE PERSONAL RESPONSE

Many observers today are appalled by the misery and degradation they can witness every day in our big cities. Is it still possible to be inspired by cities as expressions of the human spirit?

THE CREATIVE DIMENSION

What would a poem be like that is written by a latter-day Wordsworth and called "Los Angeles" or "Chicago"? What would a latter-day Blake say in a poem called "New York"?

The Limits of Language

John Masefield, "Cargoes" 622

DISCUSSION STARTERS

You might want to ask students: Can you imagine yourself being on one of the three ships in this poem? In what capacity?

THE RECEPTIVE READER

1. The first stanza might suggest adventurous trade that broadened horizons and opened up routes to fascinating exotic places. The second stanza might suggest colonial expansion and conquest, trashing distant cultures in search of treasure? The third stanza might suggest grubby latter-day commercialism, catering to prosaic everyday needs.

2. Have students freely explore the images and associations that the connotative words in this poem bring to mind. For instance, Palestine is not like any other place on the map. It is the legendary Holy Land, battleground between the true believers worshiping the God of the Old Testament and worshipers of exotic idols; it was through centuries the goal of pilgrimages and crusades. A peacock is not an ordinary domesticated bird like a chicken

or a duck—it is a gorgeous bird totally unfit to eat but associated with ostentatious, vainglorious display as it spreads its dazzling tail feathers.

THE RANGE OF INTERPRETATION

How aware are students of current tendencies to reexamine the conventional glorification of slave-owning, oppressive early civilizations and of the "Age of Exploration"?

Gerard Manley Hopkins, "Peace" 624

DISCUSSION STARTERS

What is the central metaphor in this poem? Hopkins is speaking of peace on a private, highly personal level: inner peace. For Hopkins, that inner peace is elusive; trapping it is like taming an elusive wild bird, shying away from human contact.

THE RECEPTIVE READER

1. Bringing the word *under* up front in "*under* be my boughs" highlights the shielding, protecting influence (like a shielding tree in rough weather) that the poet wants to offer the elusive, roaming wild wooddove of peace? "To *own* my heart" accentuates how intensely *personal* this poet's religious feelings are?

2. The word *plumes* helps us to see a fanning out, an unfolding of feathers. Some students may see the fanned tail of the peacock, but doves, too, can stretch their wings. Patience ultimately "plumes"—unfolds or blossoms—to Peace.

3. The work the poet is thinking of is the work of the contemplative life, or of the preaching life, or of the missionary life?

John Keats, "On First Looking into Chapman's Homer" 625

DISCUSSION STARTERS

Keats approached the poet's task with intense seriousness and a transcendent sense of mission. In the same year that he wrote "On First Looking," he determined to immerse himself in his chosen vocation "for ten years, that I may overwhelm / Myself in poesy; so I may do the deed / That my own soul has to itself decreed."

THE RECEPTIVE READER

1. Each of the more *connotative* choices in the following pairs takes us away from the ordinary to a heightened, enhanced world more glowing with suggestions of romance or legend:

Standard	Keats' choices
kingdom	realm
poets	bards
loyalty	fealty
patron of poetry	Apollo
lands	demesne
expanse	pure serene
field of vision	ken

2. This poem follows a Petrarchan rhyme scheme, its first octave following the typical *abba*, *abba* pattern, and the closing sestet the *cdcdcd*. This type of sonnet scheme often "turns" in the ending sestet. Students could argue that this one does too, because it is at this point that the poet takes the imaginative leap from his journey through the realms of literature to the excitement of the astronomer or explorer: "Then felt I . . ." (Some students might argue that the key word that makes the poem turn earlier is the *Yet* of line 7.) The wonder and "wild surmise" of the Spaniards beholding the vast expanse of the Pacific provides the climax or high point of the poem.

Dylan Thomas, "Fern Hill" 626

DISCUSSION STARTERS

Thomas' poetry should be *heard* to be fully enjoyed. You may want to have students read the poem aloud in a Quaker reading, for which students read, on impulse, as much or as little of the poem as they feel comfortable reading—then letting the next reader pick up the thread. What is the dominant drive or force behind Thomas' poem? It is a powerfully nostalgic re-creation of an idealized memory of childhood, with a steady drumbeat of such phrases as "young and easy"; "I was prince of the apple towns"; "I lordly"; "I was green and carefree"; "it was all shining"; "happy as the heart was long." In the last four lines, the implied counterpoint of an emotionally and imaginatively diminished adulthood becomes overt: "and wake to the farm forever fled / from the childless land."

THE RECEPTIVE READER

1. Was the house one where "lilting" songs were being sung by people "happy as the grass was green"? Did the child move through the days happily and excitedly as children climb trees? Students might imagine the poet as a young boy climbing atop wagons and feeling as though he were a "prince," looking out over a domain of apple trees. The phrase "Down the rivers of the windfall light" makes it seem as though he is carried downstream, floating easily, in a perpetual sunlight that is gratuitous, free like a windfall of ripe fruit? To the speaker, the sun is "young once only" because as we grow up, the sun, like everything else, comes to seem familiar and old to our jaded eyes?

2. Childhood is a time of growth, like that of the fresh green sprouting in springtime. (The child is also green—unripe, young, innocent, inexperienced, unseasoned, springlike?) Everything in that precious "golden" time is valued and treasured.

3. The poet envisions God's creatures in the first pristine days after creation as spellbound by the "spinning," living world around them, moved to "praise" by the still uncorrupted glorious world in which they find themselves. There is a parallel to the expulsion from Eden, with the farm "forever fled from the childless land"? In the original story, however, Adam and Eve were responsible for their eviction from Eden. In this poem, the children are "green and golden," innocent; it is Time that is the enemy, who allows "so few and such morning songs."

4. The chains are the chains of mortality. Even when we are "green" and still growing, we are already programmed to die; we are already "dying." There is no way to stop time, no way to hold on to childhood, no matter how golden, how green.

e. e. cummings, "anyone lived in a pretty how town" 628

DISCUSSION STARTERS

Cummings' playful attitude toward life and language is reflected in this comment by Elizabeth Cummings, his younger sister:

> My brother was great fun to be with. He could draw pictures, and tell stories, and imitate people and animals, and invent games, and could make you laugh, even when you thought you felt very miserable.

When does cummings seem to be playing games with language? When or how is he serious? Can a poet be playful and serious at the same time?

THE RECEPTIVE READER

1. The rotation of "spring summer autumn winter" adds to the feeling that life is moving, not static. The seasons change. A different one is "uppermost" or "foremost" at different times of the year. "Sun moon stars rain" are also part of the steady alternation of basic life cycles. Yet despite this changing order, the words stay the same. Despite the changing order, the elements that make it up stay the same, giving us a basic sense of underlying continuity under the surface of constant change.

2. Paired opposites echo throughout the poem: floating/down; women/men; sowed/reaped; isn't/same; sun/moon; down/up; laughed/cried; joy/grief; someones/everyones; sleep/wake; laughed/cryings. There are many such couplings that we can imagine as concrete polarities, for example

sun/moon. But there are also those that might be thought of as slant polarities, such as nevers/dream.

3. The superficially jumbled lives of these people seem to be following basic familiar patterns. The simplicity of the basic underlying patterns of life seems to fit the simple rhyme scheme of a child's verse?

THE PERSONAL RESPONSE

Are there some unexpectedly serious statements here under the deceptively childlike surface? "Children are apt to forget to remember" is right on the mark. "They / said their nevers they slept their dream" may remind us of people who live by strict rules (don't ever do this, never do that) and "fall asleep" to what they would really like to do in their lives.

THE CREATIVE DIMENSION

Quaker readings require trust on the part of the instructor. The reading is called a "Quaker reading" because it imitates a kind of reading and speaking done at a Quaker gathering—each person takes a turn when the spirit moves him or her. There doesn't have to be any particular order to the reading. People can read one line that resonates for them—and stop. Then someone else feels moved to go on.

Hugh MacDiarmid, "Weep and Wail No More" 630

DISCUSSION STARTERS

MacDiarmid says in one of his poems: "Lourd on my hert as winter lies / The state that Scotland's in the day"—"Heavy as winter the current state of Scotland lies on my heart." How much does language have to do with giving people a sense of separate identity—Southerners as against Yankees, French Canadians as against English-speaking Canadians? In this poem, the poet tells his readers: *Give over* (stop) your weeping and wailing; you *must* keep quiet to hear the dead who are making *no more noise at all* than the grass flourishing *where nobody* walks.

Poems for Further Study

Mark Strand, "The End" 631

DISCUSSION STARTERS

One poet compared life to traveling on a train and death to getting off at our appointed destination. Mark Strand compares death to getting on a ship that sails off into darkness. What would be your students' preferred metaphor for the end of life?

THE RECEPTIVE READER

1. The songlike or *balladlike rhythm* of the poem is shaped in part by the refrain-like repetition of "not every man knows," of "what he shall sing," and of "there at the end"—with the last one, fittingly, closing the poem. The repetition of these key phrases is more than just pleasing to the ear; it drives home our inarticulateness and the inadequacy of language to do justice to the ultimate reality of death: "Not every man knows what he shall sing at the end." All that anyone knows, the poem suggests, is what has happened and what is happening now: pruning the roses, stroking the cat, "the sunset torching the lawn and the full moon icing it down."

2. The song stands for any last words or thoughts. (George V, who died in 1936 and was widely reported as asking "How stands the empire?" actually exited this world after saying "God damn you" to his doctor. Stonewall Jackson, after being grievously injured in the Civil War, is said to have whispered, "Let us cross over the river and sit under the shade of the trees.") With the image of the ship, the poet may be alluding to Greek myth, where Charon ferried the dead across the River Styx to their final abode in Hades. The sea represents the great unknown Beyond, as in the Arthurian myth where the ship carrying the body of the dead king drifts out to sea.

THE CREATIVE DIMENSION

In the second and third stanzas, the poet looks back over life and presents, very briefly, the details that stand out when "the time has passed to prune the rose or caress the cat, / When the sunset torching the lawn and the full moon icing it down / No longer appear." In the next sentence he adds sky and clouds to his short list of roses, cats, the sun, and the moon: "the sky / Is no more than remembered light, and the stories of cirrus / And cumulus come to a close, and all the birds are suspended in flight." These are the small everyday details of the texture of life, not properly treasured until the end.

Margaret Atwood, "Dreams of the Animals" 631

PERSPECTIVES—ATWOOD AND CANADIAN LITERATURE

Poet, novelist, short story writer, and literary critic, Margaret Atwood has been called the most influential and widely acclaimed writer in Canada, a national icon, and Canada's "high priestess of angst." Her best-known novel, *The Handmaid's Tale* (1985), is a scathing indictment of a plastic, sterile, misogynistic society. A central recurrent theme in her writing is the inhumanity of human beings to one another (and to animals, as in this poem). A radical feminist and ecologist, she grew up as an entomologist's daughter "in the bush" without formal schooling until she was twelve. Before Atwood's forebears moved to Canada from Connecticut, one of her ancestors, Mary Webster, was tried as a witch and hanged. When the town officials came the next day to cut her down, she was amazingly still alive and was freed because of the principle of double jeopardy. One reviewer speculated that Atwood had inherited from her ancestor "a gut-level aversion to societies that presume to have God on their side." In the introduction to a collection of her nonfiction prose, Atwood said, "When you begin to write, you're in love with the language, with the act of creation, with yourself partly; but as you go on, the writing—if you follow it—will take you places you never intended to go and show you things you would never otherwise have seen. I began as a profoundly apolitical writer, but then I began to do what all novelists and some poets do: I began to describe the world around me.' "

DISCUSSION STARTERS

You might want to have students bring pictures of cartoon animals juxtaposed with pictures of their real-life, wildlife counterparts. What feelings and associations are brought in to play by the contrasting images?

THE RECEPTIVE READER

1. We may think of moles as grubby, blind, smelly creatures, but here they seem at home in their world of darkness and "delicate / mole smells." The frogs are not clammy and bug-eyed but "sparkling" and "green and golden." The "pattering" feet of the armadillo make the animal sound harmless or childlike? The "crested, royal-eyed" iguana is made to seem superior and aristocratic—like a captive king?

2. The animals in the wild are dreaming of what comes naturally to them—mostly other animals. The captive animals, on the other hand, caught in an oppressive human world, are caught in dreams centering on cages and sawdust. The dreams of the natural survival methods of the red and black striped fish—"defense, attack, meaningful / patterns"—are juxtaposed against the silver fox's dreams of "digging out"—although the baby foxes will have to be left behind, their "necks bitten." The birds' territories are "enclosed by singing." But the armadillo's territory is circumscribed by a "pattering" of its own feet, driving it insane. The frogs, atop their lily pads, sparkle "like wet suns," dreaming of things "green and golden." The trapped iguana, however, for all its regal appearance—"crested, royal-eyed, ruling"—dreams of "sawdust."

THE PERSONAL RESPONSE

The animals are made to seem not "lovable" (let alone cuddly) so much as admirable—they are vital creatures each with its own kind of distinctive beauty?

Gerard Manley Hopkins, "The Windhover" 633

PERSPECTIVES—HOPKINS' FALCON AND THE RANGE OF CRITICISM

Hopkins' "Windhover" may be the most widely analyzed poem in the English language. Much explication has focused on the symbolic meaning of the bird as an emblem of Christ. Poet and critic Babette Deutsch said, "the bird is the falcon or kestrel. While in the title Hopkins chose to give it the local name descriptive of its hovering flight, in the body of the poem he refers to it as a 'Falcon,' capitalizing the word to emphasize the symbolism, and he makes the most of the courtly associations of falconry. . . . A passage in a sermon by Hopkins the priest illumines more fully the work of Hopkins the poet. Speaking of Christ, he said: 'Poor was his station, laborious his life, bitter his ending: through poverty, through labor, through crucifixion his majesty of nature more shines.' This might be taken as the text of 'The Windhover,' or as a prose gloss upon it."

Jerome Bump, in "Hopkins as a Jesuit Poet" (*Critical Essays on G. M. Hopkins*, ed. A. Sulloway, G. K. Hall, 1990), says: "The fusion of the sublime and the beautiful in a single creature in 'The Windhover' represents another stage in Hopkins's revolt against dualism. The striking opening of the sestet, 'Brute beauty,' emphasizes through consonance, assonance, and a double stress the unity of these opposites. What is admired is both the beauty of the bird's flight patterns and its 'dangerous' brute force."

One Jesuit critic identified at least three different critical readings of the phrase "the heart in hiding." For instance, we might simply take the phrase more or less at face value: the poet is not visible or particularly noticeable—or might even be deliberately trying not to be conspicuous and scare off the bird. Or else, the poet desires to share in the natural freedom and beauty of the bird—but "hides" or shrinks from it, as an act of meritorious self-abnegation. Or else, the poet is remiss, shrinking from the labor and pain that would be the true imitation of Christ. (Robert Boyle, in *Metaphor in Hopkins*, U of North Carolina P, 1961). I. A. Richards said that the poet is "hiding from Life, has chosen a safer way"—avoiding the danger of temptation by seeking the shelter of faith.

DISCUSSION STARTERS

Make sure students hear the poem read: Hopkins' poems enchant the ear with their wonderful lines full of alliteration, assonance, and cross-rhyme at the same time that the bold, rich images dazzle the eye. Are your students able to sense the poet's "ecstasy!" as the poem sweeps the reader "off, off forth on swing"?

THE RECEPTIVE READER

1. The three words—*minion*, *dauphin*, *chevalier*—carry connotations spelled out in the second stanza: the bird suggests cherished beauty, fiery valor, action, and pride—of the kind that we might associate with the chivalric pageantry of the Middle Ages, with plumes decorating the headgear and the horses of the knights.

2. Most of the words seem to carry a feeling of mastery, particularly when listed together. *Riding*, *striding*, and *gliding* picture actions of someone fully in control and easily in command. *Sweep* suggests unresisted speed, and hurl suggests motion with extra force. In the poem, the "sweep" is the motion the skate's heel makes as it smoothly speeds in a curve, chiseling the ice with ease. As "the hurl and gliding / Rebuffed the big wind," readers may be able to feel the force and assurance of a flight that causes great winds to shift in "rebuff." The bird doesn't simply "resist the wind"—it rebuffs it, stopping it cold and pushing it back.

3. The buckling action of the vital link, "AND the fire that breaks from thee then," causes the poet to move into an exalted religious state—one of ecstasy and wonderment. This feeling is like being swept away by a lovely and dangerous knight. But all this elation or ecstasy was caused by a mere bird. Similarly, as the plain, ordinary plodding horse-drawn plow is drawn through the furrow, the earth it throws up polishes it to a beautiful shine. When a fire is dying, embers that already look like black-blue ashes may suddenly shift and break open, with the "gash" revealing a beautiful "gold-vermilion" fire. All three images reinforce the idea that even in ordinary "brute" or inanimate examples of God's creation there lurk reminders of the transcendent, dazzling beauty of the Creator.

4. The falcon is enticed or drawn along by the dappled dawn?

THE RANGE OF INTERPRETATION

Students may be ready to see the Falcon's image as a "shining knight," who rescues and frees the speaker from his "heart in hiding." This might mean freeing him from the earthly desires of his heart, from spiritual misgivings, or from his shyness about declaring his love openly and unconditionally.

Wole Soyinka, "Lost Tribe" 634

DISCUSSION STARTERS

Soyinka is an African writer who challenges the cultural rootlessness of the superficially Westernized postcolonial African. How does the poet in this poem vent his wicked wit at the expense of American pop culture? How is the way we think mirrored in the way we talk?

THE RECEPTIVE READER

1. The poet has a keen ear for the buzzwords, the slogans and clichés, that people use to create a fake "sincerity" and a superficial air of chumminess and cheerfulness in an alienated "lost" society. To the poet, there is something intrusive and officious, busybody-ish, about people who tell us (in the imperative, commanding or "barking" mode) "Touch!", "Enjoy your meal," or ("crisper still") "Enjoy." The smile and the hugging of a child become too impersonal and superficial when we offer them routinely, "by rote," in order to seem a superficially "caring" person?

2. The "incantations"—prayers or chants that should create very special results on very special occasions—lose their "magic" when they are thoughtlessly used. At the same time, people pick up their ideas and ways of talking from too many sources? Or they use a language too private and self-indulgent—cut off from the larger community? (Words minted as under a "private franchise" prove "counterfeit" and worthless in the "open markets" of larger social intercourse.) And there is too much of a babble of conflicting voices—as "incessant tongues pretend a way of thought"?

3. Soyinka's *metaphors* tend to be dramatic and intensely visual, hard to ignore? Ants move in a steady flow of purposeful motion when undisturbed. But when human steps break up the pattern, the ants scurry about in futile hysteria—like the uprooted people of the modern world, who have lost the sense of community. Instead of drawing their intellectual and spiritual nourishment from a culture with deep roots, the poet's contemporaries live with "Straws outstretched to suck at every passing broth"—taking in bits and snatches of ready-made ideas from passing trends and fads. Our gurus and "instant" media celebrities dispense pills and bromides like fake pharmacies pushing their wares. Our cults and fads are disposable like paper diapers in our throw-it-away society. Tickertapes can give only bit facts, and the slogans that have been tickertaped to people's foreheads cannot do justice to authentic human values.

4. The *imperative* form of the verb is the commanding or "barking" form: "Do this! Do that!" The concluding question is identified as a "tear-duct / Variant" of the injunction to smile—it is the tear-jerking "Have you hugged your child today?"

5. The lost tribes of Israel have been "found" by different theorists in places as distant as South America. We too in the modern world are estranged from our roots in a common culture or a common religion?

THE PERSONAL RESPONSE

Do students feel that the familiar slogans satirized by Soyinka have their place—that they serve a social or human function? Working in groups, your students might want to work out a defense of, or proposal for the reform of, the language of public friendliness or good cheer.

John Heaviside, "A Gathering of Deafs" 635

DISCUSSION STARTERS

Ask students what other languages besides words they can think of—the language of music, the language of numbers, the language of gestures, the language of colors? How do these other languages communicate, and what do they say? A student writes about John Heaviside's poem:

There are few things more fascinating than to watch "A Gathering of Deafs," as described by John Heaviside in his captivating poem about deaf culture with its celebration of community and storytelling. The poem obliquely becomes a commentary on the hearing world on several levels: (1) How the busy pace of our lives isolates us from one another; (2) How communication barriers need to be removed by reaching out to others; and (3) How we have lost the "community" we once had in America. To get at these layers of meaning, the poet uses strong kinesthetic imagery to convey a sense of a very different silent "community" of people who share their feelings and their stories. . . . The poet succeeds in giving the reader a sense of the deafs' isolation from the outside world, conveying their special creativity in using the arched eyebrow or hyperbolic gesture to communicate fully in their silent, visual/kinesthetic/tactile language. Yet the outside world is likewise excluded from the liveliness of this "gathering," since it cannot understand this "jive wild" of the hands. Language, after all, is the primary means of communication of living beings.

THE RECEPTIVE READER

1. A "congregation" (like a "community") is more than a casual group of people—its members are bonded by common experience, a common dedication, shared values. Also, a congregation is quite apart from a world of nonbelievers—the way the deaf here, in their "lively" but "serene" world, are at the opposite pole from the spastic "honking" blast of the punk rocker's radio. "Jive" (like the talk of jazz musicians) is a lively, colorful, fast-moving kind of insiders' talk—not the clumsy or limited way of communicating that outsiders might expect the language of the deaf to be. *Dexterous* means not just skillful but nimble. A "configuration" is not just a fairly simple or predictable pattern but a characteristic, unique pattern intricate enough to reward attention.

2. *Mellifluous* is derived from the word *mellifer* meaning "honey-bearing." It means flowing sweetly or smoothly. The word *staccato* is associated with music; it denotes sounds intentionally abrupt, harsh. In the poem, staccato is surrounded by words like *emphasizing*, *abrupt*, *jerking*. *Mellifluous* is linked with the adjective *delicate*.

3. The language of the deaf is expressive, human; it has its own grace and strange beauty; it allows lovers to caress the air "joining their thoughts / by the flow of fingertips."

Chapter 18 FORM Rhyme, Meter, and Stanza 639

The first fact of the world is that it repeats itself. I had been taught to believe that the freshness of children lay in their capacity for wonder at the vividness and strangeness of the particular, but what is fresh in them is that they still experience the power of repetition from which our first sense of the power of mastery comes.

ROBERT HASS

I'm thinking of the form of a poem, the shape of its
understanding. The presence of that shaping constitutes
the presence of poetry. Not tone, not imagery, not particular
qualities of content.

ROBERT HASS

Much modern poetry, like much modern art, has left formal conventions of the past behind. If you showed your students reproductions of two paintings, how would they tell the Rembrandt from the Picasso? How could they tell Michelangelo's *David* from a figure by a twentieth-century sculptor like Giacometti or Henry Moore? How can they tell whether music they hear on the radio is Beethoven or modern jazz? Modern poetic form, like form in the sister arts, tends to be more irregular, more improvisational, less locked into predictable patterns, than it once was.

For a preliminary exploration of traditional and open form, you may want to look with your students at three samples illustrating different conventions and expectations about poetic form. Ask your students which of these they would place in the eighteenth, the nineteenth, or the twentieth century. What features of form do they recognize in each? Note Pope's neatly packaged, self-contained couplet, with antithetical balance of opposites, strong metrical beat, and end rhyme (probably a more perfect rhyme with the pronunciation of Pope's time than with ours). Note the strongly rhythmical beat and the predictable end rhymes of Poe's mellifluous lines. Note the unrhymed lines or irregular length, the syncopated rhythms, and the offhand style of Lee's modern poem.

It was many and many a year ago,
  In a kingdom by the sea,
That a maiden there lived whom you may know
  By the name of Annabel Lee.

—Edgar Allan Poe, "Annabel Lee"

last week
my mother died/
& the most often asked question
at the funeral

was not of her death
or of her life before death
                                        but
why was i present
with/out
a
tie on.

—Don L. Lee, "Last Week"

Good nature and good sense must ever join;
To err is human; to forgive, divine.
—Alexander Pope, "Essay on Criticism"

Ogden Nash, "The Hunter" 640

DISCUSSION STARTERS

Hunters, boxing fans, and aficionados of deep-sea fishing may seem to the quizzical observer to be throwbacks to an earlier cycle of civilization. Why? Do we have a right to criticize them, or should we leave them alone? Effort, ingenuity, pluck, and luck are needed to assist this mighty duck-killer as Nash and his readers watch the hunter's shenanigans amused and bemused.

Gwendolyn Brooks, "Old Mary" 640

DISCUSSION STARTERS

You may want to chart the formal features of this poem for your students somewhat as follows:

My lást | defENSE
Is the prés | ent TENSE.

It lít | tle húrts | me to know
I sháll | not go

Cathé | dral-húnt | ing in SPAIN
Nor ché | rying in Mích | igan or MAINE.

First Reading: American Folk Song, "Black Is the Color" 641

DISCUSSION STARTERS

Make sure students listen to the poem and *hear* the segmenting effect of rhyme—traditionally the most basic means of transforming the flow of prose into lines of verse.

THE RECEPTIVE READER

1. The *refrain* gives the singer a chance to use and hear the magic words "true love" several times, while at the same time mentioning one striking physical detail that helps her visualize the loved person? The other repeated line is varied to make it rhyme in the second stanza?

2. The poem goes from marveling at the lover's presence to the fear of loss?

3. Does a woman singing the praises of her lover still represent an exceptional role reversal in lyrics and ballads today?

Rhyme, Alliteration, Free Verse

Jonathan Swift, "A Description of the Morning" 643

DISCUSSION STARTERS

The details of this poem have the feel of a large city. How does Swift's "cityscape" compare with Blake's or Wordsworth's? Unlike Blake's "London," which is accusing and despairing, or Wordworth's Westminster Bridge poem, which glamorizes the city, Swift looks at the city with a half-affectionate, half-sardonic eye. There are thieves, philanderers, and debt-ridden aristocrats. But there are also ordinary people who are beginning to go about their unspectacular chores: Moll cleans; "the small-coal man" advertises his wares; the "chimney-sweep" outshouts him; "bailiffs" appear to keep the peace after thieves had done their work at night. The final touch is the image of schoolboys dragging their feet in an effort not to arrive at school.

THE RECEPTIVE READER

1. Many of the *couplets* are like a freeze frame capturing some amusing or bemusing facet of city life. The most neatly packed couplets are lines 3 and 4, lines 5 and 6, lines 7 and 8, lines 15 and 16. The images in these couplets focus on a single subject, and the second line sometimes adds a humorous or ironic twist (like a punch line) to the first.

2. *Seedy sights*: Betty pretending to have slept in her own bed; thieves let out of the prison by a conniving warden (the turnkey) to ply their trade in the night. Duns are persons who demand payment, like bill collectors. Swift satirically implies that "his lordship" may be in arrears—most likely from squandering his wealth on luxuries. However, there are also many good ordinary people plying their trades?

Emily Dickinson, "The Soul selects her own Society" 645

DISCUSSION STARTERS

This powerful poem insists that the part of us we call "the soul" knows exactly what is good and right for her. No pretense, no flattery, no accommodation for the great, the rich, the flatterers. If we let the soul speak honestly, Dickinson suggests, we will choose our friends honestly.

Ask students to list key words from Dickinson's poem and play with a range of full rhymes or *slant rhymes* for each. (Dickinson was a great lover of slant rhyme.) Below is a sampling of possibilities.

Society	variety	so quietly	sobriety
Door	more	snore	dare
Majority	pejoratively	minority	most horribly
Chariots	Harriet's	carrots	
Gate	mate	mat	get
Emperor	terror	mirror	Elsinore
Mat	mate	slat	met
One	come	done	sun
Valves	halves	evolves	suave
Stone	bone	strewn	moan

THE RECEPTIVE READER

1. The only full rhymes are *Door/more*? Almost a full rhyme is *society/majority*? All others are slant rhymes—*pausing/kneeling*, *gate/mat*, *nation/attention*, or *One/Stone*. These slant rhymes make us listen for echoes rather than lulling us to sleep by too predictable pat rhymes like *nation/station*, *mad/had*?

2. The *metaphors* bring the poet's perspective to life by startling juxtapositions of the exotic or grand and the ordinary: chariots stop at the poet's "low gate"; an emperor is kneeling on her lowly doormat; the people from among whom the "Soul selects her own Society" become an "ample nation." The soul does not just fail to pay attention any longer to those not chosen; with much greater finality, the "Valves of her attention" close "like Stone." The poem makes us marvel at the pride shown and the high standards set by the "Soul"?

William Shakespeare, "Sonnet 30" 646

PERSPECTIVES—REVISITING THE "SESSIONS OF SWEET SILENT THOUGHT"

Murray Krieger's rereading of Sonnet 30, in *A Window to Criticism: Shakespeare's Sonnets and Modern Poetics* (Princeton UP, 1974) demonstrates how a familiar poem may be drastically reinterpreted when seen through the lens of modern critical conventions and assumptions. From the point of view of the modern critic, wary of the frank emotionalism of the sonnets, the poet-as-lover or the poet-as-friend who speaks to us in the sonnets may seem prone to "self-pity" and to a "sentimental" bemoaning of his "woes" as a lover. The critic may therefore ask us to distance ourselves from the persona speaking to us in the poem—whose "error and weakness of vision" Shakespeare "so carefully exposes" to us. We can thus assume the proper ironic detachment from the persona's "sentimental insistences, presented too howlingly in the most obvious and unimaginative terms of lamentation (four uses of 'woe,' three of 'moan,' alliterative emphasis on 'woes,' 'wail,' and 'waste, 'mong the many obvious devices)."

Having thus interposed the persona between poet and reader, Krieger proceeds to trace in the poem a dialectic that opposes the indulgences of the sentimental lover to images suggested by an "auditor's mentality": "Such bits of soft sentiment as 'sweet silent thought,' sighs, wails, drowning eyes, grievings and moans, are held in the businesslike framework of 'sessions' to which one is harshly summoned up . . . of 'expense,' accounts, and payments." The speaker in the poem "treats his various mournings as items to be entered in the account book (especially lines 7–12). The repetition shifts from the commonplace emotional terms in lines 9–11 (grieve, woe, moan) to that most central marketplace term, 'pay,' in line 12." The speaker-persona "tries to submit his woes to the auditor's assumptions and operations. He is so subdued by common-sense worldliness that he feels forced to render the intangible as tangible, the immeasurable sorrows as measurable items."

However, "affection cannot be reduced to ledger entries." The "auditor's mentality" does not succeed in its attempt to put the irrational sorrows of love in a rational, matter-of-fact framework. In the final couplet, therefore, "all reasonable ways out having failed, the poet turns to the present friend, and the endlessly troublesome troubles are at an end." Through the "lover's reckless leap," the "sessions of sweet silent thought" are adjourned for the speaker to "think on" his "dear friend." "The attempt to make legal and financial sense of his thought is abandoned for the sheer, unreasoning immediacy of love." It remains for the poet (Shakespeare, not the persona of this particular sonnet) to present a more mature, more successful union of emotion and control, of unreason and reason, in a subsequent sonnet.

DISCUSSION STARTERS

The translator of Marcel Proust's *À la Recherche du Temps Perdu* used a phrase from the second line of this sonnet as the English title: *Remembrance of Things Past.* You may want to ask students to cluster or freewrite for a few minutes about the word *memories.* What "remembrance of things past" is triggered by the term?

THE RECEPTIVE READER

1. Alliteration, like end rhyme, must not become a klunky, mechanical device—it must serve its bonding, echoing function naturally, subliminally?

2. Other alliterating syllables are "with old woes new wail my dear time's waste"; "drown an eye . . . hid in death's dateless night"; "weep afresh loves long since canceled woe . . . from woe to woe tell o'er." Often the alliteration links words closely related in meaning and emotional resonance: woes—wail—waste; drown—death's—dateless; and "Then can I grieve at grievances foregone."

3. The *turning point* comes with the "But . . ." that introduces the final couplet. It has been preceded by the "When . . . then . . . then . . ." pattern of the three quatrains, piling loss upon loss, sorrow upon sorrow. In spite of the heaviness and magnitude of these, the ending couplet shows they can be overcome through friendship.

Juxtapositions: The Role of Rhyme 647

1. Note alliteration: coiled/caverns; Feeds/fossils/ferns.

2. Note play of full rhyme and slant rhyme in *stair/there/fear*.

3. The poet uses end rhyme at the end of each second line: *streams/dreams*; *one/sun*. But in addition there are internal rhymes: *showers/ flowers*; *shaken/waken*. There is alliteration: light/leaves/laid; wings/ waken; rocked/rest.

Rhythm and Meter

Robert Frost, "Dust of Snow" 649

Ask students to read the poem first as if it had been written as a prose sentence, without meter and without the line breaks of verse. What would be the rock-bottom natural stresses that would seem to stand out? (Can your students hear that the prose sentence would have a more even flow, with a much less pronounced rhythm?)

Percy Bysshe Shelley, "To ———" 650

You may want to ask your students to try their hand at some trochaic couplets modeled on Shelley's. Have them start with a key word that follows the Boston rather than the DETROIT pattern. Sample:

Students, while professors teach,
Dream of going to the beach.

Denise Levertov, "O Taste and See" 653

See "Perspectives" entry on Levertov in Chapter 16 of this manual.

DISCUSSION STARTERS

A modern poem is often irregular and nontraditional but not *formless*. What features helping to shape the poem do your students recognize? Note the echoing of "meaning . . . meaning"; the insistent drumbeat of series like "bite, / savor, chew, swallow, transform"; the climactic final "being / hungry, and plucking / the fruit."

THE RECEPTIVE READER

1. Like other formal features, the *line breaks* here should be noticeable, especially since in the absence of rhyme and traditional meter they are the poet's primary means of giving shape and rhythm to the poem. However, the breaks should not be obtrusive—we must still hear a natural speaking voice.

2. Students might identify these items in *series*: "grief, mercy, language, / tangerine, weather"; "to / breathe them, bite, / savor, chew, swallow, transform."

Oddly matched items are mundane things like the tangerine or "crossing the street" that sneak up on us in a context of weighty abstractions like mercy or death. Appearing in this apparently jumbled form in the poem, they remind us that in our real lives there is no sharp break between abstract thoughts or feelings and the most concrete observations?

3. The poster asks onlookers to "taste and see," to have a concrete, sensory experience of God, as if He were physically present in our world. The poet feels the imagination should make us take in and "taste" the physical world in this same intimate way? We should be responsive to our world, savoring hungrily all that can be bitten, chewed, swallowed as it is brought to the "imagination's tongue."

4. All experience in this poem becomes a fruit that we hunger for and digest, transforming it "into our flesh." Words like *taste*, *tongue*, *bite*, and *chew* have prepared us for this central metaphor.

Juxtapositions: The Matter of Meter 654

Students should be able to identify the dominant meters in each of these lines:

1. DOUble, DOUble, TOIL and TROUble; FIre BURN and CAULdron BUBble.	trochaic tetrameter
2. My WIFE and I lived ALL aLONE, conTENtion WAS our ONly BONE.	iambic tetrameter
3. It was MANy and MANy a YEAR aGO	anapestic tetrameter
In a KINGdom BY the SEA	anapestic trimeter
4. but YESterDAY the WORD of CAEsar MIGHT Have STOOD aGAINST the WORLD. Now LIES he HERE	iambic pentameter
5. POPlars are STANDing there STILL as DEATH	dactylic tetrameter

Traditional Stanza Form

William Shakespeare, "O Mistress Mine" and "Under the Greenwood Tree" 655

THE RECEPTIVE READER

In the second song, the configuration of the stanza is especially distinctive: the line length contracts from a three-beat line to a two-beat line (in the sixth and seventh lines of each stanza) and then expands again in the last line.

MAKING CONNECTIONS—FOR DISCUSSION OR WRITING:

Pleasing repetition—of a rhyme scheme, of a refrain, and of alternation in the length of lines—is the key to our enjoyment of stanza forms such as these. Students might enjoy bringing in a tape of their favorite songs, or writing out the lyrics to one of their favorite songs. When looking for features similar to Shakespeare's, ask students to look for theme (in each of these poems—love and dalliance), rhyme schemes, and refrain. If any students have a special interest in music, they might want to work (perhaps in a small group) to put Shakespeare's lyrics to music and try singing them.

Melvin Walker La Follette, "The Ballad of Red Fox" 656

DISCUSSION STARTERS

You may want to have students plan and present a *choral reading*, with different speakers doing the questions and answers for each pair of stanzas (and perhaps a chorus of voices answering each question?). Have students explore different formats and aim for the most effective, dramatic presentation.

THE RECEPTIVE READER

1. The variable refrains in stanzas 1, 3, and 5 move from when to where to how, as we focus first on the chase and finally on its bloody end. The first two lines in these stanzas also shift from "yellow sun" in the first two refrains to "yellow sky" in the last. Students might offer reasons for this shift: a yellow sun has positive connotations of warmth and light, whereas a "yellow sky" suggests negatives? (Some may feel that the rhyme scheme is the only reason for the variation.)

2. The stanzas follow the traditional *rhyme scheme* of the ballad: *abcb*. The second stanza has a set of *two* rhymes: *abab*. Readers can almost follow the narrative this poem presents by following the rhyming words at the end of each line: *sound, gun, hound, run*; *sulphur, clay, morning, day*; *belly, eye, brush, die*. Alliteration accents the grim weighty words in the last stanza: bullet/belly/blood/brush. Other key words are the repeated words found in each stanza—they emphasize motion and drama: *When, when, when, when*;

where, where; *through, through, through*; *how, how*. The cumulative series at the end builds up to the grim climax: "with a bullet . . . a dagger . . . and blood . . . Shall red fox die."

3. The old ballad style has the power of directness and simplicity. It clears away the fog of excuses, recriminations, and rationalizations to go to the heart of the matter. It focuses on a central tension or conflict. It gives us a story that lingers in the memory. Its style has survived myriad fads and fashions. And so on.

THE PERSONAL RESPONSE

Ask students to identify words that tend to show how the poet feels about this story: the hound is "wicked"; the meadows are "hot as sulphur." The sense of threat or menace the poem builds up makes us see the event from the point of view of the victim? (Have your students heard about protests against the traditional English fox hunts?)

Elizabeth Bishop, "One Art" 658

DISCUSSION STARTERS

How is losing an art? The art is not so much the art of losing things but the art of coming to terms with our losses and putting a good face on them? The speaker appears determined to accept all losses gracefully; yet her reference to the last loss carries a heavily ironic tone: The implication is that the loss of "you" is indeed a disaster, despite her protestations that the art of dealing with loss is "not too hard to master"? You may want to ask students to write a journal entry or poem starting or ending with some variation of "The art of losing isn't hard to master."

THE RECEPTIVE READER

1. The traditional *villanelle* has six stanzas—the first five are three-liners or tercets, the last a quatrain. The rhyme scheme (counting slant rhymes) is *aba* for the first five stanzas and *abaa* for the last. Some slant rhymes are *fluster/master*; *gesture/master*. A playful forced rhyme is *last, or/master*. For the mathematically inclined, you may want to give a formula for the rhyme scheme like (5) 1–2–1 + (1) 1–2–1–1. Notice the triple rhyme *continent/evident*—here as often helping to give a poem a facetious touch.

2. The first line and a variation of the third line keep popping up in the poem until both are repeated in the ending quatrain. The first and third lines of the opening tercet are repeated three times like a refrain. "The art of losing isn't hard to master" is repeated verbatim in stanzas 2 and 4 with only a slight switch to "The art of losing's *not too hard* to master" in the final stanza. The words in the other refrainlike line—"this loss is no disaster" —vary more until the line is again slightly reframed in the ending quatrain ("though it may look like (Write it!) like disaster").

3. The speaker is tongue-in-cheek about "lost door keys, the hour badly spent," memory lapses, the idea of owning "two rivers, a continent." The loss of the "loved houses" begins to shift the poem to more serious topics? The loss of "you (the joking voice, a gesture / I love)" seems the most serious, although the poet maintains the facetious tone—modified however by the emphatic parenthetical "(Write it!)."

John Milton, "When I Consider How My Light Is Spent" 659

DISCUSSION STARTERS

By the time Milton was forty-four years old, he was completely blind. This poem was written when he was forty-seven. The talent—writing—"which is death to hide" had not really been rendered "useless," since Milton dictated his greatest poem when he was blind.

THE RECEPTIVE READER

1. The rhyming words in this poem follow a typical interlaced Petrarchan pattern: *abba abba cdecde*: (a) *spent/bent/present/prevent*; (b) *wide/hide/chide/denied*; (c) *need/speed*; (d) *best/rest*; and (e) *state/wait.*

2. The most regular *iambic* pentameter line might be the last line, which restores calm and serenity after the tension or temporary rebellion of the poem. However, students might also opt for lines 1–3 or 6–8. The *trochaic* inversions occur in the following phrases: "LODged with me useless"; "EIther man's work"; "BEAR his mild yoke." The word *lodged* stands out at the point when the poet closes in on his central theme—the tragedy of a poet denied the ability to write. The trochaic emphasis on *bear* tends to make it sound like an imperative, emphasizing the admonitory or chastising tone of the answer Patience gives to the poet's "murmur."

3. Students may find some enjambments stronger in their pull into the next line than others. ". . . to prevent / That murmur" shifts the turning point (the "But . . .") in this sonnet into the line preceding the sestet. Here are some ideas students may feel are emphasized because of the enjambment and the caesura that follows on the next line:

enjambment caesura

spent / Ere half my days || — tends to emphasize the sense of futility and wasted time?

hide / Lodged with me useless || — emphasizes the futility of *useless?*

bent / To serve therewith my Maker || — emphasizes the devotion of the poet "bent" on serving his God?

present / My true account ||	highlights the poet's sense of responsibility (or "accountability") to his Maker?
|| His state / Is kingly. ||	The caesura before and after this short but weighty sentence and the line break work together to slow down the poem and give solemn weight to this central statement of the poet's worship of his God?
speed / And post . . .	The caesura is absent—the word *speed* speeds all the way into the next line without stopping, thus emphasizing the unrelenting motion?

4. The opening two lines set up a central polarity with the term "ere half my days." Half the poet's days have been spent "in the light" and now the other half will be spent in the "dark world" of blindness. Though "day-labor" is expected of God's servants, the poet lives with "light denied." Another polarity brings us to the resolution of this basic issue: Although thousands of God's (invisible?) servants speed to do his bidding, it is as meritorious to "rest" and wait, accepting His will.

Edna St. Vincent Millay, "I, Being Born a Woman and Distressed" 660

DISCUSSION STARTERS

Millay turns the conventions of traditional love poetry upside down by not only separating sex and love but by being quite rational about her physical involvement with the man she is addressing. Does this poem nevertheless have some of the feel of a traditional sonnet? (The other person is "fair"(beautiful or physically attractive)—if in no way the intellectual equal of the woman. The poet is, or was, in "distress" and temporarily "possessed." Some of the large abstractions dear to sonneteers appear: life, love, scorn, pity, mind versus "blood.")

THE RECEPTIVE READER

1. This Petrarchan sonnet is written in iambic pentameter. The rhyme scheme of the octave is *abba, abba*; of the sestet, *cdcdcd.*

2. The two poles of passion and reason dominate the octave and the sestet, respectively. Physical passions "cloud the mind," leaving the speaker momentarily "undone, possessed." But the tide of passion recedes in the first line of the sestet with a big "Think not for this, however . . ."—the *this* being the treason of the frenzied body ("the stout blood") against the brain,

which should know better but was temporarily "staggering." In the sestet, the cool detached reason reasserts its superiority, disdaining any further entanglement or even conversation with the person who served to "clarify the pulse."

THE PERSONAL RESPONSE

Conventionally, *men* are often accused of being able to treat sex as something merely physical, without personal commitment or involvement? Is this an emancipated woman claiming equal rights to "recreational sex"?

Traditional and Open Form

William Wordsworth, "It Is a Beauteous Evening" 661

DISCUSSION STARTERS

The speaker contemplates the "beauteous evening" and concludes that the child in the poem has a spiritual nature that can intuitively sense God's presence in the world around—unlike adults, who need to reconstruct their sense of the divine in nature by "solemn thought." (It is thought that the person walking with the speaker in the poem is Caroline, Wordsworth's natural daughter by Annette Vallon.) For many Romantic poets, nature was the true "temple" and the virgin forest God's true "cathedral." Can your students see evidence of such Romantic nature worship in this poem?

THE RECEPTIVE READER

1. As mentioned in the text, the second line carries the reader over into the third without much pause (enjambment). Ask students to read the poem first with extra emphasis on this and other distinctive features that provide a counterpoint to monotonous regularity. Have them read *without* a line stop at the end of lines 2, 3, and 7—pulling the reader over into the next line. Ask them to accentuate the major breaks *within* a line. Then ask them to read the poem more naturally—with the variations and syncopations not standing out or being obtrusive but serving their function of subliminally giving life and variety to the poem.

2. This poem should be read quietly, slowly, solemnly—in a spirit of religious awe. Notice a *network* of words like *calm, holy, quiet, adoration, broods, eternal, everlastingly, solemn, divine*. Images helping to inspire religious awe include "The holy time is quiet *as a Nun*"; "*Breathless* with adoration"; lying in "Abraham's bosom"; and worshiping "at the *Temple's inner shrine*." Note that the sea—"the Mighty Being"—is in "eternal motion," suggesting the poet's (pantheistic?) belief in divine energy suffusing all creation. Iambic meter is best illustrated by line 10? ("If THOU apPEAR unTOUCHED by SOlemn THOUGHT")? But the meter should never be allowed to become a metronome beat?

Anne Sexton, "Her Kind" 662

DISCUSSION STARTERS

Diane Middlebrook's biography of Anne Sexton (*Anne Sexton: A Life*) traces the tortured life of the poet. The images and metaphors of "Her Kind" gives us an inkling of what it must feel like to be an outcast, "a possessed witch." A suicidal housewife at age twenty-eight, the poet began writing at the suggestion of her therapist. Writing helped give her seventeen years of focus and enormous productivity, ultimately earning her a Pulitzer Prize. Ask students to think about what role writing plays in their own lives. Have any of them ever written letters or journal entries that had a cathartic or therapeutic effect? Have they ever used writing to work through personal matters?

THE RECEPTIVE READER

1. The interlaced rhyme scheme of the first stanza is *ababcbc*; of the second, *dedecdc*; of the third, *fgfgcgc*. The *c* rhyme links all three stanzas with *mind*, *kind*, *disaligned*, *kind*, *wind*, and again *kind*, maintaining the focus on "her kind."

2. Ask your students to cluster the word NIGHTMARE to help them focus on such nightmarish details as the following:

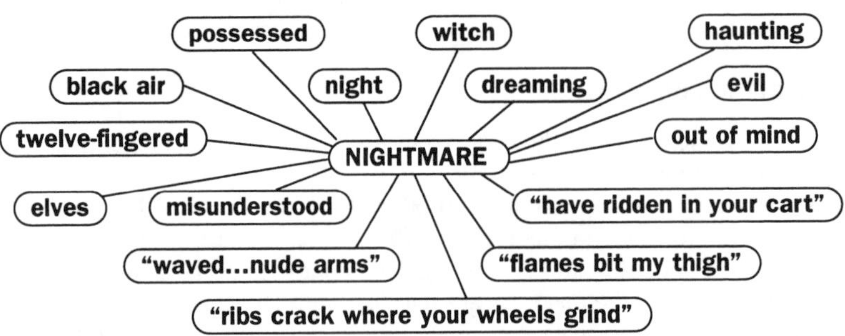

3. The refrain becomes an insistent affirmation of solidarity as the poem moves from identification with the woman ostracized and "misunderstood" to identification with the murdered victim.

4. Moving beyond the stereotype, we get a portrait of a "lonely" and "misunderstood" woman, distracted ("out of mind") but brave. She is the quintessential outsider, out of sync with the existing world of "plain houses" that tries to control her with "flames" of punishment and "wheels" of torture. We look at the ghastly ritual of witch hunting and witch burning from the point of view of the persecuted victim, who "is not ashamed to die." The poem is a powerful plea for human solidarity with people who seem "twelve-fingered" to the multitude.

THE CREATIVE DIMENSION

Why do some people have (and why do others lack) the imaginative sympathy to put themselves in the place of the outsider, of the underdog, of the unheard? How do people learn or fail to learn to put themselves in someone else's shoes?

Sharon Olds, "I Go Back to May 1937" 664

DISCUSSION STARTERS

What do the poems by Milton, Sexton, and Olds in this part of the chapter have in common? They are all three intensely personal, with the poets coming to terms with a crucial, disturbing part of their personalities and personal histories. Olds has said that she loves poetry because it allows her to go back into a time before she was even born; in so doing, and with the clarity of hindsight, she sees her future father and mother terribly mismatched to the point of destructiveness; yet as poet, she "wants to live"; accordingly, she accepts the conditions of the life she was given. She accepts it because her artistic credo is that she "will tell about it," using it as the raw material for her poems.

THE RECEPTIVE READER

1. Unconventional *line breaks* (going beyond traditional enjambment) throughout the poem break up the normal grammatical structure of sentences, pulling us into the next line from subjects to verbs, from modifiers to what is modified, and from prepositions to the rest of a prepositional phrase. These breaks set up a persistent *counterrhythm* to the more regular segmentation that might have parceled out the flow of the poet's thoughts and feelings into too neat artificial units:

> strolling out/under
> the/red tiles
> bent/plates of blood
> I/see my mother
> the/wrought-iron gate
> its/sword-tips
> are/innocent
> things/you
> go/up to them
> I/want to live
> male and female/paper dolls
> together/at the hips
> as if to/strike sparks

2. *Parallel* structure keeping up the continuous flow of closely related thoughts and feelings abounds:

• "I see . . ." (three times); "I want . . ." (three times)—these parallel elements are echoed again in the climactic "I take . . ." and "I say . . . ," with parallel structure lining up and highlighting the elements that bring out the contrast between what the speaker impulsively wants and what she rationally decides to do.

• "They . . . are about to graduate . . . are about to get married . . . are kids . . . are dumb . . . are innocent . . . would never hurt anybody"—there seems to be an ominous tone here in the reiteration of the parents' ignorance and naiveté, leading us up to the climactic "I want to go up to them and say Stop, / don't do it" ("you are going to do bad things to children . . .").

• The paired "she's the wrong . . ."/"he's the wrong . . ." emphasize the speaker's feeling that neither are to blame—and both are to blame for what will happen.

• "You cannot . . . you are going . . . to do . . . to suffer . . . to want to die . . ."—parallelism here drives home the horrid inevitability of future events.

3. The closing lines, reconciling the poet to her own personal history, might be considered her creative manifesto: "I say / Do what you are going to do, and I will tell about it."

THE PERSONAL RESPONSE

Students might start by trying to think of ways in which they resemble their parents—looks, manner, voice, values—and ways in which they do not. How happy are they with the differences? With the similarities?

Kathleen Lynch, "How to Build an Owl" 665

DISCUSSION STARTERS

What makes it poetry? The poet focuses our attention and makes us take a provocative fresh look—asking us to look at the bird from a thought-provoking (the creator's) perspective. And this is not a dispassionate objective description. Our emotions—of respect, of awe, of admiration—are strongly brought into play. Finally (or perhaps rather first of all), the poem is shot through with poetic rather than literal language: Why would the owl-builder have a "trembling thumb"? What's the symbolic meaning of the heart here? Why a "hundred hours"—and why "Stay awake forever"? Who or what whispers to the owl—with what message?

THE CREATIVE DIMENSION

How to build a lizard, how to make a rose, and how to design a hummingbird are among the many possibilities.

Edward Wolf, "Comfort Food" 666

DISCUSSION STARTERS

Do your students know, or have they observed, someone who is good at comforting the sick?

THE RECEPTIVE READER

1. Initially the poem is conversational: "And I'm no cook—but it turns out I can dish up comfort food. Know what that is? French toast, rice pudding, cupcakes; something soft, warm, sweet." The tone begins to change with the next sentence: "Of course I'm trying to be clever with this too, clever enough to get him to eat, eat anything." After that sentence, the poem turns serious when the speaker reveals why he is doing the things he is doing: "I could never have imagined what a 106 pound man would look like." Up until this point, the speaker's casual, chatty tone is so inviting, so confiding, and so appealing to the reader that what follows catches the reader unawares.

2. The speaker is empathetic, caring, and desperate. Although the desperation is well-masked, the speaker is trying to think of anything, anything at all, that will, at most, prolong the other man's life. The speaker drags an "old upholstered chair into the garden" and covers it at night so that it will be dry in the morning. Next day the sick man can then sit in a dry chair "in the morning light" and drink hot chocolate made "from scratch" while he "drifts in and out." It seems unlikely that anyone other than a lover or a very close friend would dedicate himself so fully to the care of the dying man. That the speaker would be a family member or care worker is unlikely, given the speaker's memory of "a salad of flowers" "we had once in a restaurant in North Beach."

3. The images that will linger most strongly are doubtless the images of the sick man. "The skin so stretched out—for the first time I really see where leather comes from. And bones." The sick man has shrunk so much that he is little more than a fleshless skeleton: "The wrist is so big, the cheek is so delicate." Finally, the dying man's daily life is an indelible image. He is skin and bones, he can only sit and watch, only sometimes conscious.

4. The prevailing attitude toward the sickness at the center of the poem is two-fold. The speaker shows a desperate desire to ease the sufferings of the sick man. All of the actions he describes are actions taken in an attempt to make the other man more comfortable. The speaker prepares "comfort food"; he strives to come up with something the sick man will eat, keep down, and enjoy. He pulls the chair out into the garden and keeps it dry. He probably helps the sick man out to the chair ("When he can, he sits in it"), and prepares homemade hot chocolate. At the same time, when the speaker contemplates the sick man, he has no illusions. He sees the sick man very clearly; ironically, this second aspect of the speaker's attitude makes his desperation to ease the sick man's sufferings even more poignant. For the speak-

er has no illusions about the sick man's future, and he knows the best he can do is to provide a drop of comfort in an ocean of disease.

5. Comfort food in this poem provides comfort for both the preparer and the person for whom it is prepared. The sick man derives comfort from the food because he can keep it down and it provides enjoyment and some sustenance. Furthermore, it is prepared by someone who clearly cares for and looks after the patient. For the speaker, comfort food works similarly. He does everything he can to bring comfort to the sick man; those things provide comfort for him as well.

Juxtapositions: Close and Free Translation

Rainer Maria Rilke, "The Panther" 667

DISCUSSION STARTERS

What is the archetypal appeal of this much-translated poem? The panther—a powerful, vital, fierce creature of the wild, like Blake's Tyger—is caged, as we say, "like an animal." Its condition becomes a symbol of life that is confined, constricted, thwarted, and denied by whatever forces cage it in or break its spirit?

THE RECEPTIVE READER

The two versions both preserve essentials of the original poem: the unseeing eye of the caged animal, a prison world that consists of iron bars, the animal's physical grace juxtaposed against its powerlessness, and the veiled or curtained eye that yet at moments seems to come back to life—but only for a moment. The formal, controlled pattern of the first translation might seem to emphasize the "closed world" in which the panther does his pacing. The more fluid lines of Bly's open-form version allow him to mirror the animal's "rhythmical easy stride"—evoking the animal's lost freedom?

Poems for Further Study

Popular Ballad (anonymous), "Lord Randal" 668

DISCUSSION STARTERS

Popular ballads, originating among the common people rather than in the aristocracy, first and foremost tell a story, even though they have elements of the lyric and the dramatic. All human beings love a story, especially when it contains elements of love, murder, domestic intrigue, and the supernatural. Ask students if they can think of some contemporary ballads sung by popular bands (or of pop culture classics like "Frankie and Johnny" or "Stagger Lee"). Then compare these elements from "Lord Randal" with the contemporary pieces: (a) "Lord Randal" focuses, *in medias res*, on a climactic moment, with the action developed through dialogue; (b) the words are simple, the language vigorous; (c) there is an absence of sentimentality; (d) there is no characterization or description; (e) the emphasis is on what is happening at this moment; (f) the repetition is incremental, so we share in the discovery of a terrible event.

THE RECEPTIVE READER

Listeners get the first hint that all is not well in stanza 5, when the mother asks the question about the young hunter's hawks and hounds. The stanza starting "And what became of them . . .?" strikes an ominous note and points to an unfortunate ending. Cumulative repetition is used in the second and fourth line of each stanza; the narrative unfolds through the questions and answers found in the first and third lines. There is also repetition in these "story" lines, the first always ending with "Lord Randal, my son?" and the third with the phrase, "mother, make my bed soon." This story of betrayal deals with one of the oldest themes we find in early literature—the need for loyalty and the fear of treachery. We need to trust people, but by trusting them we become vulnerable. This ballad activates that age-old fear.

Christine de Pisan, "Marriage Is a Lovely Thing" 670

PERSPECTIVES—CHRISTINE DE PISAN: MEDIEVAL WOMAN OF LETTERS

Christine de Pisan was a voluminous writer who participated vigorously in the "culture wars" and political polemics of her time. She may have worked in or run a workshop for the production of manuscripts at a time when women copyists and illuminators worked as scribes for the book trade of the preprint age. A native of Italy living in Paris, she helped introduce the great authors of early Italian humanism to medieval France, championing the subtlety and soaring poetry of her admired Dante and his *Divine Comedy*. The contested image of women was a favorite topic of medieval debates: The poetry of courtly love had romanticized the disdainful beauty on the pedestal, with the male lover perpetually humbling himself before the unattainable courtly lady. At the opposite end of the spectrum, a traditional strain of misogyny in the Catholic church was strongly reflected in Jean de Meun's sequel to or continuation of the *Roman de la Rose*, reinforcing a traditional misogynistic polemic rehearsing the list of famous temptresses and *femmes fatales* from Eve to Delilah. Furthermore, poets like Chaucer knew the Roman poet Ovid and played with his mock-serious, unromantic advice about how to win over susceptible women. Writers reckoned with female members of the audience: Authors including Boccaccio and Chaucer defended themselves against possible charges of speaking ill of women. Christine de Pisan, though calling herself "a mere woman," vigorously took Jean de Meun to task for defaming her entire sex. In her *City of Women*, she told story after story of virtuous "good women," including many female saints and martyrs. In her poem dedicated to Joan of Arc, she admonished the city of Paris not to resist Joan of Arc's party in the war that ended in the eventual defeat and execution of the Maid of Orléans. In 1402, Christine de Pisan published a first edition of her collected works.

DISCUSSION STARTERS

This is a poem of "true love," of a courteous, thoughtful husband who knows how to cherish his wife, who is a "gentle one." What might be a modern perspective on this poem? Is the implication that he is not like other men—who are known to do things that hurt, to urge against the woman's will, to put down instead of "raise up" the woman? Do your students feel that the poet is idealizing the "gentleness" of the couple's relationship—the way male poets overstated and idealized the beauty of the lady? Do they feel that putting a lover up on a pedestal only makes him or her ready for a fall?

THE RECEPTIVE READER

1. The *refrain* sustains and reiterates the feeling of thankfulness and loving appreciation that suffuses this celebration of a happy union and of the wedding night that consummated it. The poem as a whole builds up the sweet frenzy of the *envoi*, with the writer "bursting" with the sweetness of love.

2. Most early love lyrics, written from the male point of view, tell of unrequited love or idealized yearning for a beloved. Pisan, the woman, is celebrating a happy marriage—not a common theme in earlier poetry or in today's? (The contemporary poet Sharon Olds writes on the same theme of long-married love in language that is quite modern. Two of her poems are "True Love" and "The Promise." Ask your students to find one of them in the library on audiotape?)

William Wordsworth, "I Wandered Lonely as a Cloud" 671

DISCUSSION STARTERS

In this famous poem, the first sestet sets the scene: The poet alone on a hike suddenly comes upon an unexpected sight. The second describes this scene of daffodils. The third describes their happy effect on the speaker, though he lets us know that he hadn't grasped "what wealth the show to me had brought." The last stanza elaborates: The experience is special, but its recollection with that "inward" eye feeds and inspires the poet and fructifies subsequent poetic efforts. Wordsworth defined poetry as "the spontaneous overflow of powerful emotion recollected in tranquillity." Ask students: What did Wordsworth mean by *recollection*? Is it ever as strong or meaningful as firsthand experience?

THE RECEPTIVE READER

The stanza form of this poem is sometimes called a *stave of six*. Each stanza rhymes *ababcc* and is written in iambic tetrameter, a "sprightlier" meter than the more stately or weighty pentameter? Three of the concluding lines, almost like a refrain, reinforce the central image of the daffodils "dancing in the breeze," "Tossing their heads in sprightly dance," until finally the poet's heart "dances with the daffodils." The final stanza moves from the concrete images to the uplifting, consoling reflections inspired by the sight.

MAKING CONNECTIONS—FOR DISCUSSION OR WRITING

Wordsworth's sister, though she personifies the daffodils, doesn't dance with them. She responds more directly and artlessly to the experience? Her response is less self-conscious?

Thomas Nashe, "A Litany in Time of Plague" 672

DISCUSSION STARTERS

Nashe's meditation on death's inevitability is haunting in its songlike or balladlike sparseness, with no embellishments or circumlocutions to cushion us against its solemn message: Not success, not beauty, not strength, not wit can save us from death. Students need to hear this poem read aloud. Let them select some of their favorite lines. Some have said that the lines

> Brightness falls from the air;
> Queens have died young and fair;
> Dust hath closed Helen's eye.
> I am sick, I must die.

are so compressed and beautiful because there is a downward movement from the beginning "brightness falls . . ." to the final prayer of "Lord have mercy on us!"

THE RECEPTIVE READER

1. The insistent *repetition* of the "I am sick, I must die" and the cry, "Lord have mercy on us!" sets up a powerful *refrain*. Parallel construction throughout the poem sets us up for the poet's playing off of *opposites*: A line often starts with and highlights a large abstraction that sums up something human beings treasure or pursue (Gold . . . Physic . . . Beauty . . . Strength . . . Swords . . . Wit). But each of these in turn is canceled out by its powerful and unanswerable opposite (plague . . . wrinkles . . . dust . . . worms . . . death).

2. The *rhyme scheme* follows an *aabbccd* pattern through its six stanzas. Like a tolling bell, the rhymes *fly/die*, *by/die*, *cry/die*, *reply/die*, and *sky/die* sound their *memento mori*.

3. An underlying iambic trimeter runs through the first five lines of each stanza. The opening line of the poem is quite regular, establishing the beat: "aDIEU | fareWELL | earth's BLISS." In the sixth line, the meter changes to an anapestic dimeter, with the shift in pattern helping to alert us to the blunt message it contains: "I am SICK, I must DIE."

THE PERSONAL RESPONSE

Has AIDS become a latter-day plague comparable to the (bubonic) plague that swept Europe periodically beginning with the fourteenth century? Which of Nashe's sentiments might seem related to the feelings experienced by AIDS victims or their friends and families? Which of his sentiments seem archaic or strange?

Theodore Roethke, "The Waking" 673

DISCUSSION STARTERS

Critic Frederick J. Hoffman has said that "Roethke's poetry is one of the most exhaustive, vital, and vivid reports we have of a soul in the several agonies normally recorded in one human life." You may want to let students begin by discussing, in small groups, some of the paradoxical lines of the poem in order to reach some consensus about their intended meaning: "I wake to sleep, and take my waking slow"; "I learn by going where I have to go"; and "We think by feeling."

THE RECEPTIVE READER

1. The traditional format of the *villanelle* shows in the three-line, iambic pentameter stanzas, interlocked by the traditional rhyme scheme of *aba aba aba*, *aba aba*, culminating in the final four-line stanza, rhymed *abaa*. Half-rhymes show in pairs like *you/go*, *how/slow*, *do/go*, *air/near*.

2. This enigmatic, paradoxical poem blurs the barriers between sleep and wakefulness, between thinking and feeling, between shaking and steadiness, and between falling away and staying near. A note of acceptance or resignation seems to run through many of the lines? Where others learn by branching out or leaving the trodden path, the speaker learns by going where he *has* to go. He does not or rather cannot fear his fate? Thinking cannot be separated from feeling—and, anyway, what so terribly important would there be for an independent, separate intellect to know? Even when there are others close beside us, it is hard to tell them apart. "Great Nature" has its own plans for us. Being awake is a kind of sleepwalking, a kind of waking dream? Staying close to the blessed ground keeps us from futile initiatives or rebellions?

Quincy Troupe, "Impressions/of Chicago; For Howlin' Wolf" 674

DISCUSSION STARTERS

For your students, is the place where they live (or where they may have lived for a long time) just a location, or do they identify with the place—loving it, hating it, being bored stiff by it, rooting for it, feeling pride or disgust?

THE RECEPTIVE READER

1. Rhymes like "dues payers/blues players" may remind students of the improvised rhyme-patter of rap.

2. While the current generation might not recognize the old Bluesmen—Bo Diddely, Muddy Waters, the Wolfman—the blues themselves have become part of the legacy of American popular culture. Sixties rock icons (Eric Clapton, Mick Jagger and the Rolling Stones, and Robert Plant and Led Zeppelin) reinterpreted the blues to appeal to the largely young, largely white rock-and-roll audience. This poem could be called a blues poem, as it echoes standard blues lines to lament the state of things, e.g., "how many more years down in the bottom / no place to go moanin' for my baby / a spoonful of evil / back door man / all night long how many more years / down in the bottom built for comfort." The blues is typically a lament on love or luck gone wrong in a world where drugs or alcohol may provide the only (temporary) relief.

3. Realistic reflections of the Chicago scene begin with the poem's opening line as the freezing wind blows in off Lake Michigan: "the wind/ blade cutting in / & out swinging in over the lake." The frigid winter temperature, Chicago's reputation as the Windy City, and its often foul and smelly air ("the sulphuric night" and "the bituminous breath of chicago") are all alluded to. In the Polish, Irish, and other predominantly Catholic neighborhoods "the friday night smells of fish" would be a predictable occurrence. Richard Daley was mayor of Chicago for more than twenty years (1955–1976); he was a big party boss throwback who gained notoriety for his response to civic unrest during the 1968 Democratic National Convention. The poet's zany and surreal imagination keeps us from looking at the Chicago scene with the ironic detachment of the establishment journalist but instead makes us share (with hallucinatory intensity) in the emotional experience of living there, as "we came in the sulphuric night drinkin' old crow / while a buzzard licked its beak atop the head of richard nixon," experiencing "the bituminous breath of chicago / howling with three million voices of pain."

4. Two themes may stand out. The first is of life refusing to surrender: the children of Chicago who "have eyes that are older / than the deepest pain in the world" dance, play, and run over the depressed streets of the city's south side without ever cutting their feet on the "billions" of pieces of glass. The second theme reflects the standard blues lament of how much longer will this go on: "how many more years / down in the bottom," "all night long how many more years / down in the bottom built for comfort."

Chapter 19 PERSONA Masks and Faces 680

Critical doctrine shifts slowly between two poles. One is a view of the poem as accomplished impersonal artifact, speaking its own language, and having basically the same message for all trained readers. The second is a view of the poem as a confessional, cathartic sharing of the poet's personal thoughts and feelings.

- Ask students to identify poems that they consider most directly personal and autobiographical. For instance, they might choose poems by Sharon Olds, Lorna Dee Cervantes, or Li-Young Lee. Which poet they have read have they come to know and understand most intimately as a person?
- At the opposite pole, which poems do they remember in which the poet seems to remain *outside* the poem? For instance, in Rilke's "Panther," we come to know little or nothing about the poet as a person?
- Finally, what poems do they remember in which the poet speaks in the first person, but the "I" of the poem seems to speak in a special role—assuming a public persona? Does Milton speak in his self-appointed role as a religious poet dedicated to serving the Lord? Does Gerard Manley Hopkins, in poems like "Pied Beauty" or "The Windhover," speak to us as a priest?

First Reading: Rita Dove, "Flash Cards" 682

For a "Perspectives" entry on Rita Dove see Chapter 15 of this manual.

DISCUSSION STARTERS

What experience have your students had with parents who drive their children too hard? Or with parents who are too permissive, providing too little motivation or direction?

THE RECEPTIVE READER

1. Students may feel that the anxiety of the pressured kid is still too strongly felt by the adult poet to be imagined only.

2. This poem is packed with *lifelike details* that make the speaker's childhood experience resonate with the reader. The speaker's father's mantra is "*What you don't understand, / master.*" He is a man who reads a biography of Abraham Lincoln (a classic example of a successful struggle through

difficult times), who puts "up his feet after work" and relaxes "with a highball." He quizzes his child ("After supper we drilled"), and is, at minimum, a very strong motivating force in her education. There is no respite for the child. Just "one bud on the teacher's geranium, / one clear bee sputtering at the wet pane" exist for brief diversion. Like a bedraggled bird, the beleaguered child limps home in the rain: "The tulip trees always dragged after heavy rain / so I tucked my head as my boots slapped home." At school the child is known as "the whiz kid," and as a result she is allowed to be "keeper / of oranges and apples." Such status is constantly under siege and vulnerable to challenge: "the faster" the child responded to the flash cards, "the faster they came."

3. The restlessly sleeping child spinning on a wheel is still on the anxiety-driven treadmill of the overachiever. A special twist to the number the child keeps repeating in her sleep is that not only is that number the answer she is guessing in response to the flash cards of dreams, but it is also her age: "*Ten*, I kept saying, *I'm only ten*."

4. The poem tells the story of the structured, pressured life of a ten-year-old model student. The poem does open on a perhaps positive note as the speaker describes the honor of being "keeper / of oranges and apples." This positive note, however, is almost immediately superseded by the pressure and anxiety resulting from obsession with academic success and the relentlessly motivating father.

5. The poet does not sound overtly bitter or vindictive; she does not sound judgmental about the father? She is not out to condemn him? Like other successful people, she is ambivalent about the pressure that helped make her a successful person?

The Autobiographical "I"

PERSPECTIVES—REHABILITATING CONFESSIONAL POETRY

Twentieth-century critical fashions long encouraged poets (and other writers) to hide their personal agonies behind an ironic mask. In recent years, woman writers especially have returned to poetry that is more directly personal, more frankly "confessional." The act of faith in strongly personal writing is that the frank exploration of personal inner space is not merely narcissistic. It will find a strong echo in the readers, who will see the relevance of archetypal experiences and existential challenges to their own lives. This is the secret of great autobiography. As James Baldwin said, "One writes of one thing only—one's own experience. Everything depends on how relentlessly one forces from this experience the last drop, sweet or bitter, it can possibly give." Richard Rodriguez said in *Hunger of Memory*, "I write of one life only:

my own. If my story is true, I trust it will resonate with significance for other lives." Here are statements by poets subscribing to the same credo:

> I write very personal poems but I hope that they will become the central theme to someone else's private life.
>
> —Anne Sexton

> Human relationships. Death and loss. The seasons as they change. Is there anything else? These, at least, like atoms, are the building blocks.
>
> —Linda Pastan

> When I speak to you about myself, I am speaking to you about yourself.
>
> —Victor Hugo

As Robert Phillips says in *The Confessional Poets* (Southern Illinois UP 1973), "As with all good poetry, the best confessional poems are more than conceptions. They are revelations."

Ben Johnson, "On My First Son" 683

DISCUSSION STARTERS

What is expected of us when we play the role of the mourner? What rituals and procedures do we have to go through? How much in our public or private grieving is ritual, and how much is sincere feeling? How much of our true personal feeling can we demonstrate in public or share with others? Do mourners wear a mask, assume a public persona?

THE RECEPTIVE READER

1. The poet exhibits, by our modern-day standards, an almost sacrificial attitude toward death and sounds an orthodox admonition against becoming too attached to "worldly things"—even a son. The church taught that those who died young were better off (we "should envy" them). They were spared the ravages of the world, of our (sinful) flesh, and of old age. Remind students that in the seventeenth century infant mortality was high: children died frequently during childbirth, in infancy, or in childhood; people had to learn to be philosophical in order to survive multiple griefs. The father's "sin" was "too much hope of thee" when fate (or God) had something different in mind.

2. The father calls the dead son "child of my right hand," his "joy," and his "loved boy." Expression of feeling may seem especially strong in the

phrase "O could I lose all father now!" —since only complete forgetting would stop the bereaved father from lamenting. The last lines of the poem, in contrast, are didactic, advising the reader not to become too attached to what can be taken away at any moment. This is different—distanced—from the effect of the earlier outcry where the poet's feelings were expressed directly to the reader?

Maxine Kumin, "Nurture" 684

DISCUSSION STARTERS

Have students trace the recurrence of the first-person pronouns *I*, *me*, and *my* in this poem. Do they tend to make the poet sound like a self-centered or self-absorbed person? Why, or why not? Where and why does the poem shift to the plural *we* and *our*?

THE RECEPTIVE READER

1. The baby kangaroo with the pillowcase as a substitute pouch might make us smile, as the poet breaks the ice by starting with something entertaining and far-fetched—not likely to present a real challenge to readers in their own experience? But the poem has turned more serious when we come to "They are warm in the throat."

2. The poet does sound like a person who has taken in more prosaic, everyday young animals in distress? She probably does have "paw prints" from small animals she cares for on her fireside?

3. There might be a mixture of fascination and fear? We are fascinated with what human beings might be like in the "raw," without the artificial varnish of civilization. But there is also the fear that if people are left without rules or the restrictions of a community, they will exhibit only what might be called their "shadow side." This dark side seems both exciting and dangerous. The poet appears to see herself as both "same and not-same" as the wild child. The sameness seems rooted in an animal heritage that we share and that makes us "scratch, grimace, grunt," giving us the common language of the laugh and the howl. As with going barefoot in the summer, the exciting potential of freedom and the dangerous "if" of stepping on glass coexist.

4. The poet's-eye view of language seems to be that its earliest function was to express the range of basic human emotions—the sense of danger, well-being expressed in grunts, anguish or pain expressed in the howl, and relief expressing itself in laughter?

5. The poet seems a warm-hearted, caring person? She has a sense of humor that serves as a defense against charges of sentimentality? Today she might be expected to be part of an animal rights group?

THE PERSONAL RESPONSE

A much debated issue: whether women can be (or should be) "nurturing" and politically tough and effective at the same time.

Sappho, "Letter to Anaktoria" 685

PERSPECTIVES—IN SEARCH OF THE HISTORICAL SAPPHO

A. R. Burn says in *The Penguin History of Greece* (1990) that Sappho's circle gives us a glimpse "of women's life in a part of the Greek world where it was notably free." Sappho "was little and dark, typically Greek in fact, whereas the ideal was to be tall and fair." She "enjoyed fame for her poetic genius, and parents even from Ionia would send their girls to be taught by her. They left, normally, to be married; Sappho herself was married and had a daughter of her own." C. M. Bowra, in *Ancient Greek Literature* (Oxford UP, 1960), says that "about 600 B.C. the island of Lesbos gave a new poetry to the world." Sappho "lived with a circle of women and girls between whom there was little formality and no artificiality. To these friends her poems are addressed, and as she felt powerfully and deeply, her work has often the power of tense passion. Her name, maligned by the corrupting imaginations of Alexandria and Rome, has suffered from her passionate attachments and unrestrained tenderness, but no one who reads her poetry can feel that it is the reflection of anything but the purest love. She is the perfect exponent of the pangs of unrequited passion, of the regret of parting and the memory of old love. . . . She states the facts with such power that they are sufficient in themselves, and the smallest fragments of her work are still instinct with life. She has only to say 'I loved you, Atthis, once—a long time ago' or 'the spring's messenger, the love-voiced nightingale' or 'I have a lovely child with beauty like golden flowers, Cleis, my beloved,' and nothing can be added or taken away."

DISCUSSION STARTERS

Next to love and hate, jealousy may be the emotion most fully chronicled by poets and other writers. For Sappho, it crushes the spirit; it leaves her mute; it is a feverish illness and, finally, a kind of death. Ask your students what images, memories, and associations the term *jealousy* brings to mind. Have them cluster the term and then write a short passage focused on jealousy.

THE RECEPTIVE READER

The speaker is a passionate woman who is in love with Anaktoria, creating the classic triangle with the spurned or slighted third person consumed by jealousy. The speaker in the poem watches the woman she loves talking to a man who is "like the very gods"—because he is permitted to gaze at his beloved, whose sweet voice murmurs love-talk "all for him." Although the speaker wears a mask of composure when looking at her lover, "underneath" her heart is shaking, a flame seems to spread in her, and a fever shakes her body. The world is blotted out to her sight and hearing, with a sound of thunder in her ears. Are moderns too blasé to own up to the kind of feelings that Sappho expresses with fierce romantic passion?

Louise Erdrich, "Indian Boarding School: The Runaways" 686

DISCUSSION STARTERS

As Erdrich's poem suggests, a majority culture will often try to reform, or "re-form," the lifestyle and value system of a cultural minority. It takes an effort of the imagination for people representing the mainstream culture to enter into a perspective different from their own. Ask students to collaborate in planning a presentation that would project different perspectives on what happens in this poem, with participants taking turns to assume the different identities ("I am the sheriff . . ."; "I am the lame guard . . ."; "I am the runaway").

THE RECEPTIVE READER

1. Many writers from minority backgrounds leave behind fashionable academic conventions of "aesthetic distance" to project powerfully the grievances and aspirations of their people. The feelings expressed in this poem may seem too personal and too intense to make the speaker in this poem sound like an imagined person, an assumed persona? And yet they may be the intensely imagined or projected creation of someone intimately acquainted with the history of her people?

2. If we bring assumptions about the civilizing mission of the established system to this poem, they are likely to be challenged by its portrayal of the hunting down of fugitives, "the worn-down welts / of ancient punishments," the shameful green dresses and the punitive scrubbing of sidewalks, and the memory of "old injuries."

3. The fugitives from the forced "reeducation" of the Indian boarding school jump trains on the run only to be caught by the sheriff waiting for them at the midpoint of their desperate journey.

4. The railroad tracks are like scars ("old lacerations") cut into the landscape, but the children love them because they are their link with home. The highway becomes a road back to the dead end of the children's treatment by the system. The dresses and the work imposed as punishment become a badge of humiliation?

THE PERSONAL RESPONSE

The poet, by making us forget race, by mobilizing the age-old resentment of the oppressed against the oppressor, and by showing us punitive adults brutalizing children, makes it hard for us not to empathize with the runaways?

Janice Mirikitani, "For My Father" 687

DISCUSSION STARTERS

In this poem, the experience of the internment camps changed the father's life. Ask your students to wonder, what if? What if something important in their lives had not happened or things had taken a different turn? For a journal entry, can they draw up a scenario for an "alternative life"?

THE RECEPTIVE READER

1. The father's immigrant status and Japanese ancestry are almost immediately invoked: "He came over the ocean / carrying Mt. Fuji on / his back / Tule Lake on his chest." Tule Lake was one of the camps to which Japanese Americans were sent during the Second World War. Executive Order 9066, signed by Franklin Roosevelt in February 1942, gave the U.S. Army the power to arrest each and every Japanese American on the West Coast. As a result, over 110,000 men, women, and children were taken without warrant, indictment, or hearing, to internment camps. Even when released from the camps, the poet's people remained "the other" to the cornflake-eating "hakujin [white people] / whose children / pointed at our eyes."

2. The father is presented as a stern, unyielding, silent man who, through sheer force of will, turned a desert into a strawberry field. Tule Lake apparently taught the father that dreams and compassion are out of place in the bleak, harshly lit real world. When the daughter and her siblings were caught stealing strawberries, the father's "eyes held / nothing / as he whipped us / for stealing." The "desert had dried / his soul." The daughter rebelled against the silence, the harshness, of the embittered parent who was beyond his children's touch—although she has come to understand what made him what he was.

3. Strawberries are something of a miracle in this poem, as they are produced in such a hostile environment. The strawberry is a rich luxurious fruit; strawberries on cereal have more panache than cereal with bananas. Symbolic of what is delectable and desirable, the strawberries, watered by tears, are nevertheless the product of a bleak setting and a stunted life. They admonish us to think about the toil and hardship behind the good things we thoughtlessly consume.

MAKING CONNECTIONS—FOR DISCUSSION OR WRITING

Ben Jonson's "On My First Son" is the anguished lament of a parent whose seven-year-old son has died. The father vows to "never like too much" again. In the future he will protect himself from ever experiencing such grief by keeping his love under wraps. Sharon Olds' "I Go Back to May 1937" is an emotional response to college graduation photographs of her parents. In the pictures, the mother and father are on the verge of entering into what will be a disastrous union ("she's the wrong woman, / he's the wrong man, you are going to do things / you cannot imagine you would ever do, / you are going to do bad things to children, / you are going to suffer in ways you never heard of, / you are going to want to die"). However, Olds concludes that since she is a product of that miserable pairing, she cannot go back to them and urge them not to marry: "I / want to live."

Janice Mirikitani's "For My Father" is the unhappy story of a Japanese American man who was permanently affected by the circumstances of his life and times. A victim of unceasing racial prejudice, the father responds by shutting down his emotions. Like Ben Jonson's narrator, Mirikitani's father is going to shield himself from further emotional anguish by refusing to allow himself to dream, to hope, or to love. Sharon Olds' narrator is similar to Mirikitani's in that both speakers look over a parent's life, acknowledge the hardship and unhappiness endured, and end on a forgiving note?

Juxtapositions: Variations of "I"

Elizabeth Barrett Browning, "How Do I Love Thee? Let Me Count the Ways" 689

DISCUSSION STARTERS

What might be a modern reader's answer to "How do I love thee"?

THE RECEPTIVE READER

1. The *voice* we hear is that of someone striving earnestly to be entirely idealistic, soulful, dedicated, pure, and faithful beyond the grave, with a love that is an extension (or replacement?) of her "childhood faith." The person has managed to eliminate (or repress?) any trace of deplorable but very human weaknesses, such as impatience, fault-finding, orneriness, lust, or jealousy. In our modern world, the vocabulary we use with friends or lovers (revealing) is often different from our public persona (concealing). But this person is all *persona*—playing a public role in a private relationship?

2. Though the feeling expressed by the words "I love you" is universal and timeless (which might help explain why this poem is still popular in our day), the words and sentiments that follow up are so solemn and "pure" as to make the poem sound terribly old-fashioned and archaic? These words and expressions conjure up few concrete images but stay on the level of uplifting, high-minded abstractions: "to the depth and breadth and height," "to the

level of every day's / Most quiet need," "freely, as men strive for right," "purely, as they turn from Praise." At the same time, many superficially cynical moderns have a secret weakness for poetry suggesting that people are capable of a more ideal vision?

3. The "I love thee" returns in the poem with increasing insistence until it culminates in the triumphant "I love thee with the breath, / Smiles, tears of all my life!" and then comes to rest in the final "I shall but love thee better after death."

Gwendolyn Brooks, "A Song in the Front Yard" 689

DISCUSSION STARTERS

What is the key difference between the two poets juxtaposed here? Compared with Browning, Brooks erects fewer barriers between private feelings and the words she uses to describe them. The reader will readily hear and feel the girl's rebellion, frustration, anger, and wildness with the direct expressions "I want . . . "; "a girl gets sick of . . ."; "I say it's fine . . ."; "I'd like . . ." In this poem, we see strong feelings shatter protective shells or shields, leaving little distance between the self and the word?

THE RECEPTIVE READER

1. The front yard is usually the one our neighbors see. It's the one we keep up for "appearances," whereas the back yard is the one we "live" in. The back yard is less well tended, where "hungry weeds grow," and where "Johnnie Mae" hangs out. Here the suppressed real self can come to the surface. The speaker is hungry to break out of conventional behavior and go farther than the back yard—walk down the alley flaunting black lace stockings.

2. In the poem, the poet identifies with an earlier adolescent self? a person with a proper upbringing but pent-up feelings of rebellion?

3. A rose is conventionally associated with glorified passionate love, with a lover dancing attendance upon a properly feminine and ladylike object of his affections. The young woman in Brooks' poem is sick of the conventional courtship dance. The terseness of the line nicely mirrors the speaker's impatience to live more unconventionally, more genuinely, more in the diversity of "untended . . . weeds."

The Public Persona

Dylan Thomas, "In My Craft or Sullen Art" 691

DISCUSSION STARTERS

In this poem, Dylan Thomas speaks to us in his public persona as the poet-sage dedicated to his calling. A specialty of latter-day debunking biographers is to look for the private demons behind the public persona (such as alcohol and promiscuity in the case of Dylan Thomas, driving him, like a rock singer, to an early death). You may want to farm out to groups of students some exploration of the paradox of the public persona of the poet-sage and the poet's private demons in the case of Milton, Whitman, Frost, or Thomas. Add or substitute any others (Shelley?) of your or their choice.

THE RECEPTIVE READER

1. Thomas' art could be considered "sullen" in that it is difficult, demanding, not easily humored or sweet-talked into performing. (It also acts sullen or unresponsive when offered the rewards of meretricious celebrity.) Yet he sees himself laboring by a "singing light," literally the light that enables him to write (or "sing") but also a light that is symbolic of the light that poetry brings into a dark world. Students may interpret Thomas' metaphors somewhat like this:

bread	monetary reward
strut	ostentatious, smug display
ivory stages	elitist forum for approved authors (like ivory tower elitist scholarship?)
common wages	spontaneous gratitude
spindrift pages	writing that may be carried as if by the wind or ocean (not for a presold audience)
towering dead	canonized authors (writing poems about nightingales)

2. The poet's "art" is the writer's solemn, quasi-religious calling or vocation, and it rhymes with *heart*. The multiple rhymes with "wages" help the poem focus on the central question of the poet's incentive or reward.

3. The moon (here the "raging" moon) is often used as a metaphor for the subconscious, powerfully emotional and potentially destructive, part of our common humanity. It represents the dark or "shadow" side of the self as opposed to the sun's rays of light (reason and logic).

4. The solemn tone and the long-drawn-out sentences with strong breaks after the short, strongly rhythmic lines, together with the echoing multiple rhymes, contribute to the chanting, hypnotic effect that was Thomas' trademark.

Walt Whitman, "I Understand the Large Hearts of Heroes" 692

For a "Perspectives" entry on Whitman see Chapter 12 of this manual.

DISCUSSION STARTERS

Some people are caught up within their own narrow selves and maintain a fault-finding adversarial relationship with much of the rest of humanity. Whitman had a tremendous gift for broad sympathy or empathy for the kaleidoscopic range of people, motives, occupations, and aspirations that he chronicled in *Song of Myself.* You may want to send students to their dictionaries to explore the meanings and ramifications of words like *sympathy, empathy, solidarity, rapport, fellow feeling.* How do they see these qualities reflected in Whitman's poem?

THE RECEPTIVE READER

1. For the poet, human beings are not interchangeable entities that can easily become mere statistics. Instead, they are "lank loose-gowned women," "silent old-faced infants," and unshaven men. When we see, with the skipper, the "crowded and rudderless wreck," we can visualize "Death chasing it up and down the storm." The message chalked on the board makes the skipper more than a functionary doing a job?

2. Whitman is fond of large, sweeping uplifting abstractions: "the large hearts of heroes. / The courage of present times and all times." But his "I suffered, I was there" is well earned by his human sympathy for the people "boated from the side of their prepared graves"?

Audre Lorde, "Coal" 693

DISCUSSION STARTERS

"I / is the total black," "I am Black," says the poet in her public role as a spokesperson for the unheard. Whom would your students accept as a spokesperson for their generation? Whom would they nominate as the voice of their gender, ethnic group, or race? Who speaks for them as students?

THE RECEPTIVE READER

1. Words in this poem are not neutral counters but are glowing, slashing, poisonous, explosive ("like young sparrows bursting from shell"). They do not exist in a vacuum but are weighted or "colored" by the price paid by those who risk using them. Words break through resistance like diamonds that are used to cut the glass in a window or door. They breed like poisonous adders; some, like slips in a perforated checkbook, can be torn out only once, leaving behind a stublike reminder like "an ill-pulled tooth with a ragged edge"?

2. The opening up of congealed attitudes and breaking down of obstacles, achieved by passionate and searing words, is the recurrent theme of the poem?

3. The "I / is" and "come whatever wills" sound like echoes of Black English?

4. The poem has the proud, aggressive, defiant, militant tone of someone using words to break down barriers and advance causes. The collective "I" in the poem is all black people coming, like coal, "from the earth's inside," and like a diamond dug from the earth turning into a living flame "in the open light"?

Imagined Selves

Louise Bogan, "Cassandra" 695

PERSPECTIVES—BOGAN: A WOMAN POET'S BIOGRAPHY

Sandra M. Gilbert and Susan Gubar, the editors of *The Norton Anthology of Literature by Women* (1985), call Louise Bogan a "scrupulous artist" who, while a poetry critic for *The New Yorker*, "herself wrote poems that constituted a rigorous and fearless exploration of an interior 'wilderness'" and that in the words of W. H. Auden "wrested beauty and truth out of dark places." Bogan's parents had had an unhappy marriage, and she said, "I cannot bring myself to describe the horrors of the pre-1914 lower-middle-class life, in which they found themselves." Her own first marriage failed, and she described herself "as the highly charged and neurotically inclined product of an extraordinary childhood and an unfortunate early marriage, into which last state I had rushed to escape the first." After a second marriage and persisting psychiatric problems, Bogan entered into a lifelong friendship with the poet Theodore Roethke. She continued to publish collections of her poetry and won prizes, visiting professorships, and poet-in-residence appointments. She identified with the achievements of women writers from Sappho to Virginia Woolf. Gilbert and Gubar call Bogan's rewriting of ancient myth in poems like "Cassandra" a "powerful reimagining of mythology."

DISCUSSION STARTERS

Have your students encountered in literature or legend an alter ego, a character with whom they especially identify? If they were to nominate such a person from story, myth, or legend, who would it be, and why?

THE RECEPTIVE READER

1. Cassandra as the truth-teller would appeal to a poet weary of human trickery and self-deception. However, she would appeal especially to the

woman poet if the assumption is that the lust, pride, and suicidal belligerence Cassandra bares or exposes have historically been prerogatives of men.

2. If Cassandra were really mad or deranged, it seems unlikely that her spirit would express itself in such a regular (and regulated) form. The classic form of the poem subliminally reinforces the lucidity, control, and deliberateness of Cassandra's truth-telling? We call her mad because divine inspiration speaks through her? Or because she destroys the complacent illusions of her "sane" contemporaries? The second *again* seems to emphasize the recurrent, compulsive nature of her "mad" mission.

Marie Luise Kaschnitz, "Women's Program" 695

DISCUSSION STARTERS

Oppressive governments have often watched poetry, like humor, warily, aware of its subversive potential. What is subversive about this poem?

THE RECEPTIVE READER

1. The personality of the poet and the *persona* of the radio talker probably overlap considerably. It is probably the poet herself who rebels against conventional sex roles that assign to a woman the broadcasting of recipes and of advice on running household appliances? It is the poet who has subversive fantasies of sabotaging the "women's program"?

2. The subversive advice serves in part as a warning? The last lines tell us, "Don't be too sure / Evening will come / Don't be too sure / That God loves you." In a violent, irrational world, we should not take *any* continuity for granted, and God may at times seem to have abandoned His people. Pouring milk into telephones, making cats sleep in dishwashers, and seasoning food in weird combinations certainly conjure up strange images. Are these surreal gestures symbolizing the poet's refusal to accept or cooperate with what has become "normal," accepted, or approved in the world around her?

3. When she advises the listeners to "go meet the ones with the bagpipes / who come from inside the mountains," she suggests that it would be safer and saner to follow the Pied Piper (of Hamlin) than to follow the official guides sustaining the system. (About the shoes: When the Pied Piper abducted the children of Hamlin to punish their elders for defrauding him, the townspeople found only the children's shoes.)

Robert Browning, "My Last Duchess" 697

DISCUSSION STARTERS

What is "dramatic" about Browning's poem? Dramatic monologues like Browning's *My Last Duchess* are probably best appreciated and understood when read aloud—dramatically. You may want to divide the class into groups and assign portions of the poem to each group. Ask students in each group to coach a selected speaker on a "dramatic reading."

THE RECEPTIVE READER

1. The widowed duke, a connoisseur of painting and sculpture in the Renaissance vein, is negotiating a new marriage. The dowry seems to be a big issue, though the duke pays lip service to the beauty of his intended. His last wife is still there in a most lifelike painting. She had a marvelous smile, but she did not reserve it exclusively enough for her vindictive master, who had her killed.

2. The speaker's explanation that his late wife "was too soon made glad" begins to sound ominous? By the time he mentions his "nine-hundred-years-old name" we are likely to get the message? When he says, "I gave commands," we are sure?

3. The key to creating a believable persona very different from the author's own is not only to capture the speech patterns and mannerisms of the speaker but also to enter into the much more slippery designs or intentions of the speaker. The duke is intensely proud and very jealous (a murderous combination), and he isn't very good at concealing that jealousy as he describes his last duchess to his visitor. His use of the possessive pronoun *my* in the opening line may alert us to a possessive nature that reveals itself quite clearly by the end of the poem (which ends in "for *me*"). To say that the speaker didn't like it much when the duchess considered a sunrise equally beautiful as his love token at her breast is an understatement. A key passage —"Even then would be some stooping; and I choose / Never to stoop"— shows us a person who considers it beneath his dignity even to criticize offenders or explain his criticism (they should KNOW!).

4. The duke's *conversational tone* puts a civilized, suave surface on the personality of an arrogant, murderous, sexist individual? By the duke's own admission, rather than being given to chatting amiably, he was used to giving the kind of command that could stop "all smiles" together. The frequent *enjambment* helps create the effect of offhand, nonchalant conversation, which tends to stop and start irregularly—with one sentence running into the next with the same straddling effect as the lines in the poem rather than fitting into rigid segmented patterns.

5. The duke's *public persona* is that of the patron of the arts, of a person reasonable in his negotiations about the new marriage, and of a person trying to discuss rationally (and without shouting or vindictiveness) the foibles of his ex-wife?

Poems for Further Study

Yusef Komunyakaa, "My Father's Love Letters" 699

DISCUSSION STARTERS

At one time, the overmothering "Mom" came in for much criticism. Do fathers today bear the brunt of the blame for the traumas and frustrations of emotionally damaged offspring?

THE RECEPTIVE READER

1. The father is an illiterate man who works at a mill, wears a "carpenter's apron" which "always bulged / With old nails, a claw hammer / Looped at his side," and who lives surrounded by extension cords, "voltage meters & pipe threaders." In the past the father has been physically abusive to the mother, to the extent that she has left the household. In what sounds to be a Friday night ritual, the father comes home from the mill and dictates letters in which he pleads ("Love, / Baby, Honey, Please") for the mother to return. "He would beg, / Promising to never beat her / Again." The father seems an example of the cycle of violent abuse and whining regret (not to mention fruitless promises) experienced by battered women?

2. The son's feelings about the father are extremely mixed. This is a man who, despite being unable to read, could "look at blueprints / & say how many bricks / Formed each wall,"—but who also "stole rose & hyacinth / For his yard." The son is in a way relieved that the mother is gone and beyond the reach of the father's abuse: "Somehow I was happy / She had gone." In fact, he even contemplates including a reminder ("how Mary Lou / Williams' 'Polka Dots & Moonbeams' / Never made the swelling go down") that would undercut the purpose of his father's letters. The crucial last lines—"Laboring over a simple word, almost / Redeemed by what he tried to say"—illustrate the ambivalence of the son's feelings. How, on the one hand, could the son ever forgive the beatings, the mother's flight, the essential brutality of such a man? But in the "quiet brutality" of his workshop surroundings, the inarticulate, illiterate father is struggling to give expression to stunted emotions, amorphous regrets.

Countee Cullen, "Saturday's Child" 700

DISCUSSION STARTERS

Do your students remember the children's poem to which Countee Cullen alludes in his title?

> Monday's child is fair of face
> Tuesday's child is full of grace,
> Wednesday's child is full of woe,
> Thursday's child has far to go,

Friday's child is loving and giving,
Saturday's child works hard for a living,
But a child that's born on the Sabbath day
Is fair and wise and good and gay.

All things considered, would your students think of themselves as "Saturday's child"? Monday's child? Sunday's child?

THE RECEPTIVE READER

1. The first three stanzas, in particular, play off *paired polarities* highlighted by the rhyme scheme. The first two lines present *others'* destinies in bright, optimistic terms; the last two lines present *the speaker's* in terms of pain and despair. Note *silver spoon/black raccoon*, *rattle/battle*, *silk and down/sackcloth gown*, *star/tar*.

2. The *personified abstractions*—Dame Poverty, Pain, Death, and Sorrow— enhance the feeling that destiny or fateful forces have dealt the speaker a poor hand; they imply that fate determines the speaker's destiny rather than his own options or choices. Those who "gave the speaker life"—his parents—were taken from him early by death?

3. In spite of the formal language and the allegorical framework of personified abstractions, we assume the speaker is speaking directly about his own experience as an unwanted child in a poor black family with too many mouths to feed already?

Denise Levertov, "In Mind" 700

For a "Perspectives" entry on Levertov see Chapter 16 of this manual.

DISCUSSION STARTERS

How are the two women who dwell in the poet's mind related to traditional stereotypes of "good" and "bad" women?

THE RECEPTIVE READER

The playing off of opposites in this poem is mirrored in pairs like *innocence/moon-ridden*, *fair-featured/old woman*, *utopian smock or shift/opals and taffeta*. The one alter ego is "kind and very clean"; the other is "not kind" and wears rags and "torn taffeta." The first woman does indeed seem to represent a modern "utopian" ideal: She is all natural ("unadorned") and close to nature ("smelling of / apples or grass"). But—she "has / no imagination." Her innocence and smooth hair and cleanliness will turn deadly dull? The writer, at other moments, with another part of her mind, yearns for a more "turbulent" life, symbolized by gaudy adornment (opals, feathers, taffeta). This alternative persona is inspired by the moon that is the patron of the artistic subconscious mind from which her "strange songs" emerge. Each overly idealized version of ourselves leaves some part of our being unfulfilled? For each one of us, there is another, dark side of the moon that other people are usually not permitted to see?

Nikki Giovanni, "Legacies" 701

DISCUSSION STARTERS

Have any of your students aspired to be *like* their parents (or like earlier generations in their family)? Have others aspired *not* to be like their parents?

THE RECEPTIVE READER

1. The grandmother speaks her request to the little girl "proudly." She wants to pass on to the next generation humble and practical but nurturing, life-sustaining skills? The skills may symbolize for the older woman family values and making the best of your potential in a hostile world. But the girl, like many other frustrated, rebellious adolescents, may feel that by learning these humble domestic skills she will be *locked into* the domestic sphere instead of being "dependent on her spirit"?

2. The title of the poem, "Legacies," and the year in which it is written hint that the poet appears to be closest to the girl. (Also, the younger person is identified as "the girl" and the older as "her grandmother"—instead of "the old woman" talking to "her granddaughter." This helps us see the situation from the girl's point of view?)

Sylvia Plath, "Mirror" 702

PERSPECTIVES—PLATH'S "MIRROR" AND THE UNRELIABLE NARRATOR

Donna Richardson's rereading of Plath's "Mirror" (in *The Explicator*, Winter 1991) illustrates the readiness of current critics to distrust or question the overt testimony of the speaker in a poem or the narrator of a story. "The poem is often incompletely analyzed as being simply about the unavoidable horrors of growing old." However, according to Richardson, the mirror-narrator would make an odd spokesperson for the author since its "point of view is not only emotionless but also extremely limited physically as well as morally." We should not, like the woman in the poem, "concede truth and godhood to an emotionless object." Audiences tend to "split between mirror-trusters and mirror doubters," making the narrator ironically a mirror of the audience's values as well. As readers, we "can make the mirror the god it says it is, giving it depths that it does not possess," or we "can reject its claim that its superficial truth accurately reflects human worth. Unfortunately, many women (as well as men) have traditionally done the former." The fishface looking at the woman in the mirror is a reflection of her moral state—the "fixed and dehumanized" state of someone who "chooses to take the two-dimensional reality of physical appearance as the only truth."

DISCUSSION STARTERS

Sylvia Plath wrote in a journal: "My writing is a hollow and failing substitute for real life, real feeling." Her poem "Mirror" reflects her awareness of the polarities of illusion and reality but at the same time her commitment to the cruel truth. How do your students feel about mirrors? You may want to have them cluster MIRROR and then write a passage or poem sorting out the images, associations, or ideas the term brings to mind.

THE RECEPTIVE READER

1. The mirror reports on the alternation of its picture of the blank opposite wall with people-pictures as if it had no real understanding of how people live and come and go within walls. Plath's calling the mirror a "little god" may remind us of the house altar of Roman times, for instance. Is it true that many people spend time before the mirror every day the way others spend devotional time in front of a domestic shrine? At the same time, the "little god," though seeing much, is definitely limited in mobility and influence on human lives?

2. The mirror becomes more knowing and ominous as it reveals itself to be the silent participant in a lifelong drama—the woman's search "for what she really is." The young girl that the woman once was has disappeared as if drowned in the lakelike smooth surface of the mirror. The truth-telling mirror knows that candlelight and moonlight can blur and flatter aging features (or inspire romantic thoughts that make us forget harsh reality)—but they are "liars."

3. The mirror says defensively "I am not cruel, only truthful." But the truth, as the mirror knows, *is* "terrible." The poet remains distant from the tearful and agitated woman; like the mirror, the poet *is* "unmisted by love of dislike." (The poet is the mirror?) And yet her fascination with the fate of the old woman may be rooted in her deep-down knowledge that the same fate awaits her?

Chapter 20 TONE The Language of the Emotions 706

How do we make students more sensitive to tone? Like music, like the language of gestures, the spoken language is a language of the emotions. In watching a foreign-language movie without subtitles, we may not understand a word. But we can hear (and see) anger, surprise, terror, grief, resentment, hostility. You may want to have students rehearse and present an "emotional symphony," with different participants in turn performing the sounds and gestures of anger, grief, pride, terror, disdain, tenderness, glee, and the like. When we move to the spoken word, the heard overtones and undertones of feeling and attitude add an additional layer or dimension to the substratum of the dictionary meanings of words. The emphasis is on *heard*: Have students coach or critique their peers as they read the sample passages in the opening discussion with the right mournful, awed, or irreverent tone.

Irony and paradox affect tone especially in twentieth-century poetry and in the metaphysical seventeenth-century poetry that was a model for many modern poets. Irony and paradox are the poet's means of doing justice to the complexities of experience. A lively sense of irony makes the poet look for the less flattering underside when things seem too superficially beautiful. Modern poets especially have looked for the ironic counterpoint, noting with grim amusement the discrepancy between theory and practice. Can your students think of some familiar examples of the ironic contrast between the idealized façade and the unflattering truth? Examples might be the patriotic orator who stays far from the line of fire, the politician who talks about integrity but is ready to deal, the lover who swears lasting devotion to secure temporary pleasure.

While irony often delights in what undercuts or *debunks* a moralistic façade, paradox tends to recognize and *accept* the essential complications and dilemmas of life. People who love paradox have learned to live with contradictions. Life is neither all good nor bad; it is neither an idyllic utopia of benign, nonviolent creatures nor a nightmarish vision of hell. It is a paradoxical mixture of both. People attuned to paradox resist the temptation to be trapped into *either/or* choices; they opt for the *both/and*. We start making our peace with paradox when we begin to see that in some vital conflicts both sides may in some way be right: people who stress the need for law and people who yearn for freedom, parents who want to protect their children and children who know that at some point they have to be on their own. Irony and paradox are the bane of literal-minded people, of people with a one-track mind. Sören Kierkegaard said,

> One should not think slightingly of the paradoxical; for the paradox is the source of the thinker's passion, and the thinker without a paradox is like a lover without a feeling, a paltry mediocrity.

First Reading: Robert Hass, "Song" 708

DISCUSSION STARTERS

How many people in our society come home to an "empty house"? Do any of your students remember a Beatles song about "all the lonely people"? What do they make of the phrase "lonely in a crowd"? Why do so many people in the modern world have so many contacts but few lasting relationships?

THE RECEPTIVE READER

1. As with many modern people living alone, there seems little chance here that the "great crowds of family," with loving offspring hugging the dear Papa, will miraculously materialize. There is a cat for company. The speaker feels "naked," defenseless—at the mercy of loneliness and disappointment. What renders his loneliness poignant is that otherwise it's a perfect day—the bay clear, the hills baking in the sun, the red scrub oak furnishing glowing touches of color.

2. Students may sense different underlying emotions, depending on their lives or experiences. The underlying emotion may well be one shared by many moderns: the unfulfilled yearning for a fuller, richer life in the bosom of a loving family—while actually the person is cooking filet of sole for one in "an empty house."

3. The poem is *understated* in that the speaker never comes right out to say: "I'm disappointed! Feel sorry for me! I am so alone."

4. The filets of sole are not really being eaten (let alone savored gourmet-style); they stew there in their precious yuppiish tangerine sauce, and the "bone-white dish" calls up unfortunate memories of white bones bleaching in the desert. The terse short lines prevent any buildup of mushy self-pity?

The Register of Emotions

Louise Bogan, "The Dream" 710

DISCUSSION STARTERS

What is the stuff nightmares are made of? Are they highly personal or individual? Or are there recurrent, near-universal elements welling up from the collective subconscious? Are our nightmares murky and senseless, or do they make sense in a strange way?

THE RECEPTIVE READER

1. The prevailing *tone* of the poem is one of terror. Although the word *dream* can suggest a pleasant experience, this dream is the stuff of horror

movies. Highly charged emotional words and phrases include the initial "O God," followed by a network of terms like *terrible, blows, fear,* and *retribution* as we watch the "terrible horse" pawing the air and threatening to smash the "coward complete," cowering and weeping on the ground and ready to "swound."

2. The *fairy tale* quality lies in the facing of a nightmarish threat ("the terrible beast") and the miraculous rescue and redemption. Other elements reminiscent of the world of the fairy tale are the appearance of a good fairy (in the form of "another woman") and the use of a token that has quasi-magic powers (the flinging of the glove).

3. Many nightmares take the dreamer to the brink—when the dreamer wakes, drenched in sweat, with a wildly pounding heart? But here some strange parable of the taming of the wild beast (of passion?) is being played out. Is the "strong creature" that comes to the rescue an alter ego—a different and less cowering part of the speaker's personality? Nightmares go on and on, with the oppressive or horrifying images blending and merging, with no chance to get things under control and sort them out into neat segments. At the same time, the long, fluid lines of "The Dream" are not *totally* out of control—they come to a full stop at the end of each stanza, thus perhaps preparing us for the wild beast being reined in at the end.

4. Are our dreams mere "idle dreams"? Or are they, as Freudians claim, indications of subterranean turmoil in the psyche?

William Shakespeare, "Sonnet 18" 711

DISCUSSION STARTERS

How do people act when they are "hyper"? When our students are praised or loved, do they want the other person to speak moderately and "truthfully"—or hyperbolically, with the speaker going all out? Even though modern poets shy away from *hyperbole*, is the human impulse to dramatize, to heighten, to exaggerate alive in our culture?

THE RECEPTIVE READER

1. Many of us would be more than sufficiently flattered to be compared to the fresh beauty of a May morning or to the languorous sweetness of a sunny summer day. However, never content with timid or conventional comparisons, Shakespeare makes the beloved in this poem "*more* lovely and more temperate." The poem proceeds to elaborate on the shortcomings of the summer season: Even summertime is not perfect; it has "rough winds," it is too brief, its heat is intemperate, going to broiling extremes. Nature is too mutable and its pleasures too transitory to compare with the "eternal summer" that the person addressed in the poem has brought into the speaker's life—and into the annals of poetry.

2. The sestet, with the opening "But . . ." providing the conventional turning point, turns from the limited perfections of nature to the "eternal" beauty of the beloved, who will remain forever young—immortalized in "this," the poem whose lines will triumph over time and give "life to thee."

William Stafford, "Traveling through the Dark" 712

DISCUSSION STARTERS

Is *understatement* the natural tone to choose when a show of emotions would be inappropriate, impossible, or awkward? Or is it a convention—like the assumption that in our culture boys don't cry and men don't weep? Are the emotions that Stafford's poem buries or hides with its matter-of-fact voice too horrid to acknowledge—to "swerve" into? The speaker must make a swift, ugly decision; perhaps he cannot indulge in the luxury of an emotional response. Instead of telling us his feelings, the speaker thinks "hard for us all." But, paradoxically, we as readers are haunted by the unexpressed feelings in his mind.

THE RECEPTIVE READER

1. Symbolically, we all travel through the "dark" of the unknown. The dilemma in which the speaker finds himself has no right answer, yet to swerve from the practical (though emotionally wrenching) solution "might make more dead." Even after pushing the dead doe off the road into the river, the speaker is still "in the dark" as to the right answer to the question raised by the incident?

2. The dry, matter-of-fact tone is strong in the line "It is usually best to roll them into the canyon" and in expressions like "stood by the heap"?

3. Students are likely to conclude that the poet felt emotions the poem doesn't express; strong feeling is *implied* in lines like "her fawn lay there waiting, / alive, still, never to be born" and "Beside that mountain road I hesitated." Here, the less-said says more, as is often the case with deliberate understatement.

THE PERSONAL RESPONSE

Some readers will insist that it was the speaker's obligation to living things not only to "hesitate," but to "swerve." Some readers will argue they would not have the stomach to push the dead doe with the living fawn inside her into the river. Some will be pragmatic and point out that it is unlikely the speaker had proper tools (or experience) with which to save the fawn. Finally, some may describe analogous events in which a pivotal choice must be made on the spot.

Dylan Thomas, "Do Not Go Gentle into That Good Night" 713

DISCUSSION STARTERS

Here, Dylan Thomas protests against his father's coming death and calls for a passionate last stand against it (even though he knows it can't be prevented). Which, for your students, are the injunctions or incitements that most glow with passionate defiance? Have them look for the active verbs, many of them in the imperative (or command) form—"burn," "rave," "rage," "curse," "bless."

THE RECEPTIVE READER

1. This marvelous poem of rebellion against the inevitable does without familiar notes of grieving and mourning; it does not cultivate sorrowful emotions (that are often tinged with self-pity?). Instead, the poem strikes a note of fiercely passionate defiance, of glorious rage that is a last affirmation of the will to live in the face of approaching death.

2. If Thomas had spoken to his father *directly* early in the poem, it might have started the poem with a tone of personal reminiscence, rather than starting it with the grand sweep of a universal indictment of age and death. As it is, bringing the father in at the end comes as a climactic heightening of intensity, bringing the rage and defiance of the poem "close to home"?

3. The ordinary people in the poem are wise enough to know that "their words had forked no lightning"; their "frail deeds" might have been "bright" (but weren't?); the sun shook off the songs they addressed to it. But although they were held in by the limitations of mortal life, they had the passionate imagination that transforms the ordinary into the poetic. The poet wants them to be true to the bitter end to that passionate intensity. Language for Thomas is the chief agent that transforms drab reality. The emotional intensity of the poet's language is at the opposite pole from the understatement of Cullen's poem. *Hyperbole* pervades such extravagant images as "caught and sang the sun in flight," "grieved it on its way," "their words had forked no lightning," "might have danced in a green bay." Extremes of darkness and light are played off, for instance, in "*blind eyes* could *blaze like meteors* and be gay." Opposites are played off in "*curse, bless*, me now with your fierce tears."

4. *Light* (with *bright* and *sight*) and *night* are the key words that the rhyme scheme highlights and drives home; their refrainlike repetition and final juxtaposition make the poem a paean to light as the symbol of life even as it is about to be engulfed by darkness.

THE PERSONAL RESPONSE

Impious (meaning irreligious or lacking respect for God) might be an appropriate label for the poet's call to rebellion against what is presumably

God's will, especially in light of the biblical "the meek shall inherit the earth." But the poet's "rage" can also be seen as an expression of a committed, passionate love of God's creation? (Martin Luther said, "If I knew the world would end tomorrow, I would plant an apple tree today.")

N. Scott Momaday, "Earth and I Gave You Turquoise" 714

For a "Perspectives" entry on Momaday see Chapter 13 of this manual.

DISCUSSION STARTERS

In this poem, past, future, and present intermingle. Have students trace the pattern of the poem as it is reflected in the changing tenses of verbs: "I gave . . . we lived"; "I will bring . . . we will make"; "I speak . . . I go."

THE RECEPTIVE READER

Students will find different images that help them share the speaker's emotions. Very strong is the feeling of standing aside, being left out, as "they dance near Chinle / by the seven elms" and "drink coffee till morning." Students may be drawn to the unadorned, unspoiled natural images like "the wild cane remembers you"; still others will be touched by the loneliness of the speaker who goes to his "young brother's house," which is "filled" while the speaker's is empty. Some may respond to the stark simplicity of "You and I will not be there." The speaker in the poem deals with his grief by imagining a future life where he "will ride the swiftest horse" and his dead lover "will hear the drumming hooves."

THE CREATIVE DIMENSION

You may want to suggest that women in your class try a re-creation of Momaday's poem—re-created from the perspective of a bereaved woman. Here is a student-written example:

Old stories in my house
dusty in the attic
I remember laughing singing
You
planting children in my womb
Me
the moon-woman growing
as big as a mountain
The years lie heavy on my breast
I still have a lock of your hair

clipped one summer day
Sometimes I speak your name

The Uses of Irony

Martín Espada, "Latin Night at the Pawnshop" 717

DISCUSSION STARTER

Salsa bands, congas, maracas, the tambourine—what images and associations do they bring to mind? Is there something especially festive, colorful, and vital about "Latin" or Latino culture—and is it endangered in Anglo environments like Chelsea, Massachusetts? (Do students from diverse cultural traditions think of their cultural background as exceptionally rich, warm, and human—more so than the mainstream culture?)

THE RECEPTIVE READER

The poet likely was saddened and angry when he viewed these jailed objects; many urban pawnshops in fact do have wrought-iron bars on the windows in order to keep burglars out. Though the name "Liberty" implies freedom, liberation, the poem conveys a sense of defeat, of people being trapped and thwarted in their search for a richer, colorful life by economic forces. Inside, not only are the musical instruments trapped, but, by implication, an entire cultural tradition. The pawnshop becomes a morgue—these are not just pawned objects; they suggest the death of hopes.

Anne Sexton, "Ringing the Bells" 717

DISCUSSION STARTERS

In an interview, Anne Sexton said that poetry "should be a shock to the senses. It should almost hurt." In this poem, Sexton shocks us with an understated glimpse of her own private hell as we follow a very long, rambling sentence to a dead end. Have students read "Ringing the Bells" aloud—they might try to assign different student voices to different lines, chiming in the way the different bells do at the direction of the bell-lady in the poem.

THE RECEPTIVE READER

1. We think of *Bedlam* and other old-style asylums as primitive, barbaric institutions, but ironically this modern, supposedly more enlightened institution, with all its modern music therapy, in the end is apparently no better at offering sick people a cure (they "are no better for it").

2. The *music therapy* gives the attendants the illusion of doing something for their charges, although ironically the ritual is only half-understood by the disoriented patients (who have merely learned to follow orders "by

instinct") and does them no good. The smiles of both the "bell-lady" and of the "crazy ladies" seem merely painted on, helping to perpetuate the illusion that something useful is happening here. The real ironic counterpoint to the well-intentioned therapy is in the tick of the "small hunched squirrel girl" who picks forever at the hair over a lip. She is totally cut off from an "untroubled and clean" world where kitchens (unlike the make-believe kitchens in the wards) are really "workable." The circle of disoriented patients is like "bees caught in the wrong hive"; there is a show of activity, but it leads nowhere. And the speaker, although in her lucid moments aware of the futility of the exercise, goes along, because there is nothing else for her to do.

3. The *run-together lines*, held together by a loose string of *ands*, mirror the monotonous succession of days that all blur and run together without an end in sight. Although the sound of the bells is "untroubled and clean," the minds of the patients are muddled.

FOLLOW-UP—THE CREATIVE DIMENSION

You may want to ask students to think about a recurring act or deadening routine in their own lives, something they do daily, weekly, or monthly. Have them try their hand at using a long drawn-out sentence held together by a string of *ands* to mirror the monotonous grind. Here is an example:

And this is the way you're poor
and your dreams are big enough only to survive the next day
and this is the way you see the mailman coming with the bills
and your parents are out working for the next month's rent
and these are the beans which become the main course
—breakfast, lunch, and dinner—
and this is the way you see your father worn down
from a fourteen-hour job, and at dawn he's up
ready for the next workday,
and this is the way
your old blue jeans and white T-shirt become your Sunday
clothes
and your mother tells you, "just as long as you're good and
keep clean."

nila northSun, "Moving Camp Too Far" 718

DISCUSSION STARTERS

The ironic note in northSun's poem is first struck in the title: Camp has been moved "too far"—too far away from true Native American life. The poem is built around the ironic discrepancy between the authentic life of the past and today's cheap plastic tourist trade, serving pseudo-ethnic junk food for the soul. The first three statements in the poem, "i can't . . . i can't . . . i don't" regretfully evoke positive images of a Native American culture that is history. The last six statements, all starting "i can . . . i can . . . i can," are heaped with images from a cultural wasteland, where fake mementos of Native American culture are exploited for commercial purposes. Where have students encountered the trivializing and exploitation of the Native American past?

THE RECEPTIVE READER

1. Have students look up the dictionary definitions of these terms. *The American Heritage Dictionary* defines a *travois* as a "sledge formerly used by Plains Indians and consisting of a platform or netting supported by two long trailing poles the forward ends of which are fastened to a dog or horse." *Counting coup* was a means of gaining fame or standing by being the first to strike or touch an enemy. The title implies that the entire cultural camp or home as the poet knows it has moved too far off-center or too far away from its cultural roots.

2. When something one holds dear is trivialized, its effects go deeper than just surface irritation. A person's identity and self-concept are tied in subtle yet often irrevocable ways to his or her cultural heritage and background. Attack or trivialize that, and you do serious damage to the roots of individual self-esteem. The deepest irony lies in the last two lines of the poem: Although the speaker has no direct experience of the old traditions ("i can't"), she "can" participate in a pathetic substitute, "& unfortunately / i do."

THE PERSONAL RESPONSE

Have students experienced the feeling of seeing something they value cheapened or exploited?

W. H. Auden, "The Unknown Citizen" 720

PERSPECTIVES—THE AGE OF AUDEN

The thirties in Europe have been called the "Age of Auden." A product of the British prep schools with an Oxonian accent, lionized in England, Auden left Europe in 1939 to live in the United States, reversing the itinerary of famous literary expatriates like Eliot, Pound, Stein, and Hemingway. Auden's best-known poems look with a mixture of sardonic humor and desperate foreboding at a world heading for a second disastrous world war and make a mockery of the pretensions of European civilization. In a long critical tribute to Auden in the *New Yorker* for April 1, 1996, Nicholas Jenkins describes Auden as at first one of "a group of young, more or less left-wing poets." Perpetual dissident and outsider, restless wanderer and transient, homosexual, Auden participated in and became increasingly disillusioned with an intellectual scene marked by Marxism, psychoanalysis, anti-fascism, anti-imperialism, and avant-garde trends. Quoting representative portentous lines—"Something is going to fall like rain / and it won't be flowers"; "Go down with your world that has had its day"—Jenkins says: "To a generation of young readers, dismayed by the economic conditions in their country and by the long slide of history toward the Second World War, Auden seemed to possess a communal voice, an imagination that was eerily in contact with their own hopes, fears, and resentments. The thirties was a time of weak political leadership in Britain, and an early phrase of Auden's about England—'this country of ours where nobody is well'—soon became a touchstone." For a poet called a traitor by both his former left-wing friends and by the pompous voices of British right-wing reaction, Auden has had amazing staying power. Jenkins says that four American presidents—Johnson, Reagan, Bush, and Clinton —"have quoted Auden to make political points." A few years ago, a small collection of Auden's poems, titled *Tell Me the Truth about Love*, sold over two hundred thousand copies in Britain.

DISCUSSION STARTERS

What is our attitude today toward monuments and memorials? (What monuments do your students know?) What is the difference between old-fashioned war memorials and the Vietnam Memorial—a long wall of stark black marble inscribed with the names of more than 56,000 dead?

THE RECEPTIVE READER

1. One of the casualties of mass societies in the twentieth century is a sense of community—a community small enough for people to know others by name. Instead, recognition depends on "identification" numbers: on driver's licenses, credit cards, social security cards. We become numbers in a computer. Form letters treat us as faceless interchangeable entities. Instead of being validated as unique individuals, we feel like ants?

2. All the praise in this poem is ironic—as though we were patting someone on the back for being such a spineless, faceless, timid timeserver. It's a left-handed compliment to be valued simply for not being a trouble-maker—for never having been the subject of an official complaint. This "model" citizen was a regular dues-paying member of a conventional union and never had enough independent thinking to hold "odd views," let alone depart from the union line to work as a scab—going to work in spite of a strike declared by the union. The observation that this citizen held "the proper opinions for the time of year" hints that what is "proper" (our value system) changes as quickly as the season, depending on the temperament of the

"majority." This weathervane mentality is spotlighted in the citizen's attitude toward peace and war: When it was the season for peace, he, like many others, paid lip service to the cause of peace. When war came, he forgot his peace-loving sentiments and went along without resistance. He never had enough conviction to interfere in any way with what the teachers of his children did.

3. This modern "saint" is an extreme example (or caricature?) of the conformist modern citizen without a mind of his or her own. That kind of person is valued by the state because such a citizen never makes waves. The "State" becomes the great leveler, turning dynamic, ornery human beings into boring automatons.

THE CREATIVE DIMENSION

Perhaps ask students to write an ironic tribute to "The Unknown Student"?

Walt Whitman, "A Glimpse" 721

PERSPECTIVES—WHITMAN: VARIETIES OF LOVE

The following is a young woman's re-creation of the Whitman poem. How close is this student re-creation to Whitman's original in spirit, atmosphere, rhythm, substance? Is the main point of the poem gone because the lovers are no longer gay?

A hand waved through the crowd caught,
Of friends and faces in a club around the bar
late one warm spring night, and I remained at the table,
Of a young man who loves me and whom I love, loudly approaching and
touching my body as he takes the seat,
Talking the night away with all the passers-by, drink,
smoke, and sarcasm,
There we two, happy to share our friends, time, life—
mostly our youth.

DISCUSSION STARTERS

How do your students feel about crowds? What makes the difference between a loner and a gregarious person, surrounded by congenial people?

THE RECEPTIVE READER

1. The other people in the barroom are "a crowd of workmen and drivers," a group of working men who have stopped for a drink to mark the end

of a working day and to take the chill off a winter night. The working men are boisterous, noisy, and in motion: "the noises of coming and going, of drinking and oath and smutty jest." The two lovers provide a complete contrast of silence and stillness. What is ironic is that the coarse working people, who may tend to think of gays as dirty and immoral, are the ones who tell dirty jokes while the gay lovers represent tenderness.

2. The two lovers in the poem are "content, happy in being together," without saying very much of anything, "perhaps not a word." Ideally, are there times when lovers understand each other so completely they need not bother to speak aloud? On the other hand, are there times when people hunger for a tender, affectionate word?

Juxtapositions: Modern Parables

Stephen Crane, "The Wayfarer" 722

DISCUSSION STARTERS

At the center of Crane's parables there often seems to be a dense or naive individual who wonders or "understood not these things." What is gained by having someone at the center of the poem who is presumably less smart than the readers are?

THE RECEPTIVE READER

Although many pay lip service to the pursuit of truth, the path that leads to it ironically sees few or no travelers and as a result is choked with weeds. On closer inspection each weed seems more like a knife: The truth can cut and hurt both those that are exposed to its glare—as well as the truthteller who might have to pay the price for blowing other people's cover?

Bruce Bennett, "Leader" 722

DISCUSSION STARTERS

What images and associations does the word *leader* bring to mind? What personages do your students think of as "leaders"? Has the word become rehabilitated and shed the negative connotations it acquired when "leaders" like Hitler, Mussolini, or Stalin led their respective nations?

THE RECEPTIVE READER

In Crane's parables, as here, anonymous but representative human beings act out little scenarios that dramatize something very basic about how we as humans think and feel and act. What is the irony in Bennett's poem? We think of leaders as powerful individuals. But the irony is that they depend on followers who tend to be sheeplike (otherwise they wouldn't be followers).

The Uses of Paradox

Nelle Fertig, "I Have Come to the Conclusion" 724

DISCUSSION STARTERS

What does Fertig mean when she says, "we choose particular people / because they provide / the particular mirrors / in which we wish to see"? Paradoxically, we hang mirrors so we can admire ourselves in the mirror, but we hate it when they tell the unflattering truth.

THE RECEPTIVE READER

1. Which of the following have a meaning for your students? What is that meaning? Have them discuss the "mirror, mirror, on the wall" of "Snow White"; Alice in Wonderland's looking-glass; the story of Narcissus staring at his own image in the pool he uses as a mirror; Pablo Picasso's paintings of women looking in the mirror; Hamlet on the playwright's art holding "the mirror up to nature."

2. That we go for people who provide what we want to hear and see is not really "surprising" to this speaker, who refers to this insight condescendingly as a "surprising bit of knowledge"?

3. When flattery ceases or wears off, quarreling and recrimination may ensue?

Francesco Petrarca, "Or Che 'l Ciel e la Terra e 'l Vento Tace" 765

DISCUSSION STARTERS

The *abba*, *abba*, *cde*, *cde*, rhyme scheme of this poem is in the Petrarchan vein. Similarly Petrarchan is the pervasive playing off of opposites. The lover is at war with himself, although he wants to find peace in his relationship with the beloved; his beloved destroys and dazzles, caresses and slashes. The lover has "died and risen a thousandfold." Love provides food for the soul that is both bitter and sweet. Which of these contradictions "make sense," as the text claims, on second thought? Where or how are both sides of one of these paradoxes true? Have your students experienced any such contradictory emotions?

THE RECEPTIVE READER

1. The "natural" occurrences— a calm heaven and earth; winds, birds, and wild beasts asleep—seem fitting for nighttime when we expect the creation to be at rest; the paradox arises from the unnatural, very human restlessness ("I only keep vigil") of the speaker who thinks, burns, and weeps amidst the peace and stillness of darkness.

2. Clashing concepts, jostling images, and *mixed emotions* abound in this poem. The quintessential Petrarchan note is struck in the "bitter and sweet" (*dolce amaro*) rising from the same fountain. Paradoxically the night is peaceful, but the night is also agony. The beloved is both destroyer and dazzler, giver and taker. The lover both rages and longs. The lover is "caressed and slashed by the same hand." The lover is searching for the promised land, but he finds himself in a "world of ceaseless strife."

3. Phrases that mirror traditional Christian *religious imagery* are "fountain of life," "martyr," "died and risen a thousandfold," and "promised land." The quasi-religious vocabulary helps elevate the speaker's love to the level of religious worship and exaltation. But, paradoxically, otherworldly religious terms are here applied to a worldly attachment. The alternating despair and elation of the lover is compared (blasphemously?) to the death and resurrection of Christ.

William Shakespeare, "Sonnet 97" 725

DISCUSSION STARTERS

The underlying pattern of irony often is: "I thought this was true, but here is something else that called it into question." The underlying structure of a paradox is: "This is true, and yet this is also true." Ask your students which of these two best fits the pattern of this sonnet. (Ask them to find the two pivotal uses of *yet* in the poem?)

THE RECEPTIVE READER

1. The central paradox here is the sense of inner coldness, bareness in the midst of a season of abundance and growth. The chill in the poet's soul is mirrored in "freezings," "dark days," "December's bareness," pale leaves, and muted birds dreading winter. The central metaphor for the unavailing, unconsoling outward summer setting is the "abundant issue" or "wanton burthen" that springtime engendered and "teeming autumn" brought to fruition.

2. The metaphor shifts even as we view autumn as pregnant ("teeming with rich increase") and as giving birth to rich new life. The metaphor tilts to the imagery of loss and deprivation with the key phrase "widowed wombs." Paradoxically the rich imagery of gestation and fruition leads to thoughts of orphans and abandonment.

3. The leaves "look pale" just as humans do when they encounter grief or extreme shock; the leaves also dread the approach of winter. Autumn is personified as giving birth like a widowed woman after the husband's death.

John Crowe Ransom, "Bells for John Whiteside's Daughter" 726

PERSPECTIVES—JOHN CROWE RANSOM AND EMOTIONAL DISTANCE

Ransom wrote at the time of the critical revival of seventeenth-century metaphysical poetry, when his "subtle," "rich and complex," and "elusive" poems lived up to the criteria of establishment critics. Critical manifestos emphasized the need to guard against sentimentality and uncontrolled emotion; pundits lectured about the need for maintaining "aesthetic distance." Thornton H. Parsons, in *John Crowe Ransom* (Twayne, 1969), said, "In Ransom's best poems about death the technique of screening the data through a narrator is very important." In "Bells for John Whiteside's Daughter," Ransom's narrator is "capable of a considerable emotional distance from death. He is astonished at the quietness that can come over, has come over, the little girl whose energetic noisiness had disturbed him so much." In the concluding stanza, "direct statements about the dead girl are terse and restrained, and the horror of death is implicit. 'Brown study' is an effective euphemism for death because it has an ironic relevance to the personality of the girl alive; during her energetic life, the quiet, pensive mood seemed as unnatural for her as now seems the reality that so much clamorous liveliness could be permanently stilled." The narrator is "vexed"—he "is not outraged, not overwhelmed. He was resignedly distressed by her noisiness when alive, and he is resignedly distressed by her temperamentally unnatural repose in death. The implication is that death itself is vexatious to human beings. This is close to our usual attitude toward it, our recurring sense of uneasiness that our lives logically imply deaths some time in the future; and, though we grow accustomed to the inevitability, it is vaguely annoying." The motionlessness of the once violently active girl "has made her survivors motionless, has 'sternly stopped' them, has made them confront death directly and definitely. 'Primly propped' ends the poem with the emphasis upon the unnaturalness, the excessive formality, of the girl's appearance. This phrase conveys quietly and implicitly more horror than an indignant outburst would. . . . A little girl's death could readily entail a crude and trite pathos, but Ransom skillfully avoids it by limiting the reader's view of the girl to the narrator's version of her. A vivid picture of her in a characteristic moment of her life is presented in language formalized enough to keep us detached, to keep us from empathizing her persona purely: 'the tireless heart within the little / Lady with rod.' "

DISCUSSION STARTERS

Though we expect grief at a funeral, Ransom's mourners seem only astonished, vexed. Are we in turn expected to be vexed by their failure to show more conventional emotions of grief? Who stipulates the emotional etiquette for the way we are supposed to feel at funerals? (And why is an Irish wake different from other kinds?)

THE RECEPTIVE READER

1. The phrase "sternly stopped" might indicate that the mourners are well aware of the harsh reality of death and its stern, not-to-be-ignored summons that brings to a stop for a time our everyday frivolous activities. The overwhelming emotion in the poem may be a kind of numbed shock at the contrast between the bustling innocence of the girl (with the "tireless heart" and "such lightness in her footfall") and her lying, quite out of character, "primly propped" in death?

2. Goose live and talk "goose-fashion"—and their squawking and honking convey their feelings in "goose" (or goose language) just as we convey ours in English. The idea that perhaps their honking and our talking are not that far apart on the evolutionary scale is funny?

3. Are funerals archetypal occasions for mixed emotions—with grief and fear mingling with bittersweet memories of the departed?

John Donne, "Holy Sonnet 10" 728

DISCUSSION STARTERS

The recurrent note of much medieval literature was *Timor mortis conturbat me*—"The fear of death shakes me." What are conventional or familiar ways of coping with the fear of death?

THE RECEPTIVE READER

1. The self-dramatization on a large, cosmic stage is characteristic of Donne. Fate, monarchs, death, war, resurrection, and eternity all play their parts in the cosmic confrontation between Death and the defiant individual who challenges its universal sway.

2. Donne is a master at launching the kind of paradox that makes us see something we took for granted in a totally different light. Fate, fatal accidents, murderous kings, and desperate assassins can all doom people to death—and Death then has to do their bidding! He is not really omnipotent after all. He is no better than their "slave." *Sleep* is used literally in its first appearance in the poem. Donne uses it here to belittle Death, saying that "rest and sleep" are like trial runs for our final "rest," but from them we derive much pleasure (not fear). *Sleep* is used figuratively in the next to the last line of the poem for our stay in the ground (our relatively "short sleep") before resurrection.

3. The grandiloquent rhetoric of the speaker in the poem is designed to disabuse us of our notion that Death is to be feared. Major points in the supporting argument:

- Death is like rest and sleep (only more so), two states from which men gain pleasure.
- Often the best go first—so why should we be afraid to follow them and enjoy, like them, delivery and eternal rest?
- Death, rather than being "mighty and dreadful," does the bidding of any executioner or assassin (not to mention drunk driver); he is little better than an errand boy for all the lethal forces in our lives.
- His companions are unsavory characters like poison, war, and sickness, hardly inspiring respect.

4. Though we tend to think that death is the end of all things, the whole point of Christian doctrine is that there is *life* after death—put dramatically and paradoxically, "Death, thou shalt die." After the last trumpet sounds on the Day of Judgment, no one ever again will die.

Juxtapositions: Convention and Originality

Andrew Marvell, "To His Coy Mistress" 729

DISCUSSION STARTERS

How much has courtship changed over the centuries? (Or is the whole idea of courtship dead?) Is male initiative still the standard convention in courtship? Is the man expected to do most of the talking—talking the woman *into* something? Is the man expected to be the aggressor, the woman the "coy" or reluctant partner?

THE RECEPTIVE READER

1. Lovers are at times separated, but it takes extreme *hyperbole* to place one in India and the other one in northern England (when in sober fact one may have just been down the street from the other). Love may take time to ripen (and to overcome the coyness of the beloved), but it's a mind-stretching conceit to imagine it starting before Noah's flood and coming to fruition in the conversion of the Jews that pious Christians did not anticipate before the end of time. In this poem, empires are not vast enough to serve as a good point of comparison with how huge love might grow if we had "world enough, and time." And proper praise of the loved one's beauty might require time enough for several new species to evolve.

2. Learned critics remind us that Marvell's contemporaries thought of the "vegetable soul" as the lowest in the hierarchy of vital functions—it keeps us alive in a "vegetative state" when the sensitive soul and the rational soul

are already dead. So perhaps we should not "envisage some monstrous and expanding cabbage" (J. V. Cunningham). However, it is exactly the "vegetable" principle in us that makes us slowly grow (and again decay) like a cabbage. The slowly growing cabbage (or other vegetable) is paradoxically unpoetic but would be more steady, solid, and nutritious than the impetuous but perhaps short-lived attentions of the fiery lover?

3. Marvell uses a chariot, which was used as a splendid, destructive, frightening vehicle of war, to make us visualize the relentless, fierce onslaught of time, which eventually destroys all human happiness and achievement. Eternity here is not an eternity of blessed souls hymning praises but an arid desert in which nothing can survive.

4. The *graveyard imagery* is simultaneously shocking and sexual: Worms "try" the virginity of the woman. The images take the *carpe diem* philosophy from the euphemistic level of the fading rose to the level of the grinning skull and the blanching bones: Both her honor and his lust turn to dust and ashes. The morbid vision of the grave reminds us that there it will be too late to "embrace." As for *verbal irony*: The grave is a "fine and private place," indeed!

5. The *birds of prey* are ravenous creatures who don't waste time; they "devour" what time has to offer rather than wait passively for it to grind them down. The search for fulfillment in this poem is not a dance through the flowers but rather a siege, an assault, with the "iron gates of life" having to be breached "with rough strife."

6. Marvell's poem first expresses the defiant human desire to make time stand still when in the midst of a peak experience—but it then settles for the idea that the fiery intensity of the lovers will make it hard for the more slow-moving sun to keep up.

Countess of Dia, "I Sing of That Which I Would Rather Hide" 731

PERSPECTIVES—COUNTESS OF DIA: POEM AND MUSIC

The poems of the troubadours were sung or chanted, with the close alliance of poem and music found in much early poetry. The lyre and in later ages the lute were the symbolic accoutrements of poets. A beautiful rendering of this poem is included in *The Romance of the Rose: Feminine Voices of Medieval France*, performed by a group called Héliotrope on the Touch label. This recording re-creates the music of the *trovaritz* (women troubadours) of Languedoc, or southern France, and the *chansons de femmes* of northern France.

DISCUSSION STARTERS

The countess, though rejected, takes heart in her ability to love, pleased at beating her lover at "love's game." Despite his "cold" words and "slights," she never brought him shame nor hurt his name—devotion was her motto in every respect. How universal is the experience of rejection that is mirrored in this poem? Is it more common or more relevant today than Marvell's impatience at the lady's coyness?

THE RECEPTIVE READER

1. Like the early love poetry written by male poets, this poem is a "plaint"—a lament of unrequited love. But the perspective is different: For the male convention of love denied by the haughty lady, this poem substitutes the voice of love betrayed, of devotion not honored but treated callously and superficially by the "charmer" who has long since flitted on to other flowers. The woman speaking in the poem prides herself on her constancy and on her refusal to stoop to the level of vindictiveness and recrimination.

2. The finely crafted stanzas help to contain and sublimate the speaker's emotions. No outbursts of destructive passion here; no telling the callous blackguard what deep down we might really think of him. All is decorum; all is contained and under control, like the intricate interlaced rhyme scheme of the poem.

Poems for Further Study

Sir John Suckling, "Song" 732

DISCUSSION STARTERS

Who's talking? Some readers will argue that the voice is that of an older, perhaps cynical man advising a "young sinner" in the ways of love. The tone is both flippant and sympathetic toward a naive younger male. The somewhat jaded voice of experience tells us that one human being can't *make* another love him or her. At the same time, the final line, "The devil take her!" carries the cheerful suggestion that there are others to love—so none is worth being forever "pale and wan" about. Other readers may argue that the speaker is the young lover speaking to himself, arguing with himself and finally coming to his senses?

Richard Lovelace, "To Lucasta, Going to the Wars" 733

DISCUSSION STARTERS

Has "honor" become an old-fashioned or obsolete term? Who still uses it—when or where? In what cultural contexts was it a potent, weighty concept?

THE RECEPTIVE READER

The speaker is going off to war and is leaving his beloved. The tone is at first solemn and adoring (the chaste mind of his lover is pure and sainted like a nunnery) but shifts to become witty—tenderly playful and irreverent. He wants to respond to her implied objections ("True, a new mistress now I chase"). Changeable, inconstant male love becomes the metaphor for the poet's going to war, apparently abandoning his love? But the poet's clever paradoxical word play tries to make his love see that his "inconstancy" is really constancy to a higher ideal and that his love of honor honors his love of her and makes it all the more special.

Sharon Olds, "Quake Theory" 733

DISCUSSION STARTERS

In this poem, Olds likens the breakdown of a human, personal relationship to a natural disaster. Why does the central earthquake metaphor fit the situation? What would have to be different if her central metaphor were a hurricane, a fire, or the eruption of a volcano? A student, in a paper entitled "The Fault, the Father," writes of "Quake Theory":

The poem, as titled, seems to be offering a potential theory on why relationships break down. The description of earthquakes and faults, their tension causing extensive damage, works metaphorically to express the tensions so typical in bad relationships. Although Olds offers no solutions, in fact, seems to want to put into words how these things can occur, there is a sense of warning in this complex poem. The final lines describe "heavy damage" and "innocent people" being unwittingly sucked into the cracks. Perhaps Olds wants to warn us of the destruction that results when tensions are allowed to build within the structure of a family.

THE RECEPTIVE READER

The *earthquake metaphor* serves to give the poem a serious, solemn, awestruck tone—although at first we merely seem to learn what a "fault" is as if in a science lecture. But the poem throughout builds up the "terrible pressure," as two tectonic plates scrape against each other until the climactic moment when, in the emphatically set off short line, "the earth cracks." At the same time, the poet has an uncanny gift for slipping from the earthquake metaphor naturally and almost casually into the discussion of the tensions between mother and daughter, as if she were talking about the same thing. She brings in the sarcastic father, the third point of the triangle, in the same natural offhand manner. We feel tenderness for the innocent victims as things come to a head. The poet does not overtly place blame—the tension is simply called "a fault." On the other hand, the father's forehead is "sarcastic" as though it could speak sharply, the sound of his hand running over his chin is like a "faint rasp." Both of these auditory images carry a condemnatory bite. A student wrote:

Although the father is barely described, the tension he evokes is hinted at by the poet. The "faults" that get stuck for years have a ridge that "bulges up like a father's sarcastic forehead." In this mother/daughter poem, the father is an intrusive element in the structure of the poem, suggesting that he is the underlying cause of tension and ultimate breakdown in the relationship between mother and daughter. There is a strong sense that the father is an overbearing, sarcastic, dominant, and insensitive man.

The fact that the "innocent people" are left unnamed might indicate that the poet purposely meant to include everyone, including the father, although students may come to the conclusion that only the mother and daughter qualify as innocents.

Joy Harjo, "Leaving" 734

DISCUSSION STARTERS

When a break occurs in a love relationship or other human tie—when the time has come for "leaving"—is it better to turn the occasion into a melodrama or to go quietly?

THE RECEPTIVE READER

1. *The situation*: The speaker of the poem is partly awakened by a phone call in the early hours of the morning. The speaker's lover is talking to her mother in a "Something not too drastic, tone of voice." The speaker stays in bed during this conversation, and when the lover returns she says that it was her mother who had called to tell her that "Her sister was running away from her boyfriend and / was stranded in Calgary, Alberta. Needed money / and comfort for the long return back home." This story has special resonance for the speaker who also will be leaving for home within hours. The situation between the sister mentioned in the phone call and the speaker are curiously analogous: both are just beginning the "thousand mile escape homeward."

2. The speaker's *tone* seems deliberately understated and noncommittal. The speaker is "fighting to stay in sleep" perhaps because of an early departure next morning or perhaps because the lover's mother's call (at four o'clock in the morning, a time which is generally a real attention-getter) is not sufficiently compelling to cause the speaker to completely awaken. The most overt clue as to the speaker's emotions occurs with the use of the word *escape*. Though the poem is called "Leaving," the last line ("a thousand mile escape homeward") indicates the departure is more than just a visit home. Just as the lover's sister is "running away" and in need of "money / and comfort for the long return back home," so too the speaker is escaping from a relationship that, although not described, cannot be successful—else why use the word *escape*? The speaker's emotions are somewhat muted; there is a weary finality in the air.

William Shakespeare, "Sonnet 130" 734

DISCUSSION STARTERS

Should we say adoring or admiring things to people we love? Or should we be totally truthful and sincere?

THE RECEPTIVE READER

1. Shakespeare's *irony* spoofs many of the conventional images of his day: eyes like sun, red lips, snow-white breasts, rosy cheeks, sweet breath. Here the hyperbolical style of the sonneteers has begun to backfire: The more we call the beloved an angel or a goddess, the more a skeptical voice in the back of our minds is likely to point out that the real person "treads on the ground."

2. One student insisted "a reeking breath is unacceptable to me in someone I would choose to love." A few students may argue that we no longer idealize and elevate the people we love sufficiently. Most, however, will be delighted with Shakespeare's dose of reality therapy. Irony here debunks or rebels against a conventional style, but it does not undercut or sabotage the speaker's love for someone "rare" and special. The traditional "turn," here at the beginning of the final couplet, takes us from the flippant or spoofing tone to a love that does not need "false compare" to be strong.

Pablo Neruda, "The Fickle One" 735

DISCUSSION STARTERS

When people are called "fickle," they are accused of being capricious, inconstant, bouncing back and forth in irresolution. Neruda's poem "The Fickle One" highlights a paradox encountered by some people in love: A person may be totally committed to another person and yet be attracted to other people. Can one love someone and still have roving eyes? Can one lust after the daydream yet still be content with what he or she holds now?

THE RECEPTIVE READER

Students are likely to have varying reactions to this poem, depending on how tolerant they are of total candor (and of a frivolous touch) in a relationship. The speaker's fantasy life is charged with images of violent passion—no rosebuds here and candlelight but a "tail of fire" lashing out and "lightning bolts of blood." We are not surprised that no ordinary, limited person will satisfy such a passionate lover: The paradoxical yoking of contraries in the last part of the poem goes beyond the conventional idealizing of a beloved person. Whether real or imaginary, the soulmate addressed here does not fit a simple stereotype or formula. She may at times seem ugly and at others beautiful, at times diminutive and others tall. She must subsume all that is precious, lasting, and refined (like gold and silver) and all that is earthy or grown from the earth, like the wheat?

Chapter 21 THEME The Making of Meaning 739

Values, attitudes, and ideas are implicit in significant or meaningful poetry. Modern critics have generally been wary of spelling these out in too pat or too glib a fashion. In part, they reacted against a nineteenth-century tradition of versified uplifting moral sentiments. In part, they feared that any "insight" we formulate in abstract, bloodless terms easily comes to sound like a platitude. Poets will sometimes talk about the values and ideas that are acted out or embodied in the living context of their poetry. In the following excerpt, Gary Snyder talks about recurrent themes implicit in his poems. Which of these do your students recognize, understand, or share? Can they elaborate on what these themes involve or imply?

> As a poet I hold the most archaic values on earth. They go back to the late Paleolithic: the fertility of the soil, the magic of animals, the power-vision in solitude, the terrifying initiation and rebirth, the love and ecstasy of the dance, the common work of the tribe.

First Reading: Pat Mora, "The Immigrants" 740

DISCUSSION STARTERS

Have any of your students been in situations where people talk (or whisper) in one language in some contexts or for some purposes, while using another language for others?

THE RECEPTIVE READER

1. Many *all-American lists* are likely to include the Stars and Stripes, hot dogs, apple pie, football, and Barbie dolls as quintessentially American items. Other items might include drive-in movies, corn on the cob, cowboys, Hollywood, Thanksgiving, swimming pools, Coca-Cola, cheerleaders, Cadillacs, hamburgers, baseball, the Statue of Liberty, outdoor barbecues, the Fourth of July, movie stars, and parades. (What, if anything, do these items have in common?) Lists reflecting a more sardonic perspective might include guns, pot, white male police officers.

2. The immigrant parent realizes that the quicker the child is "Americanized"—cut off from the parents—the easier things will be for that child. Remembering their own struggles to understand and be accepted in this new world, they whisper between themselves in Spanish, Polish, or other original language, giving voice to "that dark / parent fear": "Will they like / our boy, our girl, our fine american / boy, our fine american girl?" The poem makes us share in the feeling and apprehensions of actual living peo-

ple, at the opposite end of the spectrum from statistics and sociological abstractions.

3. The impulse to keep children in touch with the parents' background and language may vary from group to group and perhaps family to family. Assertive ethnic pride is a fairly recent phenomenon? By the time the immigrant parents have become grandparents, their grandchildren may be so comfortably ensconced in their American-ness that they can seek to rediscover the culture and language of their grandparents.

Idea and Image

William Stafford, "Freedom" 741

DISCUSSION STARTERS

Do Americans today feel "free" or "oppressed"?

THE RECEPTIVE READER

1. Note how *un*obvious and therefore striking and provocative the *concrete images* are that keep the word *freedom* from remaining a much abused abstraction. Explorers or hikers may want to follow the course of a river (downstream toward the ocean or upstream toward the source) if that is their purpose or if they have no other clear goal or destination. But this is a decision they make—being able to make that decision is the essence of "freedom." People who are not free are forever marching in a direction set by others; they are forever following an itinerary charted for them by leaders, by habit, or by creed. If people wake up early enough (very early!), they can travel unimpeded before streets and freeways and subways are impossibly crowded, carrying people antlike to their prescribed destinations. (Freedom requires enough space so that we can be ourselves?)

2. Much of what we do is governed by precedents and influenced by experiences of long ago. However, to be truly free, we must be free to make decisions based on "what happens now." We usually think of leaders as making independent decisions, but they are really constrained to do much that is designed to ensure the loyalty of their followers and the success of their policies. While some people wrestle with their faiths and go through stages of intense soul-searching (thus affirming and using their "freedom"), many others repeat the established beliefs as if by rote?

3. To be free, we must try not to become prisoners of groupthink, ideology, creed, or tradition? We must live in the present, not in the past?

4. One possible summary: People can have freedom only when they are truly independent, self-reliant individuals, making their decisions "in the here and now," unswayed by the attitudes, expectations, or edicts of others.

Archibald MacLeish, "Ars Poetica" 743

PERSPECTIVES—MACLEISH'S "ARS POETICA": POETICS OF A NEW CRITICISM

This for a time universally anthologized and widely quoted poem served as an early critical manifesto for what was to become the New Criticism (now often called formalism), which championed the concrete image rather than the abstract idea as the language of poetry. MacLeish's programmatic poem reflected the suspicion of mere talk that made a generation of modern poets search for the eloquent image. From T. S. Eliot's "objective correlative" to John Ciardi's emphasis on *how* (rather than *what*) a poem means, the high priests of modern criticism preached that "meanings" are not prior to and separate from the actual poem. Whatever the poem "says" should be fully imagined, actualized, acted out, rendered in concrete images. According to Dan Jaffe, contributing to an assessment of the thirties (in *The Thirties: Fiction, Poetry, Drama*, ed. Warren French, Everett Edwards, 1967), the poem was widely read but also widely misread and attacked as an endorsement of art for art's sake—"a poetry that is self-sufficient, in which texture is more important than idea, a poetry removed from the relevancies of life, a poetry that exists for its own sake and for the sake of an aesthetic elite." However, MacLeish was "a poet of social consciousness"; "in desperate times he sought to revitalize American democracy." His message here is that "message does not make poetry." This does not mean that MacLeish is shying away from ideas. "Instead he indicates that that kind of 'meaning' alone is not enough." MacLeish believed "that poetry should be as real as the images of the world." The images in "Ars Poetica" are "enormously evocative, full of symbolic potential. They are images chosen not only for their sensory impact but because of the intellectual and mythical ripples they set in motion." A poem "is first of all an experience; it must have the reality of a happening, not of a statement."

DISCUSSION STARTERS

You may want to ask students what "wordless" images from their reading of poetry so far have stayed most vividly in their minds. Why do they think these images had a special impact? Do these images have a special meaning for them?

THE RECEPTIVE READER

1. There is something in the texture of the metal and in the contours of the imprint that stimulates and appeals to our sense of touch. At the same time, the raised images, numbers, or letters on "old medallions" tell a tactile

kind of story of the people who made them. Smoothly worn casements evoke sadly or nostalgically the steady lives of people now dead, who used to lean out of a window with their sleeves rubbing the stone sill?

2. A poem should be "motionless in time / As the moon climbs." Whatever the exact implications of these enigmatic lines, the poet would seem to discourage poetry that is full of sensational surface action. We can *contemplate* the moon that seems to stand still while actually moving imperceptibly in time. When seen through the twigs and leaves of a tree, as through a screen, the moon seems to let the twigs go very slowly—the way we in reading the poem slowly leave behind one by one the memories it recreates?

3. The poem does leave us with striking, memorable concrete images, like the empty doorway that takes the place of an overt outpouring of grief. But, at the same time, the poem does preach that a poem should not preach?

Walt Whitman, "When I Heard the Learned Astronomer" 744

DISCUSSION STARTERS

Whitman's poem is a famous demonstration of the gulf that separates the "two cultures"—the sequential, logical, analytical, mathematics-driven culture of science and technology and the intuitive, contemplative, imaginative culture of art and literature. You might want to ask your students if they think science/math majors and art/English majors are two separate species or races of people. Are there basic differences in outlook or personality, and how do they show?

THE PERSONAL RESPONSE

Some people find in star charts or in the mathematical language of vectors and ellipses a strange beauty of its own. (Otherwise people would not become astronomers or mathematicians?) Do any of your students own or use telescopes? How and why do they use them? A math major or science major (or a group) might want to demonstrate some particularly striking or elegant graphs or charts to the class.

George Herbert, "The Pulley" 745

DISCUSSION STARTERS

Conventionally, Christ has often been depicted as carrying the shepherd's staff (with its crooked end used to pull sheep away from danger). How do the implications and associations change when instead we imagine God using other implements to bring human beings "into the fold"—a thunderbolt, a fishnet, or a pulley—a mechanical device that multiplies limited human strength so that it can lift heavy loads?

THE RECEPTIVE READER

1. When the speaker in the poem says "Rést in | the bót | tom láy," he is speaking of the only one among His treasures that God refuses to bestow on His creatures (the others being strength, beauty, wisdom, honor, pleasure). Here the word means "peace of mind," being at peace and at rest; it is the opposite of the "restlessness" that God gave us plenty of. The first *rest* is pulled out for our attention by one of the few trochaic inversions in a predominantly iambic poem. But the meaning of the word keeps shifting: If we had "rest," we would "rest"—that is to say, stand still or be caught up—in this natural world rather than attend to the salvation of our souls. So God decided to let us have all the "rest" (all the remaining treasures) but not this one. Then we would be left restless enough to seek for our final rest not in this but in the next world.

2. The richer our society has become in material goods and conveniences that were once considered luxuries, the more our pundits and gurus seem to talk about frustration, stress, alienation, uprootedness, restlessness?

3. In a traditional religious context, we might expect the poet to put the emphasis on the natural "depravity" or innate sinfulness of human beings. But in Herbert's poem the emphasis is not on sin but on our sense of being incomplete, being profoundly dissatisfied or unfulfilled, if we do not find our way to God and are thus deprived of the blessings of religion.

John Donne, "Holy Sonnet 5" 746

DISCUSSION STARTERS

Can your students identify the familiar points of doctrine in this poem? We are made up of body (the physical "elements") and soul. Sin has brought death into the world. To save our souls we must repent (weeping bitter tears of repentance). We must cleanse ourselves of the sins of lust and envy (of the seven deadly ones apparently the two uppermost in Donne's mind). If our religious zeal is strong enough, redemption—"healing"—is possible. Millions accept these doctrines as part of their creed—without the passionate upheavals and apocalyptic imaginings in this poem. What accounts for the passionate involvement and "fiery zeal" of the true believer?

THE RECEPTIVE READER

1. The idea of the duality of body and soul is introduced in the first two lines, which identify his "little world" as composed of both "elements" and "an angelic sprite." Both body and soul have been betrayed and damned by "black sin." Other opposites are the great world outside (the macrocosm) and the little world of the human organism (the microcosm), heaven and earth, water and fire?

2. Astronomers were beginning to think of the stars as centers of new worlds, of new solar systems, thus finding "new spheres" beyond the traditional conception of the heavens. Explorers and navigators were charting new continents and new oceans—which for the hyperbolical poet become a vast resupply of liquid for the sinful poet's remorseful tears. Science and faith meet as the vocabulary of the new astronomy and the new geography is enlisted to help dramatize the apocalyptic religious struggle of sin and redemption.

3. As with Shakespeare and with Donne's metaphysical contemporaries, the key metaphors in this poem shift rapidly and escalate. Water is the metaphor for the copious tears of repentance that hyperbolically "drown" the sinner. But since God promised Noah to send no more drowning floods, water might still be used as a cleansing agent. Actually, something stronger, namely fire, might have to be the cleansing agent instead. However, this would have to be a different kind of fire from the murky fires of passion, of lust and envy, that have up to now burnt within the sinner. A different kind of fire, that of ardent, fiery zeal, will have to start burning in him. Paradoxically, in devouring ("eating") sin, it will heal the soul-sick individual.

The Committed Poet

Wilfred Owen, "Dulce et Decorum Est" 749

PERSPECTIVES—WILFRED OWEN AND ANTIWAR POETRY

Like the poetry of a handful of his friends who also served in World War I, Owen's poetry commemorates human beings sacrificed on the altar of patriotism. When the great imperialistic and militaristic powers of Europe—with Germany and Austria-Hungary allied against England, France, and Russia—embarked on their much predicted "world war," few—and no one listened to them—had an inkling of what was ahead. In the ossuaries at Verdun, the bones and skulls of many of the 600,000 French, British, and German soldiers of Owen's generation who died in the fighting around this small French town may still be viewed. In the battles of the Somme river in northern France, tens of thousands of young men were machine-gunned or torn to pieces by massed artillery fire on a single day. The slogans of flag-waving nationalistic rhetoric here had a profound and lethal effect. Owen calls Horace's "Dulce et decorum est / Pro patria mori" an "old Lie"—which is by no means dead in our modern world.

DISCUSSION STARTERS

How much do your students know about the resurgence of nationalism in today's world? Where are people today dying for the greater glory of country, nationality, or tribe?

THE RECEPTIVE READER

1. The details in phrases like "bent double," "old beggars," "coughing like hags," "sludge," "haunting flares," "trudge," "blood-shod," "lame" and "blind" stack one upon the other to produce a horrific picture of "rest-time" during war. War propaganda and political speeches would no doubt turn these martyred human beings into proudly marching troops with Hollywood smiles, ready to crush the evil foe. (George Orwell once said, "War propaganda, with its self-righteousness and revolting hypocrisy, makes thinking people sympathize with the enemy.")

2. The fact that these limping soldiers who are already half-dead and impervious to fear are jolted into "an ecstasy of fumbling" at the shout of "Gas! Gas!" says much about the horror of chemical warfare. We watch aghast the struggle of the soldier who cannot get his gas mask on: he flounders "like a man in fire or lime," "guttering, choking," "smothering," "writhing," "gargling"; the lungs are "froth-corrupted"; the dying is "obscene as cancer."

3. In the sixth line of the second stanza, we first see the soldier stumbling to his death, as Owen sees him "drowning" in a sea of green gas. In the speaker's dreams, the soldier "plunges" at him "guttering, choking, drowning." The insistent repetition of *drowning* mirrors the persistence of the nightmare that the helpless dreamer cannot shake off. Only a few years ago, the soldiers in this scene were the children who in their innocence listened to the promise of warlike glory that they too late found to be the "old Lie."

4. The many cumulative series and parallel structures drive home the horrible scene and leave it imprinted on the reader's mind: "limped . . . lame . . . blind . . . drunk with fatigue"; "was yelling . . . and stumbling . . . and floundering"; "If in some smothering dreams . . . If you could hear . . ."

5. The basic irony is that the promise of glory used to enlist impressionable young people brings not glory but inglorious, nightmarish suffering and death—a lesson that the stay-at-home patriot addressed in the poem apparently has not yet learned.

THE PERSONAL RESPONSE

Have your students seen war movies that, instead of numbing them with Rambo-style carnage, made them think of the victims of war as suffering fellow humans?

Robert Hayden, "Frederick Douglass" 751

PERSPECTIVES—THE HISTORICAL DOUGLASS

Speaking at a Fourth of July ceremony in Rochester, New York, in 1852, Frederick Douglass said: "What to the American slave is your

Fourth of July? I answer, a day that reveals to him more than all other days of the year, the gross injustice and cruelty to which he is the constant victim. To him your celebration is a sham; your boasted liberty an unholy license; your national greatness, swelling vanity; your sounds of rejoicing are empty and heartless; your denunciation of tyrants, brass-fronted impudence; your shouts of liberty and equality, hollow mockery; your prayers and hymns, your sermons and thanksgivings, with all your religious parade and solemnity, are to him mere bombast, fraud, deception, impiety, and hypocrisy—a thin veil to cover up crimes which would disgrace a nation of savages."

DISCUSSION STARTERS

What might Frederick Douglass say on the Fourth of July if he were alive today?

THE RECEPTIVE READER

1. People who enjoy a measure of personal freedom tend to take it for granted, and politicians tend to invoke freedom in self-serving fashion to show how patriotic and freedom-loving they are. But to the person who is oppressed, the need for and the yearning for freedom are as elementary as the need for air and for the fruits of the earth. Oppression chokes and starves the human spirit as surely as oxygen deprivation and famine choke and starve the body. And achieving freedom and preserving it can be a "terrible" struggle. Statues and wreaths of bronze are part of the conventional, dutiful way of honoring the ideal of liberty. However, it does not become meaningful unless people, inspired by someone like Douglass, are able to live their lives in the spirit of that beautiful and awe-inspiring ideal, "fleshing his dream."

2. Hayden speaks eloquently for people aspiring to the day when freedom "is finally ours." But at the same time his powerful rhetoric is couched in terms that are universal. One powerful appeal in this poem is to our basic human solidarity with those who are hunted down and beaten to their knees by oppressive authority. Another powerful appeal is to our idealistic hope that "love and logic" will prevail, that the love of liberty is not an empty dream but can become instinctual, as natural as our heartbeat.

Denise Levertov, "What Were They Like?" 752

DISCUSSION STARTERS

Vietnam became one of the great traumas of our history. Where does it keep resurfacing? Why is it hard to forget? Are people still taking sides?

THE RECEPTIVE READER

1. The first speaker seems to be outside the experience of the Vietnamese people martyred during the war. The questions are those of a detached cultural anthropologist (he is addressed as "Sir" by the second speaker). He is the kind of art lover or aesthete who lovingly studies the dainty ivory, jade, and silver artifacts of a culture while the people who made them and their children are burnt by napalm, smashed by bombs, until only their charred bones remain. On the other hand, it seems that the second speaker lived through the experience of the Vietnam War (or had close relatives or friends who did) because of the bitter images the answers conjure up. The second speaker's detachment comes not from lack of interest but is mocking, imitating the obtuse questioner? Or the deliberate understatement and lack of passionate indictment stem from the need to protect the speaker from the horrid images of killed children, burned mouths, and charred bones.

2. The *question-and-answer* format allows us as readers to listen and to think. We are not being harangued, accused, denounced. Rather we are in the position of judge and juror who listen to the testimony of concerned parties. We make up our own minds; we reach our own conclusions?

3. Many of the contrasts are powerful: the playing off of an artist's delight in budding blossoms against the killing of the children; the playing off of the water buffalo in the rice paddies as part of an age-old pastoral ritual against the bursting of bombs mingling with desperate screams.

Czeslaw Milosz, "Incantation" 753

PERSPECTIVES—CZESLAW MILOSZ: POEMS FROM A DIFFERENT PLANET

For critics, Milosz presents the challenge of a poet that geographically, politically, and philosophically comes from outside the boundaries of American academic criticism. He is a voice of historical and political awareness, who said in one of his poems: "Those who are unaware / Deserve to be punished: they wanted only to live." He was one of the first Eastern European intellectuals and dissidents to turn his back on the postwar Communist system; he did not "throw in his lot with the creeds of his time" (Baron Wormser). He does not have the ingrained fear of abstraction long fashionable in the West; instead, he tries to rescue terms like Truth and Justice from years of abuse by obtuse apparatchiks and time-serving politicians. Helene J. F. de Aguilar, in " 'A Price out of Thy Store': The Place of Czeslaw Milosz," in *Parnassus: Poetry in Review* (1984), is an example of a critic saying that poets who opposed totalitarianism are in style "for suspicious reasons," discovering "slightly sanctimonious" touches and "bothersome rhetorical flourishes" in Milosz's poems of exhortation, and lecturing the poet about his "habit of lecturing in the middle of a poem."

DISCUSSION STARTERS

How disillusioned, apathetic, or cynical are your students when it comes to politics, and why? Do they believe in the possibility of a fresh new beginning? Where would they look for an "incantation" that as if by a magic spell would inspire them to work for Truth and Justice? Do they believe that art or poetry can be "a friend of hope"? Are we too jaded today to respond to this poet's glorious, generous vision of a new birth of Reason, Truth, and Justice?

THE RECEPTIVE READER

1. Something that is capitalized, like our names or the names of countries or God, suggests something of greater importance than something written in all lowercase. Oppression, Milosz suggests by writing "lie and oppression with small" letters, will eventually be dwarfed or overcome by Truth and Justice. The biblical "Nothing is new under the sun" can be taken as a defeatist acceptance of things as they are; this poem is animated by a powerful belief in the possibility of a new beginning, where everything will seem new and possible. When human beings can finally open the "congealed fist of the past," new ways of being and seeing will transform their lives.

2. Rather than considering Reason, Truth, and Justice hollow abstractions, the poet considers them "friends of hope" that can be cleansed of the verbal pollution of words twisted and "tortured" from their true "austere and transparent" meanings. Philosophy and poetry will then seem entirely fresh and "young" (although actually age-old)—especially to people who have never known them in their pure, unadulterated form.

3. Milosz' opening lines—with their references to the steel bars of prisons, the barbed wire of concentration camps, the shredding and pulping of banned books, and artists and writers driven into exile—are an overt indictment of the totalitarian societies (Hitler's Germany, Stalinist Russia and its satellites) that he had known at close quarters. The humanistic open society of the future that he envisions will be free from racism (it will "not know Jew from Greek") and from the oppressive rule of an elite over enslaved populations. The "universal" ideas he invokes transcend any allegiance to nationality, class, or party; they cut across narrow political or ideological boundaries.

Juxtapositions: Poems of War

Henry Reed, "Naming of Parts" 755

DISCUSSION STARTERS

How do people protest against war?

THE RECEPTIVE READER

1. Much of what we hear the instructor say is something like the earnest, jargony talk that we would expect from the drill instructor who has doubtless gone through the identical routine with other contingents of sullen recruits: "This is the lower sling swivel. And this / Is the upper sling swivel, whose use you will see, / when you are given your slings. . . . This is the safety-catch, which is always released with an easy flick of the thumb." The *caricature* results from the total humorlessness and literal-mindedness of the droning instructions, with not even a hint that these "students" are being instructed in how to maim and kill others of their species. As we say, this is a man just "doing his job."

2. There is a steady *counterpoint* in this poem of rich flowering shrubs glowing "like corals," of fragile beautiful blossoms, of bees going about their business of "assaulting and fumbling" the flowers, and of almond-blossoms making us catch our breaths with their "silent" and unobtrusive beauty. Nature here is beautiful, rich, generative, forever self-renewing. Has our species seceded from nature with our focus on a mindless, mechanical technology of destruction?

3. This poet never provides us with a slogan that we could put on a placard and use at a protest rally. But the sense that organized, mechanized killing is *wrong* and *against nature* pervades the whole poem?

Richard Eberhart, "The Fury of Aerial Bombardment" 756

DISCUSSION STARTERS

In retrospect, Reed exercises tremendous self-control in not verbalizing the implied indictment of his poem. How far, or how much farther, does Eberhart go in spelling out the questions raised by the unspeakable brutality of war? What do your students know about the bombing raids of World War II and the Vietnam War?

THE RECEPTIVE READER

1. Human beings witnessing the unspeakable human agony and the "shock-pried faces" caused by bombing raids would call for a stop—why doesn't God? Why is there only silence from the "infinite spaces" of the heavens? Why doesn't an all-powerful and merciful God make his creatures see the error of their ways, causing them to "repent"? After the first fratricide, with Cain murdering his brother Abel, we have not advanced one step further—not only are we still killing our human brothers and sisters, but we are doing so in an infinitely more organized fashion, mobilizing multitudes.

2. In Eberhart's poem, the faceless recruits of Reed's poem acquire names and human identities. ("Of Van Wettering I speak, and Averill.") Eberhart brings in the strangely dehumanized, desensitized litany of drill instruc-

tors only as an ironic counterpoint to the apocalyptic questions he asks earlier in the poem.

3. Some students will argue that the questions the poem raises are rhetorical questions. The answers already implied in the poem are the indifference of the universe to the carnage and the "eternal truth" of our unreconstructed animal nature doing battle with our better instincts. One student wrote, "The increasingly sophisticated modern machinery of war, in the hands of the same unchanging reptilian brain of 'the Beast,' is a sure-fire prescription for the ultimate destruction of humankind."

Poems for Further Study

Bethlyn Madison Webster, "Stamps" 757

DISCUSSION STARTERS

Have any of your student been on the receiving end of charity or welfare? Have any of them been close to or involved in the administering of charity? Is it true that charity is resented both by those who give and those who receive? Is it true that it is more blessed to give than to receive?

THE RECEPTIVE READER

1. The poem is called "Stamps," and it is the experience of a young couple—tired after another week of low-paid work—paying for groceries with food stamps. As the speaker's husband produces the stamps, the thoughtlessly affluent coiffed and pink-nailed next customer in line rudely stares: "she wants / to see how her tax dollars / are being wasted today." The family's one indulgence is a bag of "store brand" chocolate chips, while the censorious "taxpaper" loads up on steak, special lettuce, and wine. At the end, the clerk lays the food stamps down like cards "and pounds them with a rubber stamp." The card analogy may allude to the capricious nature of living; life is just a crapshoot, and one who sneers at food stamps today might be begging for them tomorrow. The clerk is symbolically stamping the speaker and her family with a mark indicating losers, cheaters, frauds.

2. Much will depend on where your students place themselves on the spectrum ranging from the haves to the have-nots and on how willing they are to believe that "there but for the grace of God go I."

Philip Larkin, "Born Yesterday" 758

DISCUSSION STARTERS

Do your students think "Born Yesterday" contains good advice? What do they think of advice in general—especially from their parents? After reading this poem aloud, ask them to write a response that might start, "I wasn't born yesterday . . ."

THE RECEPTIVE READER

1. The *metaphor* of a young, tightly folded flower, a folded bud, perhaps a rose, suggests the potential and promise of the newborn girl. There is a promise that in some future she will unfold not only sexually but also emotionally and intellectually?

2. The poet, while not discounting the possibility that the girl will be beautiful, wishes instead that she might be "ordinary." Perhaps people who lead unglamorized, not overly ambitious lives have a better chance to attend vigilantly and flexibly to the pursuit of happiness. Beauty and romance all too often come with their own vexations, disappointments, pitfalls, or curses. Compared with melodrama, tragedy, and the upheavals of passionate love affairs, staying on an even keel and living a satisfying and fulfilling love may well seem dull.

Denise Levertov, "The Mutes" 759

DISCUSSION STARTERS

Much recent discussion of sexual harassment has hinged on the definition of "unwanted" sexual attentions. How do women and men decide when such attentions are unwanted? How do they let the other person know? Are men more obtuse at reading the signals than women? You may want to ask students to observe and record how men and women respond to each other in public ("on the street," in classrooms, or "on the steps of the subway"). Suggest students take a pad or notebook and write down phrases they hear and any details of the interactions they observe.

THE RECEPTIVE READER

1. The *bird metaphor* is crucial to the poem because what might have been song or music (the mysterious attraction of one human being to another) has become "ugly" and "disgusting"—as if sung by "a bird with a slit tongue." Whatever "tribute" to women the men with their wolf whistles and groans intend is inarticulate like the attempt at speech of deaf-mutes.

2. For us to be true human beings, we must transcend biology? The poetry and "seemliness" of human intercourse must transform crude sexual instinct into love.

3. The men in this poem may seem mere "reptilian brains," representing crude, disgusting sexual instinct. But according to the poem, a woman, "in spite of herself," knows that their behavior at some level is a however clumsy acknowledgment of her attractiveness as a woman. She too is likely

to respond at some primitive level, as her pulse picks up speed. True, she is "disgusted," but she sees beyond the disgust to a longing crippled by the inability to even know—much less express adequately—a deep and yearning human need for love—and for the expressiveness of "poetry."

Alice Walker, "Women" 760

DISCUSSION STARTERS

To some people, the past is a burden and the legacy of their parents something to be overcome. To others, the past is an inspiration and a source of strength. For your students, is their family background something to build on or something to leave behind?

THE RECEPTIVE READER

1. "Headragged Generals" might make readers think of women like Harriet Tubman, who still wore the stereotypical headrags of slavery days and who literally participated in the battles of the Civil War, leading escaped slaves to freedom from behind enemy lines. But the later struggles for economic and legal rights were as dangerous, with minefields and booby traps?

2. The concluding *paradox*: Like countless other parents, the earlier generation in this poem believed fiercely in the promise of education for their offspring, although they themselves had been denied the benefit of book learning. These women "battered down / Doors" to provide something better for their daughters: That something better involved learning—"desks" and "books" that they were unable to read for themselves.

3. The poem is essentially a tribute to *strong* women of earlier times, "Husky of voice—Stout of / Step"?

Claude McKay, "If We Must Die" 761

DISCUSSION STARTERS

Claude McKay was born in Jamaica and came to the United States to attend the Tuskegee Institute in 1912, the same year that the Institute of Arts and Sciences awarded him its distinguished medal. He was the first black poet to receive this honor. McKay, known for his decidedly militant voice, wrote this poem after the terrifying race riots that occurred in Harlem in the summer of 1919. Are your students surprised by the militancy and defiance-to-the-death rhetoric of this voice from an earlier generation?

THE RECEPTIVE READER

1. McKay's defiant last-stand rhetoric glorifies the honor of dying in the noble cause and is alive with passionate denunciation and contempt for the

"mad and hungry dogs" and the "monsters" who are the enemy. The lines "If we must nobly die, O let us nobly die" and "O kinsmen we must meet the common foe!" and "let us show us brave" echo the attitudes of the Spartans at Thermopylae who, though knowing with certainty they would be vanquished, held their ground.

2. 1919 and 1997 or 1999 are different stages in the struggle of race relations. Are there are some primal human responses to oppression, no matter what the particular time, what the age, what the circumstance?

Chapter 22 MYTH AND ALLUSION Recovered Memories 765

A name like Apollo, Dionysus, Helen, Lucifer, or Eve activates a whole network of images and associations. Allusions to a shared body of myth and legend provide the poet with a vast register of references that conjure up images and evoke emotions. What is the cultural literacy quotient of your students? How well do they recognize and respond to the echoes of myth and legend that they encounter in their reading, listening, and viewing? Ask students to give a shorthand version of the longer story that each of the following questions brings to mind:

- What is a Cassandra?
- What is an odyssey?
- Who were the Amazons?
- What associations are brought into play by the word *exodus*?
- What is an Oedipus complex?
- Who was Nefertiti?
- What was found in King Tutankhamen's tomb?
- Where is Nirvana?
- What non-Western myths—African, Native American, Asian—have your students encountered?

First Reading: e. e. cummings, "in Just-" 767

DISCUSSION STARTERS

The Greek god Pan, the god of shepherds and herds, had goatlike legs, ears, and horns. Although he could induce "panic" among men, in this poem he plays a happy (if "queer") role as the "little / lame balloonman," signaling the "mud- / luscious" season of "Just- / spring" with a whistle that could be heard " far / and /wee." Cummings, the ultimate balloonman, was known for his picturelike spacing and word play, and he is here playing games with the conventional pacing of sentences and running together the names of the children: "eddieandbill" and "bettyandisbel." Are adults merely a more advanced, grown-up version of the children they once were, or are children and adults really two different races of people? You may want to ask your students to write a journal entry or short poem that conjures up a scene or incident from their own childhood as seen from a child's point of view.

THE RECEPTIVE READER

1. Any child knows that mud squishes deliciously between one's toes, knows that puddles are "wonderful" for walking through, with or without shoes, especially when the spring sun is out, beginning to warm the world outside. One student wrote:

I knew it was spring when, hidden from adult eyes, I dared take off my long brown tights and high-top shoes. I remember watching my white feet, sunless for so many months and all too clean, going barefoot on the dark soil, still cold from winter's leaving and moist from rain; I remember the deliciousness of this forbidden pleasure; I remember knowing in my bones that it was really spring, even though the trees were still bare. And I remember feeling that, if I did get caught, this "mud-luscious" walk was worth the punishment.

2. The poem dances out its rhythm through pauses and changes in pace. Its weird spacing slows us down with unconventional line breaks at key words ("and it's / *spring*") and speeds us up by running together such words as "eddieandbill" and "bettyandisbel." The compound words, too, "Just-spring," "mud-luscious," "puddle-wonderful," "hop-scotch and jump-rope," and "goat-footed" add to the bouncing, hopping-and-skipping effect. The several "whistles" both have ample spacing around them, making the "s" sound whistle out in midair?

3. The whistling of the queer little old balloonman comes back three times in the poem—to make sure that we don't miss his role at the center of the poem! The key word *spring* (each time accentuated by an immediately preceding line break) bounces like a ball (or echoes like a bell) throughout the poem, being repeated three times at hop-scotch intervals. Eddieandbill and bettyandisbel first come "running from marbles and / piracies" and then again "dancing / from hop-scotch and jump-rope." The world is "just-" blooming, and the children and the balloonman sense the surge of life.

4. Most students are likely to argue that the exuberance of spring and the play of color and imagination symbolized by the "balloonman" are nearly universal in a child's experience and therefore will work for the uninitiated reader. Children love balloons just as they love visits to the zoo or a carnival. It is the well-read adult's reading pleasure that is enhanced by the perceived echo of a pagan cultural tradition that was more innocent and ecstatic in its intuitive response to the vivid, playful, buzzing, blooming natural world.

5. The allusion adds an *extra dimension* to a poem delightful in itself?

William Butler Yeats, "Leda and the Swan" 769

PERSPECTIVES—POETS AND GREEK MYTHOLOGY

Several mythological figures have been a special source of inspiration to poets. Apollo, patron of poets and musicians, is the Greek god of the daylight hours, when reason, order, harmony, and symmetry prevail. However, the night belongs to Dionysus. Called Bacchus by the Romans, he is the god of wine, wearing a tiger skin, his chariot drawn by leopards or tigers. As night falls, we hear from the hills the sounds of the drums and clashing cymbals beaten by frenzied hands. We see the satyrs, half man, half goat, romping ahead of the god. We see the ecstatic Maenads (or Bacchantes), women worshippers of Dionysus, who in a trance-like state will tear a man crossing their path limb from limb, as they did to the legendary Greek singer Orpheus, whose power of song moved the rocks and the beasts and the waters. Finally, we see "Bacchus and his pards" (John Keats)—the god in his chariot draped with clusters of grapes, holding the reins of gold, driving a team of tigers.

Orpheus' power of song persuaded Hades (whom the Romans called Pluto) to grant the singer's request to have his dead wife Eurydice return with him to the world of the living. The catch was that he was not to turn back to look at her on the journey toward the light, but he did and so lost her forever. Orpheus' song transformed the wilderness into a temple sacred to Apollo. Modern poets have seen in him a symbol of the human spirit triumphing over death and adversity, as "ever new, music, with living blocks, / In non-functional space erects her house of praise" (Rainer Maria Rilke, "Sonnets to Orpheus"). However, they have also looked at the Orpheus myth from new and different perspectives. Linda Gregg, for instance, in her poem "Eurydice," looks at the story of Orpheus in the world below from the point of view of Eurydice. Eurydice here suspects from the start that Orpheus traveled to the underworld to make the experience grist for his poetic mill, already composing in his mind the new songs that he will sing to his friends to tell how far he traveled for his dead wife and how he then finally lost her.

DISCUSSION STARTERS

Myths speak to the collective unconscious. They bring a wide range of intuitive responses into play, and they do not come with pat morals or explications. They are subject to interpretation and reinterpretation. In "A Vision," Yeats said about the ancient myth underlying this poem, "I imagine the annunciation that founded Greece was made to Leda, remembering that they showed in a Spartan temple, strung up to the roof as a holy relic, an unhatched egg of hers, and that from one of her eggs came love and from the other war." As a result of this "annunciation," according to some versions of the story, Leda gave birth to Helen, legendary beauty of the ancient world, and to Clytemnestra, wife and nemesis of Agamemnon. What do your students know about Zeus' other relationships with mortal women? What do they know about legendary figures like Helen, Paris, Agamemnon, Clytemnestra, Orestes, Electra?

THE RECEPTIVE READER

1. The swan brings into play connotations of calm, graceful beauty (very different from the connotations of a quacking duck or nattering goose). In this poem, the beautiful bird, with its "great wings," becomes a terrifying, overpowering mythic creature. This creature, though it represents "brute blood," has come from the air, and it carries the god's "knowledge" and "power." The offspring engendered here will not be ordinary mortals but larger-than-life humans precipitating the great war that destroyed Troy and the downfall of the leader of the victorious Greek forces. The swan is at the same time beast (with its webbed feet and "feathered glory"), humanlike in its attraction to a human being, and divine in its knowledge and power? (The Greeks had a less compartmentalized view than we do—animal, human, and god were all manifestations of the mystery and power of life?)

2. Are we going to admire the god in awe at his mythic power? Or are we going to agree with the student who wrote: "Yeats seems to be saying that violence begets violence: the violent rape 'engenders' war; it brings about 'the broken wall' of Troy, the violent death of Agamemnon at the hands of his wife, the destruction of lives"? Or are we going to censor this poem because fundamentalists will object to it as endorsing "bestiality"?

H. D. (Hilda Doolittle), "Helen" 770

PERSPECTIVES—H.D. AND THE LITERARY AVANTGARDE

Hilda Doolittle was an early modernist of the World War I and post–World War I generation. She was a prominent member of a literary avant-garde that hated war, defied bourgeois sexual morality, rejected a soulless materialistic civilization, and searched for sources of spiritual renewal in myth and non-Western cultural traditions. She had involved relationships with prominent men and women who served as her mentors, sponsors, and spiritual soulmates. Living mostly in London and Switzerland and traveling widely, Doolittle moved in a circle of to-be-famous expatriates and exiles. She was for a time engaged to Ezra Pound, who gave her early poems his "influential imprimatur" (Marian Arkin and Barbara Shollar) as representing the modern poetic gospel of concrete imagery, rejection of verbiage, and free verse. She was close to D. H. Lawrence, another high priest of modernism, who for a time lived in her apartment with his wife Frieda. Doolittle had early developed an interest in revolutionary modern psychologists like Havelock Ellis, and in the early thirties she journeyed to Vienna to be analyzed by Sigmund Freud. Tracing the poet's spiritual odyssey in *The Norton Anthology of Literature by Women* (1985), Sandra M. Gilbert and Susan Gubar say that in her later poetry H. D. probes the sources of female creativity and rebirth. Helen of Troy was for her "the scapegoat of a war that reveals the nihilism of a culture based on masculine values. Helen, who has been reviled as the cause of the war, must recover a less punitive sense of her self."

DISCUSSION STARTERS

The images of Helen as temptress and of Helen as victim contend in H. D.'s poem. "All Greece" sees Helen as temptress, hating her, reviling her, wishing her dead. Yet the speaker suggests a different Helen, a Helen with "still eyes," with a "wan face" and "cool feet." Can your students think of other legendary figures who have been seen from radically opposed perspectives—JFK, Columbus, Albert Schweitzer, Madonna?

THE RECEPTIVE READER

1. H. D. drives home the Greeks' unrelenting hatred by the insistent parallel opening lines of the three successive stanzas: "All Greece hates . . . All Greece reviles . . . Greece sees unmoved." That hatred is carried beyond the grave and to the very end of the poem, and it will be satisfied only when Helen's ashes are laid to rest among the mournful cypresses appropriate for a funeral site.

2. The Greeks hate Helen for "past enchantments"—the spell her beauty cast over the Trojan prince Paris—and the "ills" this disastrous entanglement brought to all concerned. But the poet calls Helen "God's [Zeus'] daughter, born of love"; she has "still" (rather than shifty or glowering) eyes and beautiful feet and slender knees. *Luster* implies a certain shining from within, or something that has been polished. In this poem Helen's eyes (?) have "luster as of olives." "Maid," as applied to the passionate Helen, has paradoxical connotations of youth, innocence, and virginity?

3. Feminist writers, such as the poet Judy Grahn, have tended to see Helen more as victim and as a maligned gifted woman than as the traditional stereotypical temptress.

Juxtapositions: The Sacrifice of Isaac

Wilfred Owen, "The Parable of the Old Men and the Young" 772

For a "Perspectives" entry on Owen see Chapter 21 of this manual.

DISCUSSION STARTERS

For centuries, biblical lore has helped shape people's thinking and feeling about fundamental questions. What to your students is the meaning of the story of Job, of the parable of the Good Samaritan, of the story of David and Goliath? Are these stories ancient history, or are they relevant to our concerns and values today?

THE RECEPTIVE READER

1. Some *common elements* in both versions are Abraham and the tools of sacrifice—wood, fire, knife; father and son journeying solemnly to the appointed destination; the childlike Isaac in his innocence asking about the sacrificial lamb; the miraculous appearance of the angel calling out to stop the sacrifice; the ram discovered in the thicket. There is in both versions the same sense of grave apprehension, the suspenseful feeling that we are approaching a momentous choice that will put the principals to the test.

2. After about the first six lines of the poem, we begin to realize that the latter-day Abram and Isaac in this modernized, updated retelling of the ancient story are journeying through a different setting. Owen has the youth bound "with belts and straps," which sound like part of the uniforms and gear of latter-day wars; Owen has Abram build "parapets and trenches," reminding us of the years of murderous, grinding trench warfare in World War I. The ram offered miraculously in the thicket has become the ram of national pride, which the older generation was unable to give up and sacrifice. So the sacrificial butchery of "half the seed of Europe"—a generation of young men—continued to the bitter end. For Owen and many of his generation, there was no miraculous release or redemption from the carnage. The old men, unable to shake off their traditional nationalism and patriotism in order to make peace with the hated enemy, sacrificed their sons.

3. The unadorned simplicity of a parable allows the poet to let the story speak for itself, without passionate indictment or showy despair. The biblical parallel helps to dramatize the solemnity and enormity of the choice for jaded readers whose sensitivities have been blunted by too many stories of war?

The Language of Myth

Judy Grahn, "They Say She Is Veiled" 773

DISCUSSION STARTERS

Hints of female deities predating male-dominated religions exist in many places. Artemis (Diana), who in Greek myth became the chaste huntress, was worshipped in pre-Hellenic times as an earth goddess associated with the wildlife of mountains and forests, with the growth of crops, and with human birth. How patriarchal or male-oriented are early religious traditions that your students have studied? What female goddesses have they read about? What is their role in the early religions? What is the role of the Virgin Mary in the Christian tradition?

THE RECEPTIVE READER

If there is a feminine divine principle at the center of the universe, it has indeed become a *mystery* to us—but that is because we are *mystified*. It is not the goddess who wears the veil. It is we who are shielded from the truth by the veil of our cultural conditioning? "They" insist that "she"—a feminine archetype, an earth goddess at the heart of creation—is a "mystery," an unknown quantity, something impossible to understand, ungraspable, something obscure and therefore fuzzy. But she is "exactly in place," that is, out in the open, unveiled, unhidden, *with* a face, thus with a clear identity. If this way of looking is true, then it is "we who are mystified," that is, bewildered, and "without faces."

John Keats, "Ode on a Grecian Urn" 774

PERSPECTIVES—KEATS' "URN" AND NEO-PLATONISM

The final stanza's famous line, "Beauty is truth, truth beauty," has given much trouble to modern critics removed from the Neo-Platonic tradition that strongly influenced the romantic poets. For the Platonist, the true, the beautiful, and the good are all ultimately manifestations of the same divine essence. The sentiments at the end of the ode echo ideas Keats expressed in his programmatic "Letter to John Bailey" (1817), where he said, "I am certain of nothing but of the holiness of the Heart's affections and the Truth of Imagination—What the imagination seizes as Beauty must be truth." Truth here is not the product of the linear, logical, analytical intellect that relies on "consecutive reasoning." What the poet senses and feels and imagines leads to a higher truth—the truth of the imagination, the truth of beauty. Unlike the scientist who tries to minimize interference from emotions or desire, the poet must consider generous feelings as sacred, honoring the "holiness of the Heart's affections." The way to beauty and truth is to trust our "sublime" ennobling passions, of which Love is the most sublime. Our feelings and our creative imagination will put us in touch with the essence of the universe. (To answer the objections of skeptics, Renaissance Neo-Platonists like Castiglione's Bembo in *The Courtier* went to considerable lengths to explain the difference between "true beauty" in the Platonic sense and corrupted beauty allied with deception or cruelty.)

DISCUSSION STARTERS

Keats said, "The excellence of every art is its intensity, capable of making all disagreeables evaporate, from their being in close relationship with beauty and truth." Paradoxically in this poem, we do not achieve intensity by speeding up the flow of time—but by arresting it. Time is suspended in this poem—protecting us against disillusionment, against the inevitable coming down after moments of "ecstasy." The dejection, the despondency, the despair that in the Romantic temperament alternates with periods of exaltation is forestalled by art that captures the fleeting moment in time. Have your students ever felt that a piece of art was *too* finished, *too* static? Have they ever felt that a statue is too "cold," too far removed from breathing reality—"all breathing human passion far above"? On the other hand, have they ever felt that art makes possible a kind of perfection that breathing, moving, changeable actual life cannot attain? Life has too much of an admixture of pain and ugliness to be truly beautiful?

THE RECEPTIVE READER

1. The poem implies that in the real world people in love (like the poet in his own life) are not likely to find calm and fulfillment. Real "breathing human passion" leads inevitably to turmoil, loss, and sorrow. It leaves us feverish and with parched lips, thirsting for lasting satisfaction that escapes us.

2. Nature is pulsating, vibrant, and alive, but it also raises exaggerated expectations of happiness and fulfilment that are sooner or later disappointed. Art only can satisfy the heart's desire—making us imagine what we cannot attain in reality. The vase has survived more than two thousand years and is still unspoiled by the passage of time. It is married to quietness and serenity; nothing has ravished or violated it. It is the "bride of quietness" and the adopted child of silence and slowly moving time. The images it contains will forever remain sylvan, youthful, and full of promise.

THE PERSONAL RESPONSE

Gwendolyn Brooks writes: "Does man love Art? Man visits Art, but squirms. / Art hurts. Art urges voyages—and it is easier to stay at home, / the nice beer ready." What did she mean?

Juxtapositions: The Icarus Myth

Anne Sexton, "To a Friend Whose Work Has Come to Triumph" 777

DISCUSSION STARTERS

Does this modern rewrite of the Icarus myth glorify or condemn "impetuous, headstrong, ambitious youth"? Does this rewrite glorify or condemn the human capacity for aspiration, for "testing the boundaries"? Does it make us share in the father's grief?

THE RECEPTIVE READER

1. Some of the adjectives early start giving an irreverent, *ironic* twist to this retelling of the myth: "sticky wings," "awkward as camels," "shocked starlings," and "plushy ocean." Some of the verbs too—"pasting" the wings on,

the starlings "pumping" past—make it hard for a solemn mood to develop. The legendary inventor and anxious mourning father of the original myth is cut down to size and becomes a latter-day "sensible daddy" (who does not seem overly grief-stricken or aching with parental love).

2. For all the irreverent ironic modern tone, the genuine challenge, danger, and exhilaration of extraordinary achievement begin to shine through: "the first flawless moment," "the fire at his neck," "wondrously tunneling / into that hot eye" (of the menacing sun), "acclaiming the sun." No condemnation of *hubris* here, but instead exhilarated sharing in the daring of the "friend whose work has come to triumph"?

3. As Sexton's sonnet plays a modern variation on the ancient myth, so her rhyme scheme plays a modern variation on a conventional *abab*, *cdcd*, *efef*, *gg* rhyme scheme. Some of the rhymes are modern stretched rhymes or slant rhymes (*on/lawn*, *casually/sea*, *wings/tunneling*); and *camels/well* are at best a sound echo. The turning point toward outright admiration and endorsement ("Admire his wings!") comes close to the traditional placement—here not at the beginning of but halfway through the first line of the sestet. And the final couplet spells out and sums up the central contrast between adventurous youth and timid, sensible age.

THE CREATIVE DIMENSION

Flight is an archetypal theme that stimulates a wide range of images, associations, apprehensions, and aspirations. You may want to ask students to write their own passage or poem on the subject. Sample student writing:

I'll play
I'll play
I'll put on the wings
I'll spread them across the canyon
I'll cast a shadow on the desert
I'll fly next to an eagle
I'll melt into a cloud
I'll touch the sun
I'll play
I'll play
        it safe
from under a tree
on the edge of a mountain.

David Wagoner, "The Return of Icarus" 778

DISCUSSION STARTER

Wagoner's version of this myth seems to question authority at all levels. The tone is a combination of sardonic and folksy. Not only does Icarus *not* die in this version, but the speaker (speaking for the anonymous "we" of the poem), who draws a portrait of an adult Icarus who is a drifter and storyteller himself, is both amused and bemused by this character who comes into town and leaves just as mysteriously as he came. You may want to have students play with re-creating the debunking modern tone in a poem or passage that retells with a new slant another myth, such as the story of Helen or of Leda and the Swan.

THE RECEPTIVE READER

1. We can tell from the beginning that the story will be thoroughly stripped of glamour and solemnity—taken down to our own level? Icarus here has not drowned but unceremoniously "shows up" decades later. Instead of the doomed daring, impetuous boy, we see a drifter scrounging for a living, his neck crooked and his hip out of joint from the injuries he suffered in the fall. The smell of wine from his goatskin makes the dogs bark madly at the disreputable stranger.

2. The father's portrait is redrawn to make him a much-honored pioneer of flight (like the Wright brothers?). The loss of his son apparently did not stop him from cashing in on the celebrity status his exploit brought him. (If the son had been around, he also might have shared in the rewards: a prestigious apartment, orchards, lots of women, invitations.) The original Daedalus was an inventive Athenian; this one is disrespectfully called a "slow learner," weighted down by his years (and, ironically, "his genius") till he finally was "gawkily airborne." Polonius-like, Daedalus gave endless half-understood advice finally tuned out by the son. At the time of the celebrated flight, the son was just a kid, who of the whole story of double-crossings that led to the killing of the Minotaur in the maze built by Daedalus enjoyed only the snorting and bellowing of the doomed bull-like creature. The son was a passive participant in his father's schemes when the wax was "smeared" on to hold the "half-stuck second-hand chicken feathers." Success-oriented go-getting modern father, alienated sullen no-account modern son?

3. Humorous parts of the retelling mock the magic of flight and focus instead on the imagined mundane realities of this absurd feat, including the fact that the father merely "flapped and flapped" or that the flight was hampered because Daedalus had not thought to provide a tail. Poseidon, the god of the sea, is disrespectfully called "the old salt"; Icarus, who notices the sagging quill-tips, can't get "a word in edgewise or otherwise" with his garrulous father. However, discounting or stripping off some of the heroic trappings of the ancient myth does not keep the poet from being serious about what to him seems to be at the heart of the story. The modern poet knows that the atmosphere gets *colder*, not hotter, as we rise. As the modern Icarus rises toward the sun, which is "cool, not hot," the wax is stiffening on his elbows—"suddenly breaking/ Away, leaving him / wingless, clawing at nothing." Sun and ocean, representing the forces of nature that science has stripped of feeling and volition, are totally "indifferent" (certainly not weeping and lamenting, as they might have been if Ovid were telling the story). And the sur-

vivors, their bones broken and badly mended, must carry on as best they can long after the heroic hoopla has faded.

4. The last line gives us the *last word* on the interplay of the polarities of flight/groundedness and fame/ordinariness. The last line ironically suggests that Icarus, in his grounded way, has stayed in touch, while Daedalus, with his flights of imagination, has spiraled out. If there is a moral, one student suggested it might run like this: "It is better to live in the now, in the real world, getting calluses and telling stories and interacting with children—and loving the earth."

5. Daedalus built the labyrinth for King Minos to pen up the Minotaur—the "snorting and bellowing" half bull, half man that was the offspring of Pasiphaë and the mythical white bull. But the king double-crossed the Athenian inventor when he did not allow him to return to Athens as promised. The king in turn was double-crossed by his daughter Ariadne, who helped the adventurer Theseus emerge from his ordeal in the maze unscathed and who plotted to elope with him. (Like the great maze itself, these double-dealings were "labyrinthine.") Other mythological *allusions*: the ravenous Harpies—half bird, half woman; Helios, the sun god, driving his chariot across the sky; Poseidon (Neptune), the god of the sea.

THE PERSONAL RESPONSE

The humorous touches in this retelling may work two different ways: Some readers may read the whole poem as a spoof and dismiss the story? But others may feel that by recognizing the ridiculous aspects of our common humanity the poet makes the characters more human and more real rather than less—and we can start thinking about what special challenging events and their aftermath do to real people.

Vassar Miller, "The New Icarus" 780

DISCUSSION STARTERS

Do your students experience flights of the imagination? (What kind? With What destinations?) Are we expected to be tolerant or intolerant of "whimsy"? Is "wishful thinking" good or bad?

THE RECEPTIVE READER

1. Slipping off the husk reveals the rich nutritious ear of corn inside. In this poem, the person in his or her imagined flight strips off the law of gravity as if it were a husk that has held in the person's spiritual essence. We are not talking about *physical* flight here—no foolish attempt to fly with fake feathers like the original Icarus, the "false-feathered fool." (Nor are we talking about latter-day flight in a fake metal bird, endangering real birds like the lark and the swift whose bridal retreat is in the sky.)

2. The telescoped phrase "plumed with metal" suggests the flight of someone inside an airplane—which is encased in protective metal rather than

in the plumage of a bird. The Alps are high mountains in Europe. We may think of the solid mountains and the unsubstantial air as opposites, but here the imagined "alps of air" ask us to think of the heavens as rising to unheard-of layers of altitude, beyond the reach of the eagle's wings.

3. The new Icarus slips through the crevices of Newton's physical laws by defying the laws of gravity and motion through emotion, through suffering, which play no role in Newton's world of the laws of physics. Through profound suffering ("plummeting all Hell") and through outsoaring "all Heaven," the "you" addressed in the poem transcends the limits of Newton's materialistic universe.

4. The religious implications are abundant enough in this Petrarchan sonnet to justify a religious reading: Christ was "pinioned to wooden pinions"; he was "naked" save for a loincloth; he was "plucked and crimson-plumaged"—bleeding from wounds and a crown of thorns. Christ, by being nailed to the cross, plummeted "all Hell"; rising again, he outsoared "all Heaven? The poet, Vassar Miller, was a victim of cerebral palsy and a Catholic. It is entirely possible that she identified with Christ's suffering and his "wreck of bone"? However, at another level, the poem can also be read as a figurative journey of the creative mind, which has the potential for experiencing ecstasy at the one extreme and profound suffering at the other.

William Carlos Williams, "Landscape with the Fall of Icarus" 781

DISCUSSION STARTERS

In Breughel's painting, Icarus is barely more than a background speck. His mythic journey, his flight to the sun, and his ultimate "splash" go unnoticed by the farmer or by the crew of the ship sailing by. And the "whole pageantry / of the year" doesn't miss a beat when Icarus hits the water. Do modern poets feel a special attraction to this painting because Breughel is so much closer to them than the original myth? Is his perspective in the painting closely akin to the modern assumption (or modern myth?) of the insignificance of the individual? In the larger cycle of the seasons, and in the comings and goings of humanity, the heroic struggle and the tragic fate of the individual mean very little—or nothing. What modern individuals do your students know who seem to have transcended the anonymity of people in the modern world to achieve mythic or heroic proportions?

Modern Myths

Sharon Olds, "The Death of Marilyn Monroe" 782

DISCUSSION STARTERS

How much are people's outlook or values affected by the flickering images of the "silver screen"? Do performers from Marilyn Monroe to Madonna affect the viewer's assumptions about what is beautiful, exciting, possible, or permissible? Or are they merely "entertainment"?

THE RECEPTIVE READER

1. Marilyn Monroe supposedly died after taking an overdose of sleeping pills. In one version of the story, she was depressed by her faltering career and committed suicide. However, her involvement with the Kennedys and underground figures has led to speculation that she may have become a liability to people who conspired to end her life.

2. Seeing an "idol" die, turned into a real-life cold statue, destroys our illusions of permanence and mythic timelessness? The myth of beauty—forever flawless and young—is shattered by the reality of the gaping mouth, disheveled hair, flattened breasts, and a body heavy as iron. This shock to our cherished dream world leaves the men—and us—permanently changed, disillusioned, shaken. If such things can happen to someone so adored and worshipped, someone seemingly so removed from the mundane world, what about us?

3. Students may argue that the stereotype of the Hollywood blonde is alive in sitcoms and B-movies—and revivals and reruns. What is different about nonstereotypical images of women created by stars from Mariel Hemingway to Sigourney Weaver? Would your students say that Madonna represents the blonde stereotype—or that she plays on and exploits the stereotype?

4. Writers from Norman Mailer to Gloria Steinem have probed (and helped keep alive) the Marilyn Monroe legend. The plethora of books and articles about Marilyn Monroe's life and speculations about what caused her death underscore her mythic status.

THE CREATIVE DIMENSION

You may want to have students get ready for writing a re-creation by jotting down phrases or details that have a special impact for them. Here is an additional example of a re-creation written by a student:

> Three ordinary men will drink in bars and
> listen to the breathing of their
> ordinary wives,
> will do their
> ordinary work
> and live their
> ordinary lives,
> can no longer meet each other's
> ordinary eyes.
> The dead, glazed good-byes of the
> dead goddess made ordinary,
> got in the way,
> and three ordinary men

will be
neverthesame.

e. e. cummings, "Buffalo Bill's" 784

DISCUSSION STARTERS

Have any of the folk heroes or legendary figures of early American history and of the American West acquired mythical proportions?

THE RECEPTIVE READER

In real life, Buffalo Bill was a pony express rider and scout named Col. William F. Cody. He represents a stage in American history, idealized and glorified in countless movies, when gunmen like Cody were clearing the continent of buffalo and the native tribes, serving as frontrunners for the tide of settlers that followed in their wake. He later ran Buffalo Bill's Wild West Show, and his exploits were made famous in dime novels and the long-running musical comedy *Annie Get Your Gun* by Irving Berlin. Buffalo Bill became a symbol of the American cult of the gun—cummings shows him shooting the clay pigeons to show his deadly marksmanship, in an early demonstration of the tendency of Americans to make gunplay their favorite entertainment. cummings derives wry amusement from a multiple killer finally meeting his own match in the greatest killer of them all.

Alison Hawthorne Deming, "The Man Who Became a Deer" 785

PERSPECTIVES—POETS AND ANIMAL NATURE

Traditionally, the "bestial" or "brutish" part of our nature has been denounced by moralists. However, in pre-Christian, pagan times, animals had often been portrayed, if not worshipped, as beautiful, vital beings, symbolizing the mythical, mysterious energies of nature. The Roman poet Ovid, for instance, celebrated the beauty of the magnificent white bull beloved by Queen Pasiphaë. Modern poets who might be called "primitivists" for their rejection of our vulgar, materialistic civilization and their rehabilitation and quasi-mystical worship of our animal heritage include D. H. Lawrence and Robinson Jeffers. In his "Snake" poem, Lawrence called the snake one of the "lords of life" and cursed his "human education" for making him think of the snake as the enemy. In his "Hurt Hawks" (1928), Jeffers celebrated the "intrepid readiness, the terrible eyes" of the "beautiful and wild," "intemperate and savage" bird and said that, except for the penalties, he would "rather kill a man than a hawk." For Jeffers, the birds and fish of the wild Pacific Coast, not yet "defaced" with urban civilization, reflected "the beauty of God."

DISCUSSION STARTERS

If they had to choose, would your students choose domesticated animals like horses or dogs, or would they opt for the animals of the wild? How would they defend their choice?

THE RECEPTIVE READER

1. Unlike what happens in the metamorphoses of traditional myth, the man did not literally become a deer: "his feet did not cleave / into hooves, his head / never sprouted antlers, / and the parts that mean / manhood did not thicken / with pelt." Despite eating deer meat three times a day to facilitate the metamorphosis, "the deer remained hidden, / disguised as a man / in the perfect camouflage / of his body." The man, however, became more like a deer in behavior, in mentality: "his patience became that / of a browser" and "his heart / that of a hart." At the close of the poem, the man awakens "one winter morning to / the heat of the blood of deer / running through its / pipes like antifreeze." This is not the first time the man tried to lose himself. He once "wanted / to become an Eskimo." He "ate raw, rancid meat / and slept on the ground."

2. People trying to leave behind the anxieties and distortions of a civilization estranged from our natural roots may first try to identify with "primitive" people (like the Eskimo) assumed to be living far more intimately and harmoniously with nature. The next logical step is to try to enter imaginatively into the world of animals, recovering fundamentals of life not yet spoiled by "the pale cast of thought."

3. Because the poet is a woman, the speaker in the poem may be assumed also to be a woman. The speaker in the poem keeps her distance: "What little I know," she says, or "That's all I know about the man who became a deer." However, for someone who just knows a little, she reveals a great deal. She knows that the man wanted to become first an Eskimo and then a deer. She knows intimate physical details about the man, for example, she knows "the parts that mean / manhood did not thicken / with pelt." Finally, the poem ends on a somewhat wistful note, suggesting the speaker and the man who became a deer had once been lovers, and that the speaker may be yearning for those times: "when he loved a woman / she tasted the forest on his lips."

Poems for Further Study

Maurya Simon, "King Midas's Daughter" 786

DISCUSSION STARTERS

The lure and glitter of gold have been among the oldest recurrent themes in the history of civilization. For your students, what images, associations, cautionary tales, historical events, folk sayings, and the like does the mention of gold evoke or bring to mind?

THE RECEPTIVE READER

Midas was the king of Phrygia (located in what is now Turkey). Because of his hospitality and kindness to Silenus, who was tutor to Dionysus (Bacchus), the great Greek god of wine and ecstatic liberation, Midas was given the golden touch. When Midas escorted Silenus back to Dionysus, Dionysus offered a reward of anything that Midas wished. Midas answered that his wish was that everything he touched should turn into gold. Although Dionysus was sorry that Midas had not come up with a better wish, he granted it. At first Midas was delighted with his new power; he touched a tree branch, a clod of dirt, an apple, and turned each of them into pure, shining gold. Unfortunately, when Midas sat down for a meal, he discovered that he could eat nothing since everything he touched turned into gold. The bread he touched turned into gold and the wine he tried to drink turned into melted gold. Midas begged Dionysus to take back the golden touch, begged to be delivered from what Bulfinch calls "his glittering destruction." Dionysus responded, telling Midas to go to the River Pactolus, where he could wash away the power of the golden touch. From that day forward, Midas renounced wealth and riches.

The poet changes the Midas story by telling it from his daughter's point of view. The daughter grieves for her father's transformation: "She sees him below in a garden among statues / that are grotesque, familiar, golden." The statues were once familiar people, and the daughter must be careful not to join their ranks. She wants "to shake this curse from his shoulders"; she wishes she could "hug his thinning body, unloosen / its cold grief, its sorrow of greed." However, in this version of the story, the soul-killing legacy of greed cannot be shaken off.

In our modern world, with its frank pursuit of the bottom line, warnings about unfettered greed have come to seem old-fashioned or square?

William Wordsworth, "The World Is Too Much with Us" 787

DISCUSSION STARTER

In the Greek world, the gods peopled the heavens and mingled with mortals. Nature was alive with lesser deities and unseen presences. We know about material poverty—is there such a thing as spiritual poverty, spiritual impoverishment? Are moderns incapable of sensing a living presence in nature? Are we "out of tune" with nature?

THE RECEPTIVE READER

In Greek legend, Proteus was Neptune's herdsman. He was known as a consummate "shape-shifter"—the first being to assume many different "Protean" shapes. He is represented in myth as an old man and fortune-teller. Triton is the son of Neptune, represented as a fish with a human head. Through his shell, he is thought to make the sea roar. In this poem, Wordsworth grieves over the loss of a world where nature was alive with such mythic, quasi-divine beings. We are so busy making a living that we no longer listen in the natural world for kindred presences; our imaginative and intuitive powers have been laid waste. The pagan religion or "creed" of the Greeks may be obsolete, but nothing has taken the place of their gift for imbuing the creation with sentient, breathing life. If there are any spiritual essences in the world around us, we "are out of tune," unable to tune in and relate to them.

Edna St. Vincent Millay, "An Ancient Gesture" 788

PERSPECTIVES—FEMININE IMAGES AND EDNA ST. VINCENT MILLAY

Sandra M. Gilbert, in "Millay and the Theater of Personality" (in *Critical Essays on Edna St. Vincent Millay*, ed. William B. Thesing, G. K. Hall, 1993) traces the evolution of Millay from the "once impudent *femme fatale*," reveling in the New Woman's "sexual liberation" and "determination to be free," to the author of "Apostrophe to Man," the angry indictment of a male-dominated culture that in the thirties was girding up to go to war again. Gilbert says, "the notably feminine images through which Millay has consistently chosen to dramatize her ideas should remind us of a constant throughout all her verse: her self-presentation as distinctively 'female.' " If Penelope in "An Ancient Gesture" is "known by her tear-stained apron, so Millay's earlier women are marked by the 'long dresses, trailing ones' in which the poet herself gave readings." However, from the point of view of an activist later feminism, Millay's anger is a helpless anger, and the curses directed at a "detestable race"—"continue to expunge yourself, die out"—are revenge fantasies that do not avail. "An Ancient Gesture" questions "the epic posturings of one of history's primordial heroes," showing Ulysses as using the tear wiped away as a rhetorical gesture. Yet even as the poem "subverts the political glamour of the itinerant Ulysses, its ultimate irony is precisely Penelope's stationary helplessness as well as the helplessness of the poem's speaker, the uncontrollably sincere weeping of both women."

DISCUSSION STARTERS

Modern feminist historians and critics have asked us to listen for the unheard voices of women relegated to minor roles in the stories about the men in their lives. What other women playing such roles do your students know? What do your students know about them? What was Penelope (or what were other women in similar roles) really thinking?

THE RECEPTIVE READER

1. According to Homer, Penelope was the wife of Ulysses (Odysseus), legendary Greek general and seafarer of the *Odyssey*. She became a byword for the long-suffering faithful wife of an absentee husband. While her husband was gone, she was beleaguered by many suitors who thought her husband dead. To escape their importunities, she promised to make a choice of one as soon as she had finished weaving a garment for her father-in-law. Every night she would undo the day's weaving in order to defer making a choice until Ulysses would return. After many years he did, wreaking vengeance on the suitors and on members of his household who had befriended them.

2. The poet, a woman, sympathizes with the fatigue and despair of the absent warrior's wife. Penelope, abandoned, fending for herself among predatory males, would spontaneously burst into bitter tears. Ulysses also wiped his tears, but "only as a gesture"—a gesture deliberately made by an accomplished orator to show that he was "much too moved to speak," a gesture designed to make the spectators choke up in turn.

Donald Finkel, "The Sirens" 788

DISCUSSION STARTERS

What "siren songs" are modern readers likely to have heard?

THE RECEPTIVE READER

This poem retells the traditional story from the point of view of the sirens—whom we usually see only through a haze of wonder, superstition, and fear. The story goes that Ulysses escaped the sirens' irresistible song (luring mariners to their deaths) by filling his companions' ears with wax while chaining himself to the mast of his ship, thinking he could best the mythical creatures. True, he is not destroyed; true, he does manage to get home to Penelope; true, in some surface sense, the cunning, shrewd Ulysses has outwitted the sirens. Yet the twist is that the sirens knew beforehand of his coming and devised a special hell for him by letting him go. For Ulysses, who was a remarkable, clever, special human, they have devised a remarkable, special punishment: He arrives at Ithaca, only to row, figuratively, in a sea of wheat "reconstructing," his mouth making the strains of the remembered overpowering melody "tumble into place." He is caught as truly as the mariners at the bottom of the sea. The poem concludes with the sirens' contemptuous rhetorical question: "Do you think / Wax could have stopped us, or chains?"

Chapter 23 THREE POETS IN DEPTH Dickinson, Frost, Brooks 793

The personal voice of a poet is like a distinctive signature. What is quintessentially Dickinson about a line like "Much madness is divinest sense"? (Possible answers: the extreme paradoxical formulation, the search for the spiritual in unsuspected places.) What is vintage Frost about lines like the following?

So Eden sank to grief.
So dawn goes down to day.
Nothing gold can stay.

(Possible answers: the closeness to basic cycles in nature, like the coming of dawn and its fading into day; the choice of basic metaphors, rooted deeply in the readers' shared cultural experience, like Eden or gold; the tendency to state large sweeping insights about life in deceptively simple terms.)

You may want to tell students: "From among the poems printed here, choose for each poet the one poem that seems to you to be most essentially Dickinson or Frost or Brooks—that makes you hear the poet's distinctive personal voice. Choose a poem that you would recognize as Dickinson or Frost or Brooks even if the poet's name were not attached to it and even if you were hearing it or reading it for the first time. Then try to explain why you identify it with the author."

Emily Dickinson: The Poet's Voice 794

PERSPECTIVES—DICKINSON: THE POET AS RECLUSE

The enigmatic real person behind Dickinson's cryptic and provocative poems continues to agitate today's critics and fellow poets. Modern revisions of the traditional picture of Emily Dickinson as an eccentric recluse approach the issue from widely differing perspectives. We may think of the poet as a young woman who was ambitious but whose growing isolation was imposed on her by social circumstances represented by a narrow-minded conventional father. In a review of Cynthia Griffin Wolff's *Emily Dickinson* (*The New Republic*, March 2, 1987), Mary Jo Salter says that Dickinson was frustrated "by the contradiction between the fine education her father had offered her at Mount Holyoke and the purely domestic life he expected her to take up on her return home. Reading Wolff's extensive excerpts from Edward Dickinson's acerbic, narrow-minded essays on woman's place . . . one can well imagine the ambition of a young woman—who happened to be both a literary genius and a devoted daughter—to prove her worth quite publicly."

Alfred Kazin in "The Haunted Chamber. Reconsideration: Emily Dickinson, 1830–1886" (*The New Republic*, June 23, 1986), describes the poet as isolated from society in a way not unusual in the old rural America but also as closer to nature than most moderns. "Intensely reflective on the immediacies of life and death (especially death)," Dickinson was "clearly the subject—above all to herself—of a certain enclosure. This died with the old rural America just as she was dying." Except for fifteen years when the family occupied another house, she lived for more than forty years in the same house and on its grounds. "Well into the twentieth century, her house was surrounded by red barns and extensive fields. Amherst was backed up by farm country on every side. One of the poet's essential activities was registering the effect of the 'blue' mountains surrounding her valley . . . the changing shades and weight of weather in every season, the light, the insects and snakes in her garden." Nature, not society, was "the most physical part of her life. Unlike us, who now know nature as a government park, a preserve, to enjoy on holiday, she had it every instant all around her. Nature was *the* event in her life, constant immitigable process in reality, the great process unrolling our dreamlike passage through existence." Dickinson was not a romantic or transcendentalist and thus "did not find God in Nature. She did not find Nature a consoling simile for His absence, or what she concluded was 'condensed presence.' God was a 'distant, stately lover.' He was one character in the eternal drama of things passing, life passing:

> I have a King, who does not speak—
> So—wondering—thro' the hours meek
>   I trudge the day away—"

Finally, we may think of Dickinson as a creative genius choosing her mission as a poet over a role in the outside world. In the essay on Dickinson in *On Lies, Secrets, and Silence* (Norton, 1979), Adrienne Rich says, "Probably no poet ever lived so much and so purposefully in one house; even, in one room. Her niece Martha told of visiting her in her corner bedroom on the second floor at 280 Main Street, Amherst, and of how Emily Dickinson made as if to lock the door with an imaginary key, turned, and said: 'Matty: here's freedom.' " According to Rich, Dickinson's "nonmarrying was neither a pathological retreat . . . nor probably even a conscious decision; it was a fact in her life as in her contemporary Christina Rossetti's; both women had more primary needs." Unlike Rossetti, "Dickinson did not become a religiously dedicated woman; she was heretical, heterodox, in her religious opinions, and stayed away from church and dogma. What, in fact, *did* she allow to 'put the Belt around her Life'— what *did* wholly occupy her mature years and possess her? For 'Whom' did she decline the invitations of other lives? The writing of poetry." "I have a notion that genius knows itself; that Dickinson chose her seclusion, knowing she was exceptional and knowing what she needed. It was, moreover, no hermetic retreat, but a seclusion which included a wide range of people, of reading and correspondence." In her "white-curtained, high-ceilinged room, a red-haired woman with hazel eyes and a contralto voice wrote poems about volcanoes, deserts, eternity, suicide, physical passion, wild beasts, rape, power, madness, separation, the daemon, the grave. Here, with a darning needle, she bound these poems — heavily emended and often in variant versions — into booklets, secured with darning thread, to be found and read after her death."

Emily Dickinson, "Ourselves were wed one summer—dear" 797

DISCUSSION STARTERS

You may want to read and discuss with your students "My Life had stood—a Loaded Gun" (J. 754), another much-discussed poem giving tantalizing hints of Dickinson's real or imaginary relationships with others.

Emily Dickinson, "Tell all the Truth but tell it slant" 798

MAKING CONNECTIONS—FOR DISCUSSION OR WRITING

For many readers, this poem is the key to the intentional obliqueness of Dickinson's poems. Dickinson votes for truth, but she says direct truth is "too bright" for human apprehension. Truth "must dazzle gradually" lest it blind us. Brooks also votes for truth, and she also knows that the truth can be overpowering. People are likely to shrink from the "fierce hammering / Of his firm knuckles." Frightened by the blinding flash of truth, people are likely to retreat into snug unawareness.

Emily Dickinson, "A Bird came down the Walk" 799

DISCUSSION STARTERS

In this poem, we can see typical garden scenes: the bird pulling up and eating a worm, beetles on the walkway, and butterflies. This was a scene Dickinson most likely saw every day—the commonplace. Yet she turns these small actions into a grander, almost mystical scene by describing the bird in quasi-human terms and transforming the sky into which he flies into a silver ocean. The commonplace is transformed into the extraordinary. Would your students stop to watch a bird, a squirrel—or, for that matter, pigeons or a stray dog? Why, or why not?

THE RECEPTIVE READER

1. "Too silver for a seam" reminds us that silver is so malleable that it does not show "seams" the way stone or wood would. (And when the sun

beams on metal, often our eyes close in a squint, fusing the different elements of what we see.) The ocean in which the bird "swims" is seamless and unsegmented—like time, like eternity. "Banks of Noon" may make us think of the passing high point of the day as if it were a river (with lazy, sun-drenched swimmers diving into the water the way butterflies glide into the air).

2. This bird is at the same time too real and too strange or alien to be superficially pretty? Though the way "he drank a Dew" might be considered cute in a different context, the fate of the angleworm and the rapidly shifting eyes looking out for danger keep the scene from becoming idyllic.

3. We usually think of birds pecking, instead of eating and drinking. Dickinson describes the bird as one that "ate" and "drank" and stopped to let a passing beetle go by, the way one pedestrian might step aside to let pass another. But the strange rapidly shifting beadlike eyes of the bird and its eating a "raw" angleworm remind us that it isn't human. Then again, its quick sense of danger makes us think of it as a fellow creature—to whom we might cautiously offer sustenance (a "crumb"). Ordinary boundaries between human beings and other creatures tend to become blurred here? After all, they are all God's creatures, and observing them might make us think about the wonder and mystery of life?

Emily Dickinson, "Because I could not stop for Death" 801

DISCUSSION STARTERS

Poet and critic Allen Tate has called this poem "one of the greatest in the English language." Dickinson takes a trip with Death, climbing into the hearse in the first stanza and driving slowly past the experiences of mortality in the ensuing lines. Death takes her right up to the grave—but only "pauses" there? Their real destination is "Eternity." Death is not so much to be feared as welcomed—it is a necessary rite of passage. Do religious people and people without strong religious beliefs have a basically different attitude toward death?

THE RECEPTIVE READER

1. Death doesn't seem frightening; rather he is a "kindly" gentleman who takes the speaker for a ride the way he might take a friend on a quiet ride to the country past "Fields of Gazing Grain." It is only right that she should "put away," or put aside, both labor and leisure for a visitor with such "Civility." Most people would find it hard to look at death in this accepting way. They are more likely to see death as something to fight against, as Dylan Thomas does in his poem "Do Not Go Gentle into That Good Night." One student wrote, "It would be lovely if I could maintain such an accepting attitude of quiet curiosity toward dying. She was a lucky woman." Dickinson seems to be quietly accepting death as a necessary stage in the journey toward the ultimate spiritual transformation that leads us "toward Eternity."

2. Readers usually associate school with learning and childhood, fields of grain with harvest, and the setting sun with aging and death. These are common associations, suggesting the cycle of life from childhood to death. The "swelling of the ground" that a freshly dug and filled-in grave makes isn't usually associated with "a house," yet it is going to be the dead person's abode until the final transformation on the Last Day?

Emily Dickinson, "I heard a Fly buzz—when I died" 802

PERSPECTIVES—AMBIGUITY IN "I HEARD A FLY BUZZ—WHEN I DIED"

Dickinson's poems are cryptic and elliptic rather than prosy and explicit. Key details in the poems may remain ambiguous, with critics accusing one another of misreading a poem, if not misunderstanding "the whole cast of Dickinson's mind." Thus Charles R. Anderson in *Emily Dickinson's Poetry: Stairway of Surprises* (Greenwood, 1960) claims that "I heard a Fly buzz" reports the final crisis in "flat domestic terms"—but in the poem the stillness in the room is like the momentous stillness before the upheaval of a storm? According to Anderson, the dying person "squandered" her last words "in distributing her 'Keepsakes,' trivial tokens of this life rather than messages from the other." However, this giving away of cherished items may instead be read as her disencumbering herself for the momentous final journey? According to Anderson, "The King witnessed in his power is physical death, not God"—but it is in decreeing death, as in creating life, that God manifests His truly awesome power?

THE RANGE OF INTERPRETATION

The fly in the room at the time of death is testimony to Dickinson's uncanny ability to place large metaphysical questions in the context of totally ordinary everyday reality. Before the days of insect sprays and sophisticated flytraps, it was perfectly natural that there should be flies in the room while a person was dying. At least it would seem natural to a poet who has no intention of turning death into a great melodrama, filtering out all that is ordinary and familiar. Many of the overtones and associations that the different critics respond to are quite compatible with this overall perspective: Flies *are* "petty irritabilities"; a fly *is* a reminder of man's final cadaverous condition"; a fly's buzz *is*, if not a "dear," then a familiar sound; the world does merely fade, instead of passing with a clash of cymbals and hosannahs of the hereafter; yes, the bluefly's "eggs *are* maggots."

What might be questionable is that Emily Dickinson "would abhor the blowfly as she would abhor the deathbed scene." The fly signals the turning point from life to death; the fly's buzz is "uncertain stumbling" just as the moment of dying might be sensed as the soul's "uncertain stumbling" toward whatever uncertain future? The buzzing comes between the dying person and the light, at the point when she "could not see to see." But there seems to be no sign of abhorrence or disgust on the poet's part: The fly is part of life, just as a butterfly is. The poet does not think in superficial categories that would classify a butterfly as beautiful and a fly as disgusting, or that would classify a bird as good and a snake as evil?

MAKING CONNECTIONS—FOR DISCUSSION OR WRITING

Robert Frost referred to Emily Dickinson as an "acute sensibilitist." Invite students to clarify this statement and to illustrate with examples from the poems "Apparently with no surprise," "Hope is the thing with feathers," and "The Soul selects her own Society."

Poems for Further Study 803

FOLLOW-UP—WORKING WITH THE POEMS (A DICKINSON READING)

You may want to stage an Emily Dickinson reading. Ask students to collaborate in selecting and presenting the poems for the reading. You may want to suggest that they group poems by theme—or that students each select a poem that means most to them personally. To set the tone for the reading, have students consider Northrop Frye's comments on the poet's "lively and exhilarating mind," her "wit and sharp perception," and her "energy and humor":

> What we find in Emily Dickinson's poetry, then, is a diffused vitality in rhythm and the free play of a lively and exhilarating mind, crackling with wit and sharp perception. . . . When the Civil War was beginning to force on America the troubled vision of its revolutionary destiny, Emily Dickinson retired to her garden to remain, like Wordsworth's skylark, within the kindred points of heaven and home. She will always have readers who will know what she means when she says: "Each of us gives or takes heaven in corporeal person, for each of us has the skill of life." More restless minds will not relax from taking thought for the morrow to spend much time with her. But even some of them may still admire the energy and humor with which she fought her angel until she had forced out of him the crippling blessing of genius.

(EXPLORING RECURRENT THEMES) One student wrote:

Emily Dickinson lived in relative literary obscurity largely because the philosophy, form, and feminism of her poems were revolutionary. She was far ahead of her time in examining these topics. Time has finally caught up with her ideas. In an age of transcendentalism she was an existentialist. In a time of even meter and exact rhyme, she relied on the subtleties of language. In face of the nineteenth-century preference for "proper women," she explored her own sensuality.

Recurrent Dickinsonian themes that students may begin to recognize include the intoxicated, exhilarated vision of immortality (214, "I taste a liquor never brewed"); the role of perception, of our angle of vision, in making reality seem either "common" or "divine" (526, "To hear an Oriole sing"); and the power of the imagination to transcend reality (1263, "There is no Frigate like a Book"). You may want to ask students to pair companion poems on similar themes, such as 67, "Success is counted sweetest," and 579, "I had been hungry, all the Years"—both of which deal with the way deprivation or denial intensifies yearning?

(FOCUS ON FORM) To Dickinson's early editors, the bare unadorned form of her poems and her idiosyncratic punctuation were a puzzlement. Besides her bold unusual images and her provocative personal perspective, her highly unorthodox punctuation helps define her personal voice. The dash (found in all the poems included here) gives her voice a questioning appeal? People pause in conversation because they've either forgotten what they were going to say or because they are privately reflecting on their next statement. Dickinson uses the dash, also, like a hand turning a page in a book—to introduce a new image. Several of the selections use exclamation points (249, 288, 526). These harken back to the voice that was prevalent in Dickinson's earliest, youthful poems—enthusiastic, eager, boldly romantic ("Wild Nights!" 249, "I'm Nobody!" 288, "No Sir!" 526).

MAKING CONNECTIONS—FOR DISCUSSION OR WRITING

You might want to suggest that students focus their library project on the current reevaluation of Dickinson's work in the light of feminist perspectives. For instance, the theme of sexuality in Emily Dickinson's poetry has been explored in Camille Paglia's "The Female Marquis de Sade of Amherst," in *Sexual Personae* (Yale UP, 1991). Albert Gelpi, in "Emily Dickinson and the Deerslayer" (*Shakespeare's Sisters: Feminist Essays on Women Poets*, eds. Sandra M. Gilbert and Susan Gubar, Indiana UP, 1979), raised the issue of "feminine" and "masculine" aspects of women poets:

> Until recently, women poets since Emily Dickinson have found themselves caught in the same quandary, and, in exchange for more public recognition, have chosen to repress the "feminine" or the "masculine" aspects of themselves. Some, such as Marianne

Moore and Elizabeth Bishop, tended to obscure or deflect passion and sexuality in favor of fine discriminations of perceptions and ideas. Others, such as Edna St. Vincent Millay and Elinor Wylie, took as their woman's strain precisely the thrill of emotion and tremor of sensibility which rendered them susceptible to the threats of the masculine "other." In the isolation of her upstairs bedroom, Emily Dickinson refused finally to make that choice; but in the first half of the century perhaps only H. D., especially in the great poems of her old age, committed head and heart, sexuality and spirit to the exploration of her womanhood: a venture perhaps made possible only through an expatriation from American society more complete than Gertrude Stein's or Eliot's or Pound's. However, in the works of poets as different as Sylvia Plath and Denise Levertov, . . . and, most importantly, I think, in the work of Adrienne Rich, women have begun exploring that mystery, their own mystery, with a new sense of calling and community. Sometimes ecstatically, sometimes angrily, sometimes in great agony of body and spirit, but always now with the sustaining knowledge that they are not living and working alone, that more and more women and a growing number of men are hearing what they say, listening to them and with them. Such a realization makes a transforming and clarifying difference in the contemporary scene. And it is an important aspect of Emily Dickinson's enormous achievement that she pursued the process of exploration so far and so long on her own.

Robert Frost: Poet and Persona 810

Robert Frost cultivated an apparent simplicity that led his readers to let down their guard—perhaps so that sudden flashes of fancy or insight could hit them the more strongly? In the first poem printed here, "The Tuft of Flowers," note the paradoxical coexistence of prosaic matter-of-factness ("I went to turn the grass"; "I listened for his whetstone") and the sudden live, provocative metaphor ("A leaping tongue of bloom"). Note the memorable exuberant phrase belying the calm, understated persona of the country sage: "sheer morning gladness at the brim." Much critical and biographical writing about Frost probes the passionate depths and the private demons beneath the often deceptively simple surface of his poems.

Robert Frost, "The Tuft of Flowers" 811

DISCUSSION STARTERS

Writing about Frost's poetry, Babette Deutsch in a single sentence used the words *homely*, *somber*, *fresh*, *intimate*, *sly*, and *wit*. Which of these labels seem applicable to this poem, and how?

Robert Frost, "Mending Wall" 813

PERSPECTIVES—"MENDING WALL" AND THE PSYCHOLOGY OF WALLS

"Mending Wall" is a prime example of Frost's gift for writing an apparently simple poem that turns out to be profoundly ambivalent. At the heart of "Mending Wall" may be our paradoxical wish to have both intimacy and individuality—to want to belong while at the same time being afraid of being hemmed in by a relationship of any sort—be it a marriage, participation in a neighborhood, or allegiance to a community. Psychologists have recognized the importance of "individuation," a process wherein a person develops his or her own unique personality separate and apart from others. Individuation requires boundaries. At the same time, however, psychologists also recognize the need for intimacy. It requires *removing* the boundaries, or walls, and becoming vulnerable to others. Finding balance between these two polarities requires the skill of an acrobat, and many suffer the scars from falling long emotional distances without a net. The Irish novelist Edna O'Brien (*Time and Tide*) describes the simultaneous humor and seriousness of battles over "walls":

> Two neighboring men, bachelors, battled daily over the course of a little stream that provided drinking for their animals. Each determined that it should be his, and sought to assert his ownership with ramparts of stone and felled logs. At night these would be taken away by one or the other, so that voices were raised, shovels were raised, blows were struck, and, in the end, a court case that followed provided our light entertainment for a month.
>
> —"Irish Eyes Unblinking," *Lear's*, September 1992)

DISCUSSION STARTERS

For your students, what are the associations and connotations of the words *border, boundary, frontier, wall, fence, limit, line of demarcation*? What images and memories does each word bring to mind? Do any of them have positive as well as negative connotations? How do your students react to signs that say "No Trespassing"? What is a "spite fence"? What was the history and symbolic meaning of the Berlin Wall? What walls "came tumbling down" in an old-time spiritual?

THE RANGE OF INTERPRETATION

While students will have their own images and associations for the word *wall*, the two critical readings tend to focus on the associations of "barrier" and "boundary." A boundary, as William Ward suggests, is a *necessary* "barrier that must exist" between one person and another "if the individual is to preserve his own soul," or independence. The first critics, Sohn and Tyre, however, feel that man erects these barriers because of a natural primitive darkness, a "primordial destructiveness in the heart of man." They feel that walls are obstructing and destructive, and we, knowing this, perpetually try to break down these barriers. Can your students see that there is something to be said on both sides—"Something there is that doesn't love a wall" and "Good fences make good neighbors"? People require both solitude and sociability in their lives to exist as healthy individuals? (One student noted indignantly that this was "fence sitting—Humpty Dumpty did it and look what happened!")

Robert Frost, "Design" 816

DISCUSSION STARTERS

The Darwinian view of nature as life feeding on other life to sustain itself made it very difficult for late-nineteenth-century and early-twentieth-century poets to maintain an idyllic view of nature. However, where Darwinians insisted that the wolf—and in this case, the spider—are not evil but are merely doing what they are by nature programmed to do, the poet in this poem cannot escape thinking of these natural processes in terms of "death and blight" and "darkness," with disturbing questions churning in his troubled mind like "the ingredients of a witches' broth." What poets do your students remember in whose poems nature seems overall a benign, healing influence? What poems do they remember in which poets express an intuitive sympathy and fellow feeling for the creatures of the natural world? Finally, what poems do they remember in which the poet seems obsessed or depressed by the predatory, destructive aspects of nature?

Ask your students: In this sonnet, what words and what keynote do the multiple rhymes tend to accentuate? (*White—blight—white—night* echo in the reader's mind.) Is there a conventional "turn" at the beginning of the sestet? (The poet here starts to spell out the disturbing questions raised by the sight of the predatory spider.) Is there a summing up or send-off in the final couplet? (Here the ultimate question is spelled out: Is the appalling carnage we observe in nature part of a divine—or diabolical—plan?)

THE RECEPTIVE READER

If we are inclined to agree with Sohn and Tyre, we are given ample evidence to do so. Students might feel that the details these critics focus on are less grotesque and frightening than, say, the nightmarish images contained in the war poems by Wilfred Owen or Emily Dickinson's buzzing fly. There is no melodramatic heightening here. But there is something shuddery about the dead pale white, drained of the true colors of burgeoning life? There is something gruesome and ironic about the dead wings reminding the poet of a "paper kite"? It is worth pointing out that Frost believed in form, in design—and the meticulously crafted design of this sonnet attests to this commitment. Wouldn't he have found it hard to accept the idea that what happened in nature around him happened without "design"? Or, if either there is no design or a "dark design," would he be left with a profound pessimism about the scheme of things?

Juxtapositions: Variations on a Theme

Robert Frost, "Nothing Gold Can Stay" 817
Linda Pastan, "Posterity" 818

DISCUSSION STARTERS

The leaf—the green leaf that is doomed to fade and wilt—is the key symbol in both poems. Frost reminds us that Eden was a garden or orchard, which offered for a time a setting of happiness and innocence, but which had to be left behind—just as the speaker in Pastan's poem had to leave behind the trees that for a time were a way of "beguiling" death, delaying its sure onset. Pastan makes the basic primordial rhythm of natural growth and decay more intensely personal as each tree stands for a child, whose burgeoning growing life for a time "reconciles" us to the certainty that eventually the golden sky of dusk will turn grey and snow will cover our tracks, obliterating any trace of our passing.

MAKING CONNECTIONS—FOR DISCUSSION OR WRITING

- Some of the features characteristic of Frost's poetry are also found in "Stopping by Woods" and in "Fire and Ice." Both poems are *understated*—almost casual or colloquial in tone and easy to grasp at the surface level. Yet they raise unanswered questions that have kept critics arguing. The woods are inviting, but the speaker has "miles to go." *Paradoxically*, death in the snow becomes beckoning, promising a respite from promises that may be hard to keep. Paradoxically, fire and ice, two opposing principles, serve equally well as destructive forces.
- Many students will recognize that Frost expresses a "dark," pessimistic view of life and Whitman an optimistic, life-affirming view. Frost's spider preys on other life, inspiring meditations on death and darkness. Whitman's spider becomes a metaphor for Whitman's soul, "tirelessly" launching forth "filament, filament, filament, out of itself," making bridges and working "till the gossamer thread you fling catch somewhere."

Poems for Further Study 818

Many of these poems, in the Frost manner, make us focus on a natural, realistic scene only to cause us to pause and reflect. Frost's voice usually maintains its cool New England reserve—even after picking all those nightmarish apples! "The Road Not Taken" might be called a quintessential Frost poem: The poet brings into focus a complicated choice (for instance, whether to join the throngs trying to prosper in business or to take the "less-traveled" road of the creative artist or poet). Frost sees this choice in terms of a striking, "basic" metaphor anchored in age-old common human experience —the branching off of the two diverging roads. The common indecisions, backslidings, and detours (as in Frost's own early life) are filtered out. The metaphor does dramatize the essential: As we look back at some basic existential choice, we realize that it "has made all the difference."

Poems that hint at Frost's darker broodings include "Acquainted with the Night" and "Once by the Pacific." The solitary nightwalker familiar with "saddest" scenes stops momentarily when from "far away" he hears an interrupted cry—but it is not the voice of someone familiar (and previously close to him?) to "call me back" or to "say good-bye." "Once by the Pacific" gives the reader an unromanticized view of nature: The menacing waters of the Pacific think of "doing something to the shore / That water never did to land before." The cliffs and their continental reinforcements had better be ready for "a night of dark intent." One student writes:

> The last lines of "Acquainted with the Night" culminate in paradox. The speaker sees "at an unearthly height, / One luminary clock against the sky," evoking the image of a bright, distant beacon or guide to an almost otherworldly future. Yet, at the same time, the "luminary clock" proclaims "the time was neither wrong nor right," as if to say there is no rhyme or reason, no predictable rhythm or logic to life's desolation, both within himself and outside himself in the impersonal city and its isolated, "saddest" inhabitants. The irony is that the human sadness and alienation described by Frost's series of negative images are "neither wrong nor right": they just *are*.

Robert Frost, "The Road Not Taken" 819

PERSPECTIVES—POET AND PERSONA IN "THE ROAD NOT TAKEN"

Critics have tried in various ways to probe beyond the persona they find in many of Frost's poems: the country sage placidly delivering homespun truths. They have tried to posit a poet behind the persona who is more uncertain, more searching, more ambivalent, more perturbed in the modern vein. Thus, Patrick F. Bassett (*Explicator*, quotes Frost as calling "The Road Not Taken" a "tricky poem—tricky." For Bassett, the poem's persona is disingenuous. The speaker in the poem "admits three times within six lines that the roads of life are the same, that they are indistinguishable: one is 'just as fair' as the other, they are 'worn really about the same,' and each 'equally lay.' Thus there are no real forked roads in life, no real choices in life." However, Frost's readers "would like to believe in a world of clear, forked-road choices." The persona in the poem therefore obliges—telling the "lie" that the readers want to hear—although even then only "ages and ages hence" when he is very old—prone to rationalize, or near senility, and stuttering: "and I / I took the one less traveled by . . ." Whereas "Frost the poet may be predisposed to modern truths," the persona in the poem "seeks a direction but discovers and speaks only a lie."

MAKING CONNECTIONS—FOR DISCUSSION OR WRITING

Frost is one of the most written-about poets. Is he an example of the alleged tendency of contemporary American culture to first create heroes and then to destroy them? How much of the current writing about Frost is exposé?

Gwendolyn Brooks: Commitment and Universality 824

Gwendolyn Brooks became one of the most fiercely proud, powerful poetic voices of a new black consciousness. In her autobiography *Report from Part One: An Autobiography*, published in 1972, Brooks writes,

> There is indeed a new Black today. He is different from any the world has known. He's a tall-walker. Almost firm. By many of his own brothers he is not understood. And he is understood by no white. Not the Wise white; not the Schooled white; not the Kind white. Your least prerequisite toward an understanding of the new Black is an exceptional Doctorate which can be conferred only upon those with the proper properties of bitter birth and intrinsic sorrow. I know this is infuriating, especially to those professional Negro-understanders, some of them so very kind, with special portfolio, special savvy. But I cannot say anything other, because nothing other is the truth.

Gwendolyn Brooks, "We Real Cool" 825

DISCUSSION STARTERS

What does it mean to be "cool"? Can a person be "cool" and still be a good student? Can a person be "cool" and hold a steady job? Can a person who doesn't do drugs be "cool"? Does a person have to be black to be "cool"? How old can a person be and still be "cool"?

THE RECEPTIVE READER

Most students will recognize the young people in this poem— whether as peers, as former peers, or as young people from the other side of the tracks. They "Left school"—how horrendous is the dropout rate in the high schools your students attended? How much "lurking" and loitering is there? How much violence is there? (Do people "Strike straight"?) What today has taken the place of the gin in the poem? The poet does not preach, moralize, or offer a sociological commentary. She does not point the finger or place blame. (Even the term *sin*, echoing a preacher's vocabulary, seems to be used ironically and at any rate does not serve as the occasion for a sermonette.) There is a tragic starkness about the poem—we watch these young people helplessly, much as we might want to help?

Gwendolyn Brooks, "Hunchback Girl: She Thinks of Heaven" 826

DISCUSSION STARTERS

Historically, attitudes toward people with disabilities have run the gamut from shunning them as unwanted reminders of life's vicissitudes to a special identification with them as challenged and struggling fellow humans. Which of these two opposed impulses is stronger in our society today? (What are the teachings of religion on this subject, and do we heed them?) You may want to have your students cluster the term disabled to see what changing attitudes and associations the term brings into play today.

THE RECEPTIVE READER

1. The girl copes with her disability by distancing herself from the emotional pain. She must put artificial guards upon the heart, to curb her natural impulse to reach out to others—out of fear of being rejected or ridiculed. She cannot meet people's eyes directly but must "look / A little to the left." Her studied pretense of casualness ("scholarly nonchalance"), her aversion of her eyes from others' stares, and the "guards upon the / Heart" are all defenses against a callous world.

2. The word *marvelous* is ambiguous because we can marvel at what is miraculous and beautiful but also at what is monstrous. There may be a bitter irony in the use of the word here to describe the gaping of people at a disabled fellow human being. The girl is stared at (or marveled at) in superstitious fear instead of arousing wonder and sympathy as a unique and precious person?

3. Although the physical heart is convoluted with its elaborate arrangement of tubes and valves, and although the girl's physical body is irregular, she has a capacity for love as direct as other people with more perfect bodies. However, there may be a larger irony: The yearning of the girl for a transformation where everything is straight, uncoiled, proper, and regular is intense, and yet it may be a mirage, since life will always have its crooked byways and paradoxical limitations? The feelings of the heart can never be coerced into a straight, regular, path, like a column of numbers?

4. We may set up ideals of "straightness," harmony, and order, but these are mental constructs that do not agree with the complications and detours of life?

THE PERSONAL RESPONSE

How much do the readers' responses to this poem depend on the strength of their religious faith? How many of your students can identify with the following lines from one student's re-creation, trying to move to the essence of the poem?

> Father, my Father, surely
> you have prepared for me
> a place
> where I shall walk straight
> and be redeemed

Gwendolyn Brooks, "Piano after War" 827

DISCUSSION STARTERS

The interlaced rhymes in this finely crafted traditional sonnet are only half-rhymes (*fingers/pink/hungers/thank*)—perhaps a hint that the piano music in this poem will not be perfectly harmonious and in tune. What is the rest of the rhyme scheme? Are there lines that are near-perfect iambic pentameter? Are there others that go against the grain?

THE RECEPTIVE READER

1. The "old hungers" are for that richer glowing world of beauty and elevated, ennobling feeling created by traditional art and music, filling us with "proud delight" and giving us "musical joy." In times when both piano and pianist may be buried under the debris of war, that art lover's world may seem dead and in its coffin—along with other luxuries that war destroys or makes seem irrelevant. "After war," the piano music may start up again, trying to revive the past splendor and "glory." But as the musician tries to "rejuvenate a past," we may be a prey to mixed feelings—as if the experience were merely a kind of afterglow, like the reflected glow after sunset that sometimes "warms the west."

2. The "But . . ." that starts the sestet is true to the traditional form in making the sonnet "turn" from the attempt to recapture the glow and glory of the past. The music is not strong enough to drown out the cries of the "bitter dead" that suddenly well up. And the concluding couplet drives home the major theme of the poem: "Culture" cannot make up for the ravages of war. The speaker's eye, just beginning to soften and "thaw" under the influence of the music, again turns to ice. The temporarily softened face will again turn to stone.

3. Some students may be taken by surprise "suddenly" as the poem turns; however, it does give clues early on that the music isn't all a "golden rose." The word *clever* is used twice, bringing to mind someone too deliberate and designing in displaying her jewelry and her talent? To "beg glory"

from the "willing keys" sounds somewhat too precious. (And the evening was "snug"—too comfortable and cozy?)

Gwendolyn Brooks, "Mexie and Bridie" 828

DISCUSSION STARTERS

In this poem, the innocence and solemn play-acting of the children for a time triumph over whatever forces may be impoverishing their environment or endangering their future. Can we today still delight in the innocence of the tiny tea-party and the fine ladies "Tea-ing" among the ants and birds? Or are these little girls playing with toys and acting out roles that will restrict their possibilities in adulthood?

Gwendolyn Brooks, "The *Chicago Defender* Sends a Man to Little Rock" 829

DISCUSSION STARTERS

How real for your students today is the rhetoric of the Civil Rights movement? How many have read or listened to one of the speeches of Martin Luther King, Jr.? What impressed them or perturbed them in Spike Lee's *Malcolm X*? What milestones and crucial confrontations like the one that occasioned this poem do they know about?

THE RECEPTIVE READER

1. For a long stretch in this poem, we do not see the hate-filled faces of bigots protecting their turf; we do not see the cross burners, the racist sheriffs with their police dogs, that we might expect. Nor do we see the outside troublemakers and "commies" that the local mythology of the die-hard segregationists had created. Instead, the mock-naive persona of the reporter for many lines marvels at the ordinariness of this American town and its people. This is the "biggest News." This reporter does not go for the sensational angle or the preachy editorializing. The "I" in the poem (and this is already a clue to the stance of the poet) is first of all interested in people as people. Here they are—the do-it-yourselfers, the churchgoers, the baseball fans, the lovers of classical music, the lovers. It is in this ordinary setting that racism in all its ugliness and brutality rears its head. If we don't understand that much, perhaps we will never understand and successfully combat racism.

2. The religious references at the end of the poem take the poem beyond the level of a merely human drama. The tricks that humans "play before high heaven" do indeed (as Shakespeare's Isabella says in *Measure for Measure*) make the angels weep. The gallant children running the gauntlet of brutish harassment become saintly—"bright Madonnas." The townspeople become like Judas, who connived in the lynching of Jesus.

3. In a poem full of outrage and accusation, the final weighty charge—of the unreconstructed lynch mentality of the segregationists—might have been anticlimactic or might have been lost in the shouting. This is a poem that has been read by a million people and that reverberates long after the dutifully outraged editorials of the liberal newspapers have been forgotten.

Poems for Further Study 832

You may want to choose one of these poems to highlight characteristic or recurrent features of Brooks' poetry. For instance, "The Boy Died in My Alley" focuses on a single haunting incident, with the dead boy becoming representative of martyred youth and with the poet feeling implicated, responsible, and yet helpless to undo what is done. The balladlike form helps reduce a situation to its essentials and to its basic human meaning. The refrainlike repetitions drive home the basic elements of the situation: "the boy died in my alley. . . . was dying in your alley . . . is dead and in your alley"; "I have known this boy . . . I have known this boy . . . But I have known this boy"; "I have always heard . . . I have always heard." Key ideas are presented in cryptic, paradoxical formulations: The speaker feels guilty of the boy's murder ("I killed him") because of her "knowledgeable unknowing"—knowing in a general way what was going on, but not wanting to know, and not knowing someone that perhaps she should have known and could have helped? The solemn significance and universal relevance of the poem are enhanced by the religious allusions—seeing the boy "Crossed" or crucified, but not taking him down from his cross; the boy crying out, like Jesus on the cross, "Father!" (but also, unlike Jesus, adding "Mother! / Sister! / Brother!").

MAKING CONNECTIONS—FOR DISCUSSION OR WRITING 837

An additional choice for a library research project might be the role of religion in the black community in which she grew up and the role of religion and religious allusions in her poetry.

Chapter 24 PERSPECTIVES The Age of Theory 846

Scholars and artists thrown together are often annoyed at the puzzle of where they differ. Both work from knowledge, but I suspect they differ most importantly in the way their knowledge is come by. Scholars get theirs with conscientious thoroughness along projected lines of logic; poets theirs cavalierly and as it happens in and out of books. They stick to nothing deliberately, but let what will stick to them like burrs where they walk in the fields.

ROBERT FROST

To a considerable extent, in American universities critical affiliations like new historicism or deconstruction or now even Marxism are not linked to systematic thought. They are like our political parties, confusing to Europeans because they are important but ideologically evasive and inconsistent.

STEPHEN GREENBLATT

This is the age of literary theory—among poets, critics, and teachers, but not necessarily among general readers or our students. The idea of multiple conflicting theoretic perspectives may be new (and unsettling) for many of them. You may want to stage a *role-playing* exercise where different students choose and impersonate the critics or poets who are presenting their views on poetry in this chapter. Ask each student to present key ideas of the chosen author to the class. Can they bring the ideas and perspectives represented here to life? You may want to have the planning for these presentations done in small groups. (One class staged a tea party at which poets appeared and held forth on the subject of poetry.)

Katha Pollitt, "Anne Sexton: The Death Is Not the Life" 847

DISCUSSION STARTERS

Katha Pollitt reviews a much-discussed biography of the poet Anne Sexton in this essay. Written by Diane Wood Middlebrook, the biography begins with the evocative question, "How did a mad housewife become a star?" Do the media—including books, television shows, movies—exploit mental illness and suicide for sensational effect? Does a famous writer (now dead) have a right to privacy?

THE RECEPTIVE READER

The biographer's use of the psychiatrist's tapes is controversial because the subject of the biography, Anne Sexton, is dead and had no say in the decision. "Thunderous condemnation" greeted that event, an event precipitated when "Sexton's first long-term psychiatrist" allowed Sexton's biographer "access to tapes of all his therapy sessions with Sexton." Despite the fact that Sexton's daughter and literary executor then gave the biographer permission to use quotations from the tapes, the response to these actions has been extremely critical. The critical response also reflects that doctor-patient communication (particularly in psychiatry) is supposed to be confidential, and in this case it is hard not to conclude that Sexton's rights as a patient were violated. Further questions need to be answered before a definitive response can be had. Was Sexton aware of the existence of the tapes? Did she assume they had been destroyed at some point? Did Sexton, knowing she was going to commit suicide, attempt to protect herself from future biographers by destroying, say, old letters?

Sexton suffered from mental illness for much of her life; in 1956 she began seeing the psychiatrist (who later released the tapes) "after the first of what would be many breakdowns and suicide attempts." The drugs prescribed to control Sexton's mental illness profoundly affected her ability to work as a poet. Pollitt notes that Sexton succeeded as a poet, despite "seemingly insuperable obstacles," not least of which was "treatment with mind-numbing drugs like Thorazine, which was first prescribed in 1964 and whose side effects she struggled against for the next eight years." Of Thorazine, Sexton herself said that it was "supposed to make the rhymer go away"; unfortunately that is precisely what it did. As a result, Sexton would go off her medication in order to regain the creative urge. Once off the Thorazine Sexton would inevitably have to endure "the consequent mania." Sexton was thus in a terrible position: in order to write she would have to cease taking her medication, but when she ceased taking her medication her ability to write would be compromised by the subsequent cycles of mania and despair.

Alfred Kazin, "Dylan Thomas and Romanticism" 851

DISCUSSION STARTERS

Romantics are stereotypically assumed to be more prone than others to act out their feelings. Was Thomas a "fake romantic"? How do you and your students feel about the "histrionic" streak in some poets—the element of showmanship that was especially strong with Dylan Thomas?

J. R. Watson, "A Close Reading of G. M. Hopkins' 'God's Grandeur' " 853

DISCUSSION STARTERS

Does the New Critical agenda for reconciling or integrating "intellect and emotion" have meaning for your students? Can they think of people who are overly intellectual and others who seem overly emotional?

THE RECEPTIVE READER

Watson finds that the emphatic word *charged* in the weighty opening sentence carries two meanings: " 'loaded,' and 'full of electricity' as a battery is when it has been charged." This implies an image of a world that is "electric" or electrified with God's grandeur as well as heavy and full with its weight, or impact. As the critic points out, this electrical image becomes an extended or sustained metaphor carried into the next line, where Hopkins uses the image of the foil that when shaken reflects light in lightning-like flashes. Here the critic as insider quotes the poet directly: "I mean foil in its sense of leaf or tinsel . . . shaken gold foil gives off broad glares like sheet lightning, and this is true of nothing else, owing to its zigzag dints and creasings and network of small many- cornered facets, a sort of fork lightning too." Many readers may need help from the critic's knowledge of a different time and setting to understand the phrase "ooze of oil." It refers to the rich squeezings of olive oil in countries where the olive trees yield rich harvests. (In our modern world "oozing" oil might conjure up images of an oil spill?) The critic becomes a trusty guide not only to the meaning but especially also the *feel* of words, as he makes us sense, for instance, the heavy treadmill-like plodding or thumping of the insistent repetition in "have trod, have trod, have trod."

H. Edward Richardson and Frederick B. Shroyer, "Freudian Analysis and Yeats' 'Second Coming' " 855

DISCUSSION STARTERS

Freudian terms like *libido*, *id*, *ego*, and *superego* were once the small change of cocktail party conversation. In the meantime, Freud and his ideas have come in for much revisionist thought. What if anything do Freud and Freudian ideas mean to your students? Have they encountered evidence of the current hostility toward the Freudian tradition on the part of feminists and others?

THE RECEPTIVE READER

In the Freudian reading, the threatening anarchy "loosed upon the world" is the feverish, chaotic state of the individual psyche unable to master the unconscious sexual impulses (the "blood-dimmed tide") mirrored in both Yeats' dreams and poetry. The falcon would be the rebellious id that no longer heeds the call of the falconer, or ego? *Ceremony* would refer to actual marriage; "the worst" would refer to an actual temptress. Personal guilt and shame would replace pessimism about the future of the world as dominant attitudes in the poem.

Richard Foerster, "Message and Means in Jane Flanders' 'The House That Fear Built' " 858

DISCUSSION STARTERS

Is the 1943 uprising in the Warsaw ghetto forgotten? What happened there? How was it part of a larger pattern of deportation and genocide? The poet keeps saying "I am (the boy, the soldier, the woman)" when identifying in turn with different characters in the picture. Where are you and your students in this picture?

THE RECEPTIVE READER

Foerster notes that Flanders "uses traditional rhymes to overthrow tradition, to give us a glimpse of the deterioration of order. Against the ironic counterpoint of the innocent children's rhyme, Flanders unfolds a widening perspective of the horrors of twentieth-century war." Flanders begins her poem with the happy beat of "The House That Jack Built" and an apparently innocent, nonthreatening picture of "the boy with his hands raised over his head." Foerster comments that such an opening lulls the reader into expecting something upbeat, playful, or whimsical. Because of such expectations the reader's shock is magnified when the complete poetic picture is revealed. As Foerster says, "The skipping rhythm introduced in the first stanza leads us to believe that the boy's arms might be raised in play. By the poem's end, however, we realize he is part of a gruesome, complex tableau of the Warsaw Ghetto Uprising of the spring of 1943."

Foerster identifies the old woman as "the onlooking crone, who in traditional nursery rhymes shakes out the world's woes from her bedding." However, "In Flanders' modern version" of this nursery rhyme staple, "the crone cannot absolve herself of complicity by pretending not to understand the nature of the tragedy occurring beneath her window." And, at the end of his article, Foerster makes a fine modern analogy between the crone "attending to her domestic chores but also hiding behind the sheets of a newspaper, the way we overlook the world from our armchairs while muttering 'What's this?' when certain headlines catch our eye."

MAKING CONNECTIONS—FOR DISCUSSION OR WRITING

Flanders uses the means of simple nursery rhyme to convey the message of the brutality of war and the almost universal complicity in the perpetuation of the horror. Denise Levertov's poem "What Were They Like" uses a deceptively simple set of questions as her vehicle for a similar indictment of complicity. Both poets seem to imply that a great show of emotion and self-righteous rhetoric would be impious here, irreverent toward the dead.

Adelaide Morris, "A Feminist Reading of Emily Dickinson" 861

DISCUSSION STARTERS

Morris examines Emily Dickinson's letters and poems to a never-identified "Master" and her "surprisingly, even suspiciously similar" letters and poems to her sister-in-law who lived next door, "across the lawn." Do students think a traditional or conventional vocabulary of love can be adapted for use in a gay or lesbian relationship? Or does a new language have to be invented?

THE RECEPTIVE READER

Morris depends heavily on the internal evidence of the letters and poems of Emily Dickinson. Of the writings addressed to her "Master," letters, "supplemented by dozens of poems," survive. As for her sister-in-law, a veritable bonanza survives: "154 extant notes and letters and 276 identifiable poems and poem fragments." Nonetheless, the written record is "probably a mere fraction of a lifetime's whole." As for biographical data, Morris has nothing to work with: "The biographical details are gone: we don't know who her 'Master' was, we know almost nothing of her sensual experience, we don't even know if those she loved loved her back." Dickinson's rhetoric of love for men and women is "surprisingly, even suspiciously similar," as if, Morris says, "Dickinson were writing to the Master and Sue out of some peculiarly elliptic book of pattern letters." Rough drafts of the letters survive; these reveal both correspondences to be "highly compressed and heavily revised." Dickinson writes with passion to both the "Master" and Sue, "both are passionately solicited, courted with imagery chosen to convey their magnetic pull. Again and again she describes herself as bewitched, overwhelmed." "The most revealing recurrence," Morris notes, "is the linked imagery of sun, storms, volcanos, and wounds that she uses in both sets of letters and poems." Indeed, there even exist love poems "with alternate sets of pronouns," and Morris cites the example of poem 494: "Going to Him! Happy letter!" begins the male version, and the female version opens with "Going—to—Her! / Happy—Letter!"

The differences, masked by the similarities in the letters and poems, in the two kinds of relationships, have to do with love. Morris says: "The kind of love Dickinson desires and develops with a woman is very different from the love she desires and develops with a man." But because there exists no "book of pattern letters" to use for love between two women, Dickinson had to use the standard model, that used for love between a woman and a man. "Western traditions offer no developed discourse for love between women and thus, in need of a precedent, Dickinson may have used conventional romantic rhetoric in the letters and poems to Sue." Despite the similarity in the written record, Dickinson's relationship to the "Master" is subordinate: "The structures of the Master's world are predominantly vertical and its dramas are largely dramas of positioning: the prostration of the woman, the exaltation of the man." Dickinson's relationship with Sue is "horizontal, not a universe but a neighborhood. Its dramas detail the flexible push and pull, the coming and going of those who live day to day, side by side." Finally there are differences in style, on the one hand the "abstract dignity of stasis in the Master material," and on the other hand the "scrappy spontaneity" in Dickinson's messages to her sister-in-law.

Geoffrey Hartman, "Deconstructing Wordsworth's 'A Slumber Did My Spirit Seal' " 864

DISCUSSION STARTERS

Of the various critical perspectives discussed in this chapter, which make the most sense to your students, and which the least?

THE RECEPTIVE READER

In happy times, the speaker in the poem gave no thought to anything fearful or sorrowful: youth and beauty and innocence seemed beyond the reach of envious Time. Unfortunately for the speaker, real life catches up to him with a vengeance in the second stanza: the young woman has died and lies buried. Buried in the earth, the beloved woman is no more now than "rocks, and stones, and trees." Perhaps that the earth continues in its "diurnal course" despite the speaker's profound loss, might be read as affirmation—but more likely as resignation. That the speaker grieves still can be seen in his lament on the irrevocable loss of all vital energy and motion.

Regarding the lightening effect, Hartman says: "For the girl is still, and all the more, what she seemed to be: beyond touch, like a star, if the earth in its daily motion is a planetary and erring rather than a fixed star, and if all on this star of earth must partake of its sublunar, mortal, temporal nature." Wordsworth's speaker says, "She seemed a thing that could not feel / The touch of earthly years," and Hartman finds the literal truth of this in the woman's forever young status. At this point, Hartman uses the German word, *aufgehoben*, to describe the point he is trying to make. *Aufgehoben* is the note the last stanza closes on, and it is an "elegiac," and "elated" note. What has been purged by the poem "is a series of flashy schematisms and false or partial mediations: artificial plot, inflated consolatory rhetoric, the coercive absolutes of logic or faith." Wordsworth, then, has allowed "concreteness" and the emotions ("shock, disillusion, trauma, recognition, grief, atonement") into the poem. He has not allowed (has "purged") greeting card sentiments or religious platitudes to detract from the sincerity of his poem.

Juxtapositions: The Range of Interpretation 866

Margaret Dickie, "Sylvia Plath and Pregnancy"
Peter Porter, "On Sylvia Plath's 'Mirror' "
Damian Grant, "Sylvia Plath's Mirror Image"
Laurence Lerner, "Plath's Mirror"
Katha Pollitt, "Plath and the Critics"
Sandra M. Gilbert, "Plath and the Divided Literary Tradition"

THE RECEPTIVE READER

Dickie counteracts the stereotype of the pessimistic, depressed poet by calling attention to Plath's humor or wit, as in the "Metaphors" poem, with its "playful regard for the grotesque quality of pregnancy." However, Porter strikes a more familiar note by looking at poems like "Mirror," where "once more death has all the best parts." In these poems, images (like the terrible fish rising to the surface in "Mirror") come before the reader like ominous, inescapable messengers in Greek tragedy, "wearing their proud colors of destruction." For Grant, Plath's mirror is a "characteristically schizoid" image; a central theme in Plath's poetry is the "divided self," "the self which is alienated, oppressed, disembodied, dissolved." However, Lerner harks back to

Dickie's recognition of Plath's wit: Where Porter sees a grim image of a woman seeing "not only her own agitation but the fate which awaits her," Lerner sees as "a witty poem," in which there is "an extra irony" in the image of a woman "not yet 30" obsessing over her potential future as an old woman. Katha Pollitt observes that the critics seem to be paying less attention to Plath's poetry and more attention to the issues that seem "pertinent to her case." These issues, for which "close reading" of the poetry is apparently not required, include: "Is life worth living?" and "Is madness admirable?" and "Are men the enemy?" Sandra M. Gilbert, like Pollitt, attempts to place Plath in critical perspective. The poet was "an extraordinarily conscious and at least semi-self-conscious student of the peculiarly new literary tradition in which she quite pivotally participated."

Poets on Poetry

Dylan Thomas, "Notes on the Art of Poetry" 869

THE RECEPTIVE READER

The poet claims he early "fell in love" with words. He loved nursery rhymes and ballads and verses that appeal first of all to the ear. He didn't care, as a young child, what the words meant; he loved their *sounds*. He remained faithful as an adult to this love, finding he could marshal words and make them do his bidding—"beat them now and then." The poet's own acute auditory imagination and acute sense of hearing show when he makes us listen to the "rattle of milkcarts, the clopping of hooves," the "fingering of branches on a window pane." Thomas is enchanted with the richness and copiousness of language; he loves sentences in which words come tumbling down in unchecked abandon—whether they be words for "the gusts and grunts and hiccups and heehaws of common fun" or for the large abstractions like "love and pity and terror and pain and wonder."

MAKING CONNECTIONS—FOR DISCUSSION OR WRITING

Taking our clue from Dylan Thomas' account of his love affair with the "shape and shade and size and noise" of words, we can see (or hear) that these poems are alive with sounds. In "Fern Hill," for instance, we hear the poet "hail" (Time lets him); he "sings" (and so do the calves); the foxes "bark" clear and cold; the sabbath "rang" slowly; "tunes" came from chimneys; the green stable "whinnies." We hear all these things (and many other sounds) as Time "in all his tuneful turning" holds the poet green and dying and singing against the chains of the sea. In "In My Craft or Sullen Art," Thomas labors by a light that sings, not, as he notes, for the "strut and trade of charms," but for the lovers beneath a moon that "rages." The echoing effect of extended repetition is the signature of a poet who loves the sound of his own words, as with the recurrence of the lines "Do not go gentle into that good night" and "Rage, rage against the dying of the light" in the villanelle.

Richard Wilbur, "Letting a Poem Find Its Form" 870

THE RECEPTIVE READER

Wilbur challenges the assumption that poets who use traditional forms force the content of their poems into ready-made patterns by describing the process he undergoes when he writes poetry. Wilbur has never set out to produce heroic couplets or a sonnet, but, somehow, during the process of writing the proper form is achieved: "A poem is something which finds out what it has to say, and in the process discovers the form which will best stress its tone and meaning." *Ad hoc* means for this specific purpose, for this case only. Wilbur combines *ad hoc* with *formally* to describe his method of "letting the words find what line lengths seem right to them." This will "result in a stanza of some sort," a stanza that "will still be flexible enough to permit the argument to move and speak as it likes." Theoretically, no two of Wilbur's poems would be the same since the form of them all is *ad hoc*. Such a condition would also rule out any sort of deliberate formal precedent, since Wilbur would not begin the writing of a poem by concentrating on what form the poem will take.

Audre Lorde, "Poems Are Not Luxuries" 871

THE RECEPTIVE READER

Poetry is "the way we help give name to the nameless so it can be thought." It is women's way of tapping "unexamined and unrecorded" resources of feeling and creativity that have remained hidden and unrecognized while the traditional European reliance on ideas rather than feeling held sway. In the traditional European mode of thought of the "white fathers," life is viewed only as a problem to be solved. Lorde calls on women to cherish their feelings and respect their hidden sources of power where true knowledge and lasting action reside. Such empowerment comes from seeing life in terms of the non-European model, seeing life as "situations to be experienced and interacted with." The hobgoblins of "nightmare and weakness" then subside. Poetry, therefore, is not a luxury for women; it the medium of "our hopes and dreams toward survival and change." It is the essential starting point for the journey from experience to language, from language to idea, and from idea to action.

MAKING CONNECTIONS—FOR DISCUSSION OR WRITING

Lorde asserts that the "woman's place of power within each of us is neither white nor surface; it is dark, it is ancient, and it is deep." The poet's power, the "I" in "Coal" "is the total black" being spoken from the deepest place known, the "earth's inside." As she reflects in the poem, "There are many kinds of open." There are diamonds, open; adders, breeding openly; young sparrows, bursting open shells. All of these different types of open come from the daily experiences of life Lorde speaks of in "Poems Are Not Luxuries." The experiences find "voice" and open a woman's consciousness, when the "sound comes into the word." Not all words are nice or pretty. As she says, "some words bedevil me." But they are open, nonetheless. They are not "stapled closed" as a result of handed-down fears or the old European mode of thinking, nor by the "white father's" distorted definition of poetry as a "desperate wish for imagination without insight."

Diane Wakoski, "On Experience and Imagination" 873

THE RECEPTIVE READER

Wakoski writes to invent a more colorful life for herself—a life, as she puts it, with people who are "more interesting and mysterious" living within its pages. She is most revealing when she states, "Perhaps I have always been the isolated lonely person living around dull or sad people, and the poems were a way of inventing myself into a new life." Paradoxically, however, stretching and dramatizing experience is her way of opening up life to exploration, to seeing the world from many different angles, searching "to understand the world truly." Wakoski believes that the poet has the same common experiences everyone else does but that he or she must find a way of exaggerating that experience through the imaginative act of creation. To break through the crust of the ordinary, she fantasizes "surrealist experiences" like "the girl riding naked on a zebra wearing only diamonds." This exaggeration makes life seem new and mysterious, enabling her to see the world from fresh and different perspectives, being open to its contradictions.

Pablo Neruda, "Childhood and Poetry" 874

THE RECEPTIVE READER

Neruda seems to travel a different route that stresses unity and solidarity with others as they are. He writes "to feel the affection that comes from those whom we do not know, from those unknown to us . . . because it widens out the boundaries of our being, and unites all living things." Neruda's writing is an attempt to get closer to "people in prison, or hunted, or alone." These people may be sad, but they don't sound as though they're dull. They have most likely lived dramatized, exaggerated, perhaps surreal lives against a background of trouble and persecution in Third World nations. Through his childhood experience, the poet learned "that all of humanity is somehow together." As Neruda points out, this boyhood realization came back to him much later in his life, at a time when he was experiencing trouble and persecution. He compares the pinecone he left for the little boy to his poems— "resiny, earthlike, and fragrant." He leaves these at the door of many who are unknown to him ("in prison, or hunted, or alone") but in need of the hope his word-gifts bring.

CHAPTER 25 OTHER VOICES/OTHER VISIONS A Gathering of Poets

This chapter presents a mini-anthology of poems without editorial apparatus—for browsing, for unrequired reading, or for work in class. Selections cover the full range from the classic to the contemporary, with balanced representation of new poets, women writers, and poets representing a multicultural perspective. The following are capsule contexts and suggested questions for a sampling of poems that you may want to select for class discussion.

Aphra Behn, "Song" 881

PERSPECTIVES—APHRA BEHN: REREADING AN EARLY FEMALE POET

Aphra Behn is prominent among female writers of earlier centuries who have been rediscovered and revalued by feminist critics. Judith Kegan Gardiner pays tribute to Behn in "Liberty, Equality, and Fraternity: Utopian Longings in Behn's Lyric Poetry" (*Rereading Aphra Behn: History, Theory, and Criticism*, ed. Heidi Hutner, (UP of Virginia, 1993). Behn was "a poet of astonishing range and accomplishment," although her later reputation is "almost entirely as a playwright and pioneer novelist" and although "today's feminists prefer her vigorous polemics on behalf of herself and other women." Behn "awed men with her talent and fluency and inspired other women to write." Although couched in conventional language of heterosexual love, her poems reveal "a longing for community, for a society where the radical values of liberty, equality, and fraternity would be possible for women and defined in women's terms." Her "longings for a more just and fulfilling life" could not be realized within the social realities of Restoration England but "only in a coterie of fellow poets and a realm of poetry."

The "great power" of "Love in Fantastic Triumph Sat" derives "from the contrast between its painful and exaggerated sentiments and a controlled and orderly form that seems to accept this situation as proper, normal, perhaps even necessary." In this and other poems, Behn "depicts relationships of equality that degenerate, perhaps because it so hard for her to imagine reciprocity and equality in a society devoid of them." In its original context in a heroic drama written by Behn, this poem "is sung by the Queen of Spain, who is foolishly in love with a disdainful Moor who became her lover only for political reasons and who now rebuffs her. The song thus sets up Behn's goal of reciprocal emotion, indicated in meter and word patterning, against a context of power that vitiates reciprocity between men and women. Even though the woman is the active wooer and a queen, she is powerless against a foolish passion for a tyrannic man, and she thus colludes in the eroticizing of power on which this poem, and perhaps modern patriarchy, are based."

Chitra Divakaruni, "The Quilt" 888

Chitra Divakaruni was born in Calcutta in India, took a doctorate in English literature from Berkeley, and has published several volumes of poetry, including *Black Candle.* She has been fascinated with the "rich cosmopolitan mix" of contemporary America and with the way race, economics, sex, and gender shape our multicultural society. Her poems often focus on the problems of adjustment faced by immigrants from Asian Third World countries, who may be caught, for instance, between nostalgic dreams of the past and their Americanized children—sons "who refuse to run / the family store, daughters who date / on the sly."

SUGGESTED QUESTIONS

1. Why did the wife fail? What was expected of her? Who replaced her?

2. Is the speaker the granddaughter of this woman "who failed"? If so, what can we read into the reference to the second wife who was "wide-hipped / for boy-children"? If not, then what is the relationship of the speaker to the grandmother of whom "there are no pictures" and whose name nobody knows?

3. What does this poem tell you about cultural expectations? How does the quilt become symbolic?

T. S. Eliot, "The Love Song of J. Alfred Prufrock" 890

Eliot published "Prufrock" in England in 1917 and in America in 1920, causing such a stir of praise and disapproval that by 1922 he probably was the most discussed of living American poets. Eliot insisted that the poet must "be able to see beneath both beauty and ugliness; to see the boredom, and the horror, and the glory" of contemporary society. Prufrock's monologue was a classic statement of the disconnectedness and alienation that were to become a hallmark of much early-twentieth-century poetry.

SUGGESTED QUESTIONS

1. How do the opening images set the stage for the mood of the poem? How would you characterize the mood?

2. What allusions can you identify? What role do they play in the poem? What is the role of music, art, philosophy in this poem?

3. What role do women play in the poem—and in Prufrock's life?

4. What is the effect of juxtaposing the quotation from Dante with the poem itself?

5. What lines echo in the poem, and with what effect?

Thomas Hardy, "In Time of 'The Breaking of Nations' " 897

Thomas Hardy wrote the poem in 1915, during the early years of World War I. His title alludes to the biblical "Thou art my battle ax and weapons of war: for with thee will I break in pieces the nations, and with thee will I destroy kingdoms" (Jeremiah 51:20). The war was to lead to the breakup of the Austrian, Russian, and Turkish empires.

SUGGESTED QUESTIONS

1. How does the poem set up and reiterate the poet's perspective on war?

2. What images does the poet set up as the counterpoint to the bloody records or "annals" of war and the glories of the dynastic families that through the generations ruled over empires? What do the images have in common? What is the common pattern they establish? Would it matter if the order in which these images appear were reversed?

Theodore Roethke, "I Knew a Woman" 922

Theodore Roethke spent his childhood in the Saginaw Valley of Michigan, an area that he called "a wonderful place for a child to grow up in." His German-born grandfather and father had developed a large area of greenhouses, and farther out in the country stood the last stand of virgin timber in the valley as well a wild cut-over second growth timber. After 1941 Roethke began to experience recurring psychotic episodes, and his struggle with the illness became a major theme in his poetry.

SUGGESTED QUESTIONS

1. What is the range of metaphor in this poem? From what areas of experience does the poet draw his metaphors? (Do they go together?)

2. How serious or how facetious is this poem? Is the speaker in the poem too caught up in the physical dimension to do justice to the role the mind or the soul plays in love?

3. Does the form of the poem seem old-fashioned to you? What is the rhyme scheme in the second stanza, which uses full rhymes consistently? What half-rhymes or slant rhymes in the other three stanzas make them depart from the pattern of the model stanza?

Cathy Song, "Lost Sister" 928

Born in Honolulu, Cathy Song grew up in a small town on the island of Oahu. Her Korean grandmother arrived in Hawaii as a "picture bride" to marry a man she had never seen. Song has written about the Chinese laborers who came to "Gold Mountain" to build the Western railroad and many of whom "had always meant to go back." Her poems re-create the world of Chinatowns, with their odors of ethnic food and spices and with old-timers telling stories on street corners. She sympathizes especially with a younger generation trying to emerge from the "steamy cauldron" of the tradition-bound world of their elders. Her poems have been collected in *Picture Bride* (1983) and *Frameless Window, Squares of Light* (1988).

SUGGESTED QUESTIONS

1. What central conflict or dilemma is at the heart of this poem?

2. What role does the tradition of foot-binding play in this poem? Why has it become for feminists a symbol of centuries-old oppression?

3. What explains the ambivalent or mixed feelings in this poem about the other sister who traveled "across the ocean"? What did she gain? What did she lose? Where does she live?

4. How or why does the person addressed in this poem "need China"? How is she like and unlike her mother?

Wallace Stevens, "Anecdote of the Jar" 930

The poem says the jar "took dominion"—by its mere presence making the surrounding "slovenly wilderness" less wild. This is not some precious heirloom or an artist's masterpiece. It is just a jar that is "gray and bare" (just as the poet's stanzas are spare and unpretentious)—but that, nevertheless, like a piece of pottery found in a prehistoric tomb, testifies to the power of the human spirit to tame the wilderness. However, the modern critic, forever searching for hidden ironies undercutting apparent affirmations, does not necessarily buy into this art-triumphing-over-raw nature scenario. Critic Helen Vendler suggests that this poem is comic, each quatrain and its rhymes "formally inept and farcical, as though the American poet, vainly trying to integrate his stoneware 'urn' with his wilderness, could only do prosodic pratfalls, scrawls defacing the classic British quatrain form." In placing "a jar in Tennessee," Stevens exalts art over nature only to find that the jar does not really fit into this wild setting.

SUGGESTED QUESTIONS

1. What is the form of the quatrain, and how does Stevens deviate from it?

2. What for you are the larger symbolic meanings of the "jar" and the "wilderness." What could each symbolize? Which becomes dominant—which wins out?

3. In what ways do you think the jar "took dominion everywhere"? What is suggested by the sentence "It did not give of bird or bush"?

Wallace Stevens, "Thirteen Ways of Looking at a Blackbird" 930

Wallace Stevens said of the constructive power of poetry that it is "a violence from within that protects us from a violence without."

THE CREATIVE DIMENSION

Ask students to do their own "Ways of Looking at a Blackbird." Student-written examples:

Unvalued, misunderstood,
the blackbird circles and swirls
through our world.

With busy, watchful eyes, the blackbird
exists whether or not we understand—
or care.

Alfred Lord Tennyson, "Ulysses" 932

Tennyson wrote at a time when the British imperial glory of the Victorian age contrasted with the intellectual malaise brought on by the advent of Darwinism and religious doubt. Tennyson epitomized for many the gospel of striving, of noble effort (without particularly clearly defined specific goals), at a time when traditional values were beginning to cut loose from their traditional religious and ethical moorings.

SUGGESTED QUESTIONS

1. How much do you know about the hero of Homer's *Odyssey*? (His Greek name was Odysseus; the Romans later called him Ulysses.) What caused his wanderings? What places did he visit? What people and creatures did he encounter? What do you know about Circe, the Cyclops, the sirens? What do you know about his wife Penelope and his son Telemachus?

2. What kind of archetypal figure was Homer's hero? What was archetypal about his mythic voyage? How much of the traditional mythic hero do you recognize in this nineteenth-century poem? What attracted Tennyson to the subject of Ulysses? How does Tennyson reinterpret the legend of Ulysses?

Part Three DRAMA

THOUGHT STARTERS

Drama is one of the great performance arts. You may want to explore with your students starter questions like the following:

- Did you see live dramatic performances while in elementary or high school? What kind of performances were they—musicals? skits? popular drama? serious drama? What do you remember about these experiences?
- What is the difference between watching television or a movie and seeing a live performance?
- Did you ever participate in a dramatic production? What was your role? What did you get out of the experience?
- What has been your previous experience with Shakespeare? Did you read *Romeo* and *Juliet* or *Macbeth*? Did you see performances, movies, or videotapes of these plays?
- What makes Shakespeare's plays "classics"?
- What is the difference between tragedy and comedy?

Overview

Rather than presenting plays in strict chronological order, the introduction to drama in this book aims at giving the reader a sense of living theater and its historical roots. Students read Ibsen, probing the familiar values of a middle-class world, before exploring the world of Shakespeare's *Hamlet* or Molière's *Misanthrope*. They read Sophocles's earlier play, *Antigone*, dramatizing the conflict between the idealistic youth and the state, as their introduction to Greek Drama, with the later *Oedipus the King* available later in the book. Plays by David Mamet, David Henry Hwang, Luis Valdez, and Marsha Norman attest to the continuing vitality of the stage.

Guide to Contents

26 PREVIEW: THE HEART OF DRAMA Selected scenes and a short play introduce students to such elements of drama as situation, character, dialogue, plot, and style. The opening chapter goes to the heart of drama, focusing on conflict as the force that drives a great play. Susan Gaspell's *Trifles* and Henrik Ibsen's *A Doll's House* both dramatize the conflict between the values of society and the needs of the individual—between who we are expected to be and who we really are.

27 GREEK TRAGEDY: THE EMBATTLED PROTAGONIST This chapter explores the hold Greek tragedy has on the human imagination—and on the conventions and traditions of theater in the West. *Antigone*, the first of Sophocles' three plays about Oedipus and his children, is also the most accessible to a modern audience. In this play, a strong-willed young woman is the embattled protagonist whose confrontation with Creon as the powerful antagonist helps us define true dramatic conflict.

28 SHAKESPEAREAN TRAGEDY: THE INNER CONFLICT This chapter seeks to bring Shakespeare to life for a new generation of students. A special new reader's edition of *Hamlet* uses marginal glosses (instead of the more usual footnotes) to facilitate close reading and study of the play. These glosses, close at hand for the struggling student reader, suggest modern meanings in the context of the line. In this introduction to Shakespearean drama, the emphasis shifts from external to internal conflict—the "conflict within." Excerpts documenting the range of interpretation—from the Romantic Hamlet to the Renaissance Hamlet and to the Freudian Hamlet and beyond—show the play to be a mirror in which we see a reflection of our own preoccupations and dilemmas.

29 AMERICAN DRAMA; THE MIRROR OF REALITY Focusing on the American tradition of realistic drama, this chapter offers new perspectives on Arthur Miller's classic *Death of a Salesman* and juxtaposes it with Lorraine Hansberry's *Raisin in the Sun*. The theme shared by both plays is the classic collision between the American dream and American reality. Critical excerpts reexamine the role of Linda Loman as one of the "unheard voices" of the American theater.

30 COMEDY: A TIME FOR LAUGHTER The chapter on comedy starts with a short play by Wendy Wasserstein, leading up to Molière's tragicomic *The Misanthrope* in a translation designed to make Molière sound more like his racy, colloquial self than like a French Alexander Pope. (Shakespeare's *A Midsummer Night's Dream* appears among the plays for further reading.)

31 NEW DIRECTIONS: CROSSING THE BOUNDARIES This chapter focuses on countertrends to the tradition of realistic problem plays that extends from Henrik Ibsen to Arthur Miller. David Mamet's *The Cryptogram* illustrates the modern genre of abrasive, shattering exposé that puts self-lacerating characters on the stage. The short plays by David Henry Hwang and Luis Valdez show how the American theater has begun to reflect the true diversity of the American experience. Wole Soyinka's *Death and the King's Horseman* reasserts non-Western myth and tradition in a powerful play taking place toward the end of colonialism.

32 PERSPECTIVES: ENTER CRITIC This chapter samples the range of drama criticism, including historical, Freudian, myth-centered, and feminist perspectives. Background materials include Aristotle's discussion of the perfect plot and a review of a memorable production (the Dustin Hoffman revival of *Death of a Salesman*).

33 OTHER VOICES/OTHER VISIONS: THE MAGIC OF THE STAGE The plays for further reading are Sophocles' *Oedipus the King*, William Shakespeare's *A Midsummer Night's Dream*, Tennessee Williams' *The Glass Menagerie*, and Marsha Norman's *Getting Out*.

DRAMA
Teaching Suggestions and Answers to Questions

Chapter 26 PREVIEW The Heart of Drama 945

Theater is one of the oldest of the communal arts. It is one of the oldest of the performance arts, often in early cultures closely allied with dance and music. Live theater—often prematurely pronounced dead by lugubrious critics—has a way of resurfacing against odds. Throughout the country, theater companies are keeping the special magic of the stage alive—with, or in anti-intellectual times, without government support. Aficionados flock to Shakespeare in the redwoods or in Central Park. Most college students have the opportunity to see stage productions with student actors and often student directors. (Support your local theater!)

Here are some questions to help you and your students explore experiences, preconceptions, and assumptions that they bring to the study of plays:

- What has been your previous experience with live theater?
- Have you participated in amateur theatricals or high school plays?
- What famous stage actors do you know or have had a chance to watch in filmed productions or on the stage?
- What is the difference between a live performance and movies or television?
- What is the difference between seeing a live play and reading a book?
- When do we call a piece a melodrama or a performance melodramatic?
- What is the difference between melodrama and "serious drama" or "real drama"?
- What is a docudrama? How is a soap opera different from real drama?

The Elements of Drama 946

PERSPECTIVES—THEATER: LITERATURE AS PERFORMANCE ART

Readers of plays must learn to use their imaginations and stage a play in the "theater of the mind." Statements like the following by theater people can help us understand the limitations and opportunities of the playwright's craft:

> What actors do in a rehearsal is equivalent to what a writer does in early drafts. You are fumbling along, making discoveries. You may be making bad choices, but the bad

choices are an attempt to understand what the hell you are getting at until you arrive at the final point.

—Jules Feiffer

What we are working for is the reaction of the audience, the interacting of the actors and the audience—that's the chemistry you're after.

—Lanford Wilson

Playwrights work eternally against limitations. At the same time, they work with them. Any theater's special limitations are part of what gives it its special intensity. The curtain rising behind the proscenium arch says, "Fix your whole attention on this little space: Everything will happen here. For these three hours, there is nothing outside it." And a sign in the lobby— "This performance will end at 10:20"—tells us, "Everything that happens will happen tonight. Our work is writ in water. Let's make the most of our time."

—Amlin Gray

Poverty of means, embraced, can be both medium and message. The Chorus of Shakespeare's *Henry V* tells his audience that, if they'll assist with their imaginations, the proceedings on his "unworthy scaffold" will be not too pitifully inferior to what he could accomplish with "a kingdom for a stage," but he implies, I think, that it will actually be better.

—Amlin Gray

(situation) Tina Howe, "Museum" 947

DISCUSSION STARTERS

What, if anything, does the term *avantgarde* mean to your students?

THE RECEPTIVE READER

A museum is usually a solemn, quiet place where we expect earnest people to look respectfully at the exhibits, watched by a "watchful" and yet "unobtrusive" guard. The guard here lives up to this part of the billing, but his sucking his teeth and hitching up his underwear prevent the right mood of solemnity from developing. The clothesline as major exhibit and the loudspeaker announcement concerning mayhem in the Uffizi Gallery have already alerted us that this museum is zanier than most and that, as you might say, at any time all hell might break loose. We are not disappointed when the photographer informed of museum rules starts losing his cool, berating and mocking the guard.

(character) ntozake shange, "lady in red" 949

DISCUSSION STARTERS

Your students may want to try their hand at writing and presenting a monologue about a terminated friendship or relationship or similar topic.

THE RECEPTIVE READER

The lady in red is a woman who is finally fed up with a relationship that she has given all the benefit of the doubt, putting up with contemptuous selfishness and neglect on the part of a stereotypically thoughtless, selfish, inadequate male. She is a person with a true capacity for devotion (see the packages, plants, homemade cards) and a real need for affection (wanting "to be wanted"), but she is also a determined woman with some pride, asserting herself, cutting her losses.

(dialogue) Oscar Wilde, "A Proposal of Marriage" (from *The Importance of Being Earnest*) 951

DISCUSSION STARTERS

Oscar Wilde evoked gales of happy laughter by the simple expedient of having his characters say out loud the silly, vain, obtuse, and self-regarding things that other people only thought. You may want to ask your students: When we laugh, do we laugh at people who are very *different* from ourselves? Or does Wilde in his own way, in the words of Hamlet, "hold the mirror up to nature"? For instance, you might ask:

- Is Gwendolen the only person who acts silly about a name? (How do parents today choose names for their children? Why did Bob Dylan change his name from Zimmermann?)
- Is Lady Bracknell the only parent who has ever taken a dim view of a marriage prospect with the wrong qualifications? (How different are the criteria of parents today from Lady Bracknell's?)
- Is Jack the only person who has ever misrepresented slightly (or grossly) who he is?

THE RECEPTIVE READER

1. *Jack Worthing* is the sort of straightman who repeatedly has to listen with a straight face to the batty statements of people he cannot afford to do without. *Gwendolen* makes us laugh because with her talk about "vibrations" she parades the yearnings for a more vibrant and inspired life that most of us keep under wraps? The hyperformal circumlocutions of people who cannot bear to be thought ordinary furnish Wilde with much grounds for amusement. *Lady Bracknell*, for instance, says simple ordinary things as if through a mouth full of marbles: "Rise, sir, from this semirecumbent posture!"

2. One example of a *cliché* or platitude turned on its head occurs when Gwendolen says they "live in an age of ideals." Her ideal is—"to love someone of the name of Ernest."

3. Many of Wilde's barbs are directed at the unearned privileges of an entrenched *upper class*? Lady Bracknell's comments on education for the masses are revealing: "The whole theory of modern education is radically unsound. Fortunately in England, at any rate, education produces no effect whatsoever. If it did, it would prove a serious danger to the upper classes." Her reply to Jack's admission that he smokes is a marvelous comment on the idle rich: "I am glad to hear it. A man should always have an occupation of some kind. There are far too many idle men in London as it is."

4. Putting up with the foibles of people we love, fending off the uninvited inquiries of self-appointed judges of our credentials or character—these are all part of the human condition?

5. The Lady Bracknell character, for instance, must be able to project a formidable obtuseness and self-righteousness.

(plot) Susan Glaspell, Trifles 955

DISCUSSION STARTERS

Ask your students: "Why did Glaspell call the play *Trifles*? What does the word *trifles* call to mind? What 'trifles' play a role in this play?" In another of her plays, Glaspell writes, "It is through suppression that hells are formed in us." This is what the women in *Trifles* discover: the suppression of Mrs. Wright's spirit led to her committing murder. The empty birdcage, the oddly stitched quilt —these "trifles" lead Mrs. Hale and Mrs. Peters to uncover a murder motive, a motive the male investigators search for in vain. The series of revelations—combined with the men's patronizing comments and the women's memories of their treatment by men—lead the women to join in a conspiracy of silence. Is this their way of obtaining some power in a society that keeps them powerless?

(You may later wish to compare Torvald's relationship with Nora in *A Doll's House* to what we learn about the relationship between Mr. and Mrs. Wright. What is the *tone* used by the men toward the women in both plays?)

THE RECEPTIVE READER

1. Hale makes it clear that Wright had a hold on his wife. Wright was the decision-maker; his wife's opinions did not matter. The *major conflict* underlying the play is foreshadowed here—that Mrs. Wright was her husband's captive in an isolated, "gloomy" house. Wright had not even wanted a phone, which suggests further his desire for isolation. But we find out through the women's dialogue in the play that Mrs. Wright, when she was Minnie Foster, had enjoyed socializing—dressing up and singing, for

instance. But apparently under the iron hand of Mr. Wright, she had no autonomy.

2. From *a man's perspective*, the sticky shelves are a result of bad housekeeping, whereas the women know the spilled preserves represent lots of hard work gone to waste. After Mrs. Peters mentions that Mrs. Wright was worried that the bottles would break in the cold, the sheriff says, "Well, can you beat the women! Held for murder and worryin' about her preserves." Here the sheriff has pitted the men against the women by scoffing at something that is important to the women. The women also begin to close ranks as the men deride Mrs. Wright's abilities as a housekeeper. "There's a great deal of work to be done on a farm," Mrs. Hale says, standing up for the absent Mrs. Wright.

Hale's statement "Well, women are used to worrying over trifles" is ironic because it is the women's very attention to detail that the men should be using in their criminal investigation. With these "trifles," these details, the women discover the murder motive that the men search for in vain. The men dismiss important elements because of their preconceived notions of the unimportance of "women's things." For instance, the sheriff says, "Nothing here but kitchen things." The title *Trifles* points to the ironic significance of "insignificant" details. This theme of "little things" mattering to women appears again when the women discuss the quilt. Little details can offer evidence about Mrs. Wright. The bad stitches in her quilt, for instance, are evidence of her state of mind before the killing. The intricate knotting required for making a quilt could evidence a "craft" and "skill" necessary for someone who used the rope "in such a—funny way to kill a man, rigging it all up like that." And of course the "trifling detail" of an empty birdcage leads the women to wonder what happened to the bird.

3. The first words Mrs. Hale says in the play are in response to the county attorney's reprove that Mrs. Wright isn't "much of a housekeeper." Mrs. Hale responds, "There's a great deal of work to be done on a farm." Mrs. Hale also defends Mrs. Wright when the attorney scowls at the dirty towels by retorting, "Men's hands aren't always as clean as they might be." She also indicates her dislike of Mr. Wright by saying, "I don't think a place'd be any cheerfuller for John Wright's being in it." However, she is careful not to help the men out with a motive; when she is asked if she means that the Wrights did not "get on very well," she says, "No, I don't mean anything."

As the men scoff at the women's concerns, and the women rebuff the men and align with each other, it becomes clear that we will see the events and issues from *a woman's point of view.* The women—Mrs. Hale from the outset and increasingly Mrs. Peters—sympathize with Mrs. Wright with statements such as "I'd hate to have men coming into my kitchen, snooping around and criticizing." Their actions also increasingly indicate their alliance with her, starting with Mrs. Hale's arranging the pans under the sink "which the county attorney had shoved out of place" and culminating in their concealment of the strangled bird.

4. The women notice the important *clues*: The table is half-wiped, which could indicate an interruption of Mrs. Wright's routine. The most recent part of the quilt Mrs. Wright had been working on is poorly stitched, as opposed to the rest of the quilt. Mrs. Hale asks, "What do you suppose she was so nervous about?" Of course their discovery of the empty cage is the prime clue. Mrs. Peters knows that Mrs. Wright is afraid of cats, and so even before finding the dead bird the women wonder about its demise, rather than dismissing an empty cage as a "trifle." They also note that the pretty box and the silk in which the bird was stored indicate that Mrs. Wright "liked the bird. She was going to bury it in that pretty box."

5. It becomes clear that John Wright squelched his wife's spirit. The women point out that Mrs. Wright "used to wear pretty clothes and be lively." But after years of living with Mr. Wright in the gloomy, isolated house—with no children, no pets—she became affected by his character: "How—she—did—change," Mrs. Hale declares. Thus we know he was a negative and controlling influence, an ironic contrast with his public image of "a good man."

6. A bird with its song and flight symbolizes freedom and beauty. At one time, Mrs. Wright was free and beautiful, as the women point out in their discussion of her. She used to like to dress up and sing. But, like a caged bird, she became trapped in the home of her husband. Thus the bird symbolizes the beauty and freedom that Mr. Wright squashed in his wife. Mrs. Hale comments, "No, Wright wouldn't like the bird—a thing that sang. She used to sing. He killed that too." When the women, to their horror, discover the strangled bird, they sympathize with Mrs. Wright. Mrs. Peters identifies with fear of violent males, recalling a boy hatcheting her kitten when she was a child. Mrs. Hale identifies with the betrayal and loneliness Mrs. Wright must have felt: "If there'd been years and years of nothing, then a bird to sing to you, it would be awful—still, after the bird was still. . . . I know what stillness is. When we homesteaded in Dakota, and my first baby died—after he was two years old, and me with no other then . . ."

7. Mrs. Peters conceals the truth about the bird, knowing that it could be an important clue. She says, "My, it's a good thing the men couldn't hear us. Wouldn't they just laugh! Getting all stirred up over a little thing like a—dead canary." The irony here lies in the discrepancy between what she says and what she means. She knows the small clues—the "trifles"—are important, for she had heard the attorney say, "But you know juries when it comes to women. If there was some definite thing. Something to show—something to make a story about." But she is hiding her knowledge from "the law." Also here is the suggestion that "the law" is male, and a "male law" could not comprehend Mrs. Wright's motive.

8. In many crime shows, the Fearless-Fosdick detective hunts down a clever killer by noticing just such "trifles" as play an ironic role in this drama?

(style) August Wilson, "How Avery Got to Be a Preacher" (from *The Piano Lesson*) 969

THE RECEPTIVE READER

1. The beauty of this short excerpt is in the way it translates religious feeling into beautifully simple close-to-home images and phrases—like seeing the three candles and being told to light one and being careful not to let it go out.

2. Some echoes of Black English here: "How you *get* to be a preacher?" (no *how did you* for question); "It *come* to me in a dream" (past tense); "Willie *don't* want to hear" (third-person singular); "told him you *was* a preacher" (second-person); "they . . . *was* making noise" (third-person plural); "they told me . . . and they *give* me" (past tense); "dreaming about *them* sheep people" (demonstrative pronoun); "I can see that *easy*" (adverb). However, most of these are also familiar features of nonstandard or working-class speech generally?

3. British accents serve as a meal ticket for various people in the pop music industry? Southern speech (which some people used to be self-conscious about) is rising in the social scale?

Conflict: The Heart of Drama

Henrik Ibsen, *A Doll's House* 971

DISCUSSION STARTERS

Ibsen's play was first performed in Copenhagen on December 21, 1879; within a few years it had been translated into fourteen languages. "That slammed door," said James Gibbons Huneker, referring to the play's end, "reverberated across the roofs of the world." This classic play dramatizes the buried tensions in a family living in society-prescribed roles. Critics argue, however, about the play's thematic focus, particularly whether or not it is a "feminist" drama. To help students get into the spirit of the play, you may want to try activities like the following:

- Are your students caught up in their own traditional gender roles? You may want to conduct an experiment: Have a male student read some of Nora's lines and a female student read Torvald's corresponding lines. Can they imaginatively enter into the point of view of someone of the opposite sex?
- The play's title centers on the play's setting. The home is the central focus for Nora, and she is never seen outside the house. In the Jane Fonda version of the film, however, Nora walks outside during her talk with Kristina. In the cold, sunny day, they walk by children sledding on a hill. Students may wish to discuss the impact of this change in set-

ting on our perceptions of Nora, as well as on the dynamics of the ending.

- Is the ending a "happy ending"? One way to have students think about the ending may be to have them imagine Nora ten years after her slamming of the door. Have them write a "Ten Years Later" letter from her perspective to Torvald or to her daughter. Or have them imagine Torvald ten years from the play's end writing a letter to Nora.
- Ibsen, a century ago, said, "A woman cannot be herself in contemporary society." Is this still true today?

THE RECEPTIVE READER

1. *Torvald*, a dominant character in the play in both the technical and human sense of the word, plays the traditional patriarchal authority figure in the house. He treats his wife Nora, his "pretty little songbird," as though she were a plaything or one of the children. Although he appears affectionate, his constant use of the possessive and diminutive ("my little lark" and "my little squirrel") are condescending and controlling. This becomes particularly clear when he admonishes her for spending money, calling her "the little spendthrift" and "you little prodigal." In self-righteous, didactic schoolmasterly fashion, he is forever lecturing her: "No debts! Never borrow! Something of freedom's lost—and something of beauty, too—from a home that's founded on borrowing and debt." He has control over the money in the household, doling out an allowance to Nora. His control over her is also exhibited early on when we learn she is sneaking candy (or macaroons), which he has forbidden her to have. His condescending reproaches and finger-pointing befit the treatment of a child, not an adult. Other revealing comments treat her as a dainty fragile porcelain doll: "You don't have to tire your precious eyes and your fair little delicate hands."

Torvald's exterior of smug bourgeois respectability imperfectly covers the insecurity of someone who has had to scrounge to achieve the comfort and stability of his present life: "Ah, it's so gratifying to know that one's got a safe, secure job, and with a comfortable salary." By the same token, any hint of irregularity is a red flag to him, and he is quick to squelch any behavior that may be a threat to his status. He says: "My little songbird must never" tell an untruth again. "A songbird needs a clean beak to warble with. No false notes." His righteous statements are particularly revealing when he discusses Krogstad with Nora. Torvald is a judgmental man who believes Krogstad has suffered a "moral breakdown," mainly because Krogstad did not openly confess his crime and take his "punishment," an ironic foreshadowing of Torvald's future behavior. Torvald is proud that his own background is "above reproach," and he passes judgment not only on Krogstad but on Nora's father as well. "I literally feel physically revolted when I'm anywhere near such a person," he states.

However, particularly revealing is Torvald's admission that he might be able to "overlook Krogstad's moral failings" if it weren't for Krogstad's embarrassing Torvald at the bank by calling Torvald by his first name. Any excessive familiarity (let alone friendship) with an inferior would detract from his dignity. When Nora tries to convince her husband not to fire Krogstad, Torvald responds, "What if it's rumored around now that the new bank manager was vetoed by his wife?" When Nora calls his reasons for not keeping Krogstad "petty considerations," he is greatly offended that she would pass judgment on *him*. He stubbornly sends out Krogstad's notice, then tries to assure Nora that his own position is the correct one, never having once taken her statements seriously. In an ironic foreshadowing he says, "Whatever comes, you'll see: when it really counts, I have strength and courage enough as a man to take on the whole weight myself." This turns out to be exactly the opposite of his response in the last act.

Much of the play's dramatic irony centers on Torvald's obtuse unawareness. The conversations that take place when he is not present reveal that most everyone—Nora, Krogstad, Mrs. Linde, Dr. Rank, and even the maid—knows something that Torvald does not. Ironically, he thinks he is in control of his life and his wife. The only secret he can conceive of her keeping is one he gives her permission to keep: "Well, you keep your little Christmas secrets to yourself."

2. *Nora* flutters around the house, singing, posing, dressing up, and reciting and dancing for her husband. She smooths over events, asks for his permission, ingratiates herself to him in order to attempt to get what she wants. Like a child speaking to a restrictive parent, Nora says to Torvald, "You know I could never dream of going against you." She flatters him and searches for his approval with statements such as, "You know, there isn't anyone who has your good taste" and "Yes, whatever you say, Torvald." Also like a child, she at times secretly rebels, but hides her "misbehavior" like the sweets in her skirt pocket.

The play slowly but dramatically reveals the real person behind the learned role of the fluttery, scatterbrained childwoman who has learned to conform to the male's stereotype of womanhood. When Nora reveals to Mrs. Linde that she borrowed money and didn't tell Torvald, we begin to see that she hides more from him than macaroons. Here Nora makes it clear that she has done something considered extremely serious in her society, and she knows that revealing what she has done "would just ruin our relationship. Our beautiful, happy home would never be the same." The real Nora is not the flighty spendthrift that Torvald calls her at the play's beginning; in reality, she has been trying to deal with the burden of debt, scrimping and scraping to make payments on the loan. Also, she secured other work, working late into the night the previous year while Torvald thought she was locked away making Christmas surprises for the family. Particularly revealing is that Nora found a certain satisfaction in her hard work. She felt useful, resourceful: "Ah, I was tired so often, dead tired. But still it was wonderful fun, sitting and working like that, earning money. It was almost like being a man." Suddenly her statements about their "lovely" life seem forced and hollow. Torvald's vision of her becomes a mirage: "Oh, how lovely to think of that, Kristina! Carefree! To know you're carefree, utterly carefree; to be able to romp and play with the children, and to keep up a beautiful, charming home—everything just the way Torvald likes it!"

3. *Mrs. Linde's* discussion with Nora in Act 1 gives Nora a chance to reveal her more complex personality. At first Mrs. Linde, like Torvald, calls Nora a child and views her as someone who knows "so little of life's burdens." Then Nora reveals that all is not as it appears on the surface. She tells Mrs. Linde the story of Torvald's illness and her secretly borrowing money.

4. Comparatively, even with her secret, Nora has not had as difficult a time as Mrs. Linde, who is a reminder of the harsh economic realities facing women on the fringes of middle-class society. Mrs. Linde had to marry not out of love, but out of grim economic necessity. Then when her husband died and his business fell apart, Mrs. Linde was left to support herself in a society in which women did not have educational and economic opportunities. So in order to support herself, she had to work various jobs, with no time off. She says, "the last three years have been like one endless workday without a rest for me."

The *Nurse* had to give away her own child in order to make a living taking care of someone else's. Evidently lower-class women did not have many choices. They had to make harsh sacrifices to keep themselves and their children alive.

5. *Dr. Rank* plays Nora's confidant, someone with whom she can share her secret wishes and desires. A familiar Ibsen type—the sardonic observer and disillusioned idealist—he is a worldly-wise man who is free of the self-righteousness and pomposity of the more stereotypical bourgeois male. Being with Dr. Rank helps her to escape the "acting" she must do for her husband. Dr. Rank idolizes Nora. He is sure that Krogstad is a "type you wouldn't know," for even he views her as a sheltered beauty.

6. *Krogstad* is the bad apple in a society that is paranoid about respectability and correctness. This society brands people who have committed one error: They are forever marked "criminal." He is a blackmailer who is paying a hypocritical society back for ostracizing him.

7. Krogstad is not a stage villain. Although not exactly a multidimensional character, he takes a turn for the good in the end.

8. Nora not only borrowed money from Krogstad, but she forged her father's signature on the loan document. She naively believed that the forgery would not matter in the eyes of the law if she just revealed the dire situation she had been in. Krogstad points out that "laws don't inquire into motives." Krogstad's actions force Nora to make her own decisions, for better or for worse, and to put her husband and her marriage to the test.

9. Nora had expected a "miracle"—that Torvald would "step forward, take the blame" and say, "I am the guilty one." Her mistake was to take at face value the smug, self-glorifying pronouncements made by Torvald, such as "You know what, Nora—time and again I've wished you were in some ter-

rible danger, just so I could stake my life and soul and everything, for your sake." However, in the *climactic confrontation* Torvald fails to live up to Nora's expectations because after reading the letter his immediate concern is his own reputation and how his wife's behavior reflects on him. He quickly condemns her behavior, righteously declaring her a "hypocrite, a liar—worse, worse—a criminal!" It is then that she realizes *he* is the hypocrite.

Torvald is mainly concerned with how Nora, as the proper wife and mother, reflects how other people view *him*. Torvald gives lip service to loving his wife and cherishing his children and household, but when it comes down to it, Torvald says, there's "no one who gives up honor for love." To Torvald, reputation and social status are the idols to which people must be sacrificed.

10. Nora points out that to be "someone's wife" or "someone's mother" does not define her as a person. When Torvald says, "So you'll run out like this on your most sacred vows," Nora responds with the modern woman's declaration of independence: "I have other duties equally sacred . . . My duty to myself." She is a pioneering modern woman in search of self-realization as a person in her own right. Her idea of a "real marriage"—utopian in Ibsen's time — is one of a partnership between equals, not one in which one person has veto power over another.

Juxtapositions: The Range of Interpretation

Joan Templeton, "Ibsen and Feminism" 1028

DISCUSSION STARTERS

What for your students are the last vestiges or strongest bastions of the traditional patriarchal male-oriented mentality?

THE RECEPTIVE READER

Templeton makes a very strong case for the role the "woman question" played in Ibsen's mind and in his circle as well as in his time. Today as a hundred years ago, the demand of women for equal partnership in the family, in society, and at work continues to mean a fundamental redesigning and rethinking of the traditional male-oriented patriarchal society. However, the fact that men often sympathize as strongly with the defiant Nora as they do may point to their ability to relate the play to a larger archetypal pattern. The play may activate sympathetic emotions in men who have been condescended to or patronized by an obtuse self-righteous boss, military superior, or influential relative. In some of Ibsen's other plays, the conflict between different definitions of the *male* role is at the heart of the drama. In *The Wild Duck*, the conflict between the compromised pragmatic father and the uncompromising idealistic son can be seen as a struggle between Everyfather and Everyson.

Chapter 28 SHAKESPEAREAN TRAGEDY The Inner Conflict 1088

What has been your students' previous exposure to Shakespeare? How much of the Shakespearean lore that used to be household words for educated people is still meaningful for your students today? How much name recognition is there for names like Romeo, Juliet, Lady Macbeth, Shylock, Hamlet, Othello, Brutus, or the shrewish Kate? Ask students to provide *capsule portraits* (or capsule plots of a play) for any of these that they recognize. (Why did names such as these become household words?)

William Shakespeare, *Hamlet* 1094

PERSPECTIVES—*HAMLET* AND SHAKESPEARE'S IMAGERY

Modern language-centered criticism has often looked closely at the characteristic or changing patterns of language in a play. It has explored the ways in which styles or modes of language shape our perception of a play's theme. One well-known study pointed out that much of what Hamlet says is worded as questions. The world of the play is "pre-eminently in the interrogative mood. It reverberates with questions, anguished, meditative, alarmed" (Maynard Mack). The bubbling up of questions and riddles everywhere in the language of the play points to one of its major themes: Hamlet is coming face to face with "the illogical logic of life"; he is discovering that he lives in an inscrutable world, a world that thwarts rational analysis.

Wolfgang H. Clemen, in *The Development of Shakespeare's Imagery* (Harvard UP, 1951) focused on Hamlet's use of images—seen not as a translation of ideas already in his mind but as a mode of perceiving reality: "Hamlet's use of imagery reflects his ability to penetrate to the real nature of men and things and his relentless breaking down of the barriers raised by hypocrisy. Many of his images seem in fact designed to unmask men; they are meant to strip them of their fine appearances and to show them up in their true nature. Thus, by means of the simile of fortune's pipe, Hamlet shows Rosencrantz and Guildenstern that he has seen through their intent, and thus he unmasks Rosencrantz when he calls him a 'sponge,' 'that soaks up the king's countenance' (4.2.15). He splits his mother's heart 'in twain,' because he tells her the truth from which she shrinks and which she conceals from herself. And again it is by means of images that he seeks to lead her to a recognition of the truth. He renews the memory of his father in her by means of that forceful description of his outward appearance which could be compared with Hyperion, Mars, and Mercury. On the other hand, another series of comparisons seeks to bring home to his mother the real nature of Claudius:

a mildewed ear,
Blasting his wholesome brother. (3.4.66–67)

a vice of kings;
A cutpurse of the empire and the rule.
That from the shelf the precious diadem stole,
And put it in his pocket!

A king of shreds and patches" (3.4.100–103, 104)

DISCUSSION STARTERS

The Shakespeare festivals, Shakespeare movies, Shakespeare productions by established theater companies, and such projects as the BBC version of the Shakespeare plays attest to the impulse of each generation to reinterpret or reinvent the classics on its own terms. How familiar are your students with the practice of performing Shakespeare plays in *modern dress*? Why do modern directors often move a play from Shakespeare's time to a more modern period? What are the problems, and what are the rewards? You may want to ask your students to write a trial scenario for a modern play using characters like the following:

Hamlet Senior	patriarch who has died under suspicious circumstances and has left the family business to his wife
Claudius	Hamlet Senior's brother who has married the widow and taken over the business
Gertrude	the widow who loves her son Hamlet Junior but has married her former brother-in-law with undue haste
Hamlet Junior	the rebellious son who expected to inherit the family business and who suspects foul play
Polonius	a talky and not very bright adviser to Claudius
Ophelia	daughter to Polonius and Hamlet's fiancée until he broke off the engagement
Horatio	Hamlet's best friend

ACT ONE—THE RECEPTIVE READER

1. (Scene 1) The modern reader—and perhaps also the more skeptical members of Shakespeare's own contemporary audience—might be inclined to explain the *sighting of a ghost* as the feverish imaginings of an unhinged mind. The playwright, however, makes us see the ghost not through Hamlet's eyes but through the eyes of qualified, well-informed, competent, hard-nosed people whose sober judgment we are led to respect. These people are punctual—they appear "most carefully" at the appointed hour for the changing of the guard; they discuss intelligently various bits of spirit lore. (For instance, though restless spirits roam at night, they have to disappear at the first cock's crow.) Horatio is the initially skeptical educated person and "scholar" (not a

superstitious country bumpkin) who at first calls the guards' vision of the ghost a mere "fantasy." However, he comes to accept the reality of the ghost upon the evidence of his own eyes.

- Before we first set eyes upon Hamlet, it is already clear that we are to take the ghost (and his later indictment of the murderous Claudius and his "incestuous" queen) most seriously.

2. (Scene 2) We see a profoundly *melancholy* young prince whose glorious adolescent vision of the world has been shattered by his father's death and the too-hasty remarriage of his widowed mother. The Eden of a sheltered childhood has turned into an "unweeded garden," rife with corruption (with Claudius playing the role of the serpent?). Even before the "To be or not to be" soliloquy, Hamlet deplores the religious prohibition condemning suicide. ("O that . . . the Everlasting had not fixed / His canon gainst self-slaughter.") The loving father he idolized has been supplanted in his mother's affections by an uncle whom he despises—a godlike "Hyperion" has been supplanted by a goatlike "satyr." And yet, in his exchange with Horatio, we see a Hamlet not temperamentally solitary or depressed but rejoicing in true friendship, sociable ("We'll teach you to drink deep ere we depart"), and gifted with a quick wit and satirical bent. ("The funeral baked meats / Did coldly furnish forth the marriage tables.")

- After Hamlet listens with grave attention to Horatio's account of the appearance of Hamlet's father's ghost, we get a glimpse of the daring, fearless, impetuous side of Hamlet's temperament: "I'll speak to it, though hell itself should gape / And bid me hold my peace." At the same time, we see that Hamlet's "prophetic soul" is more than ready to suspect "foul play" in the death of his father.

3. (Scene 3) *Polonius* and his family—more ordinary, second-echelon people than those of the king's "first family"—are doomed to be destroyed in the clash of "mighty opposites" as the principals play out the central drama of fratricide and revenge. The officious, forever talkative Polonius and the youthful *Laertes* take turns lecturing Ophelia about the dangers of giving in to her naive feelings for the prince—whose private affections would obviously have to be overruled by dynastic considerations.

4. (Scenes 4 and 5) In his call for revenge, the ghost indicts his fratricidal brother for "foul and most unnatural murder" and accuses him of incest for marrying his own brother's widow. Gertrude is charged with lust that left behind a "celestial bed" to "prey on garbage." An aggravating circumstance in the mind of the ghost is that he was sent to death without the benefit of the last rites that would have eased his passage to heaven. (But Gertrude is not *explicitly* fingered as an actual accomplice in the murder?)

- Hamlet here appears spirited and passionate? He disregards all admonitions to be cautious in his determination to ascertain the ghost's message: "I'll make a ghost of him that lets [hinders] me." He commits to the revenge enjoined by the ghost without hesitation. ("And thy commandment all alone shall live / Within the book and volume of my brain.") As the ghost goes underground, Hamlet tracks him with sardonic, macabre glee—a first demonstration of his inclination to dark humor.

- Hamlet swears his friends to secrecy concerning his *stratagem* of pretended madness. He may think it "meet" or appropriate to act "strange or odd" —in order to confuse and disorient his enemies, to gain time. He has already given his friends a taste of the "wild and whirling words" with which he will begin to deflect questions and keep others in the dark concerning his intentions.

ACT TWO—THE RECEPTIVE READER

1. (Acts One and Two) Rather than playing the role of the shifty-eyed, conniving, melodramatic villain, Claudius as Hamlet's *antagonist* presents an effective impersonation of a dignified, reasonable monarch. He makes major decisions with the concurrence of his counselors, he is concerned and reasonable in granting Laertes' request, and he is understanding and avuncular in dealing with his mourning stepson. He encounters little open challenge to his authority and has for all purposes effectively supplanted the dead king. His major misjudgment is that he thinks he can co-opt Hamlet, calling him "our son": "Be as ourself in Denmark!" Hamlet faces an entrenched, wily, personable opponent?

2. (Act Two, Scene 1) Although Polonius pompously describes himself as one of those "of wisdom and of reach," he tends to lose the thread of his endless verbal meanderings. ("What was I about to say?") He explains at tedious length that "brevity is the soul of wit." Although he is expected to be a shrewd counselor and adviser, he is wrong on such crucial questions as the source of Hamlet's apparent madness (which he ascribes to disappointment in love). To Hamlet, he is a "tedious old fool." At a time when his son and daughter are becoming embroiled in the fateful developments that will destroy them, their obtuse father is mainly concerned with shielding them from premarital sex. (The tediously moralizing Polonius sets a spy on his son who is going to be exposed to temptation as a student going abroad again.) The brow beaten *Ophelia* knows how to play the part of the dutiful daughter; only once does she seem to turn the tables on the censorious males in her household: "Do not, as some ungracious pastors do, / Show me the steep and thorny way to heaven, / whiles, like a puffed and reckless libertine / Himself the primrose path of dalliance treads."

3. (Act Two, Scene 2) Hamlet taunts Polonius with willful misunderstanding of Polonius' officious questions. ("What do you read, my Lord?" "Words, words, words.") Hamlet vents his bitterness and disillusionment by hitting familiar targets of satire: the total scarcity of men with integrity; the tendency of young daughters to get pregnant to the consternation of their parents; the physical and mental deterioration of old men (like Polonius).

Polonius, feeling the barbs contained in Hamlet's apparently disjointed talk, is not so dense as not to sense that there is a pattern, "a method," in Hamlet's seemingly unhinged talk.

- Hamlet shames his former *schoolmates* into admitting that they were sent by the king to pump him and to spy on him. He will not let them play on him the way a musician plays a flute!

- In the scenes with the *players*, Hamlet is at his courteous and generous best, showing a judicious enthusiasm for the players' art and treating them as professionals, not as lackeys. He lectures Polonius about showing liberality toward these guests, treating them not according to their desert but according to one's "own honor and dignity." Hamlet speaks up for the discriminating theatergoer who can appreciate plays not loved by the multitude (who then as now seems to go for the sensational stuff and crude humor, with the clowns playing to the groundlings by ad-libbing much that is not in the script). The players at the same time serve a central purpose in the development of the plot: They become Hamlet's means of accomplishing his overriding current agenda, which is to test the veracity of the ghost's accusation by making Claudius show signs of his guilty conscience.

4. Hamlet at one time had a glorious Renaissance vision of the world as "this goodly frame," with its "majestical roof," the heavens, "fretted with golden fire" of the sun; with humanity as the glory of creation, "infinite in faculties" and of godlike understanding. But all has turned dusty, sterile, "foul and pestilent" as his uncle's and his mother's action sent him into a disastrous tailspin of disillusionment.

5. The player's pretended passion as he declaims about the death of Priam leads Hamlet to blame himself for having been slow or remiss in executing his revenge. In the "O-what-a-rogue-and-peasant-slave" *soliloquy,* he rhetorically denounces his slowness to act—is it due to cowardice or lack of outrage? But the speech slowly shifts from Hamlet's self-denunciation to the denunciation of the "Bloody, bawdy villain!" and the call for vengeance. Hamlet resolves not to waste words but to proceed to action: The ghost may be doing the devil's work by enticing Hamlet into murdering an innocent person. ("The spirit I have seen / May be a devil.") The *play-within-the-play* will goad Claudius into revealing his guilty conscience—if he is guilty. For critics stressing Hamlet's tendency to procrastinate, this stratagem is another pretext for delay. For critics taking Hamlet's concern about diabolical temptation seriously, the mousetrap play-within-the-play is further evidence of Hamlet's capacity for ingenious plotting and deliberate action, befitting a play of intrigue and counterintrigue.

ACT THREE—THE RECEPTIVE READER

1. (Scene 1) *Claudius* senses the menace in Hamlet's perturbed, hostile behavior and refuses to ascribe it to an unhappy love affair. He is plotting to rid himself of his hostile, thorn-in-the-side stepson by sending him to

England (and to his death). Protagonist and antagonist are on a collision course that promises to lead to a bloody climactic resolution?

2. "To be or not to be"—suicide (here apparently devoid of the stigma of sin) promises release—peace of mind after our anxiety-ridden lives. Death would release us from anxiety about the calamities held in store for us by "outrageous fortune." It would forever shield us from oppression, contempt, rejection in love, interminable legal wrangles, arrogant officeholders, and the lack of recognition for true merit. However, we do not know what awaits us after death—it might be like a sleep haunted by evil dreams. To make an end would be a resolute and bold step, but the fear of retribution in the afterlife turns us into cowards, with "the native hue of resolution . . . sicklied over with the pale cast of thought." Hamlet's sober weighing of the pros and cons of death is too rational to be the expression of a feverish, deranged mind?

3. Hamlet, who according to *Ophelia* once expressed his love for her in "words of sweet breath," taunts Ophelia. In harsh and abusive language, he denies that he ever loved her and rehearses satirical commonplaces about beauty corrupting female virtue and about wives cuckolding their husbands. (His bitter indictment of women is entirely unmerited by Ophelia's own behavior—and is in fact caused by his mother's dereliction, not Ophelia's?) His railing against womanhood is mingled with self-denunciation and a revealing scathing attack on marriage: "Get thee to a nunnery!" (Although some critics see the word *nunnery* as a double-entendre because of its slang meaning of "brothel," the whole thrust of this passage seems to be his attacking marriage and recommending celibacy as the only way to forestall the proliferation of fools and sinners.) Ophelia does not rail at him in return; she in fact makes an eloquent short speech about Hamlet as the model courtier, soldier, and scholar whose "noble and most sovereign reason" has been overthrown, "like sweet bells jangled."

4. (Scene 2) In the classical (and Renaissance) tradition, the candor and genuine affection in the friendship between Hamlet and *Horatio* is to the end an antidote against the corroding pessimism poisoning Hamlet's world. The qualities Hamlet praises in Horatio are also in the classical tradition: Horatio is unshaken (in the Stoic fashion) by both the favors and the blows bestowed by Fortune. He lets reason ("judgment") rule over passion ("blood"), holding them both in the right balance and not becoming "passion's slave."

5. During the *play-within-the-play*, Hamlet taunts Ophelia with obscene double-entendres while commenting sardonically on the melodrama of a husband betrayed and poisoned taking place on the stage. Comparing notes with Horatio after Claudius abruptly breaks off the performance, Hamlet—ready now to bet on the authenticity of the "honest ghost"—says, "I'll take the ghost's word for a thousand pound."

6. "We shall obey, were she ten times our mother," says Hamlet with bitter, insulting *sarcasm*—as though it would be much easier to obey a per-

fect stranger, but one not corrupt like Queen Gertrude. "What, frighted with false fire?" is a taunt directed at the king who is frightened by a mere figment of a playwright's imagination.

7. (Scene 3) We caught an earlier glimpse of *Claudius* as a criminal with a conscience when he listened to Polonius moralizing about religious hypocrisy sugaring over villainy. ("How smart a lash that speech doth give my conscience" 3.1). Like Marlowe's Faustus, torn by guilt but unable to pray, Claudius shows an inner torment that keeps him from being a gloating stereotypical stage villain?

8. (Scene 4) The terrible logic of Hamlet's revenge ironically claims its first victim not in one of the principals but in the doddering, well-meaning, blundering *Polonius*. "I took thee for thy better," says Hamlet, who apparently thought Claudius was eavesdropping behind the cloth hanging. His treatment of the corpse ("a foolish prating knave") is contemptuous and unrepenting: "I'll lug the guts into the neighbor room." Here as later, in this confrontation of mighty opposites, no sympathy seems to be wasted on the king's flunkeys.

9. "My pulse as yours does temperately keep time," says Hamlet when his mother tries to explain his violent denunciation of her and his dialogue with the ghost as signs of *madness*. And yet there is little temperance in Hamlet's violent Puritanical denunciation of his mother's impious, shameless, corrupt lust and in his lurid imaginings of the beastly Claudius fondling her and covering her with "reechy kisses"? (It is here that Freudian critics and directors take their clue concerning Hamlet's possible Oedipal feelings toward Gertrude.) In retrospect, Hamlet's father has become a godlike figure for him: "Hyperion to a satyr."

- *Gertrude*, Claudius' partner in lust and incest, yields under the onslaught of Hamlet's passionate indictment, seeing the dark stain in her "very soul." Claudius is losing a second major ally—his own turn will come in due time. The ghost returns to remind both his son and the audience of the major point in the unfinished agenda of the play.

THE RANGE OF INTERPRETATION

Controversies like those over the prayer scene are a striking demonstration of the basic tenet of *reader response* theory: Much depends on what the critic or spectator brings to the play. We might want to settle such issues by appealing to what we know about the beliefs and assumptions of Shakespeare and his contemporary audiences—only to find that how orthodox or how skeptical Shakespeare was in his own religious beliefs is of course also a matter of dispute.

ACT FOUR—THE RECEPTIVE READER

1. (Scenes 1–3) The king, shaken by Polonius' death (and realizing that he instead of Polonius could easily have been the victim), is fully resolved on

the "present death of Hamlet." He knows that the people—"the distracted multitude"—love the young prince and are likely to take his side in an open confrontation. In the meantime, Hamlet is becoming more openly defiant, brazening out his killing of Polonius?

2. (Scene 4) If Fortinbras can march to a distant plot of land and sacrifice the lives of thousands for the sake of honor or glory, how hesitant and timid must Hamlet seem, who has a much more pressing and legitimate incentive to act? Hamlet is beginning to ask whether "Bestial oblivion, or some craven scruple" is keeping him from consummating his revenge. "Thinking too precisely on the event" echoes the earlier "pale cast of thought" and provides ammunition for the romantic critics who saw in Hamlet a thinker rather than a doer. But then again, Hamlet does sound like a Renaissance prince when he talks about greatness:

Rightly to be great
Is not to stir without great argument,
But greatly to find quarrel in a straw
When honor's at the stake.

When Hamlet concludes, "O from this time forth / My thoughts be bloody or be nothing worth," we know that we are drawing close to the grand finale.

3. (Scene 5) *Ophelia's madness* reminds us that true *tragedy* is not a simple-minded melodrama in which the righteous triumph and the vicious get their just desserts. The repercussions and consequences of Claudius' crime are beginning to destroy the just as well as the unjust. With terrible irony, righteous indignation at the death of a father and sister is going to make the young idealistic Laertes a tool of the corrupt king. As for the chaste Ophelia's descent into madness: Madness, both here and as seen from a Freudian perspective, shuts off the censoring intellect and liberates lewd imaginings usually repressed?

4. (Scenes 6 and 7) There is a confused rush of events as Hamlet, on his way to his intended death in England, discovers the plot against him and turns the tables on the perfidious Rosencrantz and Guildenstern. (They find, as Polonius did before them, that "to be too busy is some danger.") And then the intervention of the pirates allows Providence—or chance?—to bring Hamlet back to the court for the final confrontation. Hamlet says later (5.2), "There's a divinity that shapes our ends, / rough-hew them how we will."

- The king plays on Laertes' devotion to his father and sister?

ACT FIVE—THE RECEPTIVE READER

1. (Scene 1) The *graveyard scene*, with its grim jests about worms and putrefaction, is our signal that dusty death is not far from overtaking Hamlet,

his uncle-father, and his mother as the principals in the tragedy. ("To this favor" we must all come.)

2. At the *funeral*, Hamlet and Laertes give a final demonstration of the hyperbolical ardor and impetuosity of doomed youth. ("Forty thousand brothers / Could not with all their quantity of love / Make up my sum.") There is little sympathy for the pedantry of the "churlish priest," who insists on denying Ophelia the full rights of Christian burial as a suicide. (Actually she drowned when floating down the brook in her distracted state?) Queen Gertrude, strangely loving and affectionate to the end, says about Ophelia (the "sweet maid"), "I hoped thou shouldst have been my Hamlet's wife."

3. (Scene 2) Hamlet has little sympathy to waste on Rosencrantz and Guildenstern. They, like Polonius before them, came between the "fell and incensed points of mighty opposites." ("They are not near my conscience.")

4. Even on the threshold of death, Hamlet has lost neither his pride nor his sardonic wit, as he mimics the precious, dainty Osric. There will be no caterwauling or self-pity: "The readiness is all."

5. In his dealings with a peer like Laertes, Hamlet is still capable of a becoming self-deprecation and aristocratic courtesy. In the end, he kills Claudius, not as the culmination of an elaborate, conniving Machiavellian plot, but in a last improvised, impetuous gesture. He himself dies as the result of his "free and open nature"—his trust in the integrity of Laertes. As his father's ghost requested, Hamlet does not harm his mother—she, whose actions poisoned Hamlet's world, fittingly dies of the poison Claudius had intended for her son.

THE WHOLE PLAY—FOR DISCUSSION OR WRITING

Allow for free exploration and discussion of students' individual responses here. Note that the questioning of the revenge ethic and the explorations of Hamlet's misogyny are very active and very topical current critical concerns. (If Hamlet is as "sensitive" as the romantic critics claim, wouldn't he be temperamentally averse to the vigilante justice they expect him to administer? Is Hamlet's misogyny akin to that of King Lear—who has terrible problems with both his good daughter and his two bad daughters?)

JUXTAPOSITIONS: The Range of Interpretation 1195

With a play and a central character as rich and multifaceted as this, the differing critical perspectives need not be mutually exclusive. For instance, Hamlet can be seen as having a brooding Romantic streak, going from youthful idealism to profound despondency. However, he is also a courteous, generous, sociable, impulsive Renaissance prince, who loves talking with his friends or befriending the players. At the same time, he is obsessed with his mother's sexual involvement with a man he despises.

Samuel Taylor Coleridge, "The Romantic Hamlet" 1196

Charles Lamb spoke of the "shy, negligent retiring Hamlet"; he said, "nine parts of what Hamlet does are transactions between himself and his moral sense; they are the effusions of his solitary musings." There is a strong romantic strain in the solitary musings on death and corruption in Hamlet's great soliloquies and in the *memento mori* of the graveyard scene. ("There is something in his soul / Over which his melancholy sits on brood," says Claudius.)

Elmer Edgar Stoll, "The Renaissance Hamlet" 1197

Stoll's Renaissance Hamlet is sociable, popular, and resolute. Shakespeare's contemporary audience, according to Stoll, took the play for "a story, not of Hamlet's procrastination" but of "a prolonged and artful struggle between him and the king." In the more public scenes, Hamlet is indeed the "courtier, soldier, scholar" who delights in his interaction with the itinerant players, who is frank and courteous in his dealings with Horatio and Laertes, and who delights in playing cat-and-mouse with the king's flunkeys. He is in control when planning the play-within-the-play and when turning the plot on his life against his former chums. He has a capacity for harsh retaliation and an aggressive satirical wit. In short, he acts more like a gallant, impetuous, generous, proud *Renaissance* prince than a "shy and withdrawn" Romantic poet.

Ernest Jones, "The Psychoanalytic Hamlet" 1198

A Freudian perspective may seem badly needed to help us focus on elements close to the heart of the play but played down by genteel Romantic and Victorian (and post-Victorian) commentators. What do we make of Hamlet's intense sexual revulsion (seeming at times to drive him close to the brink), his love-hate for a loving mother who "lives by his looks," his harsh hostility toward the innocent Ophelia? Not too surprisingly in Shakespeare's increasingly Puritanical England, sex—illicit, criminal sex—is the serpent in Hamlet's Eden.

Sandra K. Fischer, "The Feminist Hamlet: Hearing Ophelia" 1199

Although the queen's actions and her incestuous complicity with her brother-in-law are root causes of the tragedy, she and Ophelia are mostly seen and not heard—causing feminist critics to listen for hints of their side of the story.

Steven Berkoff, "The Experimental Hamlet" 1201

Berkoff reminds us that, all critical theory aside, *Hamlet* has inspired generations of directors and actors to create spectacular live theater.

Chapter 29 AMERICAN DRAMA The Mirror of Reality 1208

This chapter focuses on realistic American twentieth-century drama. It features plays that are semiautobiographical, rooted in the playwrights' own experience in ordinary American families. Allowing for differences between lower middle-class white and black families, these plays hold up a mirror to many theatergoers' own ordinary lives. You may want to have your students work in groups to develop a *composite portrait* of an "ordinary American." (Sharing of different entries may reveal surprising differences that could provide a basis for discussion.) Other groups may collaborate to write their own version of the "American Dream." (Are we always using the term ironically now? Or does it still have some of its old appeal?)

Arthur Miller, Death of a Salesman 1209

DISCUSSION STARTERS

Arthur Miller has said about Willy Loman, "I tried to dramatize a disintegrating personality at that terrible moment when the voice of the past is no longer distant but quite as loud as the voice of the present." Willy Loman is the man "stuck at that terrible moment" in the play. Married to Linda and the father of two sons (Biff and Happy), Willy has seen none of his youthful dreams come to fruition. His sons are disappointments to him, and his job as a salesman traveling on a shoestring and a smile is slipping away from him. Like a Kafka character, he has seen others get a grip on reality while he failed: He has seen his neighbor, Charley, become a successful businessman, and Charley's son, Bernard, a lawyer. Unable to deal with reality, Willy constantly regresses into scenes of the past, rehashing the major turning points in his quixotic quest for the "American Dream." Is Willy Loman a "typical American"? Is there such a thing? Or does he have special personal problems from which other Americans are luckily exempt?

THE RECEPTIVE READER

1. Willy constantly *contradicts* himself throughout the play, because his daydreams and harsh reality are at odds. He is the archetypal dreamer who would be O.K. if he didn't have to wake up. Willy believed that to be well-liked in the business world meant success. ("Be popular and you will not want" is his version of the American dream.) Unfortunately, this theory did not work well in his life (at any rate, it failed him in the end), but he clung to the ragged dream and passed it on to his sons. While he was hovering on the verge of being a business failure, he wished his hopes and dreams for success onto his sons. When they were younger, the Loman boys took to heart Willy's advice about how to be successful. They believed that Willy was what he said he was—"well-liked." (The final irony in the play is Willy's poorly attended funeral.) For Biff, in particular, Willy's hypocrisy and

contradictions become clearer as they all grow older. Willy continues to give advice to his sons, but it is clear he himself does not follow it. He advises Biff to make no jokes when he goes to see Oliver because "no one lends money to a kidder." Soon after he tells Biff to go in with a "good story." All of Willy's advice to his sons and build-up of himself as a top, well-liked marketing wizard come crashing down when he goes to see his boss, Howard. It is then that we see the real Willy—insecure, anxious, defeated.

It is not only in regards to the business world that Willy's hopes and disappointments cause him to contradict himself. At the beginning of the play he says to Linda that Biff is a "lazy bum." Then in almost the next breath he says that Biff is "such a hard worker. There's one thing about Biff—he's not lazy." As always Willy is a wanderer between reality and illusion.

Several of the *flashbacks* play off the dream against reality: At one point he tells Linda, "I was sellin' thousands and thousands, but I had to come home." Linda says "Did you sell anything?" He then offers lower numbers, revising them lower and lower as Linda (who has to pay actual bills) punctures the balloon In the same flashback, he declares that Chevrolet "is the greatest car ever built." But when Linda tells him later that they owe money on car repairs, he shouts, "That goddam Chevrolet, they ought to prohibit the manufacture of that car!"

2. *Biff* is the archetypal alienated son. (Today we would call him a victim of bad parenting?) The turning point in Biff's life came in his discovery that all was not as he had imagined. Discovering his father's affair, Biff labeled his father a "fraud." Biff felt that his confidence in himself had been built on a lie. It was then that his life changed, for everything he had believed in he now bitterly saw as an absurd illusion. This traumatic incident is central to the play, for it greatly affects the whole Loman family. Biff no longer respects or admires his father, who is torn between blaming himself and blaming Biff. Biff, too, is torn. He moves away, but his upbringing still haunts him. He turns from the "approved stealing" of construction-site wood and school footballs to real stealing: a pen, a suit. As playgoers, we are put on the spot: Are we going to make Biff's harsh judgment of his father our own? Or are we going to see Willy as a man in agony, a man who sees that "the woods are burning"?

While the central archetypal confrontation takes place between the father and Number One son, the other son, Happy (Harold) is always trying to get his father's (and often his mother's) attention? In flashbacks, Happy's refrain "I'm losing weight, you notice, Pop?" seems to get little response. (So does his repeated comment in the present, "I'm getting married.") Happy's name seems to reflect his upbeat and essentially shallow personality? (Biff's name seems to suggest a buddy, a jock, a football star?)

3. *Uncle Ben* seems the perfect archetypal embodiment of the American bonanza mentality—the dream of striking it rich, whether by finding oil on your property or winning the jackpot in the Michigan lottery. Certainly Uncle Ben is everything Willy dreams of being: the father of seven sons and a rich, self-made man. But when Willy asks, "How did you do it?" the cryp-

tic Uncle Ben never says much more than "Oh, there's a story in that" and "When I was seventeen I walked into the jungle, and when I was twenty-one I walked out. And by God I was rich." Thus the "American Dream" remains elusive. And by constantly checking his watch, Uncle Ben reminds Willy that time is running out. He also tells Willy, "Never fight fair with a stranger, boy. You'll never get out of the jungle that way." (This is a very different theory of business success from Willy's "Be-everyone's-buddy-and-be-well-liked" philosophy?)

4. *Uncle Charley* is a kind of reality principle in Willy's universe of dreams. (When the bottle is broken, you don't get your deposit back.) While playing cards with *Uncle Charley*, Willy reveals his insecurities, stubbornness, and pride. Even though he could use a good job, Willy won't take one from Charley because that would be admitting defeat. Willy feels lesser than the successful Charley; thus, Willy rubs it in that Charley cannot handle tools, the one thing he does better than Charley. Charley's son *Bernard* serves as a foil for Biff in the past and present. The Loman men call Bernard an "anemic" and a "worm" because he does well in school but is not an athlete. Willy tells his sons, "Bernard can get the best marks in school, y'understand, but when he gets out in the business world, y'understand, you are going to be five times ahead of him. . . . Be liked and you will never want." (The Loman credo! Famous last words!)

5. *Linda*, though she has always seen through Willy's self-deceptions, is the voice of human solidarity in this play. She is the one who takes the callous, uncaring offspring to task for caring less for a father in desperate trouble than for their "lousy rotten whores." She voices Miller's central indictment of the capitalist economic system: You cannot throw a human being away after squeezing that person dry of any economic benefit the person could offer you. (In more contemporary terms, you cannot throw an employee on the dung heap, steal his or her pension plan, and allow the health insurance to be canceled after a lifetime of dedication, loyalty, and hard work.) At the same time, there is another more critical way to look at Linda. Linda is Willy's support, but she also allows him to live in a world of illusion? In Act Two, Biff—who knows the truth of Willy's affair—says, "No, you're going to hear the truth—What you are and what I am!" and she shouts, "Stop it!", as though she were afraid of the truth.

6. Some of the *women* in the play include Oliver's secretary, Charley's secretary, Willy's mistress, and the woman at the restaurant. Happy's comments to Biff about the latter reveal his view of women: "Isn't that a shame now? A beautiful girl like that? That's why I can't get married. There's not a good woman in a thousand. New York is loaded with them, kid!" When he speaks with her, he calls her "Honey." Happy says that he wants to marry a woman who is just like his mother—thus, he has two stereotypical classifications for women: attractive, promiscuous women to date (and "conquer") and virtuous women "like dear old mother" to consider as possible wives.

7. *Biff* is like the son in an Ibsen play who has to fight his way out of the miasma of lies and hypocrisies bequeathed him by the older generation. Willy hoped Biff would become a well-liked athlete, student, and business success. Biff believed in his father's teachings about life until he discovered his father's extramarital affair. Suddenly, Biff saw his father as a fraud. This caused Biff to question the very foundations of his beliefs. With his father's death, will Biff be able to explore his own meanings in life, free from his father's overblown expectations and the recriminations they bring in their wake?

Juxtapositions: Unheard Voices—Linda Loman

Kay Stanton, "Women and the American Dream" 1284
Beverly Hume, "Linda Loman as 'The Woman' " 1286

The two conflicting perspectives on Linda Loman in these two excerpts are a vivid demonstration of how our view of reality changes as we see it through an ideological lens. A *feminist* critic may see Linda as the traditional wife who is smarter and more competent than her husband but does not let on. (She is the one who basically keeps the family afloat.) A *Marxist* critic may criticize Linda for her obsession with making ends meet and feeding her family. (Linda is after Willy Loman for money the way the other woman is after him for stockings—materialists both?)

Lorraine Hansberry, A Raisin in the Sun 1287

PERSPECTIVES—TIMELINESS AND UNIVERSALITY IN *RAISIN IN THE SUN*

Robert Nemiroff, Hansberry's husband and literary executor, has said of *A Raisin in the Sun* that "it is as if history is conspiring to make the play a classic." Hansberry's play first of all had a strong impact because of its contemporary relevance. It is a classic treatment of the struggle of America's minorities to find their place in the sun. The characters in this play are symbolic of the quest of America's disenfranchised for a better neighborhood, a better education, better jobs. In addition to Mama (the black matriarch), representative characters in the play include Walter Lee, the rebellious son (whose dreams of success make him the prey of con men); Beneatha, the emancipated educated daughter (proud of her rediscovered African heritage); and Ruth, the daughter-in-law (coping with being married to an embittered young black male).

However, great plays combine timeliness and universality. They seem timely when first produced, highlighting and exploring urgent issues of a time and a place. But as time goes on, they seem to transcend particular circumstances. They may prove prophetic of developments that were still in the future when the playwright wrote. They may prove to be archetypal—exploring situations or challenges that people relive again and again. The following excerpts from a student paper focus on the issue of the play's universality:

A Dream Deferred

For a piece of literature to be considered universal in scope and depth, it must speak compellingly to the human condition. It must mirror truthfully and accurately basic human concerns, such as the struggle for dignity and hope common to all people. Lorraine Hansberry's *A Raisin in the Sun*, which opened more than thirty years ago on Broadway, qualifies on all counts. Hansberry's play won the 1959 New York Drama Critics' Circle Award, the first time the work of a black female playwright had been so honored. Rightfully so, for the drama has a prophetic quality that keeps it compelling today and established Hansberry as something of a seer. We find ourselves living *Raisin* over and over again in real life.

At the end of the play, as countless black families have done, the Youngers take the courageous and dangerous step of leaving a tenement apartment for a home of their own with a private bath and enclosed yard—a small piece of the American ideal. For their courage and determination, they will pay a dear price, for they are pioneers, trailblazers, one might say, exploring alien territory where they are unwelcome. Perhaps the playwright left their impending ordeal to the imagination of the audience for more than just artistic reasons. When Hansberry was eight years old, her parents purchased a suburban home outside Chicago. She never forgot the vitriol of their white "neighbors," the daily humiliation of being cursed and spat upon as she and her siblings made their perilous way to school. Her father won a Supreme Court decision in a landmark case against the "restrictive convenants" used to keep blacks in the ghetto and out of white neighborhoods. By day her father fought for his case in collaboration with the NAACP; by night her mother walked the house armed with her husband's luger to protect her four sleeping children as mobs of yelling whites surrounded their home.

Few pieces of dramatic art ever celebrate a thirtieth anniversary showing as did *Raisin* in a 1989 PBS presentation, which was reviewed in *Jet* (20 Feb. 1989) among rave notices for its timeless quality and its message of spiritual rebirth and hope for people of color. The editors of *Jet* quote Chicago *Sun-Times* critic Daniel Ruth:

> If Hansberry were writing *A Raisin in the Sun* today, she wouldn't have to change a word. And that's a sad commentary on the state of Chicago's race relations at the start of this year's Black History Month.

Raisin looked forward to the black feminist movement, the black nationalist agenda, and the emergence of a black middle class, foreshadowed in the tentative progression of the Younger family, embarking on a journey to bourgeois respectability that three decades later has yet to reach its destination. The Youngers endlessly move their furniture and personal belongings to a new place. The people next door keep muttering, "There goes the neighborhood." Life imitates art. Black and white Americans today remain locked together in the situation of this play, frozen in a timeless cycle of racial hatred and opposition that occasionally seems on the verge of spiraling out of control.

SUGGESTED QUESTIONS

How current or outdated is this play? Do your students agree that if Hansberry were writing today, she wouldn't have to change a word of her play? (What *would* she have to change, and why?) Do black and white Americans "remain locked together in the situation of this play"? How many of your students believe that significant progress has been made since Hansberry wrote this play? How many believe that there has been backlash and backsliding since Hansberry wrote? What views prevail today on whether minorities should militate or assimilate?

DISCUSSION STARTERS

Read to or with your class Langston Hughes' "Harlem" and ask them how or why it relates to the central themes of the play:

What happens to a dream deferred:
Does it dry up
like a raisin in the sun?
Or fester like a sore—
And then run?
Does it stink like rotten meat?
Or crust and sugar over—
like a syrupy sweet?

Maybe it just sags
like a heavy load.

Or does it explode?

THE RECEPTIVE READER

1. We are told that *Ruth* is about thirty years old. As with most of the characters, however, Ruth's physical appearance is not vividly described with concrete details. Instead, the playwright tells us that "disappointment has already begun to hang" in Ruth's face." The playwright introduces the

intense, frustrated *Walter Lee* by saying "always in his voice there is a quality of indictment."

2. *Mama* tells the family that at one time all she wanted was to be free of oppression. As a newly married woman, she wanted to buy a house, but today she still lives in an apartment. She describes her husband, Big Walter, as a hard-working man who loved his children. She says that her losing a child was harder on him, even, than on her. Certainly Mama is a strong woman, and in some ways she could be viewed as the stereotypical black matriarch. But "sentimental" implies a woman portrayed with no flaws. Mama does have flaws. While she loves her family, she also bosses them around, such as telling Ruth what to feed her child and telling Beneatha she must believe in God. "There are some ideas," Mama says, "we ain't going to have in this house. Not long as I am at the head of this family."

3. *Walter* may seem to be the most rebellious because of his contentious nature. In action, however, *Beneatha* is the one in open rebellion against her environment because she is actively pursuing a strong, non-traditional role: She is studying to become a doctor, embracing her African heritage, and rejecting materialists who buy into the "white man's dream" (i.e., Murchison). It is during the "African dance" scene (act 2, scene 1) that Beneatha and Walter come together in their desire to rise above an oppressive society. Walter is hostile and rebellious because he is a black man living in a racist society. Both Beneatha and he dislike "assimilationists." Walter sees George Murchison with his white shoes and fraternity pin as a sell-out to white society. When Murchison says that Walter is "all wacked up with bitterness," Walter agrees: "Man, I'm a volcano."

4. *Ruth's* despair over her pregnancy symbolizes the difficulties of life in her social or economic circumstances? A new child may not be looked upon as a beautiful symbol of new life but as another mouth to feed. Ruth is Mama's confidante and friend. When Mama says, "They frightens me, Ruth. My children," Ruth soothes her and boosts her up: "Now . . . you taking it all too seriously. You just got strong-willed children and it takes a strong woman like you to keep 'em in hand." While both Walter and Ruth are bitter about their lives, Ruth does not see any future in Walter's bitterness and rebellions. She would love for Walter to be educated, to try to join the establishment and better their lives. This is a source of conflict for the couple.

5. The *supporting characters* often work to offer the main characters an opportunity to express their views, reveal their characteristics. Murchison, for instance, offers Beneatha a chance to express her rejection of materialistic black men, while he allows Ruth to reveal her deference to traditionally educated, wealthy people.

6. *Mr. Linder* shows that the overt prejudice of the past that Mama speaks about may no longer openly show its face. A more sophisticated kind

of prejudice has taken its place—an insidious, subtle prejudice that has the façade of civility.

7. The ending is bittersweet, for we don't know what will happen to this black family in a white neighborhood. However, the playwright leaves us with an optimistic note: Mama takes the plant, symbolic of hope and life, with her to the new house.

Chapter 30 COMEDY
A Time for Laughter

While tragedy celebrates the hero's capacity to suffer, and thereby to earn a new and deeper knowledge of himself and his universe, comedy tends to be more concerned with the fact that, for all our individual defeats, life does nonetheless continue on its merry way.

ROBERT W. CORRIGAN

The pleasures of lamenting the decline of tragedy among us have perhaps gone stale, so for a change we might lament the decline of comedy.

DONALD SUTHERLAND

Humor is a blessed gift of the gods, but it is also volatile. You may want to ask your students:

- Do men and women laugh at different things? (What would be a typical man's joke and a typical woman's joke? Is all traditional male humor obsolete or offensive?)
- Do Anglos and ethnics laugh at different things? (Do Latinos have jokes about gringos? Do African Americans have jokes about white people? Do Americans of Polish descent tell jokes about other Americans?)
- Is there a humor gap between the generations? (Do students and their parents or older relatives have a different sense of humor?) What topics are taboo or off limits for comedians today?

First Reading: Wendy Wasserstein, *Tender Offer* 1374

DISCUSSION STARTERS

Wasserstein often satirizes people who worship the trend. Her characters are "young . . . urban . . . and professional" (the much maligned "yuppies," for short). They have given up whatever private quirky individuality they once had and now wear designer clothing, drive cars that their bourgeois parents had not heard of, eat trendy foods, and are in therapy. Is ours the society of the trend, the fad? What evidence have your students seen that we live in a society where the trend is king? Do they ever go along with the current fad?

THE RECEPTIVE READER

1. Thirty-five-year-old Paul is the father of nine-year-old Lisa. He has finally arrived at her dance studio, late, having missed her dance recital entirely. The essence of this play is how these two characters come to terms with this state of events, and, in so doing, come to terms with the state of their relationship. Not surprisingly, the generation gap appears early in this extended conversation, and never really departs. Paul tells Lisa, of her danc-

ing, "Oh. Well it looked good. Kind of sexy," and the nine-year-old answers, "Yuch!" On the subject of leg warmers: Paul asks, "Where do you think you left them?" and Lisa answers, "Somewhere around here. I can't remember." Sounding increasingly parental, Paul says, "Well, try to remember, Lisa. We don't have all night." Lisa asks, "Daddy, Miss Judy wanted to know why you were late today," and Paul's response is "Hmmmmmmmm?" This sort of parental preoccupation is a very telling indicator of a generation gap. Like a typical nine-year-old, Lisa is predominantly concerned with herself at this place at this moment. And like a typical thirty-five-year-old businessman-father, Paul's physical presence is no harbinger of his mental presence.

2. Paul has missed his daughter's dance recital; he has further compounded his sin by being late to take Lisa home. Lisa is alone in the dance studio when the play opens because everyone else has already gone home, doubtless with a parent who managed to show up on time for the recital. This immediate source of tension reflects a larger problem with the relationship, one that is summed up when Lisa says, "I wish you wouldn't make appointments to see me," and Paul can only come up with "Hmmmmmmm" in response. Lisa's parents appear to be very busy people. Not only does Paul miss her recital entirely, but it turns out they don't really have to hurry home for supper because, according to Paul, "Mother said she won't be home till late." The entire exchange regarding *Joseph and the Amazing Technicolor Dreamcoat* is indicative of a parent who is not paying particularly close attention to a daughter who has been prioritized right off of the to-do list. To begin with, Paul has to write down, in his appointment book, the fact that he is going to be spending Sunday afternoon with his daughter. Then he gets the title wrong: "Yes. Sunday. *Joseph and the Amazing Technicolor Raincoat* with Lisa. Okay, Tiger?"

3. Lisa's humor tends toward the unsophisticated, overtly manipulative, clumsily obvious nine-year-old cunning: "Talia Robbins told me she's much happier living without her father in the house. Her father used to come home late and go to sleep early." Lisa's comments about the people in her life are frequently innocently funny. Miss Judy "once danced the lead in *Swan Lake*, and she was a June Taylor dancer." Daria Feldman's mother "always talks in Yiddish to her husband so Daria won't understand." In contrast to Lisa's overt humor, Paul's humor is made more amusing by its incomprehensibility to Lisa. Daria Feldman's parents bought her a computer, Paul says, "so they won't have to speak in Yiddish. Daria will probably grow up to be a homicidal maniac lesbian prostitute." When Paul answers Lisa's "what do you think about?" he tosses in some extremely amusing lines which will doubtless go right over Lisa's head: "If you speak kindly of me to your psychiatrist when you are in graduate school." The evolution of *Raincoat* to *Dreamcoat* to *Minkcoat* is humorous. There is some funny word play, particularly with "procrastinating." Lisa says, "Why do you use words I don't understand? I hate it. You're like Daria Feldman's mother. She always talks in Yiddish to her husband so Daria won't understand." To this Paul insists: "Procrastinating is not Yiddish." Having learned the meaning of the word, Lisa is quick to pick up an opportunity to use it: "Daddy, you're procrastinating."

4. The crisis of the play occurs when Lisa says, "I can't wait till I'm old enough so I can make my own money and never have to see you again. Maybe I'll become a prostitute." Paul then says, "Young lady, that's enough," to which Lisa angrily shouts, "I hate you, Daddy! I hate you!" Lisa then "throws her trophy into the trash bin." Bitterness or estrangement could easily have followed such an emotional exchange. Paul heads that off by abandoning the parental tone and making a humorous allusion to a picture Lisa made "of Mrs. Kimbel with the chicken pox." Paul manages to defuse the situation, and he follows this up with an apology for missing the recital: "Lisa, I'm sorry. I was very wrong to miss your recital, and you don't have to become a prostitute." Lisa then gives ground with her admission that "Talia Robbins picks open the eighth-grade lockers during gym period. But she did that before her father moved out." Wasserstein then makes this situation at the dance studio memorable by having Paul introduce the concept of a "tender offer." He and Lisa agree that they spend "a lot of time being a little scared of each other," and take steps to change that.

THE PERSONAL RESPONSE

It is a measure of Wasserstein's success that there are times when the reader laughs at and with Paul and at and with Lisa. Paul as distracted businessman is something we laugh at while Paul the father pondering his future is someone we laugh with. Lisa as sulky child is something we laugh at while Lisa the earnest nine-year-old is someone we laugh with.

THE CREATIVE DIMENSION

Is it necessary to the success of this play that the gender of parent and child be different? Does the generation gap and all the misunderstanding that gap entails render gender moot?

Molière, *The Misanthrope* 1383

A note on the translation: The attempt here is to reproduce for American readers what one critic has called Molière's "sprightly and dancelike dialogue." (Other translations use the five-beat iambic pentameter line, making Molière sound like a French Alexander Pope: "Esteem is founded on comparison: / To honor all men is to honor none.")

PERSPECTIVES—GENRE: DIMENSIONS OF COMEDY

Walking into the playhouse, we may see the two masks that are the traditional symbols of the theater: the weeping mask of tragedy and the laughing mask of comedy. Whenever the classical Greek influence has been strong in the theater, tragedy and comedy have been separate *genres*. However, both in ancient Greece and sometimes later, the two theatrical forms appeared on the same playbill, with shorter comic pieces following the tragic main offerings. As Sir Philip Sidney first pointed out in his *Defense of Poetry* (1595), different traditions and different kinds of laughter appear under the umbrella heading of comedy:

- Traditionally, critics have distinguished the tragic and comic genres first of all by *social level*: Comedy takes us down from the palace steps to mingle with the populace. This change in social level brings with it a change in perspective. In comedy, we are likely to look at life from the point of view of the merrymaker rather than the peace officer, the sinner rather than the saint. Comedy often breaches etiquette to nose about taboo-ridden subjects; it catches us in clumsy moments with essential garments down. We laugh out loud at others' klutziness and our own.
- Mingled with the pratfalls and comic misadventures of low comedy, we often find the elements that relate to the *life-affirming* quality of comedy: happy laughter, our delight in things that turn out well. Comedy can mold the gray world of everyday closer to the heart's desire. When we become too bitter or cynical, it can take us from the iron world of history to the green world of Shakespeare's mythical Forest of Arden, where lovers hang love poems on trees and live "like the old Robin Hood of England." "Opposition, frustration, malice, lust, prejudice, and greed can and do inhabit the world of comedy, but these divisive powers are always overcome and assimilated into the lovers' happy world" (Robert W. Corrigan).
- Depending on the playwright's temperament, the *satirical impulse* may become the driving force of a play. In satire, ridicule is systematically used as a weapon to fight falsehood or abuses. To the extent that we recognize ourselves in the characters satirized, we may be shamed into changing our ways. A continuing strand in the history of comedy is satire directed at one outstanding trait that makes a character eccentric, destroying the desirable balance that we find in the well-adjusted individual. At least since the plays of the Roman playwrights Plautus and Terence, audiences have laughed at the miser, the hypochondriac, or the braggart soldier. In Shakespeare's time, such characters, dominated by one obsession or fixed idea, were considered *humor characters*. Their temperament was thought to be overbalanced by one of the bodily fluids, or "humors," supposedly responsible for character traits like anger or melancholy. Molière devoted several of his best-loved comedies to these comic types: *L'Avare* (the skinflint), *Le Malade Imaginaire* (the imaginary invalid, or hypochondriac), *Le Bourgeois Gentilhomme* (the nouveau riche bourgeois aspiring to sophistication and social status). When we laugh at Monsieur Jourdain's pretensions to culture and his aping of the aristocracy, we laugh with a playwright observing the neoclassical requirement that comedy should "sport with human follies, not with crimes" (Ben Jonson).

DISCUSSION STARTERS

Molière's characters are nothing if not articulate. They delight in repartee, barbs aimed at individuals or society, clever insults, verbal mimicry, and spirited gossip. He and his audiences loved *epigrams*—pointed and often barbed sayings that sum up a challenging, provocative idea. Ask students to sum up in one sentence a "last word" that a theatergoer might have after watching this play. Discuss examples like the following. How well do they sum up the play?

It's not worth it trying to suffer fools gladly.
The higher our standards, the lower our opinion of other people.
"Everybody does it" is no excuse.
Love turns wise people into fools.
Eminently rational people often have an irrational side.

THE RECEPTIVE READER

1. Alceste and Philinte, who are frank and sincere when talking to one another, early raise the central issue of the *limits of sincerity*. Should we tell creeps, timeservers, and bad poets exactly what we think of them—and thus make mortal enemies? Or should we be polite and offer the fake smiles and insincere compliments that the world expects? The irascible, short-fused Alceste is a fanatic in the service of the truth; the slimy, oily surface friendliness of his society makes him ill. He holds forth forever (in neatly turned couplets) on the need for being true to one's sincere convictions—and the consequences be damned:

Our friendship turns cheap if we ever intend
To cherish the world at large as our friend.

Esteem must select from the common run—
Esteem for all is esteem for none.

To accept wholesale friendship I firmly decline;
Who befriends one and all is no friend of mine.

No, No! We should chastise upon its detection
With merciless rigor all bogus affection.

The suave Philinte smiles at his friend's Alceste naiveté and believes that we can form our own private judgments while outwardly conforming to the ways of the world. Philinte is the perfect man of the world in a society that values elegance and manners more than honesty and loyalty:

But the world expects that we give to our acts
The civil exterior that custom exacts.

And at times, whatever strict honor requires,
We must mask the emotions the world inspires.

Society is amused at the misanthrope's angry intolerance of the prevailing social mores, while Alceste glories in society's disapproval:

PHILINTE: I'll be frank myself, and thus have you know
You amuse those you meet, wherever you go;
And your fiery anger at custom's mild yoke
Has made you the butt of many a joke.

ALCESTE: Of that I am glad. That tribute I treasure.
It's a very good sign, and gives me great pleasure.
The men of our times are so vile to my eyes
That I would be disturbed if they thought me wise.

2. Alceste has just been expressing his disgust for vile humanity when the poetaster *Oronte* enters, effusively declaring his respect and admiration for Alceste. Oronte, like other would-be writers and artists, asks for "frank" criticism when all he really wants is uncritical praise. Philinte obliges, responding as most people would when asked for such an opinion by an acquaintance. ("Ah how these verses charm and delight!") Alceste, on the other hand, is in agony at the slight, trite fashionable verses that have a pretend-shepherd recite dainty hyperbolical fake sentiments to a fake shepherdess. ("Can you shamelessly tolerate stuff so trite?") Alceste champions the sincerity of a simple country song, free of the bewigged and powdered artificiality of the court style. Oronte is not amused.

3. *Célimène* takes Philinte's distinction between private judgment and public acquiescence one step further: She flatters people to their faces and then cuts their reputations to ribbons behind their backs in the quick-witted, malicious gossip in which she delights. Alceste's and Célimène's judgment of the fops and bores is not really far apart? Alceste's main objection to Célimène's criticism of others is that she gossips behind their backs but flatters them to their faces. Alceste, on the other hand, refuses to flatter.

4. *Arsinoé* is the quintessential snooping, censorious prude who makes it her business to pry into the private lives of other people and badmouth them—her mistake is that she does so to Célimène's face. Out of pretended friendship and concern for Célimène's reputation, she informs her rival of her reputation for attracting males as a woman of easy virtue. Célimène, at her mocking malicious best, turns the tables by expressing (out of friendship) her concern for Arsinoé's reputation as a censorious dried-up prune who could not attract men if she were the loosest woman in town.

5. Part of the fun is to see old sobersides Alceste squirm in the throes of his love for a woman that deep down he suspects is not worthy? (To paraphrase a familiar French saying, "The heart has reasons to which reason has no clue.") To the end, the play stays ambivalent both about Célimène's true feelings and the playwright's own attitude toward the earnest, judgmental Alceste? (Éliante says about Célimène, "In these matters it's rare that she knows her own mind.")

6. The *minor characters* in Molière's humane and enlightened theater are not just brainless butts of other people's jokes. Here a whole gaggle of

them finally turn on Célimène for being an outrageous flirt—who leads each one on in turn only to stick the knife in their backs while playing the charmer with a rival.

7. We do not seem to be very far from where we started. Philinte, as a good and true friend, will try one more time to make Alceste soften his misanthropic rejection of humanity. Célimène, while apparently ready to make an honest effort to reform, is not ready to turn her back on society and live on a desert island.

8. As the voice of an age of reasonableness and balance, Molière may be saying that, while truth and sincerity are admirable virtues, their pursuit can be carried to an unreasonable extreme?

9. Philinte and Éliante are intelligent people of good will. They never lose their tempers or get carried away by vindictiveness, jealousy, or other unbecoming passions? They both admire the misanthropic Alceste—but they are much too reasonable to follow in his footsteps. Their eminently rational intended union, at the dawn of the Age of Reason, is the closest the play comes to giving us a *happy end*?

10. Like some of Shakespeare's darker comedies, this play takes us to the brink of *tragedy*—and then pulls back. Much depends on how bitter and angry Alceste is made to sound on the stage. In the text, he has some marvelously witty lines, as when he plays with the obtuse would-be poet and pretends that his criticism of the silly verses was really directed at someone else:

Him I asked: If you please,
What brings to your eye the ominous glint?
What devil compels you to break into print?
The only bad authors who find us forgiving
Are unfortunate wretches who write for a living.

11. Do the superficial politeness and civilized manners in this play soften or mute antagonisms? Are people who call each other contemptuous names ready to escalate to brutality and violence? Is there more of a connection between the way people talk and the way they act than we may be willing to admit?

THE PERSONAL RESPONSE

Brutal honesty and the refusal to play polite games were for several decades shibboleths of youth in rebellion against an insincere and compromised society. Is it true that today's generation is more pragmatic, more ready for compromise?

Chapter 31 NEW DIRECTIONS Crossing the Boundaries 1430

How aware are your students of the nonconformist, subversive, antiestablishment, and antibourgeois tradition in the arts, in the theater, in modern literature? You may want to discuss with them terms like *avant-garde*, *surrealism*, *theater of the absurd*, *dada*, and *degenerate art*. What information, ideas, and associations do these terms bring to mind? How much do your students know about current attacks on artists who are accused of flaunting convention or undermining traditional values? In these controversies, what side are they likely to take?

First Reading: David Mamet, *The Cryptogram* 1434

PERSPECTIVES—MAMET AND PSYCHOLOGICAL REALISM

While the tradition of realism aimed at a faithful mirroring of an external reality "out there," psychological realism recognizes that we live in a mental world our own making. When ten-year-old John in *The Cryptogram* worries about the torn blanket, his mother says, "It was torn long ago. You can absolve yourself." John replies, "I *thought* that I tore it." Del responds "Because we *think* a thing is one way does not mean that this is the way that this thing must be." Psychologists like William Gray claim, however, that "because *feelings* form the underlying structural matrix of *thought*, [italics added] they are the key to remembering, to recognizing patterns, and to generating new ideas." The writer Joan Didion would concur that feelings may dominate thought when she observes: "Perhaps it never did snow that August in Vermont; perhaps there never were flurries in the night wind, and maybe no one else felt the ground hardening and summer already dead even as we pretended to bask in it, but that was how it felt to me, and it might as well have snowed, could have snowed, did snow" (Joan Didion, "On Keeping a Notebook").

DISCUSSION STARTERS

Have your students known people who seem to live in a mental world of their own—whose assumptions and parameters cannot easily be changed or challenged by anyone on the outside?

THE RECEPTIVE READER

1. In the beginning of Act One the reader is introduced to ten-year-old John who is the son of Donny. Donny and Del, with their respective androg-

ynous names, are roughly contemporaries in age who apparently have been friends for many years. The father of John and the husband of Donny is named Robert; he is frequently referred to but he never materializes. He is supposed to materialize, however, shortly, because he and John are planning on taking a trip together to the family cabin, located in the woods. John is packed, ready, and anxious for his father to arrive. He is too wound up to go to sleep, but as the play unfolds it develops that John has a chronic problem with sleep. From the opening lines of this play it is clear that the characters do not listen to one another, talk at cross-purposes, interrupt each other, and maintain several topics concurrently. None of the three characters seems capable of sustaining a meaningful, understandable, and nonfragmented conversation. The sense that something is wrong strikes the attentive reader immediately in the form of never completed sentences and disjointed conversations. More obvious evidence also comes immediately with John's problems with sleep. Finally, the presence of Donny is preceded by the crash of the teapot which hardly seems auspicious, and after Donny speaks her first lines (consisting almost entirely of "What?"), it is clear that the situation in Donny's living room, circa 1959, is tense, not nearly so banal as it appears, and joyless.

2. *John* is a decidedly precocious ten-year-old. At the beginning of the second act he has a philosophical monologue: "Or in *buildings* we have not been in. Or in *history*. In the *history* of things. Or thought. (*Pause*). I was *lying* there, and maybe there is no such thing as *thought*. Who *says* there is? Or human beings. Are we a dream. Who knows we are here? No one knows we are. We are a dream. We are just *dreaming*. I *know* we are. Or else . . . or else . . ." What makes John real and gives the play its hallucinatory intensity is that he is the archetypal young innocent victim in the series of adult betrayals which unfold. He has been the experimental subject and cause of his parents' conflicting ideas on child rearing (Donny: "No, you're ten years too late. You know, Robert always said: we disagreed about it. From the first. And his theory was 'let the child cry.' "); and it is assumed he is asleep during very explicit conversation between Donny and Del. John's inability or unwillingness to sleep at first seems a minor and understandable result of his upcoming trip to the cabin but becomes central to the play. He sees himself in a burning room: "I said, 'I'm perfectly alone.' This is what I was saying to myself: 'I'm perfectly alone.' And I think I was saying it a long time. Cause I didn't have a pen. Did that ever happen to you?" By the end of the play, John seems ready to cross over into insanity. Again unable to sleep, his explanation is a series of chilling repetitions: "I hear voices. They're calling to me"; "They're calling me"; and "They're calling my name. Mother. They're calling my name."

3. Robert's *offstage actions* become more central as the play develops. At the beginning, Robert is due to arrive home momentarily ("He's at the Office. And he'll be home soon"), and it appears to be just another day in the life of Robert, Donny, and John. As the first act develops, lies, inauspicious symbols, and old grievances come to the fore so that at the end of the act

Robert's letter to Donny ("My husband's leaving me") is ironic, but not unexpected. Robert's absence is even more palpable in the second and third acts, especially when Del's role in that absence is revealed. Del is shown to have been lying, almost from his first line of dialogue, about being at the cabin with Robert, and he continues to lie to Donny right up until the time she realizes that it was impossible for Robert to have given Del the knife. Thus the absent Robert is the catalyst in the rupture between Donny and her friend Del. Robert's neglect of his son has an openly detrimental effect upon John, who by the second act appears to be on the verge of an adult-sized nervous breakdown. Act Three, which takes place a month later, begins with a description of a household in upheaval. The mother is the custodial parent, and one of her first acts in that capacity is to dismantle the family home. Here again Robert is having a profound effect upon the lives of his wife and child. Robert excels at the art of betrayal: He first betrays his son when he does not take him to the cabin; he next betrays his wife when he has a liaison with another woman; and he betrays Del by convincing Del to participate in his deception and then rewarding Del with a meaningless token.

4. First of the *major symbols* in the play, the broken teapot makes its appearance at the same time that the character of Donny is introduced. Teapots are classic objects of domesticity, vessels out of which comes soothing tea. In a sense, teapots are akin to old-fashioned mothers: hearth-bound deliverers of comfort. The shattered teapot could be seen as a harbinger of shattered domesticity; it could be seen as symbolic of Donny herself who is about to be shattered by events. The blanket predates John, and John at first blames himself for tearing it. In the days before John was born, Robert, Donny, and Del would go to the cabin in the woods ("When the Three of us would go. Late at night. Before the war"), where Robert and Donny would have sexual relations under the blanket. One of the more perplexing exchanges between Donny and Del occurs as a result of this: DONNY: "And *Robert* and I. Would make love under a blanket. And I wondered. After all this time, why it never occurred to me. I don't know. But I wondered. . . . Did you *hear* us; and, if you did. If it upset you." DEL: "And you've thought about it all this time." It might be that the blanket is symbolic of the torn marriage between Donny and Robert; torn, despite John's belief, before his birth. Finally, the last symbol, the knife might be seen as symbolic of betrayal since it is Del's reward for agreeing in the deception of Donny. In addition to being symbolic of betrayal, the knife might be an ominous foreshadowing of the fate of John. At the end of the play, the child is allowed to take the knife out of the room and up to the attic.

5. *Del*, Donny, and Robert share a friendship of at least a decade. There may be more to the trio's friendship than meets the eye, as evidenced by Mamet's oblique hints regarding the photograph that Donny has found in the attic. It is not clear whether or not Donny is in the photograph, but Del and Robert are, and Del is wearing Robert's shirt as well as what John describes as a "strange expression" on his face. What is strange about Del's expression, interestingly, is that he is smiling. "It's strange that I'm grinning?"

he asks John, and John answers, "It looks unlike you." When Donny has forced Del to tell her the truth, Del explodes with the real story of Robert: "What do you *think*? He'd traipse off in the *wilds* . . . with *me* . . . ? To talk about *life*? Are you *stupid*? Are you *blind*? He wouldn't spend a *moment* with me. Some poor *geek*." By this point there have been hints that Del is gay, particularly when he and Donny are talking about drinking and getting drunk. The truth is not stated until near the end of the play when Donny calls him a "fairy" and then a "faggot." Del has described himself: "Who am I? Some poor Queen. Lives in a hotel. Some silly old Soul Who loves you." Whether or not Del's homosexuality makes a difference in his role is open to debate. The relationship Del has with Donny is representative of the closeness that homosexual men and heterosexual women often share, and such a close relationship is vital to this play, with Del serving as confidant, father substitute, and family friend.

6. The central *betrayal*, in terms of its impact upon the play, is Robert's betraying his son by abandoning him in time of need? He also betrays his wife by deceiving her and beating a cowardly retreat from a tragic domestic situation. Del betrays Donny by allowing Robert to use his room and by lying to her and John throughout the play. Del then betrays Robert when he reveals the truth about the week he and Robert allegedly spent at the cabin. Donnybe trays her friendship with Del at the end of the play when she turns on him as regards his homosexuality.

7. As described in a book and as remembered by John, Donny, and Del, "Misfortunes come in threes." The book has a wizard in it, and the wizard is quoted early in the first act, "My blessings on your House." When John first introduces the idea of "the Third Misfortune," it evolves that the book has been missing for a long time. At the end of the play when Del is trying to make peace, he reappears at Donny's house with the long-lost book and says, "And take your book. It's your goddam book. I've had it at the hotel. All these years. I borrowed it and never brought it back. How about that. Eh? Years ago. That's how long I've had it. Was ever anyone so false? Take it. I hate it. I hate the whole fucking progression. Here. Take the cursed thing." Much earlier in the play, Del asks John, "Alright, what are the three misfortunes?" and John, thinking Del is talking about the book, answers, "The Lance, and the Chalice; The Lance was broken by the Lord of Night, the Chalice was burnt . . ." John never finishes listing the book's three misfortunes, neither does he ever finish his list of the teapot, the stadium blanket, and . . . He is obviously pondering the idea, though, because later he says, "But something could have been the Third Misfortune, even though it had happened quite long ago."

THE PERSONAL RESPONSE

Mamet has an uncanny ability for appealing simultaneously to different parts of the audience, as when most of the men watching the *Oleanna* play identify with the beleaguered accused sexist while most of the women cheer on the female avenger. Here, would most spectators, harking back to their own childhood, identify with the child victim? Would women tend to identify with the betrayed wife? Would some spectators sympathize with the family friend, who finds himself drawn into a bad situation not of his making, unable to help the people he cares about?

THE CREATIVE DIMENSION

Is the traditional view of childhood as the lost paradise of innocence obsolete?

The Search for Roots

PERSPECTIVES—SHAKESPEARE, MONTAIGNE, AND MULTICULTURALISM

Stephen Greenblatt is a professor at Berkeley and distinguished Renaissance scholar who has taken on the George Wills and Roger Rosenblatts of the conformist East Coast cultural establishment, forever on the barricades to defend the traditional canon from the barbarians and what Rosenblatt calls "extreme multiculturalists." When Greenblatt published his article on "The Politics of Culture" in *The Chronicle of Higher Education*" for June 11, 1991, Will had used his *Newsweek* column to attack literature professors who, worse than foreign enemies, were undermining the hallowed cultural heritage, suggesting for instance that Shakespeare's *Tempest* raises the question of European colonialism in the New World, the "brave new world" of the play. (In a later column, Will, America's leading cultural Rip Van Winkle, blamed multiculturalism for the rise of Hitler.) As Greenblatt explains, the island in Shakespeare's play has only one surviving inhabitant, Caliban, who complains about being dispossessed and who is made to fetch and carry for his European masters. Only the etymologically challenged could fail to associate his name with the Caribs, original and now extirpated inhabitants of the Caribbean islands, whose name survives in *cannibal*—and *Caliban*. (Audiences often take a strange liking to Caliban, testifying to Shakespeare's uncanny gift for promoting empathy for the downtrodden even while showing proper deference to the high and mighty.) As Greenblatt reminds us, Shakespeare had read Montaigne, including apparently his essay "On Cannibals," in which Montaigne says: "So many cities razed, so many nations exterminated, so many millions of people put to the sword, and the richest and most beautiful part of the world turned upside down, for the traffic in pearls and pepper!" Colonialism "was not simply a given of the period." Our students today read and quote sources like the great Spanish Dominican Bartolomé de Las Casas (*The Tears of the Indians*), who denounced the rapacity and murderous violence of the European invaders.

David Henry Hwang, *The Dance and the Railroad* 1472

DISCUSSION STARTERS

In stories or reminiscences of older relatives or family friends, have any of your students encountered evidence of the traditional myth of America as the land of promise, the distant golden shore, to be reached only after embarking on a perilous journey and braving daunting obstacles?

THE RECEPTIVE READER

1. *Ma, the naive newcomer*, has been in America "about four weeks," while Lone has been in America two years. Ma is full of dreams: "By the time I go back to China, I'll ride in gold sedan chairs, with twenty wives fanning me all around." Kicked out of the house by his three elder brothers, Ma, in his play-within-the-play, describes his desire to make his brothers angry and jealous of his still-to-be-realized wealth. That desire led him to listen to and believe the "white devil" and his promise of wealth in the Gold Mountain. While Ma plays and loses at dice with the other workers (who fill his head with tall tales about "warm snow" and end-of-year bonuses), *Lone* practices opera steps alone on a mountaintop. Lone's proud disdain toward the other workers and initially toward Ma is a result of betrayal and disappointment. Sent to an opera school at age ten, Lone, one of the best in his class, is "kidnapped" and betrayed by his parents, and sent to the Gold Mountain (America, which appears in quotation marks in the play) to work. Lone will doubtless never forget his mother's words to him when he returned after an eight-year absence: "You've been playing while your village has starved. You must go to the Gold Mountain and work."

2. Initially Lone is a seasoned worker on the railroad and Ma is the newcomer; then this changes quickly to teacher and acolyte. Ma is at first dismissed as an insect; gradually Lone reconsiders this first assumption. The power of the relationship, initially wholly with Lone, wavers when Ma uses Lone's dice to pay for lessons in opera and dancing, when Ma tells Lone of the strike ("dead men don't go on strike"), and when Lone recognizes Ma's ability to slip into other roles ("You change forms so easily"). At the end, after an ironic role reversal in which Ma the dreamer insists the strikers continue to hold out for fourteen dollars a month, and Lone, the bitter exile, is exhorting compromise and celebrating the rebirth of the dead men, the two part, each more understanding of the other.

3. Both the strike and Lone's devotion to opera require discipline and sacrifice. Lone realizes that the only time he is not merely a railroad slave is when he is practicing his opera. Of the other workers Lone says, "They are dead. Their muscles work only because the white man forces them. I live because I can still force my muscles to work for me." Once the other workers go on strike, Lone realizes that they are not in fact dead men: "All right, this is something new. No one can judge the ChinaMen till after the strike." Lone only develops respect for the other workers when he realizes they have

risked and sacrificed in a manner similar to the way Lone risks and sacrifices to practice opera. There are rumors that "The white devils are sending in their soldiers! Shoot us all!" The connection between the strike and Lone's devotion is that both are acts of living, proud men who refuse to accept their status as railroad slaves.

4. After hearing of the disappointment, anguish, and betrayal that dashed all hopes for Lone of a life in opera, Ma comments casually that in their present situation they have "the best of both worlds." In China actors do not make much money; the possibility exists that Lone may make a lot of money in America; thus in the best of both worlds Lone can return to China and finance his acting career with the money he has made in America. This unrealistic scenario which Ma paints for Lone attests to Ma's unsophisticated optimism. Lone then entices Ma into acting the part of a duck and then a locust. Ma protests: "Look, I wasn't born to be either of those," to which Lone indignantly replies: "Well, I wasn't born to work on a railroad, either. 'Best of both worlds.' How can you be such an insect?"

THE PERSONAL RESPONSE

This play, like the Soyinka play that follows, stretches the spectator's capacity for imaginative sympathy? Both plays test our ability to relate to non-European, non-Westerns cultural traditions and perspectives?

Wole Soyinka, *Death and the King's Horseman* 1494

PERSPECTIVES—SOYINKA: A VOICE FOR POSTCOLONIAL AFRICA

In his review of Wole Soyinka's essays and speeches collected in *Art, Dialogue, and Outrage* (Pantheon, 1994), Ousmane Keita assesses Soyinka's role as a leading voice for postcolonial Africa. Soyinka's writings in this volume chronicle the thinking of a controversial and often brutally frank polemicist from the early days of Nigeria's independence in 1962 to the fall of the Berlin Wall. As a playwright, poet, essayist, and political activist, Soyinka has dealt with key issues confronting African intellectuals: rediscovering traditional African culture, coming to terms with the legacy of centuries of European colonialism, confronting the genocidal tribal divisions of decolonized Africa, fighting the trend of African regimes toward authoritarianism and censorship of ideas and the arts, and addressing the language problems of societies splintered by linguistic balkanization. Soyinka, a Yoruba, played a militant role in trying to prevent the catastrophic Nigerian civil war, which resulted from the failed attempt at secession of the Ibo, trying to establish an independent Biafra. Soyinka tried to take over a radio station at gunpoint to counteract official government lies and spent much of the civil war in solitary confinement, an experience he described in his prison notebook

The Man Died. In Keita's words, Soyinka "traces the roots of his drama back through religious rituals and court performances in West Africa; he worries about the prospects for decolonizing African culture; and he proposes solutions to Africa's vexing language problems."

DISCUSSION STARTERS

In much of the literature about the colonial past, a central figure is the young African (or the young person from Pakistan or India) who is educated in the European style. Sometimes, in fact, like Olunde in this play and the young Soyinka himself, the person comes or is sent to Europe for his or her education. Often, the Westernized, Europeanized colonial trying to make himself or herself over into a proper Englishman or imitation European lady is caught between two worlds. To the people at home, such assimilationists may seem to have sold out to the foreigner; they are giving themselves airs; they have turned their backs on their own people. In the meantime, the "civilized" native discovers, as does Olunde in this play, that a three-piece suit does not make you white. Ultimately he or she will never be one of "them"—will never be fully accepted by white people. The archetypal quest then, as in the poetry and drama of Soyinka, is for an authentic new identity rooted in one's own culture, one's own past.

Is the struggle against colonialism ancient history for your students? How much do they know about the postcolonial history of Africa? Do names like Lumumba, Kenyatta, Mau-Mau, Ibo, Yoruba, Zimbabwe, Zulu, or Afrikaner mean anything to them?

THE RECEPTIVE READER

1. The characters in the play often talk in the language of *proverbs* and folk wisdom: the cockerel that loses its tail when it is too much in a hurry; the horse that sniffs the stable and strains at the bridle; the shoot from the tree that withers to give its sap to the new sapling. The Praise-Singer's job is not only to praise Elesin's greatness eloquently but also to remind him of his duties. Part of Elesin's vitality is that he loves to hear himself talk—often about himself: "I have neglected my women." "My fame, my honor are legacies to the living." (His praise-singer says to him at the very end: "Once you had a tongue that darted like a drummer's stick.")

2. Tribal *burial traditions*, as in many earlier cultures, involve a tremendous ceremonial heightening of the awe-inspiring grandeur of death.

3. The loving re-creation of the customs and ways of talking of the native culture helps to set off the irrelevance and superciliousness of the *British colonials*, who apparently have no real way of communicating with or understanding the people in whose country they are an alien implant. The obtuse district officer's appropriation of the ceremonial *egungun* costume as a party costume dramatizes the casual desecration and destruction of local

religion and ritual by representatives of the colonial power (roughly comparable to coming to a Mardi Gras party dressed as Jesus?).

4. Iyaloja is the strong woman who is the voice of authentic tribal tradition. In the early scenes, the *market women* are willing to grant Elesin extraordinary privileges as earned by his sacrificial mission. Their attitude changes to contempt and derision as they peg him as a coward. They crudely taunt Amusa, who obsequiously does the bidding of his white masters, as less than a man.

5. Elesin's brazen self-indulgent taking over of the young man's bride early puts the loyalty of the market women and of Iyaloja to the test.

6. *Olunde* acts out the play's central thesis that the African's native roots are stronger than the superficial layer of European mannerisms and ideas. Olunde comes home to bury an honored elder only to find that he must reaffirm by his own death the sacred duty that his father has betrayed. Olunde's European education has enabled him to see the hypocrisies of European civilization in perspective: A culture with a bloody record of religious wars, massacres of "witches" and heretics, and fratricidal wars sacrificing untold millions on the altar of nationalism presumes to shed crocodile tears over the victim of a traditional ritual sacrifice. Jane Pilkings is the white liberal who apparently genuinely believes in being kind to the natives and helping them become imitation Europeans—though even she when provoked calls Olunde "a savage." At any rate, at crucial points she is rudely shut up by her domineering husband, and the aide-de-camp abruptly reveals the brutal racism lurking under the "civilized" surface.

7. The uncompromising Olunde's telling Elesin "I have no father" may already serve as a strong hint of what is to come? Toward the end, Iyaloja's riddling speeches announce Olunde's coming. In the climactic final scene, the body of Olunde is revealed to both the audience and the father.

8. The Elesin confronts a fateful choice—and fails the test. He blames his failure in part on the contamination of his thinking by white ideas (maybe the intervention of the district officer was meant by the gods to save his life). Confronted with the body of his son, he finally and belatedly takes his life—too late to appease the vengeful bitter Iyaloja, who sees him arriving in the afterlife "all stained in dung." The true tragic hero in the play is the son?

THE PERSONAL RESPONSE

The more we look at the play from a European perspective, the more we are likely to sympathize with Elesin's being trapped as the sacrificial victim in an obsolete tribal ritual. However, it is hard not to sense in this play the strong parallel with a Henrik Ibsen or Arthur Miller play in which we see the corrupt father through the eyes of an idealistic and then disillusioned son?

Juxtapositions: A Modern Everyman 1543

Everyman 1544

DISCUSSION STARTERS

"O Death, you come when I least expected you" might be the theme song for much of the religious literature of the Middle Ages. As in the *danse macabre* dear to painters of the period, Death, without regard for prince, emperor, or pope, comes suddenly and unexpectedly and equalizes "both great and small." In *Everyman*, Death asks that we take an inventory of our lives; it plucks us from the earth and forces us all to "pay the price for the sin of Adam." To help students get into the spirit of the play, you may want to write on the chalkboard or paste up on the message board some typical medieval bulletins: *Respice finem* (Look toward the end); *Timor mortis conturbat me* (The fear of death shakes my bones); *Memento mori* (Remember that we must all die).

THE RECEPTIVE READER

1. Some modern perspectives on death seem designed to make death seem less gruesome, treating it as a natural, organic part of the life cycle. But death invokes fear and trembling in Everyman. Death here is portrayed as an inevitable overpowering certainty that Everyman accepts with little questioning or resistance. (This perspective differs from Dylan Thomas' rebellious, "Do not go gentle into that good night, / Old age should burn and rave at close of day; / Rage, rage against the dying of the light.")

2. Insistent *repetition* is the cornerstone of medieval didacticism. The way Everyman approaches Fellowship, Kinship, Cousin, and Worldly Goods repeats a pattern. First Everyman states he is in a predicament. The allegorical characters then express sympathy and devotion—which cool rapidly when Everyman invites them to join him in his final journey. The much reiterated lesson is that only one's Good Deeds go with one to the final reckoning. Good Deeds is then the one to tell Everyman, "All the things of this earth are mere vanity." This statement is a reiteration of the Messenger's statement at the beginning of the play: "Here you shall see how Fellowship and Jollity . . . Will fade away like a flower in May." Another example of repetition is Everyman's comments about being unprepared to die. He says such things as, "This sudden summons catches me unprepared," "O Death, you come when I least expected you," and "Death gives no warning."

3. In student productions (or mini-productions) of the play, students respond well to Everyman's dealing with his fair-weather-buddies. They also appreciate such touches as Death's sardonic response to naive Everyman's attempt to pay him off.

4. There is simple but powerful drama in Everyman's gradual transformation from a frivolous, thoughtless sinner to a chastened penitent. However, as in other early religious drama, the good-time-Charlies and no-accounts tend to steal the scene from the earnest preachy characters?

THE PERSONAL RESPONSE

Regardless of religious affiliation, many who used to be careless, frivolous youths experience the taking stock of one's life and coming face to face with previously ignored responsibilities?

Luis Valdez, *The Buck Private* 1556

PERSPECTIVES—LUIS VALDEZ AND THE TEATRO CAMPESINO

In an interview broadcast by Public Broadcasting Station WHYY in Philadelphia (July 16, 1987), Luis Valdez talked about the connection between his love of theater and his participation in the real-life theater of marches and political activism in the cause of the migrant farmworkers of California. Valdez recalled the miserable working conditions in the fields where he asked himself as a child: "What am I doing here? I'm a kid." He first got excited about the theater when a teacher showed him how masks are made and asked him to rehearse for a role in a Christmas play—till the father's broken-down truck was fixed and the family moved on. Valdez began to write and stage plays with other kids and eventually started a puppet theater, with a cardboard box turned upside down for a stage. After going to college on a scholarship, Valdez returned to his roots and set up El Teatro Campesino, working with César Chavez and his United Farmworkers Union. He said that a 300-mile march up the spine of California, "bearing our red flag with a Thunderbird Eagle eye," was still for him "the greatest case of theater that I've ever been involved in—theater in the world, you know, theater in reality. . . . In the evening we'd settle in some little farmworker community, put up a flatbed truck, put up our banners and our backdrop, and speeches would be given and the teatro would perform every night, twenty-five nights in a row."

DISCUSSION STARTERS

The buck private is a modern Everyman in the archetypal passage from adolescence to adulthood. In both plays, the realization and awareness of death are the end of innocence (or in the medieval play, of lackadaisical frivolity?). What gives the modern play a different feel or a different impact? You may want to ask questions like the following:

- How *aware* is each everyman of his impending fate? (Everyman comes to understand what is happening and he has a chance to make amends—to make a conscious decision to alter his fate. Is the buck private more the modern archetype of the unwitting victim, who has no chance? He blindly steps on the bus, hoping he will return, but we know he will not.)
- The medieval Everyman is a sinner. Has the concept of sin disappeared from the modern play? (Is the medieval Everyman guilty and the modern Everyman innocent?)

THE RECEPTIVE READER

1. The *central conflict* may be between the common humanity of the private and his family and the murderous ethics of the war he is sent to fight. This conflict reaches its climax in the private's last letter, where in his dream the "enemy" he is called upon to kill bears the faces of his father, his mother, and his little brother.

2. Persons of all ethnic groups are drafted and die fighting in wars—often with little commitment to or understanding of official war aims and rationalizations. Thus the play's message transcends its ethnic group and speaks to us all. However, there is a special pathos in members of a minority group who are largely outside the political process and yet are fighting in wars in whose initiation and conduct they or their representatives have had little voice?

3. In both plays, *Death* is omniscient and omnipotent. In *Everyman*, Death directly addresses the doomed, but he is impersonal and implacable. In *The Buck Private*, Death seems more human and humorous— offering commentary to the audience, powdering the young man's face, and personally selling the GI his final one-way ticket. Does this make him more or less frightening? (You may want to ask students to *mime* the two contrasting figures—what different gestures would be characteristic of each?) *Kinship* is similar in both plays in that it cannot follow the doomed into the afterlife. However, the kin of the buck private are unconditionally and naively loyal to him—making his death more poignant and his loss more keenly felt?

THE PERSONAL RESPONSE

The central message may be that the enemy is your brother? This is the message that European socialists like Rosa Luxemburg tried in vain to convey to the European working classes on the eve of World War I.

Chapter 32 PERSPECTIVES Enter Critic 1570

Drama criticism, perhaps more so than other kinds of literary criticism, exists in vital interaction with the playwright's and the director's work. Playwrights conform to or rebel against prevailing critical dogma; they revise plays in response to the reactions of reviewers and critics. Dominant critical perspectives and expectations shape a playwright's work or a director's interpretation of a classic. In this chapter, critics and playwrights look for archetypes and rituals underlying the realistic surface of a play, reread the documents of the past from a feminist perspective, see in the theater a reflection of the central myths of American culture, or respond to the multicultural concern with giving a voice to America's minorities.

Focus on Critical Perspectives

Eleanor Prosser, "Shakespeare's Audience and Hamlet's Father's Ghost" 1571

DISCUSSION STARTERS

Does anyone still believe in ghosts? Does anyone still believe in evil spirits, let alone good spirits? Is there anything to recurrent stories about Satanism and witchcraft in our time?

THE RECEPTIVE READER

Like other literary historians, Prosser tries to place Shakespeare's play in the context of contemporary ideas and assumptions, thus reconstructing for us the hypothetical reactions of Shakespeare's original audiences. She looks in the ghost for the traditional Christian virtues of humility, charity, forgiveness. She finds instead self-righteousness, vindictiveness, denunciation of sinners, wrath. She apparently assumes that these latter characteristics are alien to the Christian tradition—sending signals to the original audience that the ghost was an evil spirit sent from hell to drag Hamlet to perdition. Since Hamlet seems bent on revenge and kills Polonius without compunction (in fact, Hamlet has to be told by the ghost to leave his mother "to heaven"), he too would probably not pass muster if we expect true Christians to be meek and forgiving souls. (Very few of Shakespeare's major characters are stereotypically meek Christian souls?)

Sigmund Freud, "The Oedipus Complex" 1572

THE RECEPTIVE READER

The Oedipal drama scripted by Freud makes us watch on the stage of the subconscious the "real" psychodrama that is disguised and rationalized by the overt surface action of Sophocles' actual play. Is the overmothered boy who loves his mother and never has cut the umbilical cord still a familiar stereotype, or has he become a relic from an earlier cycle of cultural patterns and conventions? Is the stereotypical domineering, authoritarian, hated father in much of earlier autobiography, biography, and confessional literature extinct? (In the *Amadeus* movie, Mozart's father became the avenging Commander of the final apocalyptic scene, sending Don Giovanni to hell.)

Francis Fergusson, "Oedipus as Ritual Sacrifice" 1573

DISCUSSION STARTERS

When it comes to rituals or rites, do most moderns merely "go through the motions"? Or are there still modern rituals that have an intense, quasi-mystical meaning for contemporaries?

THE RECEPTIVE READER

Fergusson sees the roots of the Oedipus play in prehistoric rituals of cleansing, purgation, and redemption—which have direct echoes in the Easter story as solemnly acted out in Bach's *St. Matthew Passion*. The communal and religious dimensions of the play—its echoes of fertility rites, rites of initiation, rites to placate jealous gods—take us back to a cultural stage prior to the development of the Western tradition of individualism that make us focus on major characters as autonomous individuals. Does Fergusson's view of Oedipus as the ritual scapegoat in a way absolve us from facing the basic moral questions raised by the play? The ritual requires a scapegoat, guilty or not? (The question of free will or of Oedipus overreaching human pride, or hubris, then is no longer relevant.)

Marilyn French, "Hamlet and Female Sexuality" 1575

DISCUSSION STARTERS

Does the convention of putting women "on the pedestal" still have any meaning for the current generation? Does the tradition of denouncing women as daughters of Eve (and granddaughters of Delilah) still have any meaning?

THE RECEPTIVE READER

Feminist critics have probed the tradition of misogyny in Western culture. Like French, they have focused on the "schizophrenic" attitude toward women—worshipped as the unattainable beauty on the pedestal, denounced as the eternal Eve. What makes Hamlet incredibly bitter toward women? In the more Puritanical versions of Christianity, the subduing and sublimation of our "bestial" animal heritage becomes the touchstone of moral character and godliness. Purity, chastity, then acquires tremendous importance —and women carry the burden of either validating this male standard of purity or of proving our loathsome human depravity by their transgressions. Sexual transgression (rather than disobedience or rebellion against God) then becomes the cardinal sin. Hamlet indeed expresses intense physical revulsion when thinking about his mother's sexual relations with Claudius—whom otherwise he treats with contempt as a "king of threads and patches"?

René Girard, "Deconstructing Hamlet" 1576

Deconstructionists and New Historicists both tend to play off surface meanings against ironic counterpoints perhaps accessible only to the initiated. Girard gives a deconstructionist twist to the romantic critics' emphasis on Hamlet as the reluctant avenger, forever talking and delaying. Perhaps Hamlet is a procrastinator, not because he is an intellectual temperamentally disinclined to decisive action, but because basically the author does not believe in the eye-for-an-eye revenge ethic. Similarly, Greenblatt reads *The Tempest* against the grain: The conventional all-wise, all-benign Prospero becomes a European invader and taskmaster for Caliban, the dispossessed native of the Caribbean island.

Playwrights and Critics

Aristotle, "On the Perfect Plot" 1577

THE RECEPTIVE READER

1. Aristotle's discussion of tragedy in the *Poetics* hardened into dogma in the hands of his disciples in later ages (a common fate of great original thinkers from Aristotle to Marx and Freud). The tragic flaw, pity and terror as the tragic emotions, catharsis, and the unities of time, place, and action—all these became standard fixtures of the neoclassical tradition. All of them are defined in terms of the emotions felt by the spectator or the impact of the play upon the spectator.

2. Aristotle's main concern here is with the moral qualifications of the tragic protagonist: To see a great and good tragic hero ground into the dust was repugnant to him. However, to many modern readers that is exactly the fate of Antigone and Oedipus and Hamlet—and the essence of tragedy? If instead we can see the tragic hero as flawed (Antigone is stubborn, Oedipus is blind, Lear is irascible, Hamlet is a procrastinator), we can more easily reconcile ourselves to their fate.

Richard Schickel, "Rebirth of an American Dream" 1580

THE RECEPTIVE READER

1. The test of a classic is its tendency to resurface and reveal unsuspected new meanings for a new generation. Dustin Hoffman "reinvents" Willy

for a contemporary audience but "does not dominate or distort Miller's vision."

2. Willy's "combative relationship with reality" refers to his desire to see things as he wants them to be as opposed to the way they really are. Willy's assumptions about the way society operates often contradict reality.

3. Willy's son Biff judges Willy quite harshly? Uncle Charlie and Howard both seem to be fully aware of Willy's weaknesses?

Esther Cohen, "Uncommon Woman: Interview with Wendy Wasserstein" 1582

DISCUSSION STARTERS

How aware are your students of women playwrights, women directors, women producers—whether in the theater, movies, or television?

THE RECEPTIVE READER

1. Wasserstein says, "And I also think, to get further into humor and women, that a lot of comedy is a deflection. If you look at *Isn't it Romantic?*, Janie Blumberg is *always* funny, so as not to say what she feels. And so, I think you use it—you use it to get a laugh, but you use it deliberately too." Comedy may serve as a way of deflecting attention from real issues that might prove depressing, or of fending off both criticism and condescending unwanted sympathy.

2. Wasserstein sees that males and females use humor in different ways: "I think sometimes, men sometimes top each other. Women don't do that. Women know how to lay back and have a good time." Women do not tell each other jokes, Wasserstein says; "I don't even know how to tell a joke." What women do instead, in Cohen's words, is to "share those sorts of humorous moments." Rather than telling a joke, women will take their daily experiences and relate them in a humorous way, relying not on a joke punch line but in the small absurdities rife in everyday life. Later in the interview, Wasserstein presents the female perspective on the subject of writing, and playwriting especially. In answer to Cohen's question, "Do you think it's hard for women to get started?" Wasserstein says, "It's hard to keep one's confidence. It's hard to keep yourself in the middle, not to be a nice girl and not to be a tough girl, you know, but somehow to be yourself."

3. Wasserstein sees magazine writing as providing almost instant gratification: "And the thing about magazines is it gets published pretty quickly. I mean, a play you can write and two years from then maybe you'll work it out." She writes things for magazines that she would not write for a play: "I just write an article about manicures. I'd never write a play, a two-hour play about manicures." For her magazine writing, Wasserstein uses a first-person

narrator ("there's a persona that I elect to use"), which is a more confining format than the plays: "I mean, what's fun about plays is you can divide yourself into a lot of characters and hide yourself in different places." Not surprisingly what the reader learns about Wasserstein's relation to her audience is that when it is good, it is very, very good. Cohen asks, "Do you enjoy the audience feedback," and Wasserstein answers, "I do. I mean, when it works, it's great. When a production goes wrong, it is hell. It's really hell, it's so painful."

David D. Cooper, "Idealism and Fatalism in *A Raisin in the Sun*" 1585

DISCUSSION STARTERS

Where do your students draw the line between idealism and realism? Where is the line between realism and cynicism? Do any of them consider themselves fatalists?

THE RECEPTIVE READER

Cooper selects Beneatha and Asagai as key characters because in their penultimate scene they grippingly portray "the tension between hope and despair" that another critic described. A producer is quoted who says that the Beneatha and Asagai scene captures "the larger statement of the play—and the ongoing struggle it portends." Cooper sees Beneatha and Asagai as personally embodying, respectively, despair and hope, or "to put it in a socioethical idiom, between" fatalism and idealism. Beneatha's journey from idealism to cynicism begins when her brother "squanders, on an ill-advised investment, the life insurance money set aside for Beneatha's medical education." At this point, Beneatha "gives in to despair, even cynicism, watching her dream of becoming a doctor seemingly go up in smoke." In the critical scene with Asagai, Beneatha "comes of age, so to speak, morally," Cooper says, when she has the epiphany that becoming a doctor "doesn't seem deep enough, close enough to what ails mankind! It was a child's way of seeing things—or an idealist's." Beneatha ultimately decides to become a doctor "in Africa," thus returning somewhat to a more idealistic stance as regards the medical profession.

The division between fatalism and idealism is further illustrated with the symbolism of the circle and the line. Fatalism and cynicism are presented symbolically as a circle when Beneatha says, "Don't you see there isn't any real progress, Asagai, there is only one large circle that we march in, around and around, each of us with our own little picture in front of us—our own little mirage that we think is the future." Asagai counters with the idealistic and hopeful symbol of the line: "It isn't a circle—it is simply a long line—as in geometry, you know, one that reaches into infinity. And because we cannot see the end—we also cannot see how it changes."

sites: it "gives a first impression of beauty and harmony and fruitfulness and great delicacy" but it "includes many elements that are grotesque, threatening, ludicrous, and ugly." For instance, "romantic love is made absurd by the circular madness of the four young mortals; it is parodied in the artisans' performance of Pyramus and Thisbe." Titania's passion for Bottom is farcical; Oberon's desire for the changeling boy is reminiscent of Jove's love for Ganymede. But for all its laughable permutations, in *Midsummer Night's Dream*, "love is a principle of the universe. . . . Like the moon, it is inconstant only within a larger pattern of constancy. Regardless of the foolishness or vacillation of individual approaches to love, the earth goes on being replenished. The play asserts the supreme power of love seen from an overarching point of view, from eternity."

DISCUSSION STARTERS

Shakespeare wrote in an age when people gloried in the copiousness, the rich resources, of language. Although the compulsive punning and verbal fireworks of Shakespeare's romantic comedies are largely above the modern theatergoer's head, in a good production the high spirits of the fast-moving verbal exchanges prove contagious. Puck's pranks and the bumblings and malapropisms of the good working people of Athens are still exuberant theater. But above all, the playwright plays bittersweet variations on the audience's favorite topic: the sweet agonies and misadventures of love. We watch lovers thwarted by the obtuse self-righteousness of materialistic elders; lovers spurning someone who would dearly love them in return—and pursuing instead the unattainable other who treats them like dirt; a beautiful woman falling in love with a beast; lovers consumed by jealousy.

The basic premise of traditional comedy is that, after delightful vicissitudes, all ends well. What situations and dilemmas in this play have the potential for a disastrous or truly tragic outcome? What gives the audience the reassuring feeling that in the end all will be well?

THE RECEPTIVE READER

1. (Act One, Scene 1) This opening scene provides the *frame story* for the comedy as a whole by calling for entertainment to while away the days until the marriage of Theseus with Hippolyta, the Amazon queen. The agenda will be to cast out melancholy and create a mood of mirth, merriment, revelry, and celebration of the heart's desire.

- First obstacle on the way to the triumph of pure love: *Hermia* faces idiotic laws that make children the property of their parents and threaten them with death or life in a monastery if they dare pick their own partners in love or marriage. Surprisingly in a patriarchal society, the spirited Hermia tells off her bigoted father and the obtuse duke? (And since this is a comedy, we suspect she is going to get away with it?)

• The self-righteous, possessive *Demetrius* is bested by the ardent generous *Lysander* in their very first exchange: "You have her father's love"—go marry *him*! (The audience may not need many further clues to root for the young lovers.)

• *Helena* has been abandoned by the dowry-hunting, inconstant Demetrius and will play the stock part of the rejected lover (but we suspect she will get Demetrius in the end?).

2. (Act One, Scene 2) The uneducated *lower-class* characters are not loudmouthed, aggressive louts but amiable incompetents—and therefore no threat to their privileged betters. They cannot tell a tragedy from a comedy or Thisby from a wandering knight, and they are worried about having enough time to memorize the lion's part (which consists of roaring). They make us feel good by assuring us that there are people infinitely more ignorant and bumbling than we are? (The audience loves them!)

3. (Act Two, Scene 1) *Puck*, the "merry wanderer of the night," is the trickster who does things we perhaps would like to do but can't: He makes people do his bidding and solves potentially serious dilemmas by magic tricks.

• Oberon's and Titania's stories take us from drab, inhibited reality into a magic world where a fairy king and queen fight over the favors of a beautiful boy. Oberon's jealousy and plan for revenge seem serious and threatening enough, but since these are immortal spirits we know no real harm will result?

• In a world that keeps up the stereotype of male initiative in courtship, a woman like *Helena*, overt and stubborn in pursuing what she wants, is funny? (And in a romantic comedy likely to end in multiple marriages, the odds are on her side?)

4. (Act Two, Scene 2) *Titania* seems allied with the benign forces in nature—the forces of fertility and good fortune. She regrets that the jealous Oberon's quarrels have had evil repercussions in the world of mortals—blights, floods, disease. She is loyal to a friend who died in childbirth and is going to protect the boy—Ganymede—from Oberon. She is proud, denying Oberon her "bed and company."

• *Lysander* plays the part of the thwarted importunate young male and *Hermia* the role of the chaste maiden?

• Puck, for all his mischievousness, turns out to be as prone to bumbling mistakes as we mortals? Rather than carrying out Oberon's instructions to make Demetrius respond to Helena's love, Puck complicates the course of true love by making Lysander pine for Helena (who pines for Demetrius, who in turn is after Hermia). None of this may be believable in any literal sense, but the underlying truth may be the tendency of foolish mortals to find most unlikely objects for their affections. At this point, Helena feels mocked and Hermia abandoned?

5. (Act Three, Scene 1) The *naive* would-be actors are most needlessly concerned that their imitation sword and their pitiful imitation lion will frighten the court ladies. Rampant *malapropism* makes them ask one of their number to "disfigure" moonshine.

- The infatuation of the beautiful Titania with the man-beast (Bottom with the ass's head) is merely an extreme demonstration of the irrationality of love that is a major theme of the play? (Perhaps the scenes with Titania and Bottom should not be played too farcically or condescendingly—since many a gifted woman has been found to be in love with a jackass?)

6. (Act Three, Scene 2) Demetrius finds himself accused of having slain Lysander in a jealous rage. Oberon tries to make amends for Puck's mischief by having Demetrius wake up to find himself in love with Helena—who, after having been the rejected lover, now finds herself mocked by having two young men declaring their undying love for her. With the lovers at cross-purposes, both the two young men and the two young women are now at one another's throats. Love's complications having now gone as far as they can go, Oberon, as a kind of master magician, is ready by this time to dispel the spell of illusion?

7. (Act Four, Scene 1) Under Oberon's benign influence, the spells are lifted, and Oberon and Titania are reconciled as the "morning lark" signals the return to daylight from the nocturnal world of dreams. The fogs and cobwebs of jealousy will be cleared away, and we will emerge into a world of "amity" and reciprocal love. That world may not be the world of reality, but it is the world of comedy, in which our ordinary world is refashioned according to the heart's desire?

8. (Act Four, Scenes 1 and 2) Theseus is going to overrule the harsh laws concerning parental rights and let the lovers come together (as we suspected he would). Love will emerge from the dream world of jealousy and fears and strange desires to triumph over misunderstanding. The yokels will provide an accompaniment of innocent merriment to the marriage festival that will be the culmination of the comedy.

9. (Act Five, Scene 1) The "mechanicals" butcher the traditional tragic story with their earnest, laborious explanations of their various props and stage business, offering their audience a priceless opportunity for a running commentary of wisecracks.

- *Last words*: Theseus reiterates the theme of the triumph of the lovers' imagination over drab reality—the triumph of desire over sober reason. Puck invokes the benign influence of good spirits. Oberon speaks as a kind of pagan fertility spirit, blessing the marriage beds of the three couples, wishing them good fortune and healthy offspring.

THE WHOLE PLAY—FOR DISCUSSION OR WRITING

1. Domineering elders, jealous rivals, conniving callow youth, and mocking bystanders (Puck) are in the end all brought into the fold?

2. The lovers take turns being befuddled and being laughed at. Although Oberon in the end gets the better of Titania, she has good lines when she holds her own against him. The yokels provide the upper-class characters with consistent amusement, but even Bottom has a chance to have innocent fun with the names of the sprites and fairies—and we laugh as much at the infatuated Titania as we do at the bewitched Bottom?

Tennessee Williams, *The Glass Menagerie* 1693

PERSPECTIVES—WILLIAMS' STAGECRAFT AND THE INFLUENCE OF FILM

Critics have commented on the affinity between Williams' theater and the art of the filmmaker, pointing out, for instance, his use of spotty, shadowy lighting or the use of evocative background music (such as the circus music in *Menagerie*). As Roger Boxill says in *Tennessee Williams* (St. Martin's, 1987), Williams "belongs to the first generation of dramatists brought up on the movies instead of on plays, as the strong influence of film on his stagecraft suggests." According to Boxill, "The play's central image—light playing on a broken surface—suggests the ephemeral nature of life, beauty, and human feeling. Joyful moments flicker only for an instant within the surrounding darkness of eternity, as when Jim and Laura look at the little glass unicorn together by candlelight, Amanda wishes on the moon, or couples find brief comfort in fleeting intimacy at the nearby dance hall, whose glass sphere revolving slowing at the ceiling, filters the surrounding shadows with delicate rainbow colors. In the dim poetic interior of the Wingfield living room, the picture of the absent father with smiling doughboy face is intermittently illuminated, while outside . . . the running lights of movie marquees blink and beckon in the distance." Williams' use of barely audible circus music is "consistent with his central image of light glimmering sporadically in the void. The immutable sorrow of life persists under the superficial gaiety of the passing moment. The distant calliope with its association of sad clowns, trapeze acts, and performing animals, is an invitation occasionally to escape into a garish, itinerant world of make-believe. Indeed, the circus animals are continuous with the figurines of Laura's menagerie whose tiny size on stage corresponds to the remoteness of the fairground."

DISCUSSION STARTERS

Tennessee Williams has said, "If I am no longer disturbed myself, I will deal less with disturbed people, but I don't regret having concerned myself with them because I think most of us are disturbed." The play's title announces one of its main motifs: the beauty and ultimate fragility of illusion. When Tom invites his friend Jim to dinner, Tom's mother—Amanda—conjures up hopes that Jim will court Laura, Tom's disabled sister. Laura, the caretaker of the glass menagerie, particularly loves the glass unicorn. The unicorn, with its horn, is different from the rest of the animals, as Laura is different from the others with her crippled leg. Williams modeled Laura after his own sister. He said, "The strongest influences in my life and my work are always whomever I love. Whomever I love and am with most of the time, or whomever I *remember* most vividly. I think that's true of everyone, don't you?" The play comes full circle when both men—Jim and Tom—leave; we'd been told in the first scene that the father had left the family. After leaving, the father sent a postcard saying "Hello—Good-bye." Tom's last words are, "Blow out your candles, Laura—and so goodbye. . . . "

The original title of this play was "The Gentleman Caller." Ask students what they think of that title; does it alter their image of the play's main theme? Like Willy Loman in *Death of a Salesman*, Amanda has a difficult time seeing the present because of her idyllic vision of the past. How is Amanda's escape to the past similar to and different from Willy Loman's?

THE RECEPTIVE READER

1. We expect an archetype to be less narrow and superficial than a stereotype. There are moments when we see the unhappiness and tears, and the thwarted yearning for happiness, in Amanda's life without the intrusion of Tom's violent sarcastic commentary. Tom, in fact, at times talks "gently" to his mother who at other times exasperates him?

2. The violent frustration of the adolescent ready to break loose, sick of being nagged and treated as if he were still a child, are powerfully acted out in this play.

3. The fragility of glass serves as a kind of *leitmotif* in this play. Glass has sparkle and a delicate beauty, but, like the women in Tom's household, it is fragile and easily destroyed. The unicorn symbolizes something beautiful but utterly unattainable. Other recurrent images: When Jim reveals to Amanda that he is an engaged man, "There is an ominous cracking sound in the sky," which signifies the end of "gentleman caller," the end of "the long delayed but always expected something that we live for." At the play's end, Tom notes that "nowadays the world is lit by lightning!" Also at the end he refers to extinguished hopes by saying, "The window is filled with pieces of colored glass, tiny transparent bottles in delicate colors like bits of a shattered rainbow." In another rainbow reference, Tom describes the dance hall as a place where "sex . . . hung in the gloom like a chandelier and flooded the world with brief, deceptive rainbows."

4. References to the moon (a reflector, not a source of light) appear throughout the play. Amanda refers to the "little silver slipper of a moon," encouraging her son to make a wish on it. She does so as well. But later she yells at him, "Then go to the moon—you selfish dreamer!" In the darkness of the ending, Tom says he did not go to the moon. He still spends time in the darkness of movie theaters, which suggests his own extinguished hopes. And Laura remains behind the "dark tenement wall," her "dark hair" hiding her face.

5. For instance, the theme of abandonment is a strong unifying thread in the play. In the first scene, we're told that after leaving the family, the father sent a postcard saying "Hello—Good-bye." At the end of the play, the other man in the family—Tom—has left as well. In the last scene he admits he is haunted by the image of Laura, but he is saying farewell. His last words are, "Blow out your candles, Laura—and so goodbye. . . . "

6. Tom escapes through the movies and drinking. Amanda escapes through her stories of the past. The friction in the family suggests they are not very successful at escaping their sad circumstances?

7. Certainly Laura is physically disabled, since she talks to Tom about the leg brace she wore in high school. However, Laura's extreme shyness and need to escape reality through her glass menagerie and her victrola compound her being "different."

Marsha Norman, *Getting Out* 1742

PERSPECTIVES—THEME AND STAGE TECHNIQUE IN *GETTING OUT*

Norman's stage technique throughout uses flashbacks, juxtapositions, cuttings back from present to past. Norman here dramatizes a basic psychological truth about human beings: They carry with them their past—often hidden from or only imperfectly perceived by others. Arlene, the twenty-seven-year-old protagonist of *Getting Out*, reflects the resilience of the human spirit. Human beings, the play suggests, *can* change; they *can* rise above adversity; they cannot only survive but prevail, to paraphrase William Faulkner. However, in order to understand both the challenge the protagonist in this play faces and her resources for meeting the challenge, we have to know her history—which is ever-present in this play in Arlie, Arlene's childhood and adolescent self. The playwright writes the dialogue in such a way that two characters command the stage almost simultaneously, with the younger former self or alter ego illuminating the mature woman's life. We see the dramatic conflict of two points of view, of two converging stories, of two struggles between yes and no.

DISCUSSION STARTERS

In many societies, the prison system is a separate society or alternative universe whose workings and culture are largely unknown to the citizens outside. What do we know about the growing prison system in our own society? What images, associations, or stereotypes are we furnished by the media? Have your students read or viewed accounts of prison life—like Nathan McCall's *Makes Me Wanna Holler* or Dannie Martin's "inside stories" from San Quentin?

THE RECEPTIVE READER

1. As the play opens, Arlene Holsclaw is a young woman at the crossroads, just released from Pine Ridge Correctional Institute in Alabama. After serving eight years for murder, she has returned to Kentucky where she will make the decision about how she intends to live the remainder of her life. As she approaches thirty years of age, she must decide whether she is going to spend the majority of her life in the penal system or if she is going to live an entirely different sort of life. Arlene's upbringing has been one of violence and abuse. She was cursed with an embittered, ruthless, and unloving mother (the school principal tells Arlie: "Your mother was right after all. She said put you in a special school. No, what she said was put you away somewhere and I said, No, she's too young, well I was wrong"). Young Arlene was abused by her lazy, good-for-nothing father ("Daddy didn't do nuthin to me. . . . Ask him. He saw me fall on my bike").

Like many young women in her situation, Arlene solves the anguish of no one to love by pregnancy and childbirth: "ARLIE: 'I don't feel good. I'm pregnant, you know.' DOCTOR: 'The test was negative.' ARLIE: 'Well, I should know, shouldn't I?' DOCTOR: 'No. You want to be pregnant, is that it?' ARLIE: 'I wouldn't mind.' " Arlene's response to the abuse and neglect of the adult world is to cultivate a tough and angry persona which manifests self-hatred via continuous self-destructive behaviors: "ARLIE: 'She said I fuck my Daddy for money.' DOCTOR: 'And what did you do when she said that?' ARLIE: 'What do you think I did? I beat the shit out of her.' DOCTOR: 'And that's a good way to work out your problem?' ARLIE: 'She ain't done it since.' " Arlie's angry, extreme, and violent responses to other inmates and prison guards land her in solitary confinement, where months in the "ad-just-ment room" have brought her to the brink of psychological breakdown: "I can't read in here, you turn on my light, you hear me? Or let me out and I'll go read it in the TV room. Please let me out. I won't scream or nuthin. I'll just go right to sleep, O.K.? Somebody!"

Born into a violent and dysfunctional southern family, Arlene Holsclaw is raped and molested by her father. Her mother has raised a pack of problem children ("MOTHER: 'I could be workin at the Detention Center I been there so much'"). Not surprisingly, Arlene leaps at the first chance for love. Carl is a pimp out to exploit her, who lands both of them in serious trouble, and Arlene's stay in the Alabama prison system looks to be a permanent one once she escapes and, in a scene that must have eerily reminded her of the abuse her father inflicted on her, shoots a cab driver: "Then that cab driver comes outta the bathroom an tries to mess with you and you shoots him with his own piece."

2. When Arlene's mother arrives, she knocks and calls out from the outside of the locked door, thereby initiating a terrible flashback memory. In the flashback the mother is again outside the door, knocking and calling, and Arlie is "a very young child" who is hiding and resting in her room after her father has sexually assaulted her. The father was at one time a cab driver, but he has not done any driving in "six years, seven maybe," and he appears to fill his days by beating his wife and abusing his children. His role in Arlie's life is to teach her that she is good for nothing but sex, thereby setting the stage for the later arrival of Carl. Norman's description of Carl sums up the essence of the man: "Carl is thin and cheaply dressed. Carl's walk and manner are imitative of black pimps, but he can't quite carry it off." When Carl appears at Arlene's apartment and kicks the door in, he intends to pick up where he and Arlene left off, years before: "We're goin to the big city, baby. Get you some red shades and some red shorts an the john's be linin' up fore we hit town."

Sent first to prison for forgery and prostitution, Arlie enters crime's big leagues when she breaks out of Lakewood State Prison, robs a gas station, attempts to kidnap the gas station attendant, and kills a cab driver who tries to assault her. Carl, although he does not know it, is the father of Arlene's only child, Joey. Born in Lakewood, Joey was taken from Arlene, and in an exchange with Bennie, she tries to explain what happened: "BENNIE: 'But they took him away after he was born. ARLENE: 'Yeah. An I guess I went crazy after that. Thought if I could just git out an find him . . .' "

As far as her father and Carl are concerned, the men in Arlene's life are "all the same." Bennie is a more complicated character. Bennie has retired from his job as a prison guard at Pine Ridge, and has driven Arlene to her home to Kentucky where she has been paroled. "BENNIE: 'Yes sir, I'm gonna like bein retired. I kin tell already. An I can take care of you, like I been, only now . . . I been lookin after you for a long time. I been watchin you eat your dinner for eight years now. I got used to it, you know?" This is Bennie's way of articulating that he cared for this skinny ("You always was too skinny"), feisty ("You got grit, Arlie girl. I gotta credit you for that"), vulnerable ("I'm real fond of this little girl. I ain't goin til I'm sure she's gonna do O.K. Thought I might help some") young woman. Bennie's behavior ranges from an awkward kindness to boorishness. He was one of the few guards at Pine Ridge who attempted to understand Arlie. He helps Arlene move, tells her to take a relaxing bubble bath, and goes to get her supper. He tries to remember to call her "Arlene," rather than the "Arlie" name she had used in the prison, and does himself proud when he tells Carl, "She's callin herself Arlene." On the other hand, Bennie is having a hard time making the transition from prison guard who had an inordinately large say in Arlene's life to friend on the outside without any special powers or privileges. He grabs her arm and begins to assault her sexually. It is only when Arlene accuses him of rape that Bennie considers his actions in a different light: "BENNIE: 'That what you think this is, rape?' ARLENE: 'I oughta know.' . . . BENNIE: 'Don't you call me no rapist.' "

By desisting, Bennie confirms that he is not the same sort of man as Carl or Arlene's father. Furthermore, Bennie is willing to learn, to change, and to adjust to the presence of this new woman, Arlene.

3. Arlene's mother goes a long way toward explaining Arlene. The mother's arrival at Arlene's apartment also foreshadows the play's theme that starting over is tremendous work, and the process will be haunted by the same old disappointments. If Arlene had hopes her mother would be a bit more loving and kind, they are immediately dashed: "Moves as if to hug her mother. Mother stands still, Arlene backs off." The mother's first words bring back a disturbing flashback for Arlene. What the mother says, from her opening lines, is critical, hostile, and not connected to Arlene's reality: "You look tired"; "You always was too skinny"; "Shoulda beat you like your daddy said. Make you eat"; "You forgit how to talk? I ain't gonna be here all that long. Least you can talk to me while I'm here."

The mother carries a basket full of colored dish towels, tea, and bug spray, and sets to work cleaning Arlene's apartment—symbolic actions of a woman who tried hard and unsuccessfully for years to tidy up a messy life. "I ain't hateful," the mother says, "how come I got so many hateful kids? Poor dumb as hell Pat, stealin them wigs, Candy screwin since day one, Pete cuttin up ol Mac down at the grocery, June sellin dope like it was Girl Scout cookies, and you . . . thank God I can't remember it all." Arlene's flashbacks of the father's sexual abuse indicate that there is no way the mother escaped knowing: "Nobody done this to me, Mama," and "No, Mama, don't touch it. It'll git well. It git well before." The incestuous relationship between Arlene and her father is doubtless at least partly responsible for the mother's bitterness. In the scene set in the present, the mother resists all of Arlene's overtures ("Sunday . . . is my day to clean house now"); she delights in shattering Arlene's hopes ("ARLENE: 'When I git workin, I'll git a nice rug for this place. He [Joey] could come live here with me.' MOTHER: 'Fat chance' "); and she persists with her improbable and self-serving theories about why Arlene ended up in prison ("I always thought if you'd looked better you wouldn't have got in so much trouble"). The mother mocks the use of "Arlene," shares with her her theories about lesbianism in prisons, and assumes the worst when she sees Bennie's hat.

4. The first stage of Arlie's change begins when she gives birth to Joey. After Joey was taken away to be put in a foster home, Arlie's behavior at the prison deteriorated: "An I guess I went crazy after that." She managed to break out of Lakewood after faking a "palsy fit." The entire point of the escape was to see her son, and the plan went seriously awry when a cab driver assaulted her and Arlie shot him to death. When she is recaptured, she is sent to a different prison (Pine Ridge) where she, at least initially, spends the bulk of her time in a maximum security isolation cell. The grief over the loss of Joey plus the extended hours in solitary confinement combine to very nearly unhinge her.

The prison chaplain appears in Arlie's life when she has reached the lowest point. The chaplain gives Arlene a Bible and a picture of Jesus, but, more important, "he called me Arlene from the first day he come to talk to me." He seems to be the first human male to treat Arlene with any dignity or respect. Bennie's answer to Arlene's repeated "When does the chaplain come?" betrays his bewilderment and envy at the rapport the chaplain has established with Arlene: "BENNIE: 'Yeah, he's comin, so don't mess up.' ARLIE: 'I ain't.' BENNIE: 'What's he tell you anyway, get you so starry-eyed?' ARLIE: 'He just talks to me.' " It is only to Ruby that Arlene attempts to describe what the chaplain has done for her: "This chaplain said I had . . . said Arlie was my hateful self and she was hurtin me and God would find some way to take her away." After the chaplain's abrupt transfer Arlene attempts to stab Arlie to death and then join the ranks of those who will "inherit the earth." By the time Arlene wakes up in the infirmary, "they said I almost died," and it is at this moment that the new Arlene is born: "They said they's glad I didn't." From this moment on, Arlene is a very different prisoner than Arlie was: "An then pretty soon, I's well, an officers was sayin they's seein such a change in me an givin me yarn to knit sweaters an how'd I like to have a new skirt to wear an sometimes lettin me chew gum. They said things ain't never been as clean as when I's doin the housekeepin at the dorm."

5. Ruby has been in prison and is determined never to return. She works as a cook, plays solitaire, and watches daytime television. Her apartment door is the one with "the little picture of Johnny Cash." Ruby appears in Act Two when she bangs on Arlene's door and demands back the five dollars she had loaned to Arlene's sister Candy. Candy had given Ruby advance notice about Arlene: "ARLENE: 'She tell you I was a killer?' RUBY: 'More like the meanest bitch that ever walked.' " Ruby, who is a complete stranger, is the first person to say "Welcome back" to Arlene. The two women have a shared history in that they both have served time in prison and have both been betrayed by men. The initial meeting is made difficult because Arlene is still in the first twenty-four hours of her release from prison, and she is very leery of friendly overtures or physical contact. The situation relaxes a little when Ruby offers the information that she, too, has served time in prison, "My first day outta Gilbertsville I done the damn craziest . . ." However, the situation again gets tense when Ruby attempts to give Arlene some advice: "Well, you just gotta git over it. Bein out, you gotta . . ." Arlene responds, "Don't you start in on me," and Ruby admits, "Ex-cons is the worst. I'm sorry." Ruby immediately spots Carl for what he is: "Why don't you drop by the coffee shop," she tells him, "I'll spit in your eggs." She instructs Arlene in the harsh, yet honorable, realities of their new world: "But when you make your two nickels, you can keep both of em." Ruby's appearance is critical to Arlene's continued rehabilitation. Ruby, in essence, will be Arlene's guide into the new world, picking up where the chaplain left off.

THE PERSONAL RESPONSE

6. Statistics on recidivism and on the chances of people with prison records and a history of abuse are not encouraging. Ruby, right upstairs, a

woman who is further along in the process Arlene is about to undertake, can apparently be the hard-nosed friend who could help Arlene's successful return to the outside world. Arlene's strong desire to see and reclaim her son may also continue to motivate her. Bennie is about as close to a supportive male as Arlene is likely to encounter in her milieu, and with luck Arlene might be able to shake the rotten Carl for good. Rehabilitation, second chances, and the redemption of sinners are the straws we all clutch when confronted with the harsh unforgiving realities of life?

7. Though we might expect the play to turn into an indictment of the justice system, it can be read as mainly an indictment of the men outside the system that played a role in a girl's and young woman's life? Some of the prison guards, like Bennie, eschew violence and try to use psychology (in the form of the correct flavor of gum) on the prisoners. The prison system has an outstanding chaplain who helped Arlene get started on her new life. Arlie was a desperate troublesome prisoner who routinely threw food and tried to set her cell on fire; not surprisingly such behaviors generated animosity in some of the guards. The notion of solitary confinement seems cruel and unusual, as does the length of time Arlie spends there. On the other hand, when Arlie begins to metamorphose into Arlene, the prison authorities support her? The authorities, by proximity and experience, should be the most jaded people in the play. Ironically, they are the first to believe in Arlene's rehabilitation.

8. Like most people, both Bennie and Carl are complicated, Bennie more so than Carl. Bennie suffers from the condescending paternalism that goes with the territory of being a prison guard. He does not seem a man of malice; his behavior toward Arlene is complicated by the relationship they had in prison where she was so obviously the subordinate partner. Bennie has some old-fashioned and chauvinistic ideas about women, but to his credit, he appears willing to make changes for Arlene's sake. An example is his trying and occasionally failing to remember to call her Arlene. As far as having good in him, it is true that Bennie is a promising character. This is not true for Carl, who seems to be the cowardly pimp prototype.

9. The most outrageous example of *dark humor* in the play is Arlene's story of the little boy next door and his collection of frogs. The dialogue often has a caustic, sarcastic edge. Arlie says to Guard-Caldwell, "Ain't you got somebody to go beat up somewhere?" Arlie taunts another child: "Wanna know what I know about your Mama? She's dyin. Somethin's eatin up her insides piece by piece, only she don't want you to know it." Arlene's mother is inadvertently funny when she informs Arlene she "Don't want no bad example" in her house. A lot of what Ruby says is the ironic wisdom of one of life's survivors: "Cookin out's better'n eatin in, I say," and "Arlene's had about all the help she can stand." Life, in this play, is a difficult struggle where the rewards are frequently not related to the sacrifices made. The humor of the play is disillusioned, caustic, sarcastic, ironic, helping the characters cope with grim reality.

THE CREATIVE DIMENSION

10. Skeptical readers may easily envision alternative endings that would nip the hopeful signs of rehabilitation or redemption in the bud. Arlene might hook up with Carl again and return to a life of prostitution. She might attempt to kidnap Joey and end up in prison again. Bennie might have persisted and gone on to rape Arlene, and that would have been the end of their potential friendship.